THE ADAPTIVE ORGANIZATION

THE ADAPTIVE ORGANIZATION

Anticipation and Management of Crisis

KENYON B. De GREENE
University of Southern California

1807 1982

A Wiley-Interscience Publication

JOHN WILEY & SONS

New York • Chichester • Brisbane • Toronto • Singapore

Library of Congress Cataloging in Publication Data

De Greene, Kenyon B.
  The adaptive organization, anticipation and management of crisis.

  "A Wiley-Interscience publication."
  Includes index.
  1. Organization.   2. Management.   I. Title.
II. Title: Management of crisis.
HD31.D36   658   81-13112
ISBN 0-471-08296-1   AACR2

Printed in the United States of America

10 9 8 7 6 5 4 3 2 1

To those executives with the brilliance and imagination to see the wholeness of things, and, having seen, to have the guts to take that first precarious step that begins the journey of a thousand miles.

All our great Presidents were leaders of thought at times when certain historic ideas in the life of the nation had to be clarified.

FRANKLIN DELANO ROOSEVELT

PREFACE

Today almost everybody realizes that the nation and world are confronted with formidable and reinforcing crises. But these crises usually catch people and their organizations and institutions unaware and unprepared. The energy crisis and economic stagflation that erupted in 1973–1974 were among the first of many worldwide crises to jolt our organizations and societies. Since that time even greater international instability, failing institutions and corporations, an economy that cannot be understood using present theories and that resists all efforts at control using present methods, growing ecosystem destruction, increasing social unrest, and huge technological failures further indicate that the world has entered an important stage of historical transformation.

In short, the environments of organizations have become increasingly turbulent. New perspectives, orientations, theories, models, and designs are urgently needed *now* if most organizations are successfully to adapt to and survive in such turbulence. Managing the changing organization will be very different from the management of the present and past.

In this book I have drawn on both the latest practical systems concepts for managing complex organizations and the theories and progressive methods that are forwarding the state of the art. I have synthesized and interwoven a number of advanced theoretical approaches—to evolution of organizations and their environments, organization–environment interaction, growth and aging of organizations, cybernetics, basic laws of nature, and commonality of organism and organization. I have tried to rejuvenate and advance the use of *field theory* in societal science, a theory that has largely languished outside natural science since the death of psychologist Kurt Lewin. Using field theory, I have treated organizations and environments as fields of forces in which critical thresholds can be exceeded, discontinuities can develop, and *sudden, unexpected,* and *catastrophic* reconfigurations can occur.

Although I have based this book on deep theoretic and mathematical concepts, I have written it for maximum readability in as nontechnical a style as possible for a book of its kind. I have tried to avoid specialized jargon and to define terms with which the general reader may be unfamiliar. Most importantly, I offer the book as a guide to *real-world* problemsolving, planning, and policymaking under conditions of great complexity and uncertainty.

I have directed this book especially to top management in business and industry, but most of its message should apply also to government and nonprofit organizations. Experience shows that executives must increasingly concentrate their talents and energies on factors, forces, and problems centered *outside* the organization. Surveys in many of our largest companies indicate that external affairs and long-range planning occupy most of the executives' time. Further, experts estimate that up to 90 percent of companies have proved incapable of developing and implementing meaningful corporate strategies.

I have geared this book to the changing demands placed on top general management and its line and staff engaged in corporate, strategic, and long-range planning. Indeed, the roles of top general management and of high-level, long-range planning are becoming fused. Not only must executives be increasingly concerned with maintaining *fit* between their internally rapidly changing organizations and the turbulent external environments, they must also take an increasingly holistic, future-oriented, worldwide view of things.

Surprisingly little has been written on complex turbulent environments as such even though the word turbulent has long since been incorporated into everyday organization and management talk. The literature offers just as little on large-scale organizational failures and collapse—a look at the evening news shows the need for many more books dealing with these crises. Almost nothing has been written on comprehensively understanding the external and internal organizational environments in order effectively to anticipate crises. No books have been written, to my knowledge, that couple anticipation of emerging organization–environment configurations with adaptive-system design.

Unfortunately, few executives up to now have been educated to anticipate and manage *emerging* problems. I have designed this book to help fill these gaps. The book can be used by individual executives and planners. It can also provide a focus for organizing seminars, internal problemsolving groups, workshops, short courses, and programs dealing with emerging critical problems within the organization and between the organization and its environments.

I have also written this book with middle managers and students in schools of business administration and public administration in mind. These people will inherit the new configurations of organization and environment and the now incipient crises. Use of this book can help prepare students for the organizations and problems that will be in existence after they graduate and as they enter the formative years of their working careers. For this audience, there is little point in talking about the organization as it is or was, and little point in presenting techniques that are largely relics of the 1960s. The book can be used as a primary or secondary text in college and university courses in organization theory, systems theory, organizational design, organization and environment, corporate and long-range planning, futures research, business and society, or modeling and simulation. It may be of value in curriculum redesign. In addition, practitioners in these areas can use the book as a holistic framework against which to compare and evaluate more specific theories and practices.

The only prerequisite to using the ideas in this book is intellectual breadth and maturity. However, readers will obtain maximum benefit if they already have some grasp of how organizations actually work and don't work, some experience trying to handle organizational difficulties, some knowledge of mathematical modeling and computer simulation modeling, some knowledge of systems theory and practice, and some feel for environmental change and complexity.

Important ideas are introduced early in the book and subsequently reiterated in greater depth and in different contexts. The main theoretical concepts are presented in Chapters 1, 3, and 8, and especially in Chapter 5. A comparison and evaluation of methods of futures research is given in Chapter 4. Dynamic changes in the external and internal environments are examined in Chapters 6 and 7. An overview of present and part-oriented approaches to organizational analysis and design is given in Chapter 2. A design for an adaptive organization, which possesses the capabilities for self-regulation, self-organization, problem solving, and learning, is presented in detail in Chapter 8. This design represents a merger of models and problemsolvers in an attempt to obviate past difficulties in using formal models.

Throughout the book I have provided numerous examples of organizational problems, difficulties, and failures. I also offer examples from technological development, current affairs, ecology, world history, biology, physical science, economics, psychology, and world society. The real world is *not* compartmentalized into neat disciplines, and the book is thus *transdisciplinary*. An appendix of diagnostic questions, keyed to each chapter, is designed to help executives and planners, and other readers, determine the states of their own organizations and environments and specific problems arising therein. These questions can also be used as a source of student research, reports, and case projects. The design of the adaptive organization (Chapter 8) can serve as a base for modeling, simulation, hypothesis-testing, and research along many different lines. References, keyed to each chapter, provide guidance to the more technical literature.

I have tried to make the advanced theories and concepts as clear as possible. Nevertheless, the theory of emergence and the new field theory—except perhaps for catastrophe theory which just now is catching on—may still seem exotic and arcane. Hence, for busy executives—the first time around—I suggest starting Chapter 1 with "Who Is the *Right* Manager?"; then reading in order Chapters 7, 2, 6, and 4; then reading Chapter 8 and the rest of Chapter 1; and finally reading Chapters 3 and 5. Other readers may also wish to save Chapters 3 and 5 until last. But Chapters 3 and 5 must not be slighted—they hold the key to successful organizational and environmental monitoring, to anticipating future crises and opportunities, to building an adaptive organization, and to organizational survival.

Many of the problems discussed in this book are highly controversial. I have tried to present balanced arguments while gently pressing executives to search for new insights and stressing the relentlessness of world-system forces and the urgency of taking anticipatory strategic design and management steps. *Now* is the time for a major shift in top management thinking. Many of us may not like the way the world is going, but this is the world we are in. If we want to change the way things are going, we must first recognize underlying forces, then identify the right sets of problems at the right time, and then develop imaginative and innovative strategies at least as rich in variety as the problems are themselves. I offer no quick fixes and no panaceas, and I have pulled no punches.

A multitude of ideas, my own and those of others, have gone into the creation of this book. But the final synthesis is mine and for it I must take full responsibility.

I gratefully acknowledge the help of Ian H. Wilson of General Electric Company for his detailed review of and advice on my early tentative efforts toward writing this book, and of Gerald Papke, formerly of John Wiley and Sons, for his patience and encouragement during that stage. I also express my thanks to John B. Mahaney, and Usha Jambunathan of John Wiley and Sons for their continued support. Finally, I owe the deepest gratitude to my indomitable colleagues at the University of Southern California, who, provided strong moral and ethical collegiate support.

KENYON BRENTON DE GREENE

Woodland Hills, California
October 1981

CONTENTS

CONCEPTS OF ORGANIZATION AND MANAGEMENT

Organizations as presently known may be entering an epoch of massive and widespread failures. Organizations and their managements of course have always been buffeted by environmental forces. At this time in history, however, the stressful forces appear to be greater in number, more in variety, more interacting, and less predictable. World society, human technology, and the natural environment are each changing at extremely rapid rates, both within themselves and in relationship to one another. *It is becoming increasingly difficult to anticipate patterns or configurations of forces in even the near future of the organization, and to develop the adaptive designs and strategies indispensable to steering the organization around or through critical configurations of forces.*

The concern here is mainly with medium- to large-sized organizations that may be confronted with internal human and/or technological problems and possessed of rigid or otherwise obsolescent designs that impede top management's attempts to keep the organization healthy and on a successful course. The organization may variously be:

An information-based business such as a bank, savings and loan company, or an insurance company.

A production organization such as a steel-producing company.

An entire industry consisting of companies with closely related histories, designs, and practices, for example, the automobile industry.

A department or agency in federal, state, or local government.

A not-for-profit organization such as a university, hospital, or labor union.

These kinds of organizations possess more similarities than differences, especially as they grow larger and older. Old industrial management and old labor management think much alike. Often labor–management conflicts and business–government conflicts are merely rituals, with neither protagonist attending to the underlying problems. These conflicts may eventually lead the respective organizations into symbiotic or mutually dependent relationships, generating enormous efforts that are little if at all related to realization of the goals the organizations were set up to achieve.

There are ample indications that the world is emerging into a period both quantitatively and qualitatively much different from what has been known until very recently. This period is an era of *transition*—if not one of the great periods of historical and societal *transformation*—and these times require new philosophies, language, and practices of organization and management.

Overall, these forms must possess:

A feeling for distant stirrings in the environments, especially the future environments.

A capability for quickly assembling and integrating large amounts of qualitative and quantitative information and knowledge from quite varied sources.

A very rapid response to challenges, threats, and opportunities.

A capability to learn from experience and to feed back quickly into new designs and practices the results of learning.

Terms like feeling, response, and learning suggest analogies with nature and especially with living organisms. These and other analogies will be pursued throughout this book. The last chapter will present a detailed design for an adaptive organization based on an expansion of the above requirements.

ORGANIZATION IN NATURE

Organization is not limited to human creations. Organization is a fundamental aspect of nature. Organization or order is what ties together separate elements or subsystems into a cohesively functioning whole. The opposite is disorder, random relationship, and chaos.

One can observe many beautiful examples of organization in the physical world—in atomic, molecular, and crystal structure; in the patterns of atmospheric pressure and storms; and in the large, moving tectonic plates, which divide the Earth's crust and in turn produce the distribution of mountains, volcanos, deep ocean trenches, and so on. Examples of organization from the biological world are perhaps even more striking. Note especially the means by which the many subsystems of plants and animals are kept together, functioning as unified wholes oriented toward some purpose or goal be it only reproduction or survival, and the means by which these organisms adapt to environmental changes through chemical modifications in the germ plasm.

Both the theory and language of human organizations are changing, infused by new ideas and words from the sciences. Although there is disagreement among theorists as to how far analogies and metaphors from nature can be carried, the trend today is certainly to think of human organizations as more dynamic and less static, more functional or physiological and less structural or anatomical, and more malleable and less fixed than was the case just a few years ago. Most top managers are now familiar with such terms as organic structure, living system, and brain of the firm which highlight the new way of thinking.

Human organizations are social systems—or better, *sociotechnical* systems because of the nearly all-pervasive role of technology in the modern world. Further, social systems are closely related to biological systems, particularly with regard to:

Complexity.

Possession of an internal environment and interrelationships with plural external environments.

Fit to a given environment.

Need to adapt to environmental changes.

Mechanisms or mutations that can encourage adaptation.

Stability or instability.

Mechanisms of information processing, coordination, and control.

Further, many scholars and practitioners hold that certain basic dynamic processes underlie phenomena in all worlds—physical, biological, and social. At least some of these processes can be described by natural laws. A rethinking about organization and management along these lines can open up a renaissance of ideas and applications paralleling the explosion of knowledge over the past decade in basic physics, molecular biology, and geology. And certainly the language of organization and management will change to reflect this enriched thinking just as earlier epochs saw the introduction of "optimization," "project teams," and "management by objectives." Executives may find some of these new concepts familiar, but others are in the forefront of human knowledge and are just now being popularized.

Fields of Forces and Field Theory

Any organization, natural or person-made, and its environments, can be viewed as a *field of forces*. This approach, known as *field theory*, originated in physics, but it has had an important impact on biology, psychology, and the social sciences. One form, the topological and vector psychology of Kurt Lewin, was an important system or theory of psychology from about 1930 to about 1965. Professor Lewin's theory dealt mainly with the behavior of individuals and small groups, and was not equipped to handle the complex systems which are of concern here. Nonetheless, Lewin left a legacy that includes the group dynamics practices of sensitivity training and unfreezing-refreezing of a set of interpersonal relationships. In addition, Lewinian theory influenced the development of sociotechnical systems theory, which in a modified form provides one of the key integrating themes of this book.

Viewing a situation or event in terms of a field of forces has decided advantages, but it also places restrictions on interpretation of the situation or event. The advantages are that one can get a better feeling for such things as tension, conflict, polarization, and splitting—familiar behaviors in human organizations. A field of forces also gives an instant impression of *totality*. The major restriction is that one must renounce simple explanations of cause and effect. Situations or events occur because of a particular configuration of forces at a given time. Except as an abstraction, *A* never *causes B*. Often, however, *A* is the straw that breaks the camel's back. That is, *A* adds enough to the field so that a *threshold* is exceeded and a *reconfiguration* results. The recent revolution and continuing instability in Iran and scientific discoveries exemplify situations in which simple cause–effect thinking is quite inappropriate. In both cases a complex field of forces is involved.

The terms forces and fields of forces are widely used throughout this book. Field theory today has been greatly enriched by recent advances in particle physics and statistical mechanics. These advances help explain how *incipient* forces operate and how *collective* behavior *emerges* from standard behaviors at the individual level.

Other advances stem from *catastrophe theory*, a spinoff of an obscure branch of mathematics called topology. Topology deals with forms and structures, especially their *qualitative* features. In a far less advanced state topology was utilized several decades ago, as mentioned above, by psychologist Kurt Lewin.

Catastrophe theory incorporates a number of important concepts, two of which—*discontinuity* and *morphogenesis*—shall be considered briefly here. The terms continuous and discontinuous have precise mathematical meanings,[1] but their popular connotations are more important here. Most people think of the happenings of everyday life and work as being continuous (or continual, that is, changing in small, discrete steps). Today is much like yesterday, and tomorrow will be much like today, only more or less so. Few people think in terms of *sudden breakoffs*—that familiar trends will jump or fall or that the whole world will be qualitatively much different.

In the simplest sense a catastrophe occurs when a small, perhaps unperceived, change in one or more of the continuous control or causal variables of a system leads to a sudden and usually unexpected discontinuous jump or fall in the value or a behavior or affected variable. Phenomena like stock market crashes may be described in this manner as catastrophes.

Morphogenesis describes processes underlying the creation and destruction of form. The term has its most specific application to embryology. Indeed, French topologist René Thom developed catastrophe theory with particular attention to problems of biological morphogenesis. However, the concepts are applicable to many kinds of systems. In this book we are concerned with the evolution and destruction of form in *both* organizations and their environments. Almost all executives today are familiar with or use the terms turbulent environment and turbulent times. However, not all may be aware that the complete term is "turbulent-field environment" and that fluid turbulence is a poorly understood field-theoretic problem in physics of long standing. In a turbulent-field environment new forms emerge and sustain themselves with a life of their own.

Other recent developments are highly compatible within the broad frame of reference of field theory. One development is the extensive treatment of feedback and control processes known as *systems dynamics*. Systems dynamics is also a sophisticated computer simulation methodology, which became internationally known as the basis for the famous Limits to Growth models.

The Entropy Law

The *Entropy Law* or *second law of thermodynamics* is another way of dealing with order and disorder. As the prefix *thermo* suggests, the law originated in physics in the study of heat. However, long ago the law was generalized to include many kinds of trends from organization to randomness, from order to disorder. Now the law is one of the most universal in all science.

Entropy is a quantitative measure of disorder in a system. Thus, the second law may be stated: during any process the entropy may either remain constant or increase, but the total entropy of the universe never decreases. The most probable state of a system is complete randomness, which can be equated to an inability to do work. Furthermore, a natural process is one in which the entropy of the system *plus* its environment increases, and such processes are *irreversible*.

Living systems—organisms, organizations, societies—do have the capability for decreasing entropy, *but at the expense of increasing entropy in their environments*. Sometimes the term negentropy or negative entropy is used to indicate increasing order. Overall system order increases as long as the increase in order of low-order inputs converted to outputs exceeds the decrease in order resulting from converting these inputs to waste.

Another important spinoff of the second law of thermodynamics is *the basic statement* of the interrelationship between a system and its environment. There are three types of interrelationships. An *isolated system* exchanges neither energy nor matter with its environment. Such systems—certain laboratory models, the entire universe—are only of theoretical interest. A *closed system* exchanges energy but no matter with its environment. One must be concerned with these systems for two reasons. First, many managers, theorists, and model-builders still think largely in closed-systems terms. Second, the question arises as to the degree of openness and closedness. For practical purposes Earth is a closed system, and the finiteness of its resources and escape hatches is a fundamental reason for the predicament facing humanity and other living creatures today. Were widespread lunar and planetary settlement and mining to take place, Earth could be regarded as an open system. An *open system* interchanges both energy and matter with its environments. Organizations as well as organisms can be considered open systems.

Many of these points have been made previously in other books on systems theory and organization theory. Recently, however, it has become evident that the second law of thermodynamics and the concept of entropy in particular are even more important to problems of organizational evolution and organization–environment interrelationships than had been imagined. Two extremely important developments will be presented here.

Professor Nicholas Georgescu-Roegen has introduced some revolutionary and exciting new ideas into the staid and dismal science of economics. The essence of his thinking is as follows. Thermodynamics and biology (ecology) underlie economic processes and mechanisms. Thermodynamics—a physics of economic value—helps to clear up erroneous ideas about the *inexhaustibility and possible degree of recycling of resources.* Matter and energy must be thought of as one. Even though they remain constant, they tend to change in quality and *always by the degradation of available into nonavailable forms. The fundamental meaning of the Entropy Law is therefore: the amount of matter-energy unavailable as entropy continuously and irrevocably increases.*

For example, the amount of energy available in a gallon of gasoline and the amount of matter in a rubber tire can be used only once. The dissipated heat, molecules of rubber, and pollutants are theoretically or practically useless and even detrimental.[2] The same ideas apply on a worldwide scale—a fact that both standard capitalist and Marxist economics have failed to recognize.

Furthermore, just balancing the entropic degradation—regardless of continued growth—requires an economy to draw continuously from the environments a flow of low-entropy inputs of matter and energy. This restricts even a stationary economy. Hence, there must be actual *decreases* in some areas today and decreases everywhere, on the average, over the long term. Areas of decrease include economic demand, population, weapons, luxury technologies, and urbanization. The pricing mechanisms of market forces, far from reducing the pressures on the environment, actually intensify them. And unless melded with ecology, economics essentially rules out future generations.

The Entropy Law ties together a lot of otherwise apparently separate phenomena including energy crises, pollution, inflation, unemployment, bureaucratic growth, the differences between Haves and Have Nots, international tensions, and many more.[3] It represents a *systems economics*, as opposed to the more parochial schools of economics that affect most policy today. Many of its features may not be, at first, palatable to many executives. Nevertheless, its implications for management thinking and policymaking in the Era of Transition or Transformation are profound!

Ilya Prigogine, a Nobel Prize winner in chemistry, is responsible for the second important development stemming from the basic second law of thermodynamics. Beginning with phenomena in physical chemistry, Prigogine built models of the emergence of complex organization under conditions *far from equilibrium.* He calls such nonequilibrium structures *dissipative structures* (a rather unfortunate and misleading term to the layman). The dissipative structures represent a newly emergent organization that follows the amplification of appropriate spontaneous fluctuations in the system after the environment's damping or inhibiting capability breaks down. Prigogine's work adds new depth to the understanding of the emergence of new order associated with the transition from one hierarchical level of organization of matter-energy to another. Equally important is the insight provided as to what happens when a system loses its structural stability. All these features are pertinent to the evolution of ecosystems and societies.

Evolution and Natural Selection

Like organisms, organizations have a natural history. Like individual organisms, individual organizations pass through stages of conception, birth, early rapid growth, maturity, senility, and death. Like species, genera, and families of organisms, different types of organizations *fit* different environments at different times. During long periods of relative environmental stability, neither organisms nor organizations need change too much or too rapidly. During times of marked environmental change, however, both organisms and organizations must *adapt quickly* or face extinction. In organic evolution sudden or perhaps catastrophic changes in the atmosphere, hydrosphere, and nature of competitors, and perturbations of the total ecosystem have been particularly stressful to some organisms while encouraging others. Naturalists speak of times of Great Extinctions. These include the end of the Paleozoic Era (extinction of much of the sea life), the end of the Mesozoic Era (extinction of the large reptiles and some of the dominant forms of sea life), and the end of the Pleistocene Epoch (extinction of large mammals).

For the life history and evolution of human organizations, including civilizations and nation-states, the dynamic processes are much compressed in time and space. Human evolution has been considerably more rapid than has been organic evolution in general. This situation is due to positive feedback or mutually reinforcing relationships among biological factors (particularly brain size and development, language development, erectness in walking, and manipulative capability of the hand), culture (particularly community living and mutual cooperation among members), and technology.

Mankind by one of its definitions is tool-making. Therefore from the very beginning technology has played an overwhelming role in mankind's ability to adapt, survive, and compete with other species and members of his own species. Technology still plays an overwhelming role in the ability of organizations and nations to compete with one another and to survive. Once again, the organization must be treated as a *sociotechnical* system.

Organic evolution has been possible only because spontaneous and random mutations have opened up new options for development. The same situation holds for the most part for human evolution also. However, in the case of humanity biological evolution has greatly decelerated, and few if any significant changes have occurred in the past 100,000 years, but technological mutations have become increasingly important. Scientific discoveries, new paradigms of thought, inventions, and innovations are examples of these mutations. The extent to which these mutations can be managed is obviously of critical importance to the survival of organizations, nations, and world society. This in turn affects practical decisions as to whether and to what degree to encourage and support research and research and development (R&D) programs.

Some studies suggest a considerable degree of surficial or surface randomness in scientific discovery, new paradigms of thought, and inventions. At the same time simultaneous discoveries and inventions suggest symptoms of underlying patterns. Within a field of forces there appear to be at certain times confluences of technological and other forces favorable to creative breakthrough. These ideas obviously impart quite a different approach to technological and other futures forecasting.

Like organisms, organizations and societies can face times of Great Extinctions. As with crisis periods for organisms these times can be characterized by sudden changes in the natural environment and in the nature of competitors and by perturbations of the total ecosystem of which humanity is an inseparable part.

Paralleling demise in the animal and plant worlds have been collapses with various degrees of disappearance of human nations and civilizations. Familiar examples are classical Mediterranean civilization and the Roman Empire in particular, the Mayan empire, and classical Islamic civilization. Once mighty Europe-based empires, in particular the Spanish and British, provide further examples of severe decline.

These situations have long been of interest to historians. Oswald Spengler wrote of the inexorable *Decline of the West.* Arnold Toynbee in a *Study of History* noted that 21 civilizations had all followed certain patterns of growth and decay. Unfortunately, historians at large are not held in very high repute by most policy- and decisionmakers today. The old warning by philosopher George Santayana, that he who does not understand history is doomed to repeat it, goes unheeded. It is true that the study of history has operated mostly at the descriptive level of facts, figures, and personalities. When forces are invoked for explanation, for example, migration and industrialization, they are still at an intermediate level of profundity. Now, computer analyses, systems dynamics simulations, and field-theoretic analyses are bringing a new rigor to the study of history. It is interesting to note in passing that Leo Tolstoy wrote in 1869 in *War and Peace*:

> Only by taking an infinitesimally small unit for observation (the differential of history, that is, the individual tendencies of men) and attaining to the art of integrating them (that is, finding the sum of these infinitesimals) can we hope to arrive at the laws of history.[4]

Executives are probably more familiar with products, companies, and industries that have lost fit with their environments and that have been naturally selected out of existence. The decreased demand for buggy whips is a standard joke. But there are myriad other and much more current examples. Keuffel and Esser Company stopped making slide rules in the early 1970s. Vacuum tubes don't find much use anymore as basic units in electronic circuits. Even recently developed areas like computers are subject to overnight obsolescence. Variety among automobiles continues to decline, and one or more makers may soon disappear. The dime store is a rarity— in one case in the early 1960s, management correctly anticipated trends and spun off from Kresge the highly competitive and successful K-Marts, which in turn became the dominant part of the company.

Some companies, however, either misjudge the changing fit between themselves and their environments or by poor decisions disrupt an existing good fit. GEICO, a large insurance company, was highly successful as long as its customers consisted mainly of low-risk government employees and professional people. However, the company almost foundered after it had extended coverage to people who both had many accidents and were unable to meet their payment obligations. It appears to have been a mistake for Sears, Roebuck & Co., long thought of as a chain of stores serving mainly people with lower incomes, to have upgraded its merchandise in an effort to capture the increasingly affluent middle-class market. Peoples' perceptions do not always change so rapidly as managers expect or hope, and such strategies may yield a loss of old customers coupled with an inability to gain new ones. Deficiencies in corporate structure, corporate strategy, and market assessment characteristic of Sears in the 1970s, also applied essentially to the other two large mass-merchandisers, Montgomery Ward & Co. and J.C. Penney Co. All suffered declines, reversals, or losses, especially following the 1973–74 recession. Sluggish performance lasted until 1980, in which year Ward experienced a total annual loss of $162 million.

Like organisms, organizations can get sick. Many organizations today show symptoms of pathology—perseveration (repeatedly using problemsolving methods even though the methods are demonstrably wrong), employee spirits dulled by lack of opportunity, managements geared to optimizing their own personal chances of survival, conflicting parties locked in a spastic paralysis similar to that produced by the opposing muscles in tetanus, and total energies dissipated in simple maintenance.

Very often executives do not recognize the existence or nature of pathology in their organizations. These executives need the help of a diagnostician just as individuals often need the help of a physician or other expert of the healing arts. First the diagnostician looks for, identifies, and interprets symptoms. Next he integrates these symptoms into a pattern of causality. Finally he recommends the appropriate ameliorative measures. It should be emphasized that the diagnostician, probably an outside consultant, must always work closely in all three steps with the appropriate executive.

As with organisms, pathology in organizations is most often associated with aging or frustration—conditions that may produce stagnation and decay. A common characteristic of such organizations is a pattern of behavioral symptoms that include absenteeism, tardiness, job turnover, pilferage, vandalism, sabotage, alienation, malingering, psychosomatic disorders, and overall low and even falling productivity. The symptoms are due to low morale and job dissatisfaction, which in turn are functions of poor organizational designs. These symptoms and patterns describe a critical, perhaps eventually fatal, disease in America today. The prescribed cures have included job enrichment, job enlargement, organizational development and so on. None of these or other widely practiced attempts at cure are in themselves sufficient.

Regulation and Control

In order to function properly both organisms and organizations need mechanisms for regulation and control. Regulation and control mean that the separate elements or subsystems are brought together both spatially and temporally, so that the total system functions in an integrated and coordinated manner. Regulation and control are often, but not invariably, associated with a *hierarchical* arrangement. A given hierarchical level of organization of matter-energy regulates and controls various numbers of elements or subsystems at the next lower level, which in turn controls elements at the next lower level, and so on. In some systems there is a special structure that can be called the regulator-controller, but this need not be the case.

In the famous *World Dynamics* computer simulation model, there are five subsystems or level variables—population, pollution, natural resources, capital investment, and capital-investment-in-agriculture fraction. None of these subsystems is necessarily dominant or always dominant. Rather, control shifts back and forth as a function of other variables and of policies imposed from the outside. This is a nonhierarchical model.

The key concept underlying regulation and control is information. In most situations it is better to emphasize the dynamic *flow* of information over the static *amount* of information. The sequence of information flow in the animal organism is as follows:

1. From a *source* to a *sensor* or *receptor* which might be thought of as part of a *receiver*. Determining a source, even for so simple a stimulus as a sound, may not be an easy affair. The retina is the sensor (the photoreceptor) of the eye, but the eye as a receiver also includes the cornea and lens and other structures that bend and focus light so that it falls properly on the retina.

2. From a sensor to a *central integrating mechanism*. In the higher animal organism, for mediating interrelationships with the *external* environment, this mechanism is the brain or central nervous system (brain and spinal cord). For regulating the *internal* environment, the endocrine, involuntary or autonomic nervous, cardiovascular/kidney, and immune systems are of major importance.

3. From a central integrating mechanism to a *controlled element* or *effector* like the muscles and glands. This is a control signal or message.

Now there is something seriously deficient about our presentation so far. *In a healthy organism or organization information, communication, and control messages cannot flow one way.* The central integrating mechanism must know the effects of its control messages. This knowledge is provided by *feedback*. Information about the effects of the control messages is fed back to the central integrating mechanism. *Feedback is one of the most important concepts in systems theory and practice.*

There are two types of feedback, *positive* and *negative.* In positive feedback, system output reinforces system input, and the result is more or less of the same, that is, growth or decay. Systems dominated by positive feedback can become dangerously unstable. Recently there has been important criticism of unrestrained growth. Thoughtful people are concerned about the population problem, more and more people are worried about uncontrolled spending, and almost nobody is in favor of inflation.

In negative feedback, an attempt is made to bring system output in line with system input or *desired* system output. An integrating mechanism compares the actual output with the input or desired output. Such a mechanism is often called a *comparator.* Negative feedback is the most important means of regulation and control. It is often said that negative feedback produces goal-seeking behavior. This means that negative feedback corrects for any deviations (sometimes called "error signals") that are too far above, below, or away from a desirable or stable level or platform. Unfortunately for policymaking and for solutions to the current, much emphasized "predicament of mankind," desirable is not synonymous with stable. Correctly applied negative feedback is associated with *steering* the system in space and time toward the achievement of its goal. Incorrectly applied negative feedback can bring the system to a halt or produce oscillations and, as with positive feedback, dangerous instability. Avoiding overcontrol, delayed control, or unsteady control is usually not easy in complex systems.

All healthy living and purposeful systems possess feedback. Such systems are called *closed-loop* systems. Systems without feedback are called *open-loop* systems. Unfortunately, many people misunderstand the terms positive and negative. Some attribute absolute value judgments of goodness or badness. Other people confuse closed with closed-loop and open with open-loop. The former terms come from thermodynamics and deal with energy and matter. The latter (loop) terms come from cybernetics and deal with information. *The healthy organizations emphasized in this book are open, closed-loop systems.*

Earlier system pathology was discussed. Often pathology in complex systems is due to the breakdown of mechanisms of regulation and control. In organisms the concentrations of substances in tissues and fluids must be kept within certain, often very narrow, *ranges of tolerance.*

Disorders of the internal environment of the organism were recognized and an integrating concept formulated as long ago as the mid-nineteenth century. However, this concept is best known by physiologist Walter B. Cannon's term, *homeostasis.* Homeostasis refers to the maintenance of constancy of the internal environment of the organism.

Homeostasis is an extremely important systems concept because it helps identify and illustrate phenomena and processes of (1) stability and equilibrium, (2) regulation and control, and (3) the complexity of interacting forces bearing on a single phenomenon.

Once again nature provides examples of the operation of a field of forces and of *mutual causality*. From time immemorial the eyes, brains, and arms, and the perception of the effects of the rocks, spears, arrows, and bullets on the target, served as efficient closed-loop feedback systems for hunters and warriors. However, by World War II *system complexity had begun to transcend human capabilities and to bring out human limitations*. This trend continues in an accelerated form today and is one reason for the many problems discussed in this book.

The particular problem during World War II of interest here was to aim an antiaircraft gun *anticipating* where the target aircraft would be when the shell reached the point of contact. This required a device called a servomechanism that could compare the actual aircraft position with a predicted or desired position and aim the gun accordingly. Automatic pilots in aircraft, power steering in automobiles, and thermostatically controlled air-conditioning and heating systems are also servomechanisms.

A leader in the solution of the above problem was mathematician Norbert Wiener. In 1948 Wiener wrote his famous *Cybernetics: Or Control and Communication in the Animal and the Machine*. Cybernetics incorporated homeostasis and also the study of neurological and neuromuscular functions and disorders. Once again emphasis should focus on the essential unity and *necessary harmony* of people and nature.

The processes discussed here are extremely important to industrialization, especially to automation. The fundamental principle of the operation of digital and analog computers, and of whole industries based on automatic process control or continuous control, is as presented above—sensing actual system conditions, comparing actual with desired conditions, and taking corrective action to bring actual conditions into agreement, allowing a certain range of tolerance, with desired conditions. Abrupt, one-time-only corrective control is seldom desirable. Most corrective control is either smooth and continuous or iterative, that is, it represents a cyclic repetition of the same steps that continually reduce the disparity between actual and desired conditions. As just about everybody knows, sudden braking of an automobile or overcontrolling the roll of an airplane can lead to death and destruction.

Cybernetic ideas have been implemented since antiquity. The Greek word, *kybernetes,* from which the word governor is descended, referred to the control mechanism of an ancient sailing ship. In the Industrial Revolution, which was devoted to expanding power far beyond human and other animal muscular capabilities, an important cybernetic device was the governor on Watt's steam engine. In recent years immense advances have been made, both in the expansion of human sensory and perceptual capabilities and in the coordination of the enhanced sensory/perceptual and power and precision capabilities.

Almost all our most sophisticated technologies are in this vein. However, trends toward the increasingly small and refined parallel trends toward the increasingly large and powerful. Teleoperations (regulation and control from afar), industrial robotics, smart sensors and computer terminals, and prostheses (artificial organs) provide illustrations of sophisticated technology areas in which rapid advances are being made.

The model underlying much of the discussion here is the input-throughput-output model—or in more organismic terms the stimulus-organism-response model. Unfortunately, for complex systems like person–computer systems and organizations, advances in improving the throughput–organism link have been much more modest than have been improvements of the other links. This situation introduces one of the most formidable problems of our age—the *possible limits to human problemsolving and management of complex systems.*

In both organisms and organizations things can go wrong with the flow and feedback of information. For example, information can be:

Misidentified as to source.

Incorrect at the source, even though the source is correctly identified.

Attenuated in transmission, perhaps through filtration.

Amplified in transmission.

Noisy, that is, the wanted signals or content may be difficult or impossible to extricate from the unwanted signals or content; noise may arise at the source or in transmission.

Biased or distorted in transmission, either by the introduction of random elements or by purposeful action.

Delayed in transmission.

Incomplete when received.

Misperceived by the receiver.

Refused or suppressed.

Effective information-processing requires filtration, amplification, enhancement of signal/noise ratio, and so on. However, most of the above features can be associated with malfunctions and pathology in organisms and organizations. In fact many of the most serious problems in today's complex organizations involve such things as:

One-way communications—usually only downwards.

Breakdown of cohesiveness, leading to the formation of "isolated" open-loop systems.

Rumors—amplified information based on limited initial content.

Deliberate or inadvertent (perhaps hopeful or wishful) biasing of information on the part of employees.

Suppression of information by bosses.

Lags that produce system oscillations and instability.

Oral or written communications that are inconsistent with body language.

Perceptual filtering of information because of unconscious needs and personality structure.

Policies and decisions based on insufficent or wrong information.

Confusion of needs for appropriate information with non-needs for masses of data and information.

To summarize some especially pertinent points: human organizations are subject to natural laws and display processes in common with physical, and especially, biological systems. The organization–environment interrelationship is very rapidly changing in favor of the environment. Nature is no longer so easy to tame and control, and will become decreasingly so because organizations are confronted by fields of forces and not by easily defined and isolated problems to be solved. Hence, more and more organizations will experience difficulties and many will become sick. Executives increasingly will require the services of systems consultants to help diagnose symptoms and difficulties and work out ameliorative and adaptive strategies. Executives may not want to delve into physical laws and biological analogies, but they may wish to accept these things as givens. However, they must be able to conceive questions and invite discussions of the type: what is the health of the total information-feedback-regulation-control system in my organization?

The application of cybernetics to organizations is often called *cybernation*. However, neither cybernetics nor cybernation are felicitous terms to many people, including many hardheaded top managers. People have visions of robots and the firm's being managed by computers. This is unfortunate because cybernetics, which is usually linked intimately with systems science and research, has a great deal to offer. An organization cannot be adaptive without also being cybernetic. There is nothing about cybernetics that requires the exclusion of people from the highest and most dominant regulation and control loops. A good organizational design has people doing what they do best and machines doing what they do best.

Figure 1.1 depicts a generalized cybernetic system.

Living Systems

A great deal has already been said about living systems—organisms, organizations, and societies—and their properties. For example, living systems are open systems, decrease the amount of entropy internally while increasing it externally, are cybernetic systems, and are typically arranged in hierarchical levels of organization of matter-energy. As already emphasized, all these properties are among the most fundamental in nature.

The meaning of hierarchical order requires a little more elaboration at this point. Questions such as the following might be asked: How does order at one level arise from that at a lower level? What types of individual behavior lead to collective behavior? Why is the transition from one level to another in nature almost always associated with the emergence of new properties? Why is hierarchy in nature associated with flexibility and evolution, while hierarchy in people-made organizations is often the basis of rigidity and maladaptiveness?

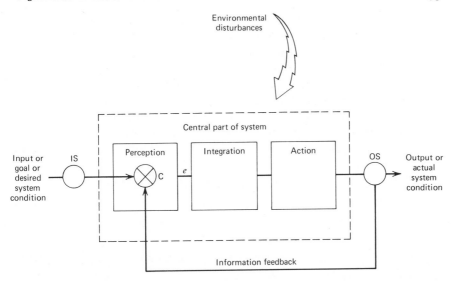

Figure 1.1. Generalized Cybernetic System. C, comparator; *e*, "error signal"; IS, input sensor; OS, output sensor.

How can we change the hierarchical structures in human organizations so that they exhibit the adaptive capabilities of natural hierarchies?

The answers to the first questions are among the most difficult in science, and attempts to answer them will be put off until Chapter 5. However, the last question can be remarked upon. Organizational hierarchies are often deficient because:

There is no emergence of new properties (functions, responsibilities) in the movement from one level to the next higher one. That is, supervisors and lower-level managers may spend their time monitoring in detail the work of employees and then redoing the work when it is perceived as *wrong*.

Top management attempts total control and allows no autonomy at successively lower levels. If, by analogy, the brain had to decide on spinal and autonomic reflexes, the organism would be paralyzed into inactivity.

A level that is not a fruit attempts control over apples and oranges. An attempt is made to create an unnatural level by bringing together immiscible constituents. These elements repel rather than bond with one another.

The interfaces between levels are impermeable.

There are too many or two few levels in relation to the natural demands imposed by the environment.

Some of these deficiencies are met, at least partially, by designs like matrix organizations and semiautonomous work groups which shall be discussed later.

Dr. James G. Miller, physician, psychologist, systems scientist, and university administrator, has probably done more thinking about living systems than has any other single person.[5] Miller employs seven hierarchical levels: (1) the cell, (2) the organ, (3) the organism, (4) the group, (5) the organization, (6) the society, and (7) the supranational system. Living systems thus bracket a number of levels along a scale ranging from the very small to the very large. Below the level of the cell are: (1) the subatomic particle, (2) the atom, (3) the molecule, (4) the complex organic molecule or colloid like deoxyribonucleic acid or DNA (which, like viruses, may possess a capability for self-reproduction), and (5) the subcellular structures like the nuclei. At the other extreme of the scale are: (1) the earth, (2) the solar system, (3) the galaxy, and (4) the entire universe.

These seemingly esoteric matters are mentioned here because:

1. Recent advances in field theory in physics are aiding in the understanding of the fundamental problem of *emergence* in the transition from one level of organization to another.
2. Advances in physics and in cosmology are beginning to unite the very small with the very large.
3. Scientists in widely separated disciplines are beginning to focus on the same kinds of basic questions, suggesting a greater trend toward the unification of science.
4. Certain morphogenetic and evolutionary processes appear to operate from the physical-chemical to the ecological and societal levels.
5. Applications of basic laws and generalization of basic processes to societal systems will place forecasting the future, now heavily dependent on the subjective judgments of experts, on much firmer ground. This in turn will enable great strides to be made in corporate, strategic and long-range planning.

For each of his seven levels, Dr. Miller identifies 19 critical subsystems that either: (1) process matter-energy, (2) process information, or (3) process both matter-energy and information. The individual subsystems generally follow either an input, a throughput, or an output classification scheme. A particularly important concept is that of *cross-level hypotheses*, that is, hypotheses that attempt to explain behavior at more than one level. This represents another step toward the unification of science. *Living Systems* is almost an encyclopedia of hypotheses, phenomena, processes, functions, and examples, many of which, especially at the higher levels, the executive would find both interesting and informative.

Symbiosis

Symbiosis is the last form of organization in nature discussed here. Symbiosis can best be defined by an example. One often sees beautiful yellow, orange, chartreuse, or brown encrustations on rocks. These are lichens, which are composite organisms. A lichen is made up of an alga and a fungus. The alga, possessing chlorophyll and therefore the capability for photosynthesis, provides nourishment. The fungus provides structural support and protection. Neither form can exist without the other.

For two decades the term person–computer symbiosis has been part of the vocabulary of the human factors and computer communities. The idea is an important one because it implies that the computer goes well beyond just *extending* human capabilities. Rather, while performing a creative, problem-solving task, the person and computer sort of merge into one another, temporarily becoming one. More specifically the human mind and the computer capabilities merge. Far in the future implanted, highly miniaturized computer-communications systems might make the person and computer permanently one. Sophisticated person–computer symbiosis is probably necessary, but even more probably not sufficient to deal effectively with the many critical problems of organizations and societies set forth here. Unfortunately, compared to the dramatic advances made in some other fields, relatively little progress has been made toward advancing person–computer symbiosis.

Symbiosis has another meaning when applied to organizations. This is, as with the algae and fungi that gradually became associated over evolutionary time to produce lichens, some organizations gradually become so intertwined as to be inseparable. Symbiosis is common in social systems in general and is increasing. Examples include relations between regulators and regulatees, cops and robbers, government bureaucracies and the institutionalized poor, suppliers and purchasers, and one nation-state and another. The bonds that connect the constituent subsystems may be economic, psychological, political, and so on and are not always evident at first glance.

Some types of symbiosis in social systems are healthy, but others are not because:

1. The constituent subsystems reinforce one another in a positive-feedback loop, producing explosive exponential or hyperexponential growth of the type discussed in Chapter 3. Such growth may severely tax the resources of the larger system at the level immediately above. The oil crises and foundering of Social Security and company pension plans provide salient examples.

2. A perturbation to or weakness developed within one of the constituent subsystems can immediately spread over the entire system, threatening its viability. Chains of job dismissals provide an important example.

3. Needed social change or reform is rendered exceedingly difficult, if not impossible. The reader will be able to think of many examples here.

SUBSYSTEMS IN MODERN ORGANIZATIONS

This is a systems book, and this fact strongly colors our orientation and presentation. Here the concern is with *wholes,* and how, when, where, and why the elements or subsystems—the *subwholes*—interact and organize so as to achieve a common goal or purpose. Many types of subwholes are dealt with in this book because: (1) these are convenient *temporary* units or levels of study, (2) we wish to establish the manner in which parts fit into the whole, or (3) we wish to demonstrate that the part approach to today's problems is almost invariably wrong.

Systems have *properties,* like openness, closedness, positive and negative feedback, linearity, nonlinearity, capability to process information, capability to process matter-energy, deterministic behavior, probabilistic behavior, and so forth. Extensive treatment of systems properties *per se* is found in a wide and growing literature.[6]

In studying organizations and other complex systems, it is often difficult to know where to begin. One tried-and-true approach is *systems analysis,* which involves primarily: (1) identifying the proper hierarchical *level* of concern, (2) identifying the system *boundary* with its environment, (3) identifying the relevant *subsystems,* and (4) identifying the *interfaces, cause–effects,* and means of *dynamic interaction* between or among the subsystems. Needless to say, systems analysis is not easy. Even more important, dissociated from *systems synthesis,* it may be completely *wrong.* Systems analysis is also extensively treated in the literature. The broad framework listed above provides a unifying theme to this book. One type of systems analysis, computer simulation modeling, receives particular attention in Chapter 4.

Consider a fairly simple system such as an airplane. For convenience in analysis, design, production, trouble-shooting and maintenance, and management, it can be regarded as consisting of several subsystems. These include:

1. The structural subsystem, consisting of the fuselage, wings, and tail assembly. (In turn, the tail assembly, say, could be broken down into such *sub-subsystems* as the rudders and elevators.)
2. The power or energy subsystem, consisting of the engine(s).
3. The communications subsystem, consisting of the radio, radar, selective-identification feature, and so forth.
4. The control subsystem, consisting of the stick or wheel, the pedals, the throttle, and the electromechanical and hydraulic connections to the flaps, ailerons, rudders, elevators, engine, landing gear, and so on.
5. The crew subsystem, consisting of the pilot and usually the copilot, flight engineer, and stewards and stewardesses (or navigator and other military crew members). The total *personnel subsystem* of course also includes the maintenance crews and the service crews in addition to the flight crews.

Even as long ago as World War II, aircraft, radars, and so forth had become so complex as to tax the capabilities of the operating crews. Later, new generations of aircraft and missiles, satellites, spacecraft, and the associated ground communications-and-control capabilities greatly accelerated the degree of complexity. New means of design, production, and management were sorely needed. Systems engineering, human factors engineering, operations research, and systems management were among the new fields that emerged to meet the demands of the times.

Many of these and other developments have served us well indeed, but with the changing nature of world problems, many formerly useful approaches and techniques have not transferred well. Some are inherently closed-system and rigid, and are not generalizable from circumscribed applications or adaptable to new situations. These approaches and techniques have a momentum, however, and continue to be misapplied in areas where the emergence of new orientations, suitable to today's problems, is critical. The modern organization, with some exceptions where technology plays a minimum role, should be seen in terms of the following dynamically interacting subsystems:

1. The *social subsystem,* consisting of the *collective* aspects of human behavior ranging from the small group to the total organization. Included are interpersonal relationships, interdependent task and job performance, collective bargaining and strikes, cultural attributes, team problem-solving, cohesiveness, expected roles, and so forth. It is especially important to note that the social subsystem *emerges* from the psychological subsystem, with contributions from the technological and power subsystems. The social subsystem is *not* a mere aggregation of individual behaviors. One might well debate whether a given behavior is psychological or social—psychologists, social psychologists, sociologists, and economists have been doing this for quite a long time. Such concepts as values, morale, and alienation perhaps should be in the social subsystem rather than in the psychological subsystem. *One* individual might place a low value on productive work, hate his job, and be alienated from others, but these behaviors are relatively unimportant to the organization until they become a way of life for *many* people. Likewise, there appears to be in many situations a collective perception, a collective consciousness, or a collective intelligence—in each case the whole is greater than the sum of the parts.

2. The *technological subsystem,* consisting of the *collective* aspects of machines and their ancillary and support features and methods of use, as well as certain nonmachine-based activities. Included are pieces and subsystems of primary equipment, computer programs, tools, job aids, work-flow and process-flow methods, documented and undocumented operating and maintenance procedures, facilities, environmental (thermal, humidity, and so on) control sub-subsystems, physical communications links, psychotechnical methods of behavior assessment, modification, or control and so forth. One of the most important dimensions of the technological subsystem is the degree of *mechanization* or *automation.* Today, technology seems to have developed an autonomy or life of its own, that is, to be not completely under human control.

3. The *psychological subsystem,* consisting of *individual* needs, motivations, emotions, personality structure, values, attitudes, beliefs, perceptions,

intellectual abilities, perceptual and perceptualmotor abilities, learned skills, creative thinking, and so forth. As applications, these areas have long been the concern of clinical psychologists, psychiatrists, industrial psychologists, human factors experts, training experts, and behavioral scientists. At the operating level there is not too much concern with individual human behavior in this book, but at the level of top management and its associated expert advisors, there is great concern with individual human behavior. The underlying needs and personality structure of the chairman of the board, the company president, a senior vice-president, the secretary of a large government bureaucracy, or a leading technical expert can have marked effects—for good or bad—on plans, policies, and decisions. In a related sense the question arises as to whether planning, policymaking, and decisionmaking ever are or ever can be completely *rational.*

4. The *political subsystem,* consisting of the structures, resources, and support capabilities that encourage and facilitate the use and growth of power and influence, the roles thereby created, and the people who temporarily occupy these roles. One should note carefully that the structures that facilitate power and influence may be as formal as constitutions and charters, but that they need not be. New technologies and technological expertise often provide unexpected new sources of power in organizations. Some organizations can dispense with their top management much more readily than they can get rid of their computer and information-system personnel. Furthermore, the legitimacy of formally defined power is increasingly being challenged—in the family, in the church, in the schools and universities, in business and industry, in the military, and in government. This means that the executive will increasingly have to rely more on his own resources than upon the authority vested in his position. Now there is nothing intrinsically good or bad about power and influence. However, excessive power and influence have often not been accompanied by equivalent responsibility. The inadvertent or mischievous misuse of power and influence in organizations has exacerbated many of the woes of the world today.

In summary, the subsystems of the modern organization consist of the subsystems of a person-machine system plus those of a sociotechnical system plus a political subsystem.

Both organisms and organizations age differently with respect to time. That is, one organism or organization may age much more rapidly than does another in the same number of years. Functional integrity of an organization requires the maintenance of *congruence* among the subsystems and also between the system and its environment. Congruence is the fit or harmony between or among the relevant entities.

Establishing and maintaining congruence is one of the single most important aspects of both organizational design and management. This requires constant monitoring of even subtle changes. Marked incongruence is a major indication of sickness. An aged technology can severely constrain the performance of an otherwise healthy organization just as a differentially aged or damaged heart, lung, liver, or other organ can threaten the viability of an otherwise healthy person. Alternatively, the newest technology may produce setback rather than progress if it is imposed on an organization with an aging or inappropriately skilled workforce or with a management that does not know how to use the technology. Or an archaic vertical management may impede the influx of independently minded but creative young persons needed for innovation.

THE ORGANIZATION AND ITS ENVIRONMENTS

The concept of organization and environment is one of most critical to modern management. Up to 10 to 20 years ago, most thinking about organizations was closed-system. That is, while the environment was recognized as a source of raw materials and workers and as a destination for products, the structure and function of the organization were thought to be determined internally. Few, if any, people bothered to think about or care whether the external environment had an impact on the organization, if there was such a thing as an internal ✳ environment, and what the effects of the organization on the external environment might be. Such dramatic happenings as social and technological change, pollution, and the energy crises have gone a long way to change most peoples' thinking. Recently organization-environment interrelationships has become one of the hottest topics in organization theory and practice.

The concept of dynamically changing external and internal environments of the organization and continuing interaction between these and organizational structure, function, and management provides another key integrating theme of this text. *Maintaining congruence or fit between the organization and its environments has emerged as probably the single most important function of top management. Maintaining fit cannot be done without anticipating changes in the internal and external evironments and in the organization-environment interrelationships.* ✳

For our purposes here the external environments of the organization are the following:

1. The *natural environment*—population, resources, pollution, and so on.
2. The *technological environment*—scientific discovery and invention, innovation, impact, transfer.
3. The *human resources environment*—abilities and skills, values and attitudes, and other elements.
4. The *political environment*—legislation, regulations, labor unions, international instability, and so forth.
5. The *social* or *socioeconomic environment*—new obligations and responsibilities toward society, macroeconomics, and so on.
6. The *market environment*—consumer behavior, competition, saturation.

The internal environment consists of the four subsystems discussed in the previous section and their interacting contribution to total organizational performance. Of particular importance are the following:

Productivity

Motivational dynamics, morale, and job satisfaction

Value and attitude change

New organizational goals

Effects of new technologies

Uses and misuses of power

FIXED VERSUS RELATIVELY ADAPTIVE ORGANIZATIONAL FORMS

For several decades it was popular—and possible—to cite certain examples of the design of twentieth-century organizations as nearly universal models to be widely emulated. Particular favorites were the functional structure of Henri Fayol, the efficient work design or scientific management of Frederick W. Taylor and the Gilbreths, the bureaucracy of Max Weber, and the decentralization of authority and centralization of control of Alfred P. Sloan, Jr. at General Motors.

These designs were in many ways highly appropriate for the times. Collectively, the designs applied to organizations that were characterized by:

1. Specialization of functions, jobs, and personnel.
2. Personal accountability associated with the learning of specific skills, procedures, and rules.
3. Tight hierarchical structure and control, perhaps slightly mitigated by decentralization.

This organizational structure was well fitted to an environment characterized by:

1. Clear patterns of dominance and subordination among nations, races, and social classes.
2. Relatively low average educational and skill levels.
3. Apparently unlimited natural and personal resources.
4. Relatively low rate of social and technological change.
5. Relatively great separation of peoples in space and time.

Several seminal studies carried out in the period from 1962 to 1975, and extension of the original ideas made subsequently, provided a bridge between the above classical and contemporary, *but still vastly incomplete,* organization theory.[7]

Arthur D. Chandler, Jr.[8] made one of the few comprehensive studies of the evolution of large, multidimensional organizations. He analyzed changes in structure at Sears Roebuck, Du Pont, General Motors, and Standard Oil (New Jersey). He concluded that the rate of environmental change in supply sources, technology, and markets yielded opportunities for strategic decisions by key men that in turn led to changes in organizational structure. In other words, Chandler emphasized strategic choices among needs and opportunities presented by changing environments.

John Child[9] continued Professor Chandler's line of thinking, and stressed strategic choices by powerful persons (the dominant coalition) in organizations as the major source of variation among organizations. Organizational structure can thus reflect order, security, power, and status—features the powerful refuse to upset. Existing power structure and associated values give a perceptual filter through which environmental changes in opportunity and threat must pass. By modifying organizational goals, the powerful can also change the size, technology, and location of the organization.

Joan Woodward[10] studied 100 British firms and found a relationship between management structure and certain technological variables. The firms were placed on a continuum that expressed predictability and routineness of, and degree of control over, operations. At one extreme were unit processors, that is, producers of tailor-made, one-of-a-kind, or prototype articles. In the middle range were large batch- and mass-production firms. At the other extreme were process-control industries.

Success in the large batch- and mass-production firms depended on *mechanistic* management rules in which duties were cleary indicated on paper. Standardization had eliminated from production tasks the need for perceptual and cognitive skills, but skills requiring strength and dexterity were still required. In many of these mechanistic firms objectives changed in erratic ways—this apparently was consequent to the fragmentation of decisionmaking and control among the specialist departments with regard to quantities, schedules, standards, and costs. Even planned changes followed internal tension. Eventually the primary goal of the firm became sheer survival rather than provision of goods and services, an indication of pathology as discussed earlier.

In the unit-production and process-control firms at either end of the continuum, management was *organic*. In the unit-production companies, problems of prediction and control were related to greater decisionmaking at every level, but an integrated control system was nevertheless maintained. In the process-control firms, routine tasks were highly automated. The remaining labor force was mostly personnel specializing in *exception-detection*, that is, the more highly educated maintenance persons and supervisors. Company objectives and procedures were repeatedly reappraised.

Just a little earlier, Tom Burns and G. M. Stalker[11] had analyzed 20 British firms and found that, of the two basic types of structure, organic structures were most effective in rapidly changing markets and mechanistic structures were effective under stable environmental conditions. Firms that successfully adapted to the changing (electronics) industry had a more holistic concept of their main task and a more varied capability to communicate the information required for innovation. Flexibility was maintained by introducing new market and technological information to reprogram routine operations. These organic firms had no rigid definition of duties, methods, and powers. Performance was continually reevaluated in the course of ongoing interactions with the environment.

In the mechanistic organizations, in contrast, work was successively shredded into smaller and smaller portions. Work was strictly controlled by the decisions and instructions of superiors. The managerial chain of command was vertical, and information flowed upward to perhaps the one person who "understood" the entire organization.

A little later Paul R. Lawrence and Jay W. Lorsch[12] studied 10 organizations in the plastics, food, and container industries. They looked at three environments differing in the amount of technological and market change and how these environments affected internal differentiation and integration. Organizations were also compared both within and between industries with regard to performance differences. The high-performing plastics company, operating in the most diverse and dynamic environment, was the most differentiated. Commensurate integration was achieved by using both an integrating unit and cross-functional teams that greatly aided the resolution of conflict among the differentiated units. Managers of all levels and specialties participated greatly in decisionmaking.

The high-performing container organization, at the other extreme, operated in a relatively homogeneous and stable environment. Functional units were not highly differentiated, and the only integrating capability was the management hierarchy. Nevertheless, this structure produced effective decisions and resolution of conflicts.

Thus, each of two quite different types of organizational structure was effective in dealing with its own external environment. Interestingly the managers of the successful plastics company appeared to have different personality attributes (greater independence and tolerance for ambiguity) than did the managers of the successful container company (greater dependence on authority and anxiety in the face of ambiguity). It is important that management personalities be congruent with the organization and its environment.

Collectively, these and related studies have led to the development of the *contingency theory* of organizations.[13] Various contingencies have been studied, and some of these have been discussed above. Contingencies include:

1. Features of the external environments, particularly the market and technological environments, for example, diversity or variety, complexity, and rate of change.

2. Technology in the internal environment.

3. Size or scale of the organization.

4. Types of employees.

5. Management strategies and political behavior.
6. Management personality types.

Briefly contingency theory holds that there are complex interrelationships among environmental certainty and diversity, internal differentiation and integration, and conflict resolution. If the following features are present, the organization will be effective in dealing with its environment: (1) internal differentiation consistent with the complexity, diversity, and rate of change of the external environments, (2) internal integration consistent with demands for interdependence imposed by the external environments, and (3) resolution of conflict at the level at which there is the necessary knowledge about the environments. Put another way, if certain important factors or variables can be specified, the best form of a given organization can be indicated. However, there is no single, universal best form, and any particular form is not equally good for all organizations or for the same organization at different stages of its life history. This important topic will be discussed more fully in Chapter 3.

As with other themes mentioned thus far, contingency theory has contributed to the ideas underlying this book. However, contingency theory by itself has a number of limitations. These include:

1. There is a tendency of some authors to interpret the contingencies deterministically. But technology, for example, does not *determine* organizational structure in any 1:1 manner. Similarly, a complex environment does not determine organizational structure. For example, some organizations can influence and even dominate their markets through advertising or acquisition of competitors or resource inputs.
2. Cause-effect relationships have been difficult to decipher. Does an inappropriate structure cause low performance, or does low performance lead to a bad structural design? In other words there has been too little appreciation of *mutual causality* and of the types of situations embodied in, say, a systems dynamics cybernetic model.
3. Variables are hard to define and measure operationally. Studies often reveal more about the backgrounds of the researchers than they do about the organizations purportedly studied. As shall be seen in Chapters 3 and 4, linear regression analysis has some major drawbacks as applied to systems that many people think are nonlinear, dynamic, mutually causal, and characterized by incipient, subtle fields of forces.
4. Evolutionary processes are difficult to discover because, as with many social systems, *longitudinal* perspectives and data are lacking, and most studies are *cross-sectional*. This means we see organizations at disconnected thin slices of time.
5. Overall, there is a need for much better integration of individual studies, which often present inconsistent, contradictory, or hard-to-reconcile findings.

To summarize, contingency theory is one systems approach to the study of organizations, but by itself it is incomplete and insufficient.

This section concludes with a brief look at one other view of adaptive organizations.

The approach is partially descended from the early contingency studies and from some classical sociotechnical systems designs. This approach is now quite familiar to top management. It involves attempts to build flexibility and rapid response into organizations, but the result is usually the superimposition of other designs onto a basic bureaucratic structure.

The rigid, restrictive aspects of a tightly-coupled hierarchical structure can be reduced, for example, by introducing *slack* into the organization, by modifying persons, and by restructuring groups. Slack resources can be produced by increasing person-hours, money, or time scheduled for a given job. By using organizational slack, the tolerable ranges of performance can be increased and the detection of exceptions made less necessary and less urgent. Top management is often reluctant to invest in slack resources, but the results can well be an improved cost-effectiveness ratio.

Individuals can be modified by proper selection and training and the use of less formal and liaison-type interpersonal relations. Several types of behavioral science techniques, for example, behavior modification and organizational development, continue to be very popular.

Groups can be restructured into *semi-autonomous work groups, ad hoc groups, project teams, program offices,* and *matrix organizations.* Some of these groupings are by necessity short-lived because they are set up as task forces to deal with specific problems with short-term solutions.

Project teams and matrix organizations have been particular favorites and have often been thought of as panaceas. They are based on the concept of *lateral* decisionmaking. Instead of bucking problems up the hierarchy, managers attempt to solve them at their own level, that is, where information originates. In theory this makes good sense and is consistent with the cybernetic regulation and control discussed earlier.

Matrix designs provide a valuable means for reintegrating planning, deciding, and doing—activities long separated in hierarchical structures.[14] Matrix organizations, in pure form, have no built-in status differences. It is assumed that each member of the organization shares values with the other members and that each member has a specialized role and a range of competence that partly overlaps the competence of the other members. Any member can assume a leadership role depending on the nature of the task.

The use of matrix organizations enables management to redeploy people flexibly, for example, in quick adjustment to technological change. Matrix organizations thus provide a means to solve one of the most formidable problems facing today's organizations—how to create self-sustaining and continual learning, at both individual and organizational levels.

At a given level in an organization a matrix can be formed when a person, say a manager or a professional, becomes a member of both a technical resource department and a product or program office. He has two bosses. Many researchers report particular success in using matrix forms. For example, Jay Galbraith[15] has found that businesses with matrix forms are more successful in developing and introducing new products than are businesses without these forms.

Unfortunately, matrix organizations, project teams, and program offices do not always work so well in application as theory would predict. For example, there may be manpower limitations, and a matrix organization may be saddled with over a hundred projects! Conflict is also common between the project manager and the line manager, who fills out one's rating form.

INFORMATION—ACQUISITION, PROCESSING, DISPLAY, AND CONTROL

Information is the key idea of cybernetic systems and a key concept of all living systems. Information in these systems must not be thought of as a fixed, static quantity but rather as a dynamic, variable flow. The flow involves the acquisition, processing, display, and control of information (in organizations) and the regulation and control of policies, decisions, and processes.

Collectively, the flow of information is often simplified as information-processing. In today's environments an organization cannot remain healthy and adaptive or even survive without a good capability to process information. Unfortunately, in organizations information-processing effective to continued high performance is not easy. Information systems are typically specialized and incomplete. They do not involve the whole corporation. They are often wrong, unusable, and unused.

Fortunately, however, there are prototypes of information-processing systems that represent the best that people have been able to create so far. These are military and space systems, and they were first called *command and control systems* and are now usually called *common, control, communication, and intelligence* (or *information*) (C³I) *systems*. These systems are among the most complex of human creations. They require the most advanced sensors, computers, techniques of information refining and communication, and control of aircraft, missiles, spacecraft, and so forth.

C³I systems are used by the U.S. Air Force, Army, and Navy and NASA (National Aeronautics and Space Administration) at tactical, strategic, and political levels and for research, research and development (R&D), and operational missions.

A typical tactical operational mission, for example, involves the following sequential and iterative (repeated with successive refinements) functions (note that command has two meanings):

1. *Acquisition* of raw data and information by direct *surveillance* and *monitoring* and from other sources.
2. *Processing* of these acquired data, for example, by *filtering, compressing,* or *enhancing,* using various computer and person-computer methods.

3. *Integration* of data and information into applicable knowledge or intelligence.

4. *Identification,* for example, of friendly, hostile, and unknown forces and weapons. This function is so important in many C³I systems that it is treated separately from general decisionmaking.

5. *Communication* of data, information, and knowledge through the several operational steps from input to the system through output from the system and then back to the input to make a closed-loop process.

6. *Display* of information for decisionmaking.

7. *Coordination* and *integration* among several levels of organizational *command.*

8. *Decisionmaking* based on formally displayed information coupled with other knowledge.

9. *Issuance* of *command* decisions for *control* of ground forces, aircraft, missiles, satellites, or spacecraft as appropriate to the system.

10. Overall *monitoring* of *tactical* operations with quick to near instantaneous *response* based on *feedback* on *performance* and on new *strategic* or other inputs. (Such military terms as tactical can also apply to peacetime space missions, for example, and in any case they have widely infused the organizational literature.)

11. *Reconfiguration* of the entire system to reflect new qualitative and quantitative inputs.

This listing is obviously an embellishment on the input-throughput-output and stimulus-organism-response paradigms presented earlier.

The outputs of C³I systems are integrated with espionage information and the results of situational and area studies by intelligence and other agencies to produce a composite body of knowledge to be used by the highest levels of national policy- and decisionmakers.

Overall C³I systems are among the most successful creations. This is to a considerable extent due to the necessarily high priority placed on national defense and to the excitement of, and consequent funding for and applications of the latest technology to, space exploration.

C³I systems have a lot to offer the business, industrial, and government organizations which are the major concern here. However, as was demonstrated as long ago as the mid-1960s, there is no easy transfer of practices and technology from weapons and space to civil systems. (Earlier I have discussed this problem extensively.[16])

A rather amusing example of an attempt to create a C³I system for automotive traffic control can be seen in Los Angeles. First a number of large, elevated visual displays were built along the Santa Monica Freeway. Next these displays were connected to a control center that received inputs from subsurface sensors and from helicopters flying over the Santa Monica, San Diego, and Harbor Freeways. The would-be system was supposed to be experimental; if the results were successful, they could then be extended to the entire Los Angeles freeway network. Soon the displays began to flash such messages as "slowing ahead" and "accident ahead." But motorists complained that the information was useless because nothing could be done about the situation. Even getting off the freeway came to be a formidable task. And if one did get off, he found the surface streets congested and just once again finding and getting back onto the freeway so time-consuming as to be not worth the effort. Today the displays remain but serve mostly sort of a public-relations function—frozen messages warn of smog conditions, admonish the motorist to save gas by joining a car poor or taking the train, or wish the motorist a happy day!

Nor are the C³I systems themselves lacking the problems found in all very complex, highly technological systems. For example, automation, introduced to simplify tasks of military enlisted men, has actually made these tasks more difficult for the types of low-skilled persons available. And many other kinds of human factors engineering problems are endemic—problems of design of displays and controls, communications nets, and so forth.

Nevertheless, quite apart from naive expectations of 1:1 transfer of practices and technology, C³I systems can provide other organizations with a sophisticated philosophy of information-processing. For example, the concept of *functions* can be greatly enriched. Many businessmen still think of such broad activities as R&D, engineering, production, accounting, and marketing, as *the* functions of the organization. In order for most people really to understand an organization, it is necessary, formally or implicitly, to successively decompose the broad activities of the organization in input-throughput-output-feedback terms. This analysis will reveal such *basic* functions as sensing, monitoring, continuous control, and so on.

C³I systems have been widely studied by human factors experts, and the results of these studies could provide a wealth of knowledge about designing, for example, the person–machine interface. Unfortunately, human factors has seen little application to organizations as organizations although it has been widely applied to the weapons and space systems and other products of corporations and industries. With the increasing installation of computerized systems in organizations and with promises of automated offices and offices of the future, it is absolutely necessary that human factors play a significant role in the design and redesign of organizations.

Computerization in organizations may have been launched on the wrong trajectory. In the early 1950s general-purpose computers were developed into two specialized branches, scientific (and military) and business. Business computers took over what had been manual clerical, bookkeeping, and routine accounting and financial tasks. Business computers used simple concepts and algorithms (rules) and performed the same simple operations over and over again on masses of data. Often called number-crunchers, business computers become the main elements of data-processing. Even today the accounting and financial units of organizations are the major demanders and consumers of so-called management-information systems, which may be little more than large, clumsy COBOL (a business-oriented computer language) programs.

The critical problems facing organizations today—as emphasized already in this chapter—are problems of complex systems and environments. They are *not* problems of needing more and more data to be processed in routine, repetitive, completely preprogrammed, and unimaginative ways. Therefore, the historic developments in the scientific and military use of computers, including the C³I system, may be more relevant to modern managements than the precedent set by using business computers has been. Further, the dazzling proliferation of computer devices today is *no guarantee* of the effective use of these devices in organizations.

For the long-range intelligence and planning that are crucial to the adaptation and survival of organizations, a vastly improved implementation of theories and models is required. But this presents one of the greatest challenges humanity has as yet faced.

In C³I systems the laws of aerodynamics and celestial dynamics have long been well known. Mathematical equations can be written to describe these laws, and the equations can be solved exactly. Computer programs can be written in turn to express exactly the equations as instructions the computer can follow. Data typically involve vehicular positions, orientations, velocities, and accelerations, conditions of the physical environment, or patterns like landscapes. These data are usually exact or can be improved by various enhancing techniques.

In organizations, societies, and ecosystems, in contrast, there is a potpourri of incomplete, often contradictory theories, seemingly generalizable natural laws, unrelated subsystems possessing apparently explanatory cause–effect relationships, pockets of precise measurement, and masses of unorganized or poorly organized data.

The problem is not one merely of the lack of data. Actually in many cases there are too many data. The problem is the lack of complete, consistent, meaningful, and usuable data organized according to a theory of cause–effect interrelationship. Executives are very familiar with one type of data—*economic indicators*. Executives are also very familiar with—and watch carefully—certain subsets of economic indicators, for example, the *leading* and *cyclic* indicators. For a long time economic theory, one of the strongest in the social sciences, seemed to underlie these indicators. Recent happenings suggest that this is not the case, and economic models have lost much of their credibility. The situation is even worse for *social indicators*. Collected largely for administrative purposes, for example, by the Census Bureau, social indicators have never been much integrated by theory. These matters are of great concern to the design and management of continually adaptive organizations.

WHO IS THE *RIGHT* MANAGER?

At one time many people believed that a good manager could manage any company at any time. This was never completely true and is decreasingly true in today's climate of rapid social and technological change. Stated most succinctly a good manager is one who is *congruent* with the subsystems of his organization at a given time in the life history of his organization under a given set of external environmental conditions. A good manager must *fit* his changing organization and the changing world outside. There is no universally good manager, and any one person must be *right* for a particular pattern of circumstances.

Most executives have observed that some people are not appropriate for certain top management roles. These are the executives who have become frozen in time or space. In the simplest sense the main reasons why top management lacks or loses fit to the organization are *psychological*. The basic, underlying psychologcal dynamics can be expressed as varied and often apparently unrelated symptoms.

An executive can fail to possess or lose fit to the *type* of organization. Organizations might be contrasted as organic versus mechanistic or problem-solving-oriented versus production-oriented. An executive who requires definite rules and procedures, definite cause-effect explanations, a definite chain-of-command with associated absolute accountability, and definite answers to questions will feel anxious and ill at ease in an organic, problemsolving-oriented organization where there are no definite answers and much trial and error is required. It would be a mistake for an organic organization to hire an executive with strong psychological needs for structuring his surroundings. The reverse situation is of course also true.

An executive can fail to possess or lose fit to a given stage of organizational growth and evolution. The predominant pattern is growth and evolution from an organic structure/problemsolving orientation to a mechanistic structure/mass-production orientation to an increasingly incongruent structure/function beset by crises and the urgent need for a new design. A familiar example of loss of fit involves the scientist or engineer who founds and entrepreneurially guides the early growth of a company, and who continues to enjoy participating personally in product design and development, but who is at a loss when trying to deal with the increasing supervisory and paperwork loads of the growing company.

An executive can lack or lose fit to the overall *organizational climate*—a collective and emergent set of properties, mostly behavioral-social in nature and unique to a given organization, that can be sensed or perceived, often the first moment a person walks into an unfamiliar organization. In some organizations one may sense spontaneity, happiness, creativity—a place on the go. In other organizations the climate may almost crackle with tension. Organizational climate can provide one immediate indication of the health or sickness of an organization. Further analysis of the latter usually reveals such things as value conflicts, low morale, and capricious and arbitrary uses of power. As an example of loss of fit to organizational climate, an executive may experience a midlife crisis in which he loses confidence in himself and doubts all he once stood for. He feels and is increasingly isolated and is often increasingly hostile toward his colleagues and subordinates—he is more and more at variance with the dynamic organization that is leaving him behind. The opposite situation, involving an energetic executive and a deteriorating climate, is of course also true.

Much has been written about the needs and personalities of managers. One commonly described need is the need for *achievement,* which most simply is the need to perceive problems to be solved, to come up with practical solutions like engineering designs, and to receive nondelayed feedback information that one is doing a good job. The need for achievement is most important to individual designers, technology experts, and managers of technological activities in which people problems are few and minor. Many a good design engineer has been rendered incongruent through promotion to supervisor.

Another frequently suggested need is the need for *power.* This is unquestionably a major need, if not the predominant need, of top management. Power is pervasive is both organisms and organizations and is inherently neither good nor bad. It is the conscious or inadvertent misuse or abuse of power that can lead an organization into difficulties and dangers. A distinction can be made between two different types of power needs: (1) the need to accomplish personal and/or collective *goals through* control over people and resources, and (2) the need to control people *directly* just for the sake of control. As long as there are reasonable checks and balances and the powerholder is aware of and held accountable for the short- and long-term consequences of his actions, fulfillment of the first type of power need may contribute greatly to the health of some organizations. In other organizations power must be shared. Under any conditions, if the goals of the executive and of the organization as a whole begin to lose congruence, both the executive and the organization can expect trouble.

The second type of power need is pathological, and the organization can do without such people.

Other important needs for many executives are those of security, status, and prestige. These terms are more direct than the general or universal categories that may stem from attempts to classify needs or motives. One such attempt, familiar to almost every manager today, is the famous Hierarchy of Needs of Abraham Maslow. As an illustration here, an executive with a very high need for security is likely to be absolute and rigid in his thinking, require a formal and predictable structure in his surroundings and in the behavior of others, and be afraid to take risks and make decisions under uncertain and risky situations. An executive of this type is incongruent with an organization in which ambiguity, uncertainty, and risk-taking are the dominant features.

Two more global personality characteristics required of many executives are *empathy* and *charisma.* Empathy is the capability to put oneself into the other person's position. Without empathy an executive is emotion-blind and is neither able to perceive correctly nor identify with the increasing behavioral problems of modern organizations. Such executives usually seek rational solutions which only aggravate matters. Charisma is the ability to inspire in others confidence, trust, and relatively unquestioning belief and to focus and mobilize the energies of others into a common goal. This type of leadership ability is especially required during times of crisis. In many stable organizations performing predictable tasks, possession of charisma may be a disadvantage and charismatic persons seen as dangerous boat-rockers. And of course charismatic dictators and cult leaders are heartily condemned by people outside their following.

Executives may lose fit with their organizations through letting their abilities and skills become *obsolete*. Managerial obsolescence is increasingly common in these days of seemingly instantaneous social and technological change. It is well known that people's personalities are significantly shaped by the times when and places where they grew up. People who grew up during times of adversity like World War I and its aftermath, the Great Depression, and World War II and its aftermath tend to have different needs, values, and perceptions from those of people whose personalities were shaped during the roughly 1950–1975 Age of Affluence. The interpersonal skills of older executives often become obsolete. The needs and values of one generation are not necessarily better or worse than those of another generation. However, an executive who has strong opinions about authority, selfless sacrifice, patriotism, and the lesser status of women and minorities may experience some tough sledding if his employees increasingly consist of the young, women, and minority-group members.

Almost everybody today will run into the danger of being technologically obsolete, and executives are no exception. Entire sciences like geology, physics, and biology have been revolutionized in just a decade or so. Generations of equipment, computers, for example, last only a few years. Engineers and scientists, particularly if they specialize in changing technologies, can become obsolescent by age 30. Many of the perceptions of organizations and management and technical practices in organizations, which were developed and widely utilized in the 1960s and 1970s, may simply not be up to the challenges and opportunities of today and tomorrow. Top managements that do not keep current with the latest relevant technologies and their implications will very likely preside over organizations that fit their environments less and less.

Technology, however, is not by itself the answer to any organization's woes. Indeed, management itself has been rapidly changing in the direction of much greater dependency on technology experts and advisers. Some organizations are in effect run by these experts although they are not part of line management. Technologists almost always see the world as *rational*—once again, without feeling or emotion—and problems amenable to rational or formally logical solutions. But the world seldom if ever operates this way. Attempts to deal with behavioral/social problems in both organizations and societies by using rationalized approaches and methods have without question helped create many of our present crises. A major reason why the United States did not win the Vietnam War was the confusion of a complex social and cultural problem with a situation requiring only enough money and enough personnel and weaponry. In a similar vein foreign aid—enough money, technical advice, and help—has largely been a failure in the so-called underdeveloped world. The same limitations apply to welfare programs.

Top management often falls into *traps* because of self-delusion and misjudgment of the dynamics of a situation. Traps are costly, generate animosity, and eventually defeat the entrapped managers. An extremely common type of trap results from the overestimation of organizational power and the underestimation of the power of the forces of change. For example, a lot of time and effort was wasted and a lot of friction generated in both civilian and military organizations over the issue of young men's long hair, beards, and moustaches—which had a *symbolic* meaning to the wearers and in no way degraded either performance or neatness. The U.S. automobile industry has fallen into a very serious trap by variously believing that they knew consumer needs better than did the consumers, by deluding themselves that they were building only what the customer wanted, and by fooling themselves that they had the power and resources to outlast seemingly aberrant fluctuations in consumer tastes until times returned to "normal"—that is, bigger and costlier is better.

A third example of a managerial trap is the attempt to lock the barn door after the horse has been stolen. This is the attempt to return to earlier times, or to resimplify things and restore an earlier order, to pretend that value and other societal change never occurred, and to return to simple relations of cause and effect. Crackdowns are a common expression of this behavior. Because such behavior runs against the grain and the opponent is really a field of forces, attempts to reverse the irreversible are in the end doomed to failure.

Few executives today would be considered either robber barons or fire-and-brimstone authoritarians. In fact most executives condemn the excesses of the past. Nevertheless, the *equivalent* perceptions of current critics of large organizations and their managements pose threats to the performance and sometimes even the survival of these institutions. Large numbers of people are both antibusiness and antigovernment. Institutions will be increasingly evaluated in terms of new criteria such as overall contributions to society, conservation and protection of the environment, quality or working life, and so forth. These new criteria increase the burden of maintaining fit. Executives will increasingly want to ask questions like: Are my actions congruent all along the line—with my own best interests, with the best interests of my organization today, with the best interests of my organization in the long term, and with the best interests of society and the natural world at large? These questions may raise considerable soul-searching and personal conflict in many executives. If only the first or first and second parts of the question can be answered affirmatively, it might be that the executive will want to consider new orientations to his life and career.

In conclusion, top managers must possess fit to their organization and must maintain fit to rapidly changing organization-environment conditions. But can managers and anybody else change or be helped to change? The answer is yes—and no! There is a wealth of theoretical and clinical evidence that demonstrates unquestionably the importance of early childhood experiences in the shaping of personality and of unconscious (below the level of awareness) or preconscious (bare awareness) motivational processes in guiding behavior throughout one's life. Executives, and also many technical advisors, acknowledge these processes when they use terms like "hunch," "intuition," "subjective judgment," and "creativity." Indeed, it is interesting to note in passing that in many cases executives who base their decisions on an intuitive but holistic grasp of a situation do a better job than do executives who base their decisions on objective, rationalized information about components that in reality articulate poorly.

Human behavior *can* be modified, but *permanent* change involves a deep analysis, a long time, a high commitment to change, and often a change in environment. Many executives, feeling they do not have the time or cannot make the commitment, seek overnight cosmetic changes. But behavior cannot be permanently changed by weeklong sensitivity training or encounter sessions, behavior-modification programs, or many so-called management-development programs.

Holistic psychoanalytic, Gestalt psychological, and field theories of perception, motivation, and personality are more congruent with the complex-systems theme of this book than are the reductionistic (reduction to basic components) orientations of behaviorism and test-and-measurement psychology.

The *transactional analysis* of the late psychiatrist, Eric Berne[9] is a down-to-earth, modern descendant of Freudian psychoanalysis. Transactional analysis has caught on in management thinking, and several books on the subject relevant to management have been written on the subject. Berne wrote of a *hierarchy of decisions,* with the first decision made early in life and each successive and more specific decision dependent on all previous and higher-level decisions. How then can human behavior ever be completely free, autonomous, or rational?

ORGANIZATIONAL CRISIS—ANTICIPATION, MANAGEMENT, AND EXAMPLES

So far a body of theory, practical experience, and examples from many different sources has been presented that collectively provides an overview of the properties of adaptive, nonadaptive, and maladaptive organizations. In particular, the similarity among natural and person–made organizations and the necessity for establishing and maintaining congruence or fit among the four subsystems of the organization, the organization as a whole, and the several environments of the organization have been stressed. Organizational crises will continue to increase in frequency, variety, number of different sources, magnitude and intensity, and integration and amplification of isolated and small disturbances into large fields of crisis. Organizations that are other than adaptive will find it difficult to weather these crises.

A crisis is a *turning point* in the evolution of an organization; beyond this point the organization either continues along a generally desirable path or suffers a serious decline in capabilities and performance, perhaps to the extent of extinction. Because the exact point is usually difficult to determine, thinking should be in terms of critical *intervals* and *stages*.

A major, perhaps fatal deficiency of many organizations is that they *wait* until crisis descends upon them before *responding*. The opposite situation—stressed in this book—is the *anticipation* of potential crisis and the *preplanned management* of the crisis if it does occur. The terms, anticipation and preplanned management require further elaboration.

Anticipation demands first and foremost that the organization have a sophisticated information-processing system such as that outlined earlier. The adaptive and anticipatory organization must be able to:

1. Sense and measure the *present* state and dynamic processes within the organization, that is, the four subsystems and their interactions that collectively make up the internal environment. (Because of limitations of knowledge about complex systems, we may have to depend on temporary and makeshift methods until better techniques are developed.)

2. Provide *alternative future* configurations of the organization, based on an understanding of dynamic processes, expert judgments, and the methods of futures forecasting (presented in Chapter 4).

3. Sense and measure the *present* state and dynamic processes of the relevant external environments.

4. Provide *alternative future* configurations of the relevant external environments, based on the approaches indicated for Item 2.

5. Provide a dynamic, easily modifiable, easily updatable, integrated *model* of ongoing yet alternative organization–environment interrelationships. Designing such a model will be a formidable job, which will demand a great deal of our attention throughout the remainder of this book.

6. Assess present and future *goals*, conflicts between or among goals, and the *disparity* between desired goals and actual organization–environment conditions.

7. Provide a repertory of flexible *plans*, the use of any one or more of which is contingent on the factors mentioned in Items 1 through 6, the relevant level of the organization, and the strategic or long-range, tactical or short-range, or operational nature of the problem. Preplanned in the rigid sense that has traditionally been associated with practices in the Communist countries is not meant here. Needs for regulation and control keep changing.

8. Provide a repertory of flexible *actions* that are contingent on the factors mentioned in Items 1 through 7 and designed to minimize the disparity between desired goals and actual conditions.

Obviously such a program cannot be implemented overnight. Also the steps or items are iterative rather than strictly sequential.

The program will require commitment by top management and a willingness to develop new insights. Some of the insights are quite sophisticated, but others, fortunately, are common sense. For example, anticipatory management is like preventive maintenance and health care. These days most managers and professionals don't wait for their car (or their factory) to break down before servicing it. The new view of health care emphasizes staying healthy through exercise, diet, good daily habits, and so on, rather than the treatment of diseases.

The program will require the embedding of flexible equipment in a flexible organizational structure. Only advanced computer-communications equipment coupled with advanced sensors will have the necessary capability. Forms like matrix organizations, which in reality are usually superimpositions on or fine-tunings of basically bureaucratic structures, will be, by themselves, insufficient. Further, there will be necessary a much greater *rapprochement* between equipment design and organization design. Once again, the importance of taking a *sociotechnical systems approach* is stressed. Chapter 2 will discuss the many deficiencies consequent to focusing on the isolated parts of the organization.

The adaptive, anticipatory organization must figuratively be all things to all men and everywhere at once. Literally it must be both a *learning system* and a *self-organizing/self-adaptive system.* Many organizations have short memories. They do not appear to learn from their own experiences or the experiences of other organizations. This can be fatal. The organization must be capable of continuous learning, and this learning must be continually reflected in updated plans, policies, and decisions. The organization must keep its eyes open with respect to the factors outlined above. Information must be digested, integrated, and presented in a form that enhances comprehension and therefore learning of complex situations. Because much organizational behavior—and crisis—will be in the future, if the organization continues to exist, learning must come from the future as well as from the past and present. This will require a sophisticated modeling and computer simulation capability that presents the alternative configurations mentioned above and answers what if? types of questions about strategies, policies, and so on.

Self-organization/self-adaptation also reciprocally requires anticipation, preplanning, and predesign. A *potential* for quickly and flexibly assuming new configurations must be built into the organization. The organization cannot wait for a major pertubation or crisis and *then* start from scratch in assuming a viable new form. The human brain, probably the best example of a self-organizing, self-adapting, learning system, possesses a prestructure and a potential.

One type of system of course that possesses a very high potential for self-organization/self-adaptation is a cybernetic system. Cybernetics ties together much of what has been considered so far and provides a main basis for the detailed design presented in Chapter 8. Most executives are already familiar with the relatively primitive systems at the *operational* level, for example, automatic process control. The problem is to extend the concepts *as relevant,* to the organization as a whole.

Many good ideas about adaptive, anticipatory organizations are thus just waiting for further implementation. And fortunately some organizations have already put into practice certain features of adaptive organizations. Before truly adaptive organizations can be designed, however, great improvements are necessary in two main areas: (1) the enhanced development of the features now present in more or less embryonic form, and (2) much better understanding and therefore models of the organization as a whole.

For example, the *boundary-spanning* or *boundary-sensing* capabilities of the organization must be both greatly expanded and greatly refined. Boundary refers to the interface between the organization and its external environment. Market research, corporate intelligence-gathering, some technology assessments, futures research, and some planning are examples of boundary-spanning activities. Refinement refers to the elimination of deficiencies in information and knowledge like those discussed earlier. Managers must manage their organizations, not the *surrogate models* of their organizations produced by information distortion so aptly described by British cybernetician Stafford Beer.[18]

A great deal already has been said about feedback. Another example of a concept with a potential for further application is *feedforward.* Feedforward is closely associated with anticipatory goal-setting, control, and planning. It is therefore closely associated with forecasting changes and reconfigurations in the environments. Feedforward was implied in the eight items listed earlier. In the simplest sense feedback provides information on, or reinforcement or regulation of, *past* activities even though these past activities are part of an (extrapolative) computer simulation model of the future! In feedforward nothing has happened yet—things are only anticipated—and planning actions are taken to circumvent, counteract, or overcome some bad occurrence—a crisis. In feedforward planning it is usually necessary to design for better feedback. So the two are inseparable. In practice feedforward may take the form of bypassing certain operations or adjusting behavior to accord with a constraint such as distance, time, or budget.

This discussion has considered mainly the adjustment of organizational goals to meet actual and forecast environmental conditions. As every executive knows, this is only part of the picture—an organization can also adjust or try to adjust its environments to meet organizational goals. Advertising, lobbies in Washington and in state capitals, and vertical consolidations (with suppliers and/or customers) are familiar examples.

Planning has been mentioned before. Unfortunately, planning, especially in government organizations at every level and worldwide, is deficient to the extent of *guaranteeing crisis.* Some of the best organizational planning at least up to now, is done in financial institutions like banks and in innovative, broad-based corporations that utilize high technologies and have organic structures.

The single greatest reason for faulty planning is the failure to understand the organization or system as a whole and in interrelationship to its environments. Although this has been said many times before, the message bears reemphasizing. Other reasons include: (1) planning is not taken seriously and receives little if any backing from top management, (2) people don't know how to plan, (3) the tools for planning are deficient or missing, (4) the short-range almost always seems more important and more demanding than does the long-range, and (5) planning can rock the boat and therefore be dangerous to one's position.

The ability to anticipate crisis is often limited by the very human perceptions and beliefs of some top managers. For example:

1. *Managers discount.*   This means that they place a lower value on people, resources, situations, and events that are removed in time and space than they would if these same entities were here and now. Discounting of course militates strongly against long-range thinking and long-range planning.

2. *Managers think in terms of linearity and continuity.*   Tomorrow will be very much like yesterday and today. Changes, if they occur, will be small, predictable, and easily managed by making small, incremental responses, that is, by making quick fixes and muddling through. This thinking also militates against long-range planning.

3. *Managers rely overly on technological solutions to complex organizational and societal problems.*   Technology will always be able to find and exploit new natural resources, create new products and markets, feed the hungry, provide jobs for the poor, and so on. These managers ignore both the possible limits to technological implementations and the harmful side effects of technology.

4. *Managers are unaware of the momentum of faulty practices that organizations develop.*   Once detected, these practices are hard to stop. Both the continuation and rectification of faulty practices leads to numerous brushfires and a preoccupation with the past and present rather than with the future.

In its most severe and acute form organizational crisis leads to extinction through bankruptcy, involuntary acquisition or merger, or abolition by a higher authority. In a less fatal form crisis is expressed in terms of loss of an important subsidiary, for example, by U.S. government antitrust action or foreign nationalization; loss of market share; loss of access to resources; loss of return on investments, often expressed as wastage of hundreds of millions of dollars; paralyzing strikes; major accidents; and so on. In an insidious and chronic form, organizational crisis is associated with stagnation and gradual decay, often followed by precipitous decline.

In dealing with actual cases it is almost always difficult to resolve cause-effect relationships and almost always wrong to define simple unidirectional, linear, A-causes-B relationships. In peforming organizational analyses, answers to questions like the following usually pose difficulties: to what extent did corporate arrogance lead to faulty worksystem design that led to deteriorating morale and poor training that lead to the major accident that led to decreased public confidence that led to loss of support or market share? Did an organization with an ingrown, closed-system style of thinking choose a new executive, who made essentially preprogrammed maladaptive decisions, precipitating crisis?

Why did productivity start to decline? Was an executive action the major cause of crisis, or did it merely break the camel's back, that is, exceed a predetermined threshold?

Obviously the scale, number of dimensions, causal dynamics, and immediacy of crises differ. The following list is an arbitrary sampling of organizational crises which roughly cover the decade, 1970–1980. The organizations listed below have variously perished, survived in reduced form, snapped back, become better from the experience, suffer chronic illness, or are so acutely ill as to be almost hopeless. In each case the organization, date or period, and major critical symptom, and some associated conditions are given:

Penn-Central.   June 21, 1970, loss of $4 million and collapse in bankruptcy. Formed earlier by merger of several railroads to become the largest transportation system in the United States; collapse followed abuses of corporate power; largest company ever to enter bankruptcy proceedings.

Rolls-Royce.   (British), February 4, 1971, collapse in bankruptcy. Collapse associated with attempts to contract the manufacture of engines for the Lockheed 1011 Tri-Star aircraft; closed down previously successful airplane-engine-making capability.

Lockheed Aircraft Corporation.   Late 1971, government-guaranteed bank loan of $250 million to stave off bankruptcy. Near collapse followed severe cost and schedule overruns involving the Tri-Star commercial aircraft (and Rolls-Royce), the C5A military transport aircraft, and other aircraft; followed by years of high debt ($700 million in 1973); L-1011s did not recoup their development costs; bribery scandals in mid-1970s led to government changes in Japan and Holland.

Boise Cascade.   Early 1970s, suffered $200 million loss. Followed unsuccessful expansion into recreational land and houses.

Pan American World Airways.   Late 1960s to mid-1970s, in the red from 1969–1974 with total losses over $170 million ($107 million in 1974). Misjudged markets, with overexpansion of routes and purchase of costly equipment; many routes turned out to be unprofitable; most routes overseas; hit by increased competition of U.S. and foreign airlines; hit by energy crisis and rising fuel costs; reputation of poor service and low employee morale; merged with National Airlines, but still lost $108.5 million during the first half of 1980.

Litton Industries.   Early to mid-1970s, plunges in earnings and stock values, increased deficits, with final losses of about $200 million. Followed bad acquisition policies; some of the acquisitions were duds.

Eastern Airlines. Mid-1970s, large dollar losses ($50 million in 1975). Reputation of low morale and low productivity.

W. T. Grant & Company. October, 1975, entered bankruptcy proceedings (second largest company ever to do so). Followed policies of major overexpansion and broadening the merchandise base to include higher-priced items; items priced beyond means of established customers; big backlog of inventory purchased on credit.

(GEICO) Government Employees Insurance Company. Mid-1970s, lost $124 million in 1975 and $40 million in the first half of 1976, planned to declare bankruptcy in 1976. In 1974 had been the nation's fifth largest automobile insurance company; near demise had followed a pattern of growth-mania including insuring poor risks; hard hit by inflation in costs of automobile parts and services and of medical claims; survived following massive cuts and retrenchments.

Rohr Industries. Late 1960s to mid-1970s, large dollar losses (lost $52.1 million in fiscal year 1976, more than that of any other company on the *Fortune 500* list). Failed to assess the market properly and to understand the intricacies of complex technology; had unwisely expanded from its role as a successful manufacturer of aircraft engine pods and other components; greatly misjudged the difficulty of transferring aerospace know-how into the civil sector; sustained losses from the production of buses and trains for BART (San Francisco Bay Area Rapid Transit) and Washington, D.C. Metro systems; cost overruns and large debts; retrenched to its former role.

A&P. Early to late 1970s (and ongoing?), continual decline in sales, profits, and stock values. The oldest and once the largest grocery store/supermarket chain; heavy top-down management and widespread organizational obsolescence; rigid formulas for improvement; continued deterioration accompanying expensive consultant advice; decisionmaking lagging behind real-world changes; in 1979 Tengelmann, a well-managed German retail grocery chain agreed to buy 42 percent of A&P stock shares.

British and French governments and aerospace industries. 1962 to present (and ongoing), Concorde supersonic commercial transport aircraft. Loss of $4.28 billion with little chance to recoup; huge cost overruns, overoptimistic sales estimates, poor cost controls, political meddling; hit by inflation and rapidly rising fuel prices more than were competitors.

Electric Boat Division of General Dynamics. Late 1970s, huge cost overruns and serious delays in production of the Trident submarine threatening to lead to unfavorable changes in the contracts with the U.S. Navy (which must share the blame). Each submarine exceeded the original cost estimate by over 50 percent; attempted to make the submarine far bigger and faster than required to meet mission requirements; corporate overenthusiasm in obtaining contracts for both Trident and attack submarines led to too-rapid expansion of the workforce (which included a large number of low-skilled persons) which led in turn to decreased productivity and severe personnel problems; apparently no workable management-information system for ordering and stocking parts and materials; these difficulties followed by a massive crackdown.

New York City. Mid- to late-1970s (and ongoing?), near bankruptcy. Poor tax structure and loss of tax base; large numbers of indigent persons; massive overspending on education, welfare, and other services.

New York City and Con Edison (electrical utility). July 13, 1977, electrical power blackout followed almost immediately by widespread and extremely costly looting. Poor contingency planning, control room design, operating procedures, and training on the part of Con Edison; societal forces creating a field just waiting to be ignited; monetary costs running into the hundreds of millions of dollars; a grim omen of things to come.

Complex involving the nuclear power industry, several government levels and agencies, and Metropolitan Edison (the local utility). March 28, 1979 and following days (and ongoing), nuclear reactor failure and near meltdown at Three Mile Island near Harrisburg, Pennsylvania. Poor control room design, personnel selection and training, and operating and maintenance procedures; generalized confusion; poor evacuation plans; followed by major inquiries and rediscovery of points made by human factors experts and critics of nuclear power years earlier.

McDonnell Douglas and American Airlines. May 25, 1979, crash at O'Hare International Airport, Chicago of a DC-10 killing 271 persons. Apparently faulty aircraft design, faulty maintenance procedures, and poor visibility from cockpit; followed by grounding of large numbers of DC-10s and disruption of flight schedules and loss of operating revenues all over the world.

Chrysler Corporation. Mid-1970s to present (and ongoing), near bankruptcy followed by a government-guaranteed bank loan of $1.5 billion plus a follow-on loan of $400 million. Poorly planned releases of new automobile models; heavy debt loads; large inventories of unsold cars; insulated thinking; massive failure to heed warning signs regarding changes in markets, human values and beliefs, foreign competition, and energy sources; failure pattern symptomatic of pervasive illness in the U.S. automobile industry.

First Pennsylvania Bank of Philadelphia. April 1980, imminent collapse staved off by government-backed $500 million loan. Had misjudged the time of peaking of interest rates leading to poor longer-term investments and a shortage of operating capital; possibly only the first of nearly 300 banks that are nearing collapse.

U.S. military. April 25, 1980, failure of attempt by multiservice team to rescue American hostages held at U.S. Embassy, Teheran, Iran. Cost eight lives, seven RH-53 helicopters, one C-130 transport, and $25 million in operating expenses, as well as incalculable losses in prestige and faith, both at home and abroad; failure attributed to bad weather, communications blackouts required for security, too few helicopters, improper maintenance, and lack of preparation and training; more significantly and more ominously, there was, according to one senior military man, no single action or lack thereof that led to the failure.

U.S. Postal Service.   Continuing deterioration of benefit-cost ratios. Decreasing services and increasing costs despite changes in management, expansion of facilities, and addition of large amounts of automated equipment; serious morale problem; hampered by obsolescent regulations; facing increasing competition from more efficient, more reliable private carriers and from electronic transmission.

U.S. Social Security.   Continuing deterioration. Inflation and demographic changes to the ratio of active to retired workers have seriously jeopardized this program of transfer of payments from one generation to another; private pension plans in corporations are also in jeopardy; one more example of the failure of yesterday's good ideas to survive the turbulent environment.

U.S. Labor Unions.   Mid-1970s to present (and continuing), decreasing confidence and decline in bargaining power. Old leadership and obsolete ways of thinking; loss of contact with younger constituency; many goals incompatible with changes in turbulent environment.

The Departments of U.S. Government, especially Housing and Urban Development and (using the older term) Health, Education, and Welfare.   Overall poor performance and low benefit-cost ratios. The typical bad features of large bureaucracies; failure to meet established goals; actual exacerbation of many problems (for example, the institutionalization of poverty and urban decline); often the playthings of power groups and vested interests; although founded with good intentions, these organizations continued and amplified many features of bad design that are ages old, and they appear to have contributed materially to the present woes and perhaps the irreversible decline of the United States.

These synopses of course only scratch the surface.[19] Nor do the critical points or intervals necessarily end within the times indicated. Hoped-for corrective action may lead to worse difficulties in the future. It seems to be in the nature of much human thinking to search for and find for every event a cause close by in space and time, and then to find a culprit to blame and to punish. Thus, as every executive is well aware, the time-honored response to organizational crisis is to fire the CEO and perhaps sweep clean all top management. These actions may be accompanied by a general crackdown and waves of firings or punishments throughout the organization.

Such thinking and behavior are most maladaptive. It is hard to pin the blame on a mutually causal system or on a field of forces. Yet that is the way the world really operates. Unfortunately, this systems thinking goes against the grain of most people. And, unfortunately, systems thinking has not really caught on outside the circles of systems scientists, engineers, and management academics. So, many organizations will continue to *respond* to crises with firings and crackdowns rather than to *anticipate* and to *plan* for possible future crises.

The remainder of this book will be devoted to looking at the many reasons why organizations fall into the difficult straits exemplified above.

THE ORGANIZATION—1981–2001

January 1, 2001 will inaugurate the twenty-first century. The world on that day will be quantitatively and qualitatively different from the world today. It will less resemble the world of today than today's world resembles the world of January 1, 1961. This is because of two major types of dynamics: (1) high rates of change—and changes in the rates of change—and therefore short doubling times in large sociotechnical systems (sociotechnical macrosystems) and in the natural environment, and (2) reconfigurations of fields of forces.

The world of January 1, 2001 will be a function of unpredictable random events like some accidents and discoveries. But even more so it will be a function of forces, variables, policies, and practices that are operating today. No one is yet aware of all these factors and how they combine and interact, and designing the appropriate explanatory and forecasting models therefore becomes an indispensable planning function for the adaptive organization and society.

Wide experience with most types of complex systems—weapons, space, transportation, urban, and others—shows that *lead times* for planning and development range from 10 to 20 years. This means that the organization must start *now* to think about what it wants to be in the year 2001. This *does not mean* that the organization casts its plans in concrete.

Whether long-range planning and control will work or not will depend on the answers to some tough questions. Three of them are posed here rhetorically: Can changes in the turbulent environmental field be predicted with enough advance warning to permit appropriate action by maximally anticipatory and adaptive organizations? Can such organizations actually be constructed? Can the appropriately congruent and motivated top managements be found?

The last twenty years of this century will witness the outcomes of many of the stresses and strains and conflicts that we witness today. Favorite ideologies and practices will increasingly be seen as exhausted. More and more people will become disillusioned with the promises and practices of Marxism, capitalism, organized religions, Keynesian economics, sudden new solutions and counter-solutions, and so forth. The world will increasingly split into the Haves and Have Nots, both within and among nations. Countless numbers of people will resent the status quo and will seek alternatives. Leaders will become panicked and will attempt to crackdown and return to simpler times of law and order. Repression and violence will beget more violence. The natural environment as a whole will be increasingly degraded, and many natural resources will become exhausted. Technological solutions will help here and hurt there. The world system will oscillate dangerously. The likelihood of a coalescence of deliberate acts and miscalculations leading to a threshold and

World War III sometime during the next two decades, assuming the continuation and acceleration of present forces, is very high.

This is not an optimistic scenario. Chapters 6 and 7 will discuss environmental configurations that would favor this or alternative scenarios. Properly designed, properly managed organizations will play major roles in encouraging the unrolling of desirable scenarios.

Here, for now, are some of the elements, both desirable and undesirable, that must be considered in planning for adaptive organizations and desirable futures:

Broadening of the concepts of organizational ownership, performance, and ethics to include all *stake*holders and obligations toward society and the natural environment.

Continuing instability and transformation of the world economic system.

Achievement of some of the limits to growth of world population, the economy, resource utilization, and environmental degradation.

Achievement of some of the limits to organizational size and complexity.

Achievement of some of the limits to technological development and application.

Great increases in the relative levels of worldwide education, coupled with appropriately rising expectations and a relative scarcity of desirable jobs.

Continued changing of values, including possible *reversal* of some values, toward the self, individual rights and freedom, the organization, authority, status, rank and privilege, bigness, the nation-state, other people, and the natural environment.

Erosion of the bases for hierarchical designs in many organizations.

Changes in management ethics.

Changes in the *symbolic* value of products.

The exhaustion of the concepts of mercantilism and mass-consumption as anomalous stages in the evolution of world societies.

Spread of alienation and the disruptive power of the alienated, leading to polarized groups and populations.

Shifts in the international distribution of political or economic power, coupled with demands for more equitable distribution of resources.

Increasing political instability throughout most of the world.

Finally, the point at which perception leaves off and reality begins is usually blurred, and the more complex the situation, the more diffuse the relationship between perception and reality. Thus, for purposes of planning, if large numbers of people perceive and believe that large corporations are degrading the natural environment and pocketing huge profits at the expense of the people, it is almost immaterial whether these perceptions and beliefs are accurate or not. Under either condition, popular ire will be expressed in attempts to get back at the big companies through litigation, legislation, collective bargaining, strikes, and so forth.

MAJOR PITFALLS: PART APPROACHES TO ORGANIZATIONAL ANALYSIS AND DESIGN

As seen in Chapter 1 increasing complexity has become one of the pervasive problems of the modern world. Technological advances and solutions to prior difficulties often spawn new and unexpected problems. The organization has become highly dependent on the advice of experts in specialty areas. Often experts are consulted *after* a crisis has arisen. On other occasions a widespread organizational problem is severely and improperly delimited in passing through the specialists' perceptual filters. Too infrequently is expert advice solicited, within a holistic framework, in an anticipatory rather than a reactive mode.

Specialists provide different foci and attend to the needs of different audiences. The main lines of distinction include:

An emphasis on people as opposed to an emphasis on things.

An emphasis on the individual person as opposed to an emphasis on groups.

An emphasis on the work system as opposed to an emphasis on the product of that work system.

An emphasis on internal organizational processes as opposed to an emphasis on external environmental processes.

A rational usually mathematical, as opposed to an intuitive usually clinical approach.

The specialty areas can be classified into three broad categories—psychological, mathematical or technological, and environmental.

THE BEHAVIORAL SCIENCE APPROACH

The term behavioral science was coined during the Cold War when certain scientists felt that social science sounded suspiciously like socialism. Earlier, psychology, under the influence of the theory called behaviorism, had received one definition as the science of behavior. Today in the systems sense behavioral science has a much broader connotation than psychology.[1] However, in the organizational sense the behavioral scientist is not only nearly always a psychologist, but he is also a special kind of psychologist. He is usually a specialist in motivation, personality, or group dynamics; less frequently his specialty is learning or testing and evaluation. In contrast, the human factors expert, when his background is psychology, is usually an experimental psychologist. These distinctions are important because specialization within a discipline, let alone that between disciplines, biases the way the problem is perceived and attacked. Rarely have specialists, even different kinds of psychologists, successfully collaborated on projects. Organizations, particularly large think tanks, *do* employ specialists of different types, but the skills of these people are usually channeled into separate projects.

The behavioral science approach, the earliest version of which was called *human relations,* arose largely as a reaction to what many persons considered to be the excesses of the first Industrial Revolution in general and the scientific management of Frederick W. Taylor in particular. The criticized industrial changes included dividing jobs into isolated tasks, separation of action from decision, homogenization of workers into mass-production systems, loss of control by people not only over their jobs but also over much of their lives, subordination of people to the machine and to mass-production technology and to a parallel impersonal bureaucracy, and an overall dehumanization of work. Human relations also had origins in the famous Hawthorne studies and in the humanistic psychology of Abraham Maslow. Human relations sought to impart a friendly atmosphere to the job. It stressed the motivational importance of friendship with one's co-workers. It also stressed to management that workers respond favorably to personal attention and discussion of their needs and that the carrot-and-stick is not the only worker-motivation scheme and maybe not even a good one. The human relations movement was too simple and it didn't work, but it did do two important things. First, it pioneered some good ideas that subsequently have been greatly expanded by the newer behavioral science and psychology-related management approaches. Second, it triggered reactions that have led to much more sophisticated conceptual models of work, management, and the organization.

Job Enrichment

Job enrichment is an approach to motivation, morale, job satisfaction, and increased productivity that is oriented to the *individual* worker. It is the application of the *two-factor theory* of Professor Frederick Herzberg.[2] The two factors are motivators (satisfiers) and hygiene (dissatisfiers). Only the former are held to motivate workers. Hygiene is at best neutral; however, bad hygiene can demotivate people. Motivators apply to the personal relation between the worker and his job. Hygiene usually applies to the job context. A motivating job is one that provides challenge, responsibility, enjoyment, earned recognition, feelings of achievement, and opportunities for growth and advancement. Hygiene consists of work-environment factors which frustrate realization of the motivators and such specific factors as behavior of supervisors, pay that is thought to be unfair or discriminatory, work rules, company policy and administration, physical working conditions, and fringe benefits. It can be readily seen that if management accepts the motivator/hygiene theory many long-favored corporate plans and policies are on the wrong track.

Job enrichment stresses expansion of the decisional, discretionary, and personal-accountability aspects of the job. The individual job becomes more self-contained, less dependent on outside control. Ideally, supervision and management themselves become enriched. Freed from the need to monitor and control individual employee behavior in detail, supervision can concentrate on providing support for motivated behavior and the satisfaction of maintenance needs. Management in turn, faced with fewer brushfires, has more time to spend on long-range plans for the design of better jobs and worksystems.

Job enrichment programs have indeed been implemented in such large companies as Texas Instruments and Britain's Imperial Chemical Industries. Positive results on both job satisfaction and productivity have been reported for a wide variety of employees including scientists, engineers, laboratory technicians, manufacturing supervisors, sales representatives, and hourly technicians and assemblers. However, not everyone wants his job enriched. Because of personality factors, some people seek hygiene and find their greatest satisfactions outside the job. Some jobs, especially in such important areas as assembly-line operations, are capable of little if any enrichment. Most important, the long-range effects of such programs are unknown. Yesterday's novelties become today's accepted state of affairs. Do motivation programs produce a sustained yield? Or does the system swallow such perturbations and return to its old steady state?

Behavior Modification

Behavior modification is based on stimulus–response (S–R) learning theory and on the viewpoint that motivation must be studied in terms of objective external behavior rather than in terms of internal drives or consciousness states. Behavior modification has roots, going back to the early years of this century, in the work on conditioning by the Russian physiologist Pavlov and the American psychologist John B. Watson. Behavior modification is based on a specific form of conditioning called *operant conditioning,* which today is particularly the creature of psychologist B. F. Skinner.

The key idea of operant conditioning is the reinforcement or reward of desired behaviors. Behavior is a function of or contingent on the effects imposed by the environment. Students of this field look for relationships between the antecedent stimulus, the response or behavior itself, and the consequences of behavior or contingencies of reinforcement. There are four main types of reinforcement: (1) positive reinforcement, (2) negative reinforcement or punishment, (3) no reinforcement, (extinction), and (4) avoidance or learning to avoid an undesirable stimulus. Behavior modifiers usually say that they prefer to use the first type.

The focus of behavior modification is the individual or small group (rarely a small organization). Four or five steps are typically followed:[3]

1. Identify such critical behaviors as job turnover, absenteeism, or performance relative to the quality or quantity of work.

2. Measure the behaviors objectively, for example, by using unobtrusive observation or analysis of existing records. Record frequencies of each behavior.

3. Identify the antecedent stimuli and contingent consequences of each behavior. The antecedent stimuli may arise either inside or outside the work situation and therefore may not always be under direct management control. However, behavior is held to be a function of its consequences, and these consequences can be under management control.

4. Intervene in order to enhance the desirable behaviors that contribute to improved performance and to discourage undesirable behaviors. Positive reinforcement is usually employed, incorporating feedback of information on performance and such natural reinforcers as attention and recognition. Extinction or punishment may be used to discourage undesirable behaviors.

5. Evaluate the results of the program. First, it is ascertained using an interview or questionnaire if the participants like behavior modification as an approach to human resources management. Then it is determined if the intervention is changing behaviors in the desired manner. This is done by comparing postintervention behavioral frequencies with those baseline frequencies obtained in Step 2.

Behavior modification as an approach to organizational change cannot be evaluated outside the context of the decades-old school of psychology known as behaviorism. And behaviorism has received some harsh criticisms.[4] As an analytic-reductionistic theory, behaviorism runs counter to the holistic theme of this text. Although behavior modification is currently popular as a practice, it provides nothing new conceptually. Indeed, it may simply be a new veneer for the old carrot-and-stick philosophy of management (reward the good guys and punish the bad guys). Behavior modification can also be easily reconciled with the operations research-management science approach and other analytic approaches which many critics consider to be modern-day Taylorism. Collectively, purely analytic approaches convey a mechanistic impression of the organization, a throwback to earlier times. Unfortunately, mechanistic models still appeal to some managers.

There is no evidence for long-term and sustained organizational improvements that can be attributed solely to behavior modification. Routine use of praise, recognition, and feedback can quickly lead to loss of potency of these reinforcers. Initial improvements reported by behavior modifiers may simply be Hawthorne effects due to selecting employees for special attention by management and by outside consultants. Dramatic results, such as those at Emery Air Freight which supposedly saved the company $3 million over three years, often reflect the confounding effects of technological change and market expansion.

Assessment Centers

The focus of the assessment-center approach is the individual potential manager, management trainee, or candidate for promotion. The most sophisticated tools are various manual, individual or group games and simulations which purport to mimic the real-world operations of the organization. Probably the most familiar game is the in-basket game which can involve some 30 items all of which require attention, assignment to categories, setting of priorities, and decisions. Typical items might include a civil rights case, resignation of a valued employee, cancellation of a project, and negotiation with a union. Group exercises can be exemplified by teams which compete for limited resources.

Participants can be rated along a number of behavioral dimensions such as leadership, judgment, risk-taking, sensitivity, stress tolerance, decisiveness, creativity, independence, communication, and problem analysis. The raters usually consist of mixtures of behavioral scientists, assessment-center staff, and managers above the level of the participant. Ratings typically range from one through five. Exercises can be tailor-made to various organizational levels. Assessments are composites of observations during the exercises, follow-up interviews, analysis of the written and oral presentations of the candidates, and interpersonal interactions with the evaluators.

The assessment-center approach is currently very popular and is apparently accepted at face value by management. Some 2000 companies and government agencies use or have used the approach, including General Motors, Ford, Sears, IBM, General Electric, HUD, HEW, the FBI, the Social Security Administration, the Civil Service Commission, and the U.S. Air Force. Yet the literature shows very little evidence for validity. Indeed, studies have shown that far simpler and less costly traditional judgments by executives can yield equally good or superior predictions of future performance.[5]

In addition to possessing a very questionable validity, assessment-center methodology introduces two other serious problems. First, assessments when seriously utilized may yield a self-fulfilling prophecy; that is, assessment results may form the basis for promotion and salary-increase decisions while the latter are used as major criteria for effective managerial performance. Managers selected for promotion and high salary increases are those with high assessment-center ratings. Then later it is pointed out that managers who had had high ratings now have high positions and salaries. Second, the behavioral traits and dimensions are to a considerable extent arbitrary, and many of them are subjective. Even granted that they can be and are correctly defined and measured, there is no evidence that these are the only or necessary traits of managers in adaptive organizations. The situation may be one of the old's reinforcing itself by selectively eliminating those who do not fit a known and predetermined mold. In this way, incipiently dangerous positive feedback loops can be generated and perpetuated, which leads eventually to loss of organizational stability and adaptability.

Sensitivity Training and Related Methods

Sensitivity training (also known as the T-group approach and laboratory method) grew out of scientific research on group dynamics, performed by Kurt Lewin and others in the late 1940s. Carl Rogers's nondirective, client-centered therapy also played an important role. The focus is on the development of individual self-awareness and awareness of the impact of one's behavior on others in the context of small groups of about 10 to 15 persons. The groups vary in amount of structure and degree of relationship to real-world work problems. Emphasis is on emotional rather than intellectual learning and on attitude change. A leader attempts, usually nondirectively, to guide the group toward the realization of its goals and to ensure that all members have an equal opportunity to participate. The training is done away from the work environment.

As is the case with other approaches, sensitivity training can be criticized both in terms of inherent deficiencies and in terms of lack of evidence as to persistent and long-term positive effects. Sensitivity training is inconsistent with every theory of personality that holds that personality is structured in the first several years of life. It is not credible that needs, traits, perceptions, values, and attitudes that have been shaped over many years can easily and permanently be changed by training sessions lasting one to three weeks. Personality represents a dynamic steady state, established in the face of pressing needs, frustrations, and conflicts. The confrontation characteristic of T-groups has proved to be traumatic to many persons. Self-confidence can be undermined, and anxieties and hostilities generated which find no resolution back at the workplace. As stressed throughout this book, the behavior of any system is a function of interactions between the system and its environment. The work environment is much different from the laboratory environment, often a pleasant retreat or resort, and behavior induced in the simpler environment can hardly be expected to carry over to the more complex work environment. And years of psychological research demonstrate that under stress people frequently regress to previous forms of behavior.

Experience in many organizations has shown that the mean old boss's new interpersonal skills are perceived by employees as being, like misuses of consultative and participative management, just one more form of manipulation. The heyday for sensitivity training was the period 1965–1975 during which untold millions of dollars were spent on T-group programs. Management today is less enamored of this approach for three main reasons: (1) unfulfilled promises and bad experiences, (2) the approach was after all a fad, and (3) the approach has to some extent merged into and been supplanted by organizational development.

Organizational Development

Organizational development (OD) can be all things to all persons. Ideally, OD is an integrated, holistic approach to problemsolving and planning for the psychological, social, and political subsystems of the organization, which also interfaces well with the technological subsystem. It can be applied to any or all levels of the organization. In reality, OD is usually a potpourri of approaches and techniques that may be conceptually and practically incompatible. At one extreme OD may be simply a synonym for, say, sensitivity training. At the other extreme OD may incorporate some or all of the behavioral science techniques already discussed—often to the chagrin of the authors of the individual orientations—as well as familiar management approaches such as management-by-objectives (MBO).

A key goal of OD is the integration of individual and organizational goals. Another key goal is to encourage and facilitate necessary organizational change. Consultants called *change agents*, playing catalytic roles, help organizations diagnose and solve their own problems of communications, conflict, interpersonal difficulties, participation in decisionmaking, career growth, and general job dissatisfaction.

Although OD lacks a comprehensive theoretical framework, many of its practitioners follow the conceptual sequence of Kurt Lewin—*unfreezing* of attitudes, poor interpersonal relationships, counterproductive behavior, and so forth, *changing,* and *refreezing.* Unfreezing involves making participants aware of the contribution of their own dysfunctional behavior to the previously diagnosed organizational problems of absenteeism, high job turnover, low productivity, lack of competitiveness with other organizations, loss of market share, and so forth. The group methods discussed earlier can be utilized here. Changing involves the application of one or more of the techniques or programs indicated below. Refreezing requires the reinforcement of the desired new attitudes, procedures, insights, and behavior patterns.

Most executives today have been exposed to the major change programs. Here are some of the commonest:

Team-building
Career and life planning
Management-by-objectives
Conflict resolution
Mutual goal-setting
Specific training
Specific reward structures
Participative management

Overlapping groups

Provision of feedback

Multiple management

The effects of OD, like those of the behavioral science approaches discussed earlier, are difficult to evaluate. Certainly it is trite to remark again that most of the intractable problems in organizations appear to be people-generated or people-related. Many managers are desperate for any help they can get in grappling with these problems. And OD is itself big business today. Many top companies in the United States and abroad have utilized OD programs and most of these have reported positive results. Companies using OD have included General Motors, U.S. Steel, TRW, Texas Instruments, Union Carbide, Polaroid, Kaiser Steel, Weyerhaeuser, Esso, Royal Dutch/Shell, Corning Glass, FIC (Mexico), and Donnelly Mirror. The program at the last company has been frequently cited as a success story; yearly gains in productivity and profits were reported over many years, and these gains were fed back to the workers in the form of salary bonuses.

The biggest impact of OD, however, may not be on objective organizational outputs like productivity and profits in specific companies, but rather on maintaining, perhaps even increasing, the collective momentum toward more humanistic organizations. There is evidence that OD works better in institutions that are *already* oriented toward more organic structures. There is also evidence that OD does not work so well during hard times. In some companies OD may even have hindered adaptation to changing environments. Indeed, some companies have abandoned their OD programs during socioeconomic setbacks when executives felt that they were losing control. During stress both individuals and institutions often revert to earlier more rigid and authoritarian types of behavior. It should be noted in passing that some of the companies mentioned above have recently experienced difficulties. Some industries as a whole, among them the American steel and automobile industries and industries *dependent on them*, are currently being buffeted severely by turbulent environmental forces.

The experiences of companies will differ. Some will discover that, in spite of having invested large sums in OD programs, their ability to anticipate and adapt to crises will not have improved. Others will find that the OD programs have contributed to weakening their adaptive capabilities. Still other companies may discover that, because their programs were correctly managed, their adaptive capabilities have been improved. A well-managed organizational development program must possess three characteristics: (1) *consistent* top-management interest and support, (2) integration with long-range planning, and (3) updating on a continuing basis in order to incorporate the newest knowledge, methods, and experience.

Finally, in keeping with the theory underlying this book, it is likely that the behavioral science approach in toto has hastened value and attitude change, the institutionalization of humanistic thinking, and the conversion of privileges into rights. Such changes in system state will not be easy to reverse should future managers decide that it is in the best interests of their organizations to try to do so.

THE CLASSICAL SOCIOTECHNICAL SYSTEMS APPROACH

By the early 1950s it became evident in several industries that mechanization and automation were not always yielding the desired results. Indeed, introduction of new technology often resulted in lowered productivity, decreased morale and job satisfaction, and increased alienation and psychosomatic difficulties.

The term *sociotechnical system* was coined by Eric Trist and his colleagues from the Tavistock Institute in London, who, in studies of newly mechanized but problem-ridden British coal mines, determined that the social system and technical system could not be designed apart from one another. A production system must be viewed therefore neither as a purely technical system to which any workers can adapt nor as an aggregation of workers whose human relations must be satisfied.

The concepts of sociotechnical systems can be applied to three levels: the work system, the organization, and the society. Most studies have dealt with industrial production systems, white-collar operations in businesses and service industries, mining, and transportation systems. Examples include automobile and other assembly, banking, hospital operations, Indian automatic looms, coal mining, bus operations, and the design of cargo-container ships.

The behavioral science approaches emphasized interactions between and among people and between the individual and his job. Sociotechnical systems analysis and design look at the interactions between the technology and the working group. One type of work-system design (or more frequently redesign) is job *enlargement,* as opposed to the job *enrichment* examined earlier. Most readers are familiar with the Volvo assembly plant at Kalmar, Sweden. This plant lacks an assembly line and was designed in an attempt to reintroduce into mass-production industry some of the atmosphere of a craftsman's shop. In such designs workers rotate among the different functions and tasks, and much of the monotony inherent in specialization is reduced.

Critics maintain that job enlargement does not provide for an increase in decisional responsibilities as does job enrichment. However, protagonists of the two approaches have largely studied different audiences, and job enlargement for certain less-skilled personnel and job enrichment for higher-skilled and professional personnel appear to be more complementary than antagonistic.

Sociotechnical systems theory has several origins. In practical studies of work systems, however, the sociotechnical approach most directly interfaces with—and conflicts with—industrial engineering. Over the years this relationship has evolved somewhat. At first the technical subsystem was regarded as essentially fixed, and different social subsystems were considered in an attempt to match best the given technology. Today most sociotechnical systems specialists agree that both subsystems must be capable of modification in order to achieve an optimum total system design. Optimum designs are of course much more likely when the total system has been planned and developed from scratch than when changes and human adaptations must be made to an extant technology.[6]

Some of the key points and areas in current sociotechnical systems practice include:

1. *Autonomous* (**more recently,** *semiautonomous) work groups.* The social subsystem is designed so as to minimize the fragmentation of jobs, tasks, and skills in space and time. Deciding is reunited with doing. Operations, maintenance, supply, inspection, quality control, and even supervision are reunited in one job. The need for specialists in inspection, quality control, time-and-motion study, and so on is reduced or eliminated. Emphasis is on knowledge and capability rather than on fixed status. The functions of supervision and management become largely those of providing resources to the working groups, and providing information on organizational goals and plans.

2. *Matrix designs.* These designs are familiar to most readers. Although not limited to the sociotechnical approach, matrix designs are favored by sociotechnical systems experts as major alternatives to hierarchical, bureaucratic structures. Autonomous work groups may be of matrix design as may be the entire organization. Key features of matrix designs are lateral as well as vertical decisionmaking, reunification of decision and action, and the setting up of ad hoc problemsolving teams that can react quickly to emergencies. Matrix designs are viewed as self-adaptive, learning systems. Pure matrix designs have no built-in status differences; it is assumed the members share each other's values. Leadership roles change depending on the nature of the tasks.

3. *Minimal critical specification.* The minimum set of conditions or variables necessary for creation of viable self-maintaining or self-adjusting production units is specified. Ideally, the unit will require no external supervision and control of its internal processes. Once critical specifications are made, the remaining functions and tasks are allowed to develop in an evolutionary manner as experience indicates.

4. *The basic sociotechnical unit.* This is the lowest level at which decisions with regard to the environment can be taken toward joint optimization of the social and technical subsystems.

5. *Unit operations.* A unit operation is a stage in a technological process in which a change in state of the material or information originally input can be identified. Unit operations are seen as mutually exclusive and the technical subsystem to be analyzed separately from both the tasks of the workers and the supervisory and control functions.

6. *Action research*. Action research is usually contrasted both with academic research and with the roles played by most organization consultants. Academicians, frequently motivated to publish or perish, do research in organizations, and the results disappear into archival journals. Consultants study organizations, and the results disappear into files. In both cases the people to whom answers mean the most—the organization members—do not participate *directly* (although they may be repeatedly consulted, interrogated, and observed) in problemsolving and learning experiences. In action research the sociotechnical systems consultant, like some organizational development specialists, serves as a resource person and as a catalyst to team or organizational problemsolving. Action research is *action forcing*.

The classical sociotechnical systems approach, like the others, has experienced difficulties. Experimental autonomous work groups may be resented by other groups that see the gains of the former as being due to favoritism. Supervisors, managers (particularly middle managers), and staff specialists may resent loss of control and power and shrinking differences in status. One person's enrichment is seen as another's impoverishment. Diversification of decision-making may be viewed as a threat to the role, even the continued existence, of labor unions.

The sociotechnical systems approach represents continuing reaction against bureaucratic designs and scientific management. And justifiably so! However, it appears that most of the creative new ideas expressed by this school have been applied to improvements of the social subsystem with attendant neglect of the technological subsystem.

Quality-of-Worklife Programs

The spread of concepts of equality, civil and human rights, and social justice and changes in worker expectations from hoped-for privileges to demanded rights have led in turn to demands for improvements in the quality of work life and for democratization of the workplace. Declining productivity and increases in symptoms of worker alienation have added impetus to these societal changes.

Professor Robert Guest of Dartmouth University has helped implement a quality-of-worklife program.[7] In the early 1970s the General Motors automobile assembly plant at Tarrytown, New York had one of the poorest production and labor-relations records in the entire corporation. Absenteeism, job turnover, and operating costs were high. Nearly 2000 labor grievances were under consideration. Mutual hostility existed among management, labor, and the union. Things appeared to be going from bad to worse. Nevertheless, appreciation of the need for new approaches, although small, was growing. A quality-of-worklife program was initiated.

When the company decided to stop assembling trucks at Tarrytown, it became necessary to redesign the plant. At first changes were introduced as usual. Industrial and manufacturing engineers and various technical specialists designed the new layout, developed blueprints and charts, planned every move, and presented the results to supervisors. One supervisor suggested asking the workers themselves, as experts in their own right, to become involved in the move. When proposals for the new design were submitted to the workers, hundreds of suggestions were made and many of these suggestions were adopted. For the first time, management, the workers, and the union collaborated in solving future problems. Such cooperation continued. By December 1978 over 3300 workers had taken part in the quality-of-worklife training program. The Tarrytown plant became one of the best among 18 in the division.

In the Tarrytown case success stemmed from mutual cooperation among the workers, management, and the unions and from large-scale worker participation, which led to increased motivation, morale, and job satisfaction. Fundamental changes in the sociotechnical production system and in organizational structure were slight. The nature of the repetitive conveyor-paced jobs, 60 cars per hour, was not changed substantially. Hierarchical structure remained intact.

Industrial Democracy

Today in most Western countries there are strong social pressures to extend democracy to all facets of life. Deep value changes and changes in attitudes toward work are evident from almost daily accounts in the popular media. As the famous 1972 strike at the Vega automobile-assembly plant in Lordstown, Ohio showed, young workers do not share with their elders the same values and attitudes toward work, and both management and labor unions can misperceive the intensity of social change.

Industrial democracy is one response to pressures for social change. However, it does not constitute a uniform body of programs, techniques, and philosophies. It is superimposed on underlying cultural and historical patterns and therefore differs somewhat from country to country. Most studies and applications have been made in Western Europe, but there has been considerable interest in industrial democracy in Yugoslavia and Israel and there is new and growing interest in the United States.

Industrial democracy may possess one or more of the following features:[8]

1. Greater worker decisionmaking and control at the level of the shop floor or office. Autonomous work groups may be part of the design.
2. Extension of egalitarian practices such as use by workers and executives of the same parking lots, lavatories, dining facilities, and living quarters.
3. Experiments on and implementations of quality-of-worklife programs. Elimination of assembly lines in various industries, flex-time, and reduced working hours when production quotas are met are representative approaches.

4. Participation by workers, usually through elected representatives, at all levels of corporate decisionmaking.

5. Ownership of companies by the workers, usually through mass stock purchases.

Industrial democracy has proceeded at different rates in different countries. Final decisional power and company ownership essentially remain longer-range goals.

Programs in industrial democracy are variously initiated and sponsored by management, labor unions, and government. In some countries industrial democracy is institutionalized by legislation. European management seems committed to industrial democracy, mainly as a means of increasing productivity and profits in which workers share, but also as a social obligation to improve worker happiness. Management, however, is resisting loss of final decisional authority and loss of ownership of companies.

Some observers view industrial democracy, if the radical extremes are ignored, as a successful blend of capitalism and socialism. Most companies would remain under private ownership, with top management making the final decisions. However worker representatives would participate at the highest corporate levels in all decisions regarding plant moves, design of new plants, major equipment purchases, shutdowns, layoffs, transfers, employee housing, work schedules and rules, and planning. The quality of worklife would be greatly improved, so that workers, even if they cannot be made to enjoy their jobs more, would at least not grow to dislike them more. High levels of productivity, and profits shared by all, would continue to be sustained because the nearly equal share of power and decisionmaking would make all participants feel a vested interest in the success of the enterprise.

Industrial democracy, like other approaches has not been without difficulties. Some of these could have been predicted from experiences with the other approaches. For example:

Workers lost interest in a program at Norsk Medisinaldepot, a government-owned drug company in Oslo, Norway. In spite of having made such concessions as autonomous work groups, job rotation, and elimination of foremen, management ignored the workers' advice on design of a new plant. The new building included suites with view windows and other amenities for executives. On the plant floor the only windows were just below the high roof!

A program at the Volkswagen assembly plant at Salsgitter, West Germany was canceled because the labor union and the leaders of the established works council protested that the new autonomous work groups were usurping their roles as intermediaries between management and the workers.

The Eaton Corporation, a textile manufacturer in the southern United States, has been accused of using industrial democracy in order to keep unions out of newly built plants.[9]

THE HUMAN FACTORS/ERGONOMICS APPROACH

The term *human factors* is often popularly used to denote any human characteristics, usually detrimental ones. In the systems field, however, human factors applies to an established set of principles and practices. The focus of human factors is mostly on large systems and, to a lesser extent, products as ends in themselves. This emphasis distinguishes the human factors approach from those discussed earlier. The human factors practitioner is not concerned with whether the systems analysts, designers, and production workers are motivated to do their jobs.

The term *ergonomics* was coined in Poland in the past century. This term is widely used outside the United States. Ergonomists are concerned with the physical dimensions of work, including health, hygiene, endurance and fatigue, stress, posture, lighting, sound, humidity, temperature, and task structure. While human factors experts often have backgrounds in experimental psychology, ergonomists tend to have been schooled in medicine, physiology, or anthropometry.

These are some of the key concepts of human factors/ergonomics within the larger context of systems engineering:[10]

1. The *systems development cycle,* an iterative cycle beginning with a system concept and extending through design, production, test and evaluation, installation, operations, senescence, and replacement.

2. The *personnel subsystem*, a separate subsystem devoted to the personnel, staff, manpower, or crews, which is developed in parallel and interacting with the structures, power, communications, and other subsystems. The personnel subsystem consists in turn of such *elements* as human engineering, staffing, and training.

3. The *person–machine interface* and *person–machine interaction,* entities requiring special attention and optimization. An extension of these ideas is *5-M interaction,* in which the *M*s are man, machine, medium or environment, mission, and management. Human performance will be a function of these complex interactions.

4. *Design tradeoffs* among people and machines; operations and maintenance; human engineering, personnel ability and skill levels, and training; and so forth.

5. *Systems analyses* applied to successively finer levels of detail. Mission, requirements, functions, task, and task-element analyses are performed. Task analysis is the workhorse of human factors, providing data for the human engineering design of equipment, for staffing, for training, and for special critical or environmental operating conditions.

6. Total system *reliability* as a consequence of the contributions of elemental reliabilities.

7. Means of classifying, anticipating, and dealing with *human errors*.

8. The definition of *systems performance criteria* associated with attempts to

assess the contributions of human, equipment, environmental, and other factors to overall systems performance.

Human factors/ergonomics is now being applied to increasingly diversified areas including the automobile, the home, the office, and consumer products ranging from power lawnmowers to sports equipment. Unfortunately, this approach does not take in the total person. Based on the stimulus–organism–response (S–O–R) model, primary emphasis is on sensory and perceptual–motor behavior, with too little concern for higher mental processes and motivation. The approaches discussed earlier place a great emphasis on motivation, morale, and job satisfaction, but neglect the areas in which human factors/ergonomics is strong.

Human factors/ergonomics has not had the impact it should have had, considering the four decades or more of effort and the many practitioners. Legislation on product safety and occupational health and safety may eventually stimulate interest and concern, but because of the way government regulations are handled the jury is still out on this matter.

Dramatic accidents like the New York City electrical power blackout of July 13, 1977, the near meltdown in early April 1979 of the nuclear reactor at Three Mile Island near Harrisburg, Pennsylvania, and the May 25, 1979 crash of an American Airlines DC-10 at O'Hare Airport, Chicago do attract popular and official attention. But after months of special investigations, often involving special commissions, the findings usually reveal what human factors/ergonomics experts have been saying all along.

Ironically, many key decisionmakers feel that human factors is just common sense, automatically taken care of in the hardware design of systems and equipment. Yet these same executives may without question accept the latest bill-of-fare of management development or behavioral science programs.

THE OPERATIONS RESEARCH/MANAGEMENT SCIENCE APPROACH

Operations research (OR) originated in England just before World War II in the work of P. M. S. Blackett and others. An interdisciplinary team was set up to study problems of radar, which did not behave in the field as it did in the laboratory. Another problem was the determination of the priority and sequence of bombing enemy cities. In the heyday of OR many more problems were defined and methods developed for their solution.

Management science (MS) is a term that was devised later when OR theory and methodology began to diffuse into the functional specialties of business schools. Today few people try to differentiate between OR and MS.

In its heyday, which lasted until the early 1970s, OR/MS was hailed as the application of the scientific method to decisionmaking. Great emphasis was placed on objectivity and quantification and on the development of specific solution algorithms or rules.

Some of the *problems* to which OR/MS has seen application are these:

Scheduling and sequencing.

Search.

Product mixes.

Allocation.

Waiting lines and bottlenecks.

Stocking and replacement.

Inventory control.

Facilities planning.

Logistics.

Routing.

Conflict.

Most readers have heard of these commonly used *techniques:*

Mathematical programming (for example, linear programming, dynamic programming).

Network flow and path methods, for example, PERT (program evaluation and review technique) and CPM (critical path method).

Queueing theory.

Game theory.

Decision theory.

Regression analysis.

Simulation.

These techniques are usually considered to be *mathematical models,* which are often further subdivided into *deterministic* and *probabilistic* models or into *analytic* models which are capable of an exact solution and *simulation* models which can provide answers through repeated approximations.

In the most basic or classical OR/MS model some measure of system performance, called an *objective function* or *criterion function,* is defined. An attempt is made to maximize or minimize this function, subject to certain constraints. The performance measure is related both to factors or *decision variables* under management control and those not. An attempt is made to find those decision variables which optimize performance. A large model may contain hundreds of variables and constants or even hundreds of equations.

Obviously, some of these techniques are used by persons who would not consider themselves to be OR/MS specialists. OR/MS has in fact lost much of its original individuality. Most practitioners have given up trying to define the terms. OR/MS is what OR/MS people do—it ranges from arcane theory-building and search for new algorithms in academia to any use of mathematics and statistics in business to applications resembling those of industrial engineering.

In the last decade OR/MS practitioners have subjected their field to a healthy reevaluation which could well be emulated by other specialists. Among major criticisms of the field:[11]

1. It is no longer interdisciplinary, but rather has become inbred.

2. Academicians talk mainly to themselves and are preoccupied with abstruse concepts that sell well to journals, leaving practically-oriented workers bereft of new theoretical groundwork.

3. The field no longer generates exciting new ideas. It has lost a main focus. Most problems it is capable of solving have already been solved. Many organizations have abandoned centrally located OR/MS groups, and their members have been dispersed to the separate branches or to the functional areas of production, finance, marketing, etc.

4. It no longer takes a systems approach and is of little value to strategic planning and decisionmaking. Its main contributions are at the tactical level.

5. Practitioners filter real-world problems and bend data to fit the rigid requirements of their models. Models are largely closed-system and mechanical.

6. Practitioners cannot communicate with management (or communicate in a negative manner) for a variety of reasons including overuse of mathematical abstractions and jargon, insensitivity to organizational climate and politics, and conveying an impression of knowing it all and of intellectual arrogance.

7. Increasing systems complexity renders it unlikely that optimum solutions based on a single objective function will make any real-world sense. Attempts to define problems in terms of multiple criteria—for example, by ranking objectives, combining criteria into a single weighted criterion, or converting objectives into constraints—may do little to alleviate underlying limitations. Even if an optimum solution can be found, it is unlikely that it will have persistent value in a turbulent environment.

8. Practitioners find themselves embroiled in organizational "games" and in conflicts of interest which may violate basic ethical and moral codes. The practice of specialists for hire to the highest bidder has come under especially scathing attack.

9. The field, *overall,* has become increasingly method-centered and specialized. Proposals are hard to sell and solutions even more difficult to implement. Practitioners are expected to deal, in some depth, only with narrow, clearly defined problems, but there aren't many of these left. Each problem is interlinked with myriad other problems in what Professor Russell Ackoff calls "messes." Attempts to reduce messes to problems and to treat problems in isolation lead variously to suboptimizations, the right answer to the wrong problem, and trivial or useless results.

10. In complex systems the most important factors may be undefined, unmeasurable, qualitative, or subjective—and OR/MS is poorly equipped to deal with such factors.

11. The field, mired in a code of rationality, may be a cultural relic from an earlier way of thinking, the Machine Age of Professor Ackoff. Similarly, but from another quarter, OR/MS is open to attack as "Taylorism." Behavioral and social factors are poorly handled—and usually ignored—and such favorite OR/MS practices as balancing the assembly line and the layout of facilities may actually introduce the kinds of problems calling for the interventions discussed earlier in this chapter.

Many of the above items are not limited to OR/MS but apply as well to the other specialty areas of this chapter. Further, a number of OR/MS workers, aware of the limitations just discussed, have gone on to make important contributions to other areas of systems science and management. In other chapters we consider further such topics as modeling and simulation and decision-making. We also treat these topics briefly below.

THE INFORMATION SYSTEMS APPROACH

It is difficult to trace precisely the origin of the idea of management-information systems (MIS). There appear to be two main reasons for this situation. First, early MIS were unplanned by-products of the application of electronic data-processing to business. Large amounts of data, especially financial data, were output from computers, and observant persons felt that these data should be put to some use in the service of management. The ad hoc nature of MIS still exists to a considerable extent, which continues to limit the usefulness of these systems.

A management-information system need not be computerized; indeed, in some situations a manual system may be cheaper, more flexible, more usable, and generally preferable. Computers introduce many new problems into organizations, problems quite apart from those presented by MIS themselves. Computers introduce problems of cost, scheduling, threats to old personnel, and needs for new personnel. The commonly experienced problems with MIS, therefore, are partially problems with computers, which cast a pall on the overall problem of automation.

The second main reason for the murkiness of the concept of MIS is the persistent lack of understanding of both what constitutes information and how a system is organized to provide useful and usable knowledge.

Information has a very precise mathematical definition in *information theory*, where it deals with the probabilities of occurrence of alternative states or elements. Information gain is equal to uncertainty loss. Information theory has been applied almost wholly at the technical level, that is, in terms of how accurately the symbols of communication can be transmitted and whether a given delivered message is one in a set of messages that could have been transmitted. Whether a transmitted symbol conveys a desired meaning and whether the message affects human behavior is irrelevant. Therefore, aside from spinning off such concepts as channel capacity and information overload, information theory has failed to live up to its early expectations in areas beyond the purely technical transmissions of messages. It is interesting to note, however, that the mathematical formula for information is the negative of that for the thermodynamic measure of entropy. Loosely then, information means order and organization; entropy means disorder and the chaos of complete randomness.

Further, information is often confused with data, knowledge, and wisdom. These can be thought of as sequential steps in collection, processing, refinement, and utilization of experience. Data are isolated observations, recordings, or facts or local organizations of the same, for example, by relating as time series or graphical or statistical summaries.

Information consists of, *or should consist of,* qualitative and quantitative, formal and informal, data *organized for some useful purpose,* in this case management planning, policymaking, or decisionmaking. Most MIS lack such thorough organization and are therefore more data collections than management systems. Knowledge can be thought of as the actual application of information to fulfill a purpose such as decisionmaking. Wisdom is cumulative knowledge tempered by experience.

Have MIS been great successes? The answer would appear to be a resounding *NO*. As long ago as 1967 Professor Russell Ackoff referred to them as "management misinformation systems".[12] Many other observers have also commented that MIS do the wrong things for managers and are not used. Henry Lucas[13] studied over 2000 information system users in 16 organizations and reported widespread system failures.

A look at the problems directly associated with the design of MIS, whether manual or automatic, will show that they are primarily *human factors* problems. They are problems of mission, requirements, and task analysis and of interfacing human cognitive and perceptual-motor capabilities with the capabilities of the subsystem producing information. The steps or activities that follow are very much like those pursued by the systems engineer and human factors expert in the design of any person–machine system.

The first step in acquiring MIS is for top management to determine if acquisition is solely for prestige or because of pressure from computer vendors. If either of these reasons is true, resources could be expended better otherwise.

MIS should be acquired only if it can be clearly demonstrated that acquisition will aid in doing things better. Unfortunately, this is not always easy to do. Managers often feel uneasy about their oganizations, yet cannot articulate their problems and especially the solutions in operational terms. It is almost a truism in both person–machine systems and in organizations that users do not know their own requirements. As a result three consequences are possible: (1) the manager states what he *thinks* his requirements to be, (2) the designer makes up requirements in inverse proportion to the amount of manager participation, and (3) the designer gives the manager every bit of information or data he can possibly crowd onto a display sheet or screen.

Requirements are performance factors related to the overall mission of the organization or to the mission of one of the organization's divisions or subsystems. The mission is usually defined in terms of goals or objectives, which themselves are often hard to define either absolutely or in terms of avoidance of conflict. Loose, nonoperationalized definitions of goals, objectives, and requirements—such as "to make more profits," "to cut down costs," "provide better data," and "improve communications"—both make design more difficult and concede to the designer a power to change the system in a way management may not really want.

Once goals and requirements are operationally defined, the basic task-analysis model should be employed:

$$\text{Information input} \longrightarrow \text{Decision} \longrightarrow \text{Action output}$$

Feedback of performance adequacy

In other words what actions or tasks must the user perform? What decisions must be made preliminary to taking action? What information—and only that information—is required preparatory to making a decision?

In human factors task analysis involves a number of other questions. For example, the good designer asks questions about criticalities, priorities, sequences, dependencies, special demands, indications of system error or variance (being outside tolerance limits), and means of alarming the user as to critical circumstances. The good designer also analyzes for conflicts among tasks and for information and task overload.

Task analysis is prerequisite to the human engineering of displays (in the present case usually computer printouts and cathode-ray tube [CRT] screens) and controls (usually keyboards and ancillary devices like light pens).

In short, if a management-information system does not meet what a manager perceives to be his requirements, he will not use it. If the MIS makes the manager feel uncomfortable, he will not use it. If the MIS fails to display information in a properly filtered, compressed, and organized format, when and where the manager needs it, he will not use the system.

Systems that are ancillary or supportive to MIS do not in themselves overcome the deficiences pointed out. *Data banks* present many of the problems of data in general. *Information storage and retrieval* systems do likewise and besides are subject to certain rigid codes and identifiers that reduces their utility.

In practice actual implementations of MIS take place mostly at lower levels of the organization. From the perspective of the organization as a whole, one is likely to get the impression of a patchwork design. Yet one should expect easier and more successful implementations in such older, more circumscribed functions of organizations as production, sales, accounting, and finance. The interrelating of these and other functions in a corporate-level system presents formidable difficulties.

THE COMPUTERIZATION APPROACH

In one of the greatest technological achievements of all time, the *logic* underlying the operation of stored-program, binary, digital computers and the electronic *parts* necessary to implement this logic came together just after World War II. By the early 1950s developments of digital computers had divided into two main branches, scientific and business, and computers were finding applications in the United States to science, the military, business, and government. Ever since developments of computer capabilities, varieties, and applications have expanded almost explosively.[14]

Computer evolution is often described in terms of *generations*, which are based on successive developments of hardware and, to a lesser extent, software or computer programs. The first generation was characterized by electronic circuitry based on vacuum tubes and by machine-language and assembly-language programming. The second generation was characterized by solid-state or transistor circuitry and compiler-language and more user-oriented programming. The third generation featured integrated circuits (the parts such as transistors, resistors, capacitors, and so on were integrated onto the boards that made up the components of the computer); increased complexity, diversity, and at the same time specialization and standardization of programs including special operating systems and programs to control other programs; and diversification of user-oriented languages beyond the familiar FORTRAN, COBOL, ALGOL, and others.

The third generation also saw the widespread use of *multiprocessing* (simultaneous execution of two or more computer programs) and *multiprogramming* (interleaved execution by one central computer of two or more computer programs). Further, designers began to link computer systems into computer networks and computer networks into networks of computer systems. The use of such networks was associated with a proliferation of remote terminals and *time-sharing* capabilities.

To digress briefly, computer developments up to the early 1970s were characterized by an order-of-magnitude increase in speed, memory-storage capacity, and reliability and decreases in access and processing time and in costs. Computers became big business, with annual sales in the United States at that time approaching $15 billion. As with other industries the goal of the computer industry was to maximize the sale or lease of its products and services.

Thus, a major reason for the acquisition of computers was the market pull of rapid technological change and the persuasiveness of computer salesmen. The salesmen emphasized the power of computers, their increasing availability at competitive costs, and the prestige of having one. Many organizations purchased or leased computers which they did not know how to use and the installation of which produced unexpected and undesirable side effects in the organization. For example, first-generation MIS were being implemented on third-generation computers and new systems, with a fiftyfold increase in throughput capability, were producing only a twofold improvement.

Does this mean that having computers was and is bad? Not at all. Many advances in science and technology in the past 30 years would not have been possible without computers. Computer simulation models are an important feature of the adaptive-system design. However, the programming of mathematical equations and those logical operations and decisions that can be expressed as algorithms is relatively straightforward. Most aspects of human behavior cannot be so readily programmed, and it is here that many people run into trouble in trying to use computers.

As more and more nonexpert people began to work with or became exposed to computers, a number of problems became evident—problems which prevail today. Several of these interrelated problems include:

1. The *person–computer interface.* Terminals and consoles may be poorly human engineered. However, the worst problem is with the software. User-oriented languages are still not easy to learn and use effectively. This is partly due to rigid rules, the ease with which errors can be made, and the difficulty in detecting and correcting errors.

2. The *incompatibility of equipment* produced by different manufacturers and the related fact that software may be system specific.

3. The *differential capabilities* of the central-processing unit (CPU) and the input-output (I-O) element. Most of the advances described above have been made in the memory, arithmetic, and control elements that comprise the CPU.

4. The *recalcitrance of software to innovative breakthroughs.* Dr. Ruth M. Davis, an expert on the history of computers, states that since 1947 programming has not changed in its basics, the correctness of software still remains the most elusive goal of computer science, and the cost of developing software now approximates 90 percent of total computer system costs.[15] One way to get around this difficulty has been to build as much of the software into the hardware as possible.

5. The *awe of computers and the fear of computerized automation.* Awe of computers leads people, including many managers, to accept the computer and its output on faith. But, sometimes simultaneously, many persons fear the mysterious power of the computer and of the impact of automation on their jobs. Attempts to implement computer systems in organizations have often led to the need for sociotechnical or OD interventions. The long-term effects of automation on jobs remains moot.

6. The *effects of computers on organizational structure* also remains moot. Major impacts on industrial production and clerical *operations* cannot be questioned. These are exemplified by the familiar applications to *process control* in the refinement of petrochemicals and to banking, respectively. There appears to be an upward shift in the locus of decisionmaking in the corporation. There is also a subtle transfer of power from line managers to computer experts. Other subtle changes may either augment or diminish organizational adaptability.

In the late 1960s a major split occurred. The trend toward *maxicomputers* and networks was paralleled by the development of small, inexpensive, stand-alone computers *(minicomputers)* and by very small components called *micropro-cessors*. A microprocessor contains circuitry for doing basic data-processing. When augmented with I-O, memory, and so forth it becomes a hand calculator, *microcomputer*, or personal computer.

Microprocessors and their descendants described below have provided essentially a qualitatively new dimension to computer evolution. Two characteristics of these devices are particularly important: (1) their use as control mechanisms embedded in other machines—or, as prostheses, in people, and (2) their use as basic building blocks making possible any number of tailor-made applications.

A *computer-on-a-chip* is a thin sheet of silicon, about one-inch square or less, onto which circuitry has been imposed by a delicate and rather complicated process. The capacities of these chips, variously defined in terms of basic electronic units, logic gates, memory, or instructions, range from the tens of thousands to the hundreds of thousands and are expected to increase greatly in the future.

It is interesting to note in passing that the large, established manufacturers of computers did not originally see much of a future in developing smaller and smaller computers.

The present fourth generation of computers is characterized by a *continuum* of computers from very small to very large and by a great variety of users and applications. Large-scale integrated circuits (LSI) are the main components of large computers, and LSI grade into microprocessors and computers-on-a-chip. Online, interactive systems find numerous applications.

The capabilities of computers and computer-communications networks continue to be improved by research. *Josephson junctions* are much faster and require considerably less power than do conventional transistor circuits. *Magnetic-bubble memories* may permit even denser packing and better control over and faster retrieval from memory. *Fiber optics* communications links carry much more information more reliably. Two or more chips can be combined to form a *wafer*. Chips may be designed to contain analog as well as digital circuits.

These and other new developments should continue to enhance the flexibility of organizing *equipment and components*. However, whether human activities can be organized in parallel remains open to question. Some computer enthusiasts predict "offices on a chip," "libraries on a wafer," "MIS on a wafer," and so on. However, it is better to send a well-thought-out, well-articulated message by Pony Express than to transmit nonsense nearly instantaneously by the lastest technology.

THE MODEL, SIMULATION, AND GAME APPROACH

A *model* is an abstraction or mimicry of a real-world system, situation, or process. Models can be classified in many ways. The main distinctions are these: all models start as *conceptual* models, and almost everybody makes conceptual models. The continuing difficulty is that the concepts cannot always be articulated or operationalized so that measurement is possible. Models and *theories* grade into one another when it is possible to define a situation operationally so as to test, validate, or falsify the underlying assumptions or hypotheses. An *iconic* model such as a scale model of a building or ship is of course not a theory. If the relevant state, variables, and interrelationships can be expressed with enough precision, it may be possible to construct a *mathematical* model. Most of the mathematical models of operations research are *analytical* models, that is, they can be solved to give exact or optimal results. Often today the term *paradigm* is used interchangeably with the term model.

A *simulation* is also a mimicry of the real world. Simulations can be manual, computer-aided, or completely computerized. In this book we shall not consider such *simulators* as those used in aircrew training. For our purposes a simulation is an experiment based on a formalized model and run on a computer. These *computer simulation models* resemble case histories and do not provide the exact solutions of analytic models.

The term *games* has several origins of interest to management. The *mathematical theory of games,* originated in 1944 by John von Neumann and Oskar Morgenstern, deals with situations of competition and conflict in which players attempt to make rational choices of actions. These actions, based on probable states of the opponent, seek to maximize or minimize some final outcome, payoff, cost, or expected value. The opponents may variously be people, computers, or a problem. When the problem is, say, a disease, the unfortunate term game against nature is often used. Game theory has helped spur developments in *decision theory*. For our purposes both theories are part of academic systems theory and operations research and are not applicable to the type of problems emphasized here.

The *transactional theory of games* (*Games People Play*) of psychiatrist Eric Berne describes preconscious psychological interactions, usually destructive, involving two or more persons. I consider transactional analysis (TA) to be a particularly well-thought-out and substantiated psychoanalytic theory and psychotherapeutic practice. Obviously an executive or planner who seeks opportunities to play these games, and who is unaware of deficiencies in his personality, may reduce the adaptability of his organization.

Manual *war games* have been played for decades. War-game and game-theoretic studies of large-scale military and political problems attracted considerable attention from the end of World War II to the early 1960s, particularly at think tanks like the Rand Corporation.

It is probably this last use of the word game that is associated most with the development of *business games*.

Business games are used more in business schools than in business organizations. Their major purpose is to provide a capstone course or integrating experience. That is, students learn considerable detail in courses in accounting, finance, marketing, production, research and development, and so on, but they do not learn how to put these subsystems together or how the subsystems interact. They learn neither systems management nor top management.

Other purposes of business games are to provide exposure to or hands-on use of computers and data-processing and to provide experience in team problemsolving and decisionmaking. These games may be manual or, more usually, computer-aided (for example, using a batch-processing mode) or completely computerized (using a time-sharing mode).

As with the other approaches discussed in this chapter, it is difficult to evaluate the results of business games. The separate approaches, almost by definition, involve so many exogenous factors and variables that evaluations based on traditional comparisons of experimental and control groups or of two or more different approaches are seldom if ever possible. Critics maintain that business games produce no better learning results than do lectures or textbook reading and that the games possess no particular validity for predicting subsequent occupational success. Much of what was said earlier about assessment centers appears also to apply to business games.

Nevertheless, designing and selling business games is still pretty good business. The potential of simulation games, albeit much more sophisticated ones, for ongoing organizational learning should not be dismissed out of hand. For example, games may bring out differences in the orientations of teams to problems; some teams may rely heavily on intuition, others on procedures. Team composition can be an important attribute of organizational adaptation and survival.

Of much more importance are *corporate simulation models*.[16] However, business games can be thought of as gradually phasing into corporate simulation models. Both represent attempts to integrate the subsystems of the organization and both can provide learning experiences for the users.

Corporate simulation models are becoming increasingly important because of explosive sociotechnical change and of the turbulence of the external environments. Organizations are much less likely to be confronted with single isolated problems capable of optimum solutions than with *coalescences* of intersecting and mutually reinforcing problems (Russell Ackoff's messes). However, models of the entire corporation are still rare. Models of specific functions of the corporation and of lower-level operations still provide the commonest examples. This is because of the recalcitrance of complex systems and especially of systems involving human behavior to ready specification of structure, variables, interrelationships, and measures.

Executive management provides a framework for activities at successively lower levels of hierarchically structured organizations. Failures of any subsystem or at any level may precipitate the organization into an unmanageable crisis. However, we must accept some things as givens, for example, that the construction of internal accounting, financial, and production process-control models is fairly straightforward. Most of these models represent extensions of principles that have been known for many years. On the other hand, marketing models and models of sociotechnical work and production systems are not so easy to construct.

The truly corporate-level models which are stressed in this book must provide the following overlapping capabilities:

Top-down integration of subsystem models whenever model compatability permits (incompatability is usually the case), or alternatively the potential for describing the entire organization starting from scratch.

Use in strategic planning.

Use in long-range planning.

Expression of organization–environment interactions.

Expression of alternative configurations, present, past, and future of the organization, environment, and system–environment interrelationships.

Use in policy formulation and analysis.

Facilitating the organization's adaptability as a learning system.

User online, real-time (as applicable) interaction with the computer system and interrogation of the system with what if ? questions.

Futures forecasting.

Processing of deterministic, probabilistic, objective, and subjective inputs.

Fulfilling all these requirements will be a tall order. Yet with thousands of organizations now planning or using models that do one or more of the above-mentioned things, it is necessary to think in such holistic terms.

Present models may not live up to expectations because of a number of reasons, including:

Lack of or poor participation in model development and implementation by the user.

Poor understanding, even incomprehensibility, of the model by the user.

Lack of an action-research orientation on the part of the design team.

Lack of full and sustained support by top management.

Model rigidity.

Obvious lack of validity, especially face validity (being in the user's eyes a reasonable representation of the real-world system he knows).

Poor human engineering, for example, of computer printouts and documentation.

Too great model cost in relation to perceived limited benefits.

Too much time is required both to learn to use the model and to use it on a continuing basis.

Making simple errors may bring the model to a halt.

Use of the model interferes with, rather than facilitates, discharge of the main perceived tasks of the user.

THE INDUSTRIAL OR SYSTEMS DYNAMICS APPROACH

Professor Jay W. Forrester of the Massachusetts Institute of Technology is the father of industrial dynamics, which he developed in the early 1960s. Forrester created industrial dynamics out of the confluence of three bodies of knowledge: (1) practical difficulties organizations face and practical experience from managing organizations which dates back to time immemorial, (2) cybernetic (information-and-control) theory that provides guidance as to system structure and information-feedback loops, and (3) developments of digital computers that permitted rapid, reasonably priced simulations of complex systems.

Forrester emphasizes that by far the largest proportion of existing knowledge, information, and data is collectively in peoples' heads. This amount far surpasses that stored in verbal form in libraries and especially far exceeds the quantitative data and information in archives, data banks, and MIS. This is a very important point in view of the ongoing controversy between industrial dynamicists and econometricians discussed in Chapter 4.

Most people organize the information and knowledge in their heads into some sort of cause–effect relationship called a *conceptual model*. The trouble is that conceptual models are imprecise, and that people do not readily perceive feedback interrelationships and therefore the mutual causality characteristic of complex systems. The role of the industrial dynamicist is to bridge the gap between management's awareness of an organizational problem and a computer simulation model designed to provide policy guidance toward rectification of the problem.

Typical organizational problems are those of growth, growth followed by decline or stagnation, oscillations among production, sales, and inventory, and loss of market share due to delivery delay.

Beginning in the late 1960s the theory, philosophy, and methodology developed as industrial dynamics were expanded to problems of the cities *(urban dynamics)*, health, ecology, the limits to the growth of population, industrialization, and the use of resources (*world dynamics* and the famous Limits to Growth models), and the national economy of the United States. The broader field is called *systems dynamics* (SD). Although industrial dynamics is still a viable term representing a specialty within SD, it is the latter term which is used here.[17]

Systems dynamics is not easy to learn or to practice except at a trivial level. Indeed, Forrester speaks of its being the basis of a new profession, which, like medicine and other older professions, would take about a decade for preparation. It is important to differentiate among (1) the cybernetic and control-systems engineering theory which contain many esoteric concepts (for example, stability and gain), (2) the philosophy (for example, the downplaying of a purely quantitative approach), (3) the model-building methodology, and (4) the actual working with the computer. Without making these distinctions, the novice is unlikely to understand such things as the sources and corrections of errors in the model or whether the computer output represents some actual dynamic behavior of the system or merely an artifact from writing the program. For example, a major fluctuation appearing on the printout might reflect an important policy change or merely the selection of an inappropriate solution interval.

Complex systems are composed of variously superordinate or subordinate information-feedback and control loops. The system tries to maintain a steady state, so dominance among the loops may shift unexpectedly, unknown to human observers and participants. Attempts to change the behavior of the system through policy changes may have no effect because the system, in attempting to maintain steady state, swallows up the policies. Sometimes intervention from the outside greatly strengthens or weakens given feedback loops exacerbating the original problem. Because of their structure, complex systems may behave *counterintuitively,* that is, in a manner opposite to what our initial expectations of cause–effect might be. These and related ideas are embedded in the structure of this book.

SD consists of a number of basic constructs or conceptual building blocks. First, the system to be modeled is considered to be a *closed* system. Right away confusion arises because the system is not thermodynamically closed; that is, matter and energy do cross the system boundary. However, feedback loops do not cross the system boundary. The system, therefore, is a *closed-loop* system.

In all systems analyses determining the system boundary is easier said than done. This book contrasts the system/organization and its internal environment with the external environments of the system. However, a systems dynamics model almost always neglects part of the internal environment and includes part of the external environment, for example, the market environment. Whatever factors or variables can be meaningfully interrelated within feedback loops are considered to be internal to the model.

Second, within the system boundary there are two types of feedback-loop structures. If one thinks in terms of action *(A)* and result *(R)* or cause *(C)* and effect *(E)*, then *positive feedback* occurs when an increase in *A* or *C* leads to an increase in *R* or *E* which in turn increases or reinforces *A* or *C*. In *negative feedback* an increase in *A* or *C* can also lead to an increase in *R* or *E* but this increase now leads to compensatory decreases in *R* or *E*. Uncontrolled positive feedback can lead to a vicious circle of growth or, substituting decrease for increase, decay or decline. Negative feedback loops are goal-seeking, but can if uncontrolled produce stagnation. Uncontrolled alternating positive and negative loops can produce various kinds of system oscillations.

The dynamic behavior of the organization is a function of the types, combinations, and dominance of its feedback loops. Certain random inputs that are harmonious to the internal dynamics and certain human policy interventions may reverse the sign and shift the dominance of the feedback loops. The systems dynamicist has a feeling for these things and tries to translate organizational symptoms or pathology into model structure. He of course works with top management in the model construction.

The third major construct defines the two basic kinds of variables of SD models. These are *level* and *rate* variables. Level variables indicate the state of the system at any given time. They are accumulations of rates of flow or (mathematical) integrations. Rate variables are flows that regulate the amounts of the levels. Rate variables are sometimes called policy variables because through them policies, in one usage of the term, can be enacted.

The fourth major construct further delineates the role of rate variables in controlling system behavior through policies. This is the information-decision-action sequence associated with the rate variable. There are four elements of this structure: (1) a *goal* or desired outcome, usually a desired level, (2) an *observed condition,* usually an actual level, (3) a *discrepancy* or *disparity* between actual and desired conditions utilizing information feedback of the actual level (in other cybernetic systems such a disparity is often called an error signal), and (4) a *desired action* expressed as an action stream, say, of some form of matter from a source or to sink outside the system boundary.

In SD *decisions* are embedded in the circular structure just implied. Decisions are made on the basis of policies; they can be viewed as specific implementations of policies.

Within this framework model construction progresses through the iterative identification of all the variables that are thought to be relevant. These variables are at first simply listed. Then cause–effect interrelationships are identified. A *causal* or *influence diagram* depicts the variables, with the direction of causality indicated by curved arrows, and the nature of feedback loops indicated by placing a + or − near the head of the arrow. Once again, this sounds easier to do than it actually is. It may not be immediately evident which variables are level variables and which rate variables or *auxiliary* variables which are extensions or more detailed specifications of rates.

A causal diagram leads to an SD *flow diagram* which uses special symbols. For example, a level variable is represented by a rectangle, a rate variable by a valve symbol, and an auxiliary variable by a circle. Flows of matter are shown by solid arrows—sometimes broken by, say, dollar signs to indicate the flow of money. Flows of information are shown by consistently broken arrows.

The flow diagram can serve as a basis for writing the equations that comprise the computer program. Equations, which have certain requirements and restrictions, are written for each variable and for the constants that represent initial conditions, inputs from outside the system, instructions to the computer as to how to print or plot, and so on.

Equations are usually written in the DYNAMO compiler/simulation language. These equations mimic the difference equations which, in the underlying mathematical model, approximate the differential equations of a continuous-variable system.

Model-building, SD as well as other approaches, is replete with difficulties. Some of these difficulties are academic or very technical and as such are mostly beyond the scope of this book.

The output of the SD model is a computer printout which shows tables or plots. Examination, especially of the latter, provides considerable under-standing about the dynamics of the system and the results of policy implementations. Unfortunately, the printout may be the only portion of the model to which the user is exposed. Under these conditions, the utility of SD, like that of the other approaches discussed may be far less than desired. Nevertheless, even a cursory look at a printout may show how one variable leads another, how two variables are 180 degrees out of phase, how a variable has exploded to its limits, or how oscillations are being damped.

THE ECONOMETRIC APPROACH

The econometric approach is one of several methodologies commonly used to forecast changes in economic conditions, for example as indicated by Gross National Product (GNP), inflation, industrial production, investment, and—increasingly—energy use or demand. Other economic forecasting methods include the subjective-judgmental and trend-extrapolation ap-proaches. However, the econometric approach is worth special consideration here because: (1) it incorporates many of the features and limitations of judgmental analysis, time-series analysis, and so forth, (2) it is increasingly popular at the same time its accuracy is being increasingly questioned, and (3) it is frequently contrasted with systems dynamics as a modeling approach.

The focus of econometric modeling is mostly on the economic or socioeconomic environment external to the organization. Most large corporations now employ the services of one or more of the major consulting firms such as Chase Econometrics, Data Resources, or the Wharton Economic Forecasting Unit. However more and more firms use small internal models, which, for example, permit the study of the effect of advertising on sales.

Like SD and other modeling approaches, econometrics is faced with the problems of definition of system boundary, selection of appropriate variables, determination of direction of influence or causality between variables, quantification, validation, and use. However, in discharging the requirements of model-building, econometrics displays three characteristic features: (1) heavy dependence on time-series data, (2) close association with regression analysis, and (3) use of simultaneous equations.

Time-series data are those in which a historical sequence or pattern seems capable of projection into the present or future. Such data may, for example, exhibit upward trends, downward trends, seasonal fluctuations, or cyclical behavior as, for example, in business cycles. Much effort has been expended in recent years in improving the quality of time-series data through averaging, smoothing, and decomposition into components. Many of the techniques for the analysis and improvement of time-series data are mathematically quite sophisticated and beyond the scope of this book.

Regression analysis is closely related to *correlation,* that is, a statistical indication of the degree to which a variable (the dependent variable) changes (increases or decreases) with changes in another variable (the independent variable). If points common to both variables are plotted on a sheet of graph paper, the familiar *scattergram* results. One can then ask the question: What straight line gives the best fit to the points? The line of best fit is called the line of regression, which is obtained as follows:

Let $y = mx + b$ be a typical straight line, where m is the slope and b is the point at which the line intercepts the y axis. For the i'th value of x, the line has ordinate $mx_i + b$. We search for the line that *minimizes the sum of the squares* of the differences between y_i and the ordinate of the line at x_i. These differences are squared so as to avoid negative numbers. We search for the unknowns m and b that minimizes the function just implied. Minimization involves using the calculus technique of partial differentiation and setting the result equal to zero.

Least-squares methods are widely used in the refinement of time-series data and for *estimating parameters* or constants like the m and b above. Of course most applications are more complicated than the simple example given above. The example represents simple linear regression. Most models utilize multiple linear regression; some utilize curvilinear regression. In multiple regression the contribution to the variance (a statistical measure of variability) of the dependent variable by two or more independent variables is estimated. For example, management might want to know how sales of a product are dependent on advertising dollars, research and development dollars, and GNP.

Computer techniques such as *stepwise multiple regression* are available to help solve equations with large numbers of independent variables. Variables are added to the equation only if it can be demonstrated that they are making a significant contribution to the variance of the dependent variable.

The *coefficient of determination, R^2* (where R is the multiple correlation coefficient) is usually used as an indication of the reliability of a multiple regression equation. R^2 indicates the proportion of the variance of the dependent variable that is explained by the model. The bigger the R^2, the less the error and the more reliable the model.

Simultaneous equations are used such that the dependent variable in one equation functions as an independent variable in one or more other equations. Thus each equation describes for a given point in time the relationship of a dependent variable to different independent variables. Both current and previous values of variables are used. The equations collectively describe the interactions among all such interrelationships at specific points in time. The value of each variable is updated at each successive point in tme.

Econometric models have two types of equations: (1) *identities* and *definitional equations* which are true simply by definition, and (2) *behavioral equations* that are hypothesized or empirical relations between or among variables (for example, the "Law of Demand" relating price to quantity). The more behavioral equations, the more sophisticated a model is supposed to be. However, a great deal of unproved or outmoded theory as well as intuitions and hunches go into the construction of behavioral equations. And with enough parameters any model can be made to describe a given period whether it predicts the future or not. Such models are said to be *overparameterized.*

For these reasons and others to be considered later, econometric models seem poorly equipped to handle periods of major change in the structure of the economy and of society as a whole.

THE NEW CHANGING-ENVIRONMENT APPROACHES

As pointed out at the beginning of this chapter, the purpose of this chapter is to summarize and interpret most of the perceptions of the organization as put into practice by consultants. The problems facing the organization, however, are changing, often dramatically. Some of the areas in which new expertise is available of can soon be provided include:

Business and society.

Business and the natural environment.

New worksystem designs to accord with changing values, expectations, and motivations.

Changing and increasing government regulation.

Occupational safety and health.

Natural resource usage and limits (right now, especially energy).

Changing roles of minority groups and women.

Volatile foreign socioeconomic and political environments which close old opportunities (Iran) or open new opportunities (China).

Changing or increased foreign competition.

Changing products and markets in an era of limits to growth.

As always executives should take a holistic approach both to problems and to offers of expert advice. Some of the above areas, while very important during a specific period, may be immaterial to the design of an adaptive organization.

WHY ACADEMIC AND CONSULTANT ADVICE MAY NOT BE FULLY OR EFFECTIVELY USED

The expert advice provided to executives by internal and external consultants has not produced the results that many people have desired and expected. This is true in spite of years of theory- and model-building, financially well-supported academic research, and numerous attempts at application.

Some of the reasons for failure to implement the recommendations of consultant teams or failure of implementations to produce the desired longer-term impacts have been discussed throughout this chapter. Here is a summary:

1. *Communications difficulties.* Top management and the consultants may

be of different age groups, educational backgrounds, or educational levels. Consultants may talk jargon. Through body language or subconscious cues, consultants may convey an impression of intellectual arrogance. Conscious of their great power, executives may view the consultants with scorn.

2. *Living in different worlds.*   The worlds of the executive and the consultant may barely intersect. The executive is typically concerned with brushfire problems or with recognized declines in capability which may threaten the existence of the organization. He may want usable results—yesterday. He may have little patience for long studies or indeed for more studies. He knows his organization but may not know how to define or solve his problems. The consultant may have little understanding of the organization, and his heart may belong to academia. Therefore he may really be interested only in those problems and studies that can both be constrained to fit his models and phrased in the abstruse language that sells well to academic journals. Threatened with career survival, the consultant may find himself caught between the pressures to publish or perish in academia and the need or desire both to augment his academic income and to be of service to the organization.

3. *Lack of interest by executives and susceptibility to "snow-jobs."*   The executive may want something done about his problems but may feel uncomfortable with new concepts and technologies. Or he may simply feel that he lacks the time to spend on things that will show results tomorrow when he is overpowered by the pressures of today. Such an executive lays himself open to snow-jobs. If he is technically trained, he may accept without question both the latest good behavioral science and the most recent pseudopsychological fad. If he received his education before, say, 1960, he may be overawed by computers and mathematics.

4. *Threats to power and status.*   The very process of probing into—questioning, interviewing, observing, measuring—may reveal a problem of inadequacies of management. Computerization and the design of MIS may overtly or covertly shift power within the organization. Therefore top management may pay only lip service to organizational change attempts, and the major purpose of solutions may be to serve as window-dressing for the maintenance of the status quo.

5. *Not related to the real world.*   Consultant recommendations may be so theoretical or unrealistic (for example, because of high costs) as to be impractical. Or the recommendations may not fit into the political environment of the organization, and executives may view them as "not invented here."

6. *Only part answers.*   The organization is a dynamic whole, the parts of which must be well articulated. Patching up one part or strengthening one subsystem by itself is unlikely to produce sustained improvements in performance.

7. *Unforeseen side effects.*   A change in one part of the organization almost always has impacts elsewhere in the organization or in the external environment. The effects of automation and technological change on worker motivation, morale, and productivity and environmental pollution are perhaps the best known examples.

8. *Saturation and exhaustion of the field.*   In some cases all the *types* of applications were recognized a long time ago, and even most of the *opportunities* for application exploited. In such cases specialists may find themselves offering the same old models and talking mainly to themselves.

9. *Organizational decline in spite of or because of specialist advice.*   Some of the approaches may turn out to have been fads, totally irrelevant to any time or place. Other approaches, potentially successful at one time, may themselves have failed to adapt to explosive sociotechnical and environmental change. In some organizations—indeed whole industries—neither management nor consultants may have correctly diagnosed an underlying pathology, so that no approach would have succeeded. The present decline in the United States automobile industry and the general decline in productivity in the developed English-speaking world provide salient examples.

It is likely that the nature of these difficulties will change with the passage of time. Some may disappear, perhaps to be replaced by even more serious difficulties. Others may be aggravated. Management itself is changing. More and more managers are receiving technical, specialized, or advanced educations. This may make the new managers more congruent with technical and rationalized solutions. However, rational thinkers are often emotion-blind and may resist translating ideas into risky actions.

Even some of the most recent and advanced approaches, such as the computer simulation modeling of complex systems, may face some of the same old difficulties.

Finally, the present era of crisis and transition sets requirements for major new breakthroughs. Many present endeavors continue to coast on breakthroughs made at times of earlier crisis and transition—the Great Depression and World War II.

ORGANIZATIONAL DYNAMICS

Dynamic organizations proceed through definite stages of growth, whereby the interrelationships between the organization and its environments are constantly changing, but it must be kept in mind that organizational growth can be confronted by definite limits.

EVOLUTION AND GROWTH FORMS OF ORGANIZATIONS[1]

Until recently the predominant view of the organization was that it is a static, closed system. Most studies were cross-sectional rather than longitudinal. Although well-defined organizational *outputs* like sales and profits have long been seen as time-varying, organizational structure and most aspects of function and behavior have not.

Organizations, as living systems, grow and decay. It is convenient to represent changes over time as mostly two-dimensional growth curves. Actually these curves are usually aggregates of underlying processes that may be fundamentally dissimilar. Also changes in living systems are rarely two-dimensional, but rather involve all four real dimensions.

Growth curves can be interpreted more precisely through the use of algebraic and differential equations. Changes involving two or more dimensions can often be expressed by using topology, a once-obscure branch of mathematics suitable for depicting geometric forms and qualitative relationships. In both graphical and mathematical-equation representations of systems change, time may appear explicitly or implicitly as an independent variable. Of course time by itself is not a causal factor or variable.[2]

The simplest form of growth is *linear,* expressed graphically as a straight line. A constant increase in time is associated with a constant or proportionate increase in, say, size or money. Most people think in linear terms, and under many conditions this may present no difficulty. Linear models are commonly used to describe and sometimes control processes in the organization and its environments. Linear approximations of nonlinear processes are often necessary because of the intractability of nonlinear models. The danger, however, comes from believing that complex real-world processes are indeed linear. Sometimes the world presents a deceptive impression of linearity. Things tomorrow will be seen as straightforward extensions of today. For example, things look linear during the interval around the inflection point where the slope of the logistic curve (described below) changes. Policies and decisions made at such times may be extremely faulty.

Many of the most important types of growth are *exponential*. Examples are legion and include population growth of living organisms, human use of natural resources, manufacture and sales of many products, economic growth, and increases in numbers of educated persons, scientists, patents, and published materials, and so on. Most people become familiar with exponential growth through the concept of compound interest. With each succeeding constant time interval, the amount increases by a constant percentage or fraction of the whole. In other words the quantity changes—either growing or decaying—at a rate proportional to the quantity itself. In systems dynamics exponential growth is a characteristic of *positive feedback* loops.

Two very important ideas associated with exponential growth are *doubling time* and *limits to growth*.[3] For example, a growth rate of two percent would result in doubling a quantity in about 35 years; a rate of 10 percent would double the quantity in about seven years. The doubling of very large quantities within short periods can have major consequences, the desirability of which depends on both the nature of the quantity and one's particular biases. Obviously, without limits various living organisms would long since have grown in number to occupy every square meter of the earth's surface and every cubic meter of the oceans' volume.

The environments of living systems do of course impose limits to growth. Sometimes the system naturally grows or decays toward an equilibrium value. A quantity defined by the *difference* between the quantity at any given time and its final equilibrium value changes at a rate proportional to itself.

More often limits are set by exhaustion of resources, saturation of an area or volume, exhaustion of a process through built-in checks, or competition with others. The applicable growth curve is usually the *logistic, sigmoid,* or *S-shaped* curve. Actually this is a composite curve with two or three segments—an initial state of increasing growth, a middle quasilinear stage, and a final stage of decreasing growth dominated by negative feedback. In the theoretical sense the limit is a value—called an asymptote—which the curve approaches ever so closely but never quite touches. The inflection point occurs at half the limiting value; that is, at this point the inhibiting processes begin to slow the growth rate.

In most systems of concern here, however, a smooth, natural approach to asymptote does not occur. This is because of the negative feedback processes which can be thought of as goal-seeking or regulatory. The system tries to stabilize itself around some value. But stability is made difficult by earlier periods of prolonged growth and by under- and overcontrol. Depending on the specific (feedback) mechanisms and times involved, systems behavior can be described as *growth with overshoot of a limit and collapse, growth with overshoot and recovery,* or *oscillatory.* The last is represented by sinusoidal waves. If the amplitudes of the waves gradually decrease toward a limit or stability level, the oscillations are said to be *damped.* If the amplitudes progressively or suddenly increase, the system shows *expanding* or *explosive* oscillations. Ordinary oscillations have identical amplitudes. Systems dynamics specializes in trying to reveal the structure underlying such behavior.

In *hyperbolic* growth the growth rate *itself* increases with time.[4] Such growth is faster than exponential, and an *acceleration* of history or of evolution can be spoken of. Hyperbolic growth has been attributed to human evolution from about 2 million years ago to about the first quarter of the twenty-first century. The curves predict that by about the year 2025 earth's human population will be more than 20 billion persons or even have reached infinity! Obviously famine, disease, and societal breakdown and chaos would impose limits on the growth of such huge populations.

Nevertheless the concept of hyperbolic growth is extremely important. The underlying mechanism involves positive feedback interrelationships among population numbers, biological structure (for example, cranial capacity), and technology and culture. Evolution can be thought of as a series of logistic curves. As one of these three dimensions of growth levels off, another *relays* it through the ceiling or limit. The overall curve enveloping the many local S-curves (the *envelope curve*) is hyperbolic. Hyperbolic growth provides one key to understanding emergent phenomena.

When one organ of an organism grows more rapidly than does another, such differential growth is called *allometric*. However, mathematically time is usually eliminated from the relevant equations, and the allometric law is more concerned with the relative pattern of growth than with the speed of growth. The allometric law implies certain requirements for function, coordination, and control. The large numbers of servers in relationship to those served and the large numbers of people receiving certain pensions and retirement benefits in relation to the tax base would appear to be examples of allometric growth.

Figures 3.1, 3.2, and 3.3 show most of the growth curves discussed in this section.

INTERPRETATIONS OF GROWTH STAGES

Before proceeding further a few more words about growth need to be said. Growth is an exceedingly important concept in organic evolution to which is linked organizational evolution. Growth has been inherent in industrialization, and most people still believe growth—of population, GNP, communications, product numbers and diversity, and so forth—is good. In an era of limits to growth, the concept assumes, if anything, even greater significance. However, growth is a blanket term that may be manifested in different ways and reflect different underlying structures.

The concept of organizational growth and of course stability and decline cannot be dissociated from the concepts of organizational effectiveness and adaptability and maintenance of best fit to a turbulent environment. Further, growth should be at least measurable along one or more dimensions and preferably relatable both to performance criteria and to underlying structure.

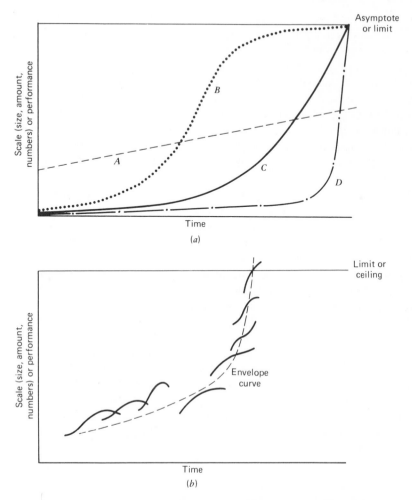

Figure 3.1. Representative growth curves: *(a) A,* linear; *B,* logistic; *C,* exponential; *D,* hyperbolic. *(b)* exponential or hyperbolic envelope curve of separate logistic curves shoots through a limit or ceiling.

Unfortunately, this is not always possible. Some of the examples discussed below utilize the mathematical methods presented above and/or provide structural interpretations. But some of the most interesting studies of organizational growth and evolution are based on expert observation (that is, are empirical) and are purely qualitative.

Some of the indices of growth and performance criteria of organizations can be noted here. Most simply growth can be measured by number of employees, size of assets, productivity, and size of markets. A little deeper probing gives measures of amount of internal differentiation, diversification of products or services, specialization of functions and personnel, integration, and coordina-

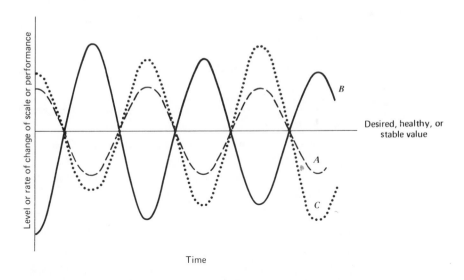

Figure 3.2. Oscillations: *A*, ordinary; *B*, damped; *C*, expanding.

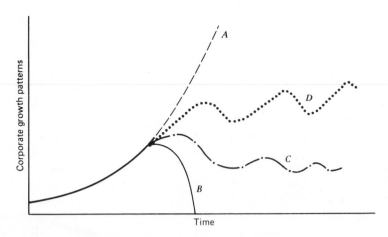

Figure 3.3. Corporate growth patterns: *A*, high-technology, high-innovation; *B*, bankruptcy or forced merger; *C*, stagnation; *D*, sustained growth punctuated by intermittent crises. (From blackboard sketch by Jay W. Forrester, System Dynamics Course, Massachusetts Institute of Technology, Summer, 1976.)

tion and control. The most subtle indicators of growth and evolution are changes in organizational climate and increases in complexity that may break through the ceilings of manageability.

Measures or criteria of organizational performance that can be linked to stages of growth or evolution include:

How well the organization recognizes its own goals and how well it achieves its formal, informal, conflicting, and changing goals.

Behavioral manifestations of low morale and job dissatisfaction like rapid job turnover, absenteeism, tardiness, pilferage, vandalism, and sabotage.

Efficiency in utilization of resources—natural, human, economic, and temporal—perhaps defined simply in output/input terms.

Maximization of desirable impacts on the external environments and minimization of undesirable impacts.

This list is not meant to be exhaustive. As shall be seen, interpreting organizational growth and evolution requires understanding of factors and variables at several levels of profundity.

Mathematical Models

Paul Strassmann uses the concept of stages of growth, and specifically the (aggregated) S-curve, in corporate planning at Xerox Corporation for computers, data processing, telecommunications, and information systems.[5] Strassmann believes that the driving force in evolutionary growth in the data-processing industry lies in the ability to find innovative and profitable investment opportunities. He relates four stages of growth—initiation, expansion, formalization, and maturity—to various features of data-processing technology, applications, management, costs, benefits, and personnel. He is particularly concerned about what happens after maturity, that is, when computer and data-processing technology have been well assimilated into existing applications. However, maturity may be more imagined than real. Thus the glamor of traditional data processing may have overshadowed the possibility of potentially lucrative new developments. Strassmann forsees a change in the shape of the S-curve caused by breakthroughs in office automation and improvements of white-collar and professional productivity.

In brief, what policy or policies is or are best for a given stage in organizational evolution, especially today for the mature, stagnant, old, or declining stages? Before implementing policies, however, it is necessary to dissect the qualitative changes associated with growth curves and stages of evolution. Professors John Freeman and Michael Hannan differentiate between processes in growth and decline of organizations.[6] They performed mathematical analyses using both multiple regression analysis and differential equations.

Professors Freeman and Hannan studied the growth and relative sizes of administrators and producers-workers in 805 California school districts, but their results appear to be generalizable to other organizations as well. In addition, their study used longitudinal or time-series data rather than cross-sectional data. In this study the use of longitudinal data brought out the fact that the causal processes in decline were not simply the opposite of those in growth. In Chapter 5 our discussion of *hysteresis* or path irreversibility will aid us in understanding such phenomena in a broader context.

Professors Freeman and Hannan studied *administrative intensity,* the ratio of administrators to teachers, as a function of size. Variations in environmental demand drove the system. The regression equation relating teachers to enrollment was identical for growing districts and declining districts. However, there were dramatic differences between growers and decliners with regard to the administrative component. Also there was no direct effect of enrollments on the number of administrators. In other words, teachers were hired and fired as a direct response to numbers of enrollments, but administrators, because of bureaucratic processes, were hired rapidly during the growth stage but let go slowly during the decline stage. Thus, administrative intensity can actually increase during stages of organizational decline.

The same qualitative differences between growth and decline stages can be generalized to apply to other organizational dimensions such as horizontal and vertical differentiation, formalization and use of rules and procedures, and centralization.

The bureaucratic processes in these systems are protective of administrators and involve a large featherbedding element. The larger the size of the administrative component, the less outside critics can obtain information, the less outsiders can find ingress to the system, and the better the bureaucrats can defend their policies and programs against opponents who lack the facts. Power structure in an organization therefore can reduce resiliency and adaptability to changing environmental demands.

Systems dynamics routinely deals with the growth forms discussed earlier (except hyperbolic, allometric, and catastrophic) but specializes in sinusoidal or oscillatory forms which recur over relatively long times—in some instances decades or even centuries. Some of the elementary features of the structure–behavior relationship can be summarized here:

A first-order system, that is, a system consisting of one level variable and one or more rate variables, cannot overshoot or oscillate. System behavior reflects a limit which restricts initial exponential growth, and the curve is logistic. For example, population *level* in a closed system initially increases exponentially because of a high birth *rate* but later approaches an asymptotic limit because of a high death *rate* associated with negative feedback pressures.

A second-order system with two level variables can produce undamped oscillations. However, the presence of two or more levels does not guarantee oscillations. Such a simple system could have levels of inventory and salesmen and order rate, production rate, and sales rate equal or proportional to one another. At the beginning the system could be in equilibrium in the sense that desired inventory equals actual inventory. Suppose there is a sudden (step-function) increase in order rate or sales rate. Over time oscillations could develop and remain indefinitely whereby inventory level and production rate are exactly out of phase, that is, their curves show right-angle crossovers. The system is unstable, reflecting expanding the rate of inventory at the times when desired inventory once again equals actual inventory! Managers would have overlooked the fact that production would be excessive once an inventory shortage had been eliminated. Addition of some minor feedback loops, however, could damp the oscillations.

A third-order system can produce expanding oscillations. Addition of certain delays, for example (delays are viewed as levels), can induce oscillations in inventory, workforce, and production rate. All these oscillations expand. A new hiring policy, for example, can damp the oscillations.[7]

Managers often face problems of this type, but of course in much more complex systems. Changes in policy can have quite *unexpected* effects on system equilibrium and stability as well as equally unexpected dynamic effects. The many interacting feedback loops can variously yield product growth, stagnation, or decline. Delivery delays, for example, can result in a corporation's losing a large part of its market share. How the feedback loops are balanced will determine whether a product is or remains profitable or not.

Managers' perceptions and judgments, however, are almost always limited by time in office and inability to see all interrelationships of the real world. Organizations pass through certain stages of instability and vulnerability. During these stages the organization may be especially sensitive to certain policy and parameter changes.

Professor Jay Forrester states that one such parameter—a change in which can convert decline to growth—is the volatility to reallocation of resources, for example, the time constant of reallocation of manpower between marketing and production. It must be made smaller or faster. However, even if a manager has this parameter identified for him, he will not, without further interpretation, know whether to make it bigger or smaller.[8]

Systems dynamics is also sensitive to intangible, poorly measurable variables such as goals, traditions, and pressures. Pressures are ways of equalizing troubles throughout an organization. Suppose that a company has traditionally made a product at a given high level and that now pressures impinge on the R&D unit from outside. Actual quality may then be reduced by a certain amount. Personnel may want to do what was achieved in the past but may have little incentive to do better. They may not want to take risks. After a year or so goals become adjusted to coincide with the lowered quality. The dominant theme is to accomplish what was done in the recent past. But the pressures remain and quality, observed quality, traditional quality, and goals continue to deteriorate. Ideals adapt to performance. Through positive feedback a downward spiral develops. People rationalize, but they do not understand what is happening to them or to their organization.

In this way subtle changes can develop a new, unhealthful organizational climate. Psychological theories—for example, level of aspiration theory and achievement motivation theory—can back up empirical observations of such organizational changes.

Professor Edward Roberts of MIT has spent many years studying aging research and R&D organizations.[9] Like other systems dynamicists he emphasizes that an organization's problems are natural consequences of its own structure, activities and policies. As in the above discussion the R&D organization may for various reasons show a decline in its technical effectiveness. Management may then lower the level of its goals so that the unit now produces less or produces at a lower level of quality. Through positive feedback loops the vicious downward spiral begins.

Top management may, for example, decide to cut back on the R&D unit. This is followed by a slowdown in recruiting rate, a stabilization of manpower levels, a reduction in technical effectiveness, an aging of personnel and presumably also of ideas, a reduction in attractiveness of the unit to outsiders, and decreased success in marketing. Management has, by its own efforts and probably without realizing it, hastened the decline of the R&D organization.

Professor Roberts cautions: "Management must see in the initial decline a warning signal that the organization needs an infusion of revitalizing influences."

These interpretations apply to entire industries—indeed to entire societies and cultures. The United States steel and automobile industries are examples of aging industries. United States production industry in general increasingly shows signs of aging and infirmity. The underlying dynamics are subtle and presently understood by very few people. In many cases top management corrective actions aggravate the underlying pathology.

There are of course mathematical models for studying growth processes other than those considered so far and based on regression analysis, differential equations, and difference equations. Some observers, for example, are critical of systems dynamics because systems dynamics, although it has the capability to generate random noise exogenously, is internally a deterministic modeling approach. One way of overcoming this deficiency—*probabilistic systems dynamics*—will be discussed later.

Some models are wholly probabilistic or stochastic. *Stochastic* models deal with events that occur randomly over time. One widely used family of stochastic models is that of *Markov processes* or sequences of such processes known as *Markov chains*. The techniques represent a blend of matrix algebra, probability theory, and differential (or difference) equations originally invented by A. A. Markov, a Russian mathematician who lived in the late nineteenth and early twentieth centuries.[10]

Markov processes deal with situations in which the state of the system can be represented by a set of mutually exclusive, qualitatively different categories. From empirical or experimental observations or theoretical assumptions the probabilities or rates of going (transitioning) from one system or organizational state to another are determined. Time can be viewed as either discrete or continuous, which produces somewhat different kinds of models. Markov processes have a property—sometimes called *ahistoricity* or being *without memory*—which requires that the future state of the system be dependent only on the present state and on no past states.

Markov processes have been used to study workforce movements (mobility), mobility through social strata, loyalty to product brands, and changes in attitudes. These models of change processes may be limited in many applications because of the assumptions of ahistoricity and discrete time as well as because of other assumptions not mentioned here. Many attempts have been made to improve the basic models, but the resulting equations are usually impossible to solve. Nevertheless, advanced Markovian models are very important to the theoretical understanding of evolutionary and ecological processes. For example, they help explain how new self-organizing systems emerge from older systems stressed by being in a position far from equilibrium.

Empirical Models

Professor Larry Greiner postulates that growing organizations pass through five distinguishable phases of evolution, each of which is terminated by a revolutionary crisis.[11] Each phase is strongly affected by the previous phase. The future of the organization is much more a function of past historical forces and decisions than it is of present environmental (for example, market) dynamics.

Organizational structure, management practices, reward systems, and control systems differ in appropriateness as the organization grows in size and age. The passage of time results in the institutionalization of organizational practices, managerial perspectives, and employee behaviors. These become both more rigid and predictable and more resistant to change when they become outmoded. Top managers who are unaware of the growth phase of their organization with its associated characteristics and problems are likely to preside over an organization frozen in time and unable to take advantage of opportunities or an organization unable to adapt to predictable crises. And organizations that cannot anticipate and adapt to crises have good chances of failing.

Professor Greiner regards each phase as an effect of the previous phase and a cause for the succeeding phase. Each evolutionary period possesses a dominant managerial style used to accomplish growth; and each revolutionary period is highlighted by a major management problem that must be overcome before growth can continue. Each set of problem solutions eventually paves the way to decay which leads to the next revolution.

Professor Greiner's phases can be briefly interpreted as follows:

1. *Evolutionary growth through creativity terminated by a revolutionary crisis of leadership.* Typically, scientists or engineers develop a new product, entrepreneurially found a company, and seek to market their product. Communications are informal as is organizational structure, and people are motivated by the intrinsic nature of their work. However, the company

grows in number of employees and amount of production output, and new requirements emerge for better coordination and control. The founders continue to think like technologists and to eschew management responsibilities. A professional manager is needed, but the founders may not want to give up control. If this crisis can be weathered—there is a foundering of organizations at each stage—the company moves on to the next phase.

2. *Evolutionary growth through direction terminated by a revolutionary crisis of autonomy.* Bureaucratization begins. Engineering, production, and marketing become separate organizational functions, and work becomes specialized. Accounting systems for inventory and purchasing are instituted. Rules and procedures proliferate. A hierarchical organizational structure is instituted, and communications become formal. However, increased efficiency yields to increased rigidity, which is inappropriate for managing a larger, more diverse, more complex organization. Lower-level managers and employees come to know internal operations and outside markets far better than does top management. There are cries for more autonomy at the bottom, but top management may resist delegation. Feelings of alienation and behaviors consequent to alienation develop if autonomy is denied. The organizational climate deteriorates.

3. *Evolutionary growth through delegation terminated by a revolutionary crisis of control.* The company is decentralized, and the managers of the separate units and territories are given far greater independence and responsibility. Top management may be by exception. The decentralized units are much better able to penetrate new markets, develop new products, and respond to customers. Overall motivation is greatly improved. Communications from headquarters to the field may be infrequent and fairly informal. However, eventually, top management perceives that it is losing control over the entire company. Top management then tries to regain control, perhaps by reinstituting centralization which usually fails.

4. *Evolutionary growth through coordination terminated by a revolutionary crisis of red tape.* A number of new formal systems or programs for achieving better coordination and control are introduced. Headquarters expands its staff and augments its capabilities through addition of a formal planning capability and centralization of data-processing. Decentralized units may be merged into product groups, viewed as investment centers, which may be encouraged to compete with one another. Profit sharing and stock options encourage identification with the corporation as a whole. All in all the corporation is better able to allocate its limited resources. However, demands for accountability eventually produce a deluge of paperwork. Rules and procedures take precedence over problemsolving, and innovation falters. Conflict breaks out between line and staff and between headquarters and field. In short, the organization has become too big and complex to be managed by formal and rigid methods.

5. *Evolutionary growth through collaboration possibly terminated by a revolutionary crisis of employee burnout.* Strong interpersonal cooperation, collaboration, and conflict resolution are emphasized. Greater managerial spontaneity is attempted through organizational development, management development, and related programs. Interdisciplinary and cross-functional teams are used, and matrix organizations are favored designs. Problemsolving is seen as a primary and global function of the organization. Real-time information systems are utilized as aids to decisionmaking. However, the line managers who rely on formal methods and the experts who created the coordination and control systems may resent and resist the new behavioral science approach. Some managers may conclude that management is not for them after all or that it is better to transfer to another company whose phase of growth is more congruent with their own personalities. Employees may become physically and emotionally exhausted from the pressures of teamwork and the demand for innovative solutions to problems. New organizational designs would then be necessary so that employees can periodically revitalize themselves.

A graphical representation of these five phases is shown in Figure 3.4.

Although the Greiner model is an excellent attempt to portray the qualitative changes in an organization longitudinally, it possesses a number of limitations as seen from current perspective. For example:

1. The emphasis on internal processes and management actions and associated neglect of the turbulent environment.

2. The appearance of linearity of growth (even though Professor Greiner suggests in his article that such change is nonlinear) and the associated equal spacing of phases.

3. The failure of psychological exhaustion or burnout to materialize as a foremost problem confronting present organizations, at least as detached from other behavioral factors like alienation.

4. Being dated; that is, based on observations and case histories of actual organizational happenings up to the time of the writing but ignoring (theoretical) undercurrents that might produce emergent forms in the future. The model is a good *descriptive* model of actually observed stages many organizations passed through during a period of relatively stable environments. It was a good *predictive* model for organizations yet to pass through these defined stages. However, its predictive value today is starkly limited by the turbulent environments and emergent phenomena of the present.

5. Apparent assumptions of continued growth with associated neglect of decay and decline, which have become the most important concerns of many present organizations.

Partly based on the Greiner model, scientists at Stanford Research International have developed a rather detailed model that deals with the

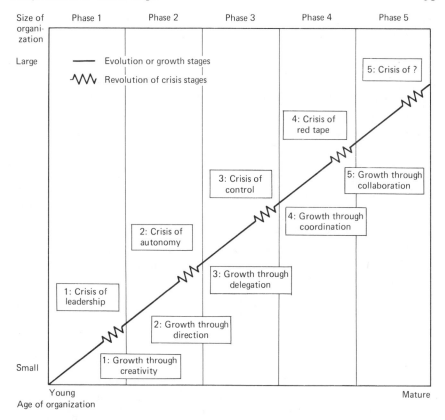

Figure 3.4 Growth phases in organizations as a function of age and size. Reprinted by permission of the *Harvard Business Review*. Exhibit from "Evolution and Revolution as Organizations Grow" by Larry E. Greiner (July–August 1972). Copyright © 1972 by the President and Fellows of Harvard College, all rights reserved.

extremes of growth, decline, and the limits to manageability of complex social systems.[12] Although the model is directed mainly to problems of government bureaucracies at the federal, state, and local levels, it is applicable to numerous difficulties found in business and industry as well.

The model utilizes 17 propositions that characterize social systems that have grown to extreme levels of scale, complexity, and interdependence. These propositions are then related to four stages of growth. Four possible fifth stages of growth are then hypothesized, each contingent on one of four possible managerial strategies. The 17 propositions are shown in Table 3.1.

A summary of the four stages follows:

1. ***High growth.*** Growth in scale, complexity, and interdependence contributes to greater efficiency. Creativity is high and management entrepreneurial. However with increasing growth there arises a need for

Table 3.1   Characteristics of Social Systems at Extremes of Scale, Interdependence, and Complexity

Diminishing relative capacity of a given person to comprehend the entire system	Declining system resilience
	Increasing system rigidity
Diminishing public participation in decisionmaking	Increasing number and uncertainty of crisis events
Declining public access to decision-makers	Decreasing diversity of innovation
	Declining legitimacy of leadership
Growing participation of experts in decisionmaking	Increasing system vulnerability
Disproportionately growing costs of co-ordination and control	Declining system performance
Increasingly rationalized person–system interactions	Growing system deterioration that is unlikely to be perceived by most members
Increasing alienation	
Increasing challenges to basic values	
Increasingly unexpected and counterexpected consequences of policymaking	

Source.   Reference 4.

greater coordination and control and more predictable patterns of relationship among system elements. Some managers desire even greater efficiency, but the increasingly rigid organizational structure drives away many creative persons (including perhaps the founders of the organization), and new workers seek security rather than outlets for creativity. This stage is akin to Greiner's Phase 1.

2. *Greatest efficiency.*   System output is increasing but at a decreasing rate. A rational self-organizing, self-limiting organization would not grow beyond this stage. However, an impetus toward even more growth prevails. The organization changes in a manner described by Greiner's Phases 2 and 3.

3. *Diseconomies of scale.*   This stage is based on the economic law of diminishing returns: at some size nothing is to be gained from even greater size, and if size does continue to increase diseconomies will emerge. In this stage total system output is declining. However, the pressures of societal and organizational forces push the system into even greater scales of activity. The large increments in efficiency derived from centralization, decentralization, and technological innovation are approaching limits of saturation or exhaustion. With arithmetic changes in scale, there are geometric increases in interdependence and complexity. Managers apply simple decision rules to complex problems. Short-term partial solutions generate formidable long-term problems. System performance enters a degenerative spiral downwards. The system is increasingly out of control. This stage is related to but transcends Greiner's Phase 4.

4. *Systems crisis.*   The problems of the preceding stage are amplified to intolerable extremes, and internal and external forces contribute to precipitating the system into crisis. The system cannot long endure unchanged, but large systems possess such inertia as to render change exceedingly difficult if not impossible. Tension between the need for change and impediments to change threatens to break the system apart.

A fifth stage that might involve renaissance, oscillation, or continued downward spiral can be hypothesized as a function of four possible management strategies:

1. *Muddling through.*   This is an incremental approach often associated with the name of Charles Lindblom. It is a cautious approach which does not question the soundness of underlying premises—what was successful in the recent past should be equally successful in the near future. Muddling through is at best a means of borrowing time. However, while time is being borrowed the system may continue to deteriorate covertly so that future policymaking is rendered even more difficult. Overemphasis should not be placed on muddling through in conjunction with a hoped-for rescue from outside the organization—for example, from a government bailout or technological breakthrough.

2. *Descent into chaos.*   If managers do not understand the dynamics of the system, and cannot or will not heed the handwriting on the wall, persistence in implementing dysfunctional policies can heighten the descent into chaos. Clearly, anticipatory design of alternative systems would greatly reduce this danger. Under certain conditions a pervasive sense of crisis could stimulate innovation.

3. *Authoritarian response.*   A time-honored response to tumultuous social change, inefficiency, threat, and crisis is an authoritarian crackdown. However, increased authoritarianism may be gradual as coordination and control structures are simplified and rationalized. This response is highly probable in many organizations and societies, but in the longer term the response will create a schism between the system and its environments. Thus, strategies 1-3 are not good long-range strategies.

4. *Transformational change.*   The Stanford Research International authors do not have much to say in this area, perhaps because it involves emergent phenomena. Management strategies that have been successful up to now, and the supportive techniques such as those we discussed in Chapter 2, may be exhausted. Thinking about a world in transformation requires innovative ways for thinking about complex systems as well as new techniques and designs. The SRI growth curve is a logistic curve which reaches a limit and decays. It is shown in Figure 3.5.

As an example of some of these dynamics, consider what happened at International Harvester. Long a family-owned and -directed business, the company in 1977 acquired a professional top manager. However, efforts to

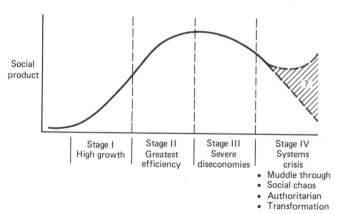

Figure 3.5 Growth, decline, and crisis in organizations. (Social product is defined as the aggregate improvement in well-being of the members of that society produced by that social system.) (Modified from reference 4, page 45).

redirect the company led to a confrontation with the United Auto Workers. The 172-day-long strike eventually led to a loss of $397 million in fiscal year 1980 and another $96.4 million in the first quarter of 1981, more than the losses of any other company outside the automobile industry. Market share has been lost, short-term debt has increased, and a major refinancing is required.

ORGANIZATION/EXTERNAL ENVIRONMENT DYNAMICS

The organization is neither a closed nor an open-loop system. People, raw materials, finished products, money, credit, energy, and information cross the permeable organizational boundary. Today the interrelationships between and among the organization and its external environments are changing much more rapidly than in the past, and both the organization and its environments and the external environments among themselves are becoming more tightly coupled. This means that a purposeful activity or a spontaneous change anywhere in the overall world environment can trigger a succession of events that spread rapidly across the entire environmental *field* and impact on the organization in unexpected ways. Models of organizational growth and change that rely mostly on internal processes are not realistic.

Relations between the organization and its external environments are of course two-way. Here we will consider how these environments:

Serve as major sources of organizational change.

Limit growth in size and form of the organization.

Potentially introduce crisis into the organization.

Modern organizations are very dependent on *new technology*. Improved generations of technology have overall helped production organizations do things faster, in larger quantities, more cheaply, more efficiently, and usually more safely. Data-processing technology has similarly improved rationalized processes in all organizations and services in service organizations. However, these improvements have not been without some unexpected costs and side effects, and it is possible that the types of improvements made in the past may not carry over into the future.

Sudden introduction of new technology into an organization can be a major disruptive force and yield an actual lowering of productivity, efficiency, morale, and so on. Top management should anticipate disruption and plan for gradual introduction of change. Employees usually feel uneasy about the unknown. Planning and preparation for technological change can variously include working with trade unions, training programs, introduction of new employee incentives and benefits, and sociotechnical or organizational development or other behavioral science designs.

Even planned introduction of new technology can have subtle and long-term effects, some of which may be undesirable. New technology, almost inherently, affects the way work is structured and jobs are performed. Automation and technological change shift required ability and skill levels, eliminate some jobs, and create new jobs. Many organizations are eager to automate because they find people problems difficult to solve. Many manual, sensory, perceptual-motor, logical, computational, and decisional functions can now be performed better by machines than by people. Advances in pattern perception, industrial robotics, and computer problemsolving should maintain this generally upward trend in ability and skill levels for jobs. The functions of the few remaining personnel in automated factories are almost limited to exception-detection and to preventive and corrective maintenance.

Over the longer term some organizations may find themselves in the paradoxical position of having eliminated jobs at lower skill levels and then being required by government regulations to make work for people otherwise unemployable. Of course the government itself may be, as is often stated, the employer of last resort.

New technology can change organizational structure both overtly and covertly. Simple data-processing and information systems usually are associated with centralization of at least some functions, but use of computer-communications networks can lead to great decentralization. Centralization of data processing often means keeping corporate power at or restoring it to headquarters. However, there is often a shift in de facto power from line managers to technical experts. In many organizations the introduction of new technology has rendered top managers obsolescent, and the question of who or what controls whom or what has become increasingly moot.

Although in the long run new technologies have the potential for increasing organizational flexibility, technology so far has mostly increased the formality of organizations. Both the assembly line and the computer are hard taskmasters. In addition, poorly designed automated systems can cast into concrete the worst features of preexisting manual systems, thereby greatly reducing organizational adaptability.

In this book we pay considerable heed to aging and obsolescent organizations. Two extremes of the application of technology can contribute to the aging of organizations. At one extreme organizations can fail because of, for example, lack of capital, hostility of labor unions, or ingrained and outmoded thinking, all inimical to the introduction of new and required technology. These organizations eventually lose to more innovative competitors and contribute to lowering industry and national productivity.

At the other extreme organizations may have an unfounded faith in technological solutions and technological bailouts. Applications may be reaching a level of qualitative and quantitative saturation or exhaustion. A *reorganization* of technology and ways of thinking about technology may be vastly more important than procuring another machine to do things even faster and in greater amounts.

Behavioral and social forces also have an impact on the organization from the outside. In the last generation large numbers of people have changed their *values* and *attitudes* toward work itself. For these people work is no longer the major driving force of their lives. Indeed, for many people work is no more than a necessary means for supporting the things in life that really are important and fun. Of course some types of work have always been oppressive, dreary, monotonous, or dangerous. But workers seem less willing to take these deficiencies for granted today.

It has become almost a cliché to state that the Protestant ethic—that hard work, thrift, and frugality are inherently good—has eroded greatly. Similar erosion has taken place with regard to the belief that what is good for the individual is in turn good for the corporation and in turn good for the nation. Nevertheless, management in both industry and labor is shocked at the vehemence of some strikes. The classic example is the strike at the Vega-assembly plant at Lordstown, Ohio in 1972. Young workers, who wanted more control over their jobs and a better quality of working life, had quite different values from those of their fathers and the older leaders at General Motors and the United Auto Workers, who tended to think in terms of the older rewards of job security, pay increases, and increases in fringe benefits.

At least a decade ago, and probably earlier, there were warning signs that both the automobile industry and the trade unions were aging. Both were ingrown in ideas as well as leadership. These ideas apply to Britain as well as to the United States. The maintenance of supportive cultural patterns as well as the implementation of innovative means of recovery from the destruction of World War II have enabled West Germany and Japan to become fierce economic competitors to the United States and Britain. Yet even in West Germany signs of inicipient socioeconomic decline are becoming more evident.

New workers, especially younger ones, bring new *motivation* into the organization. Younger workers want to get ahead faster and start at higher levels; they are less tolerant of obstacles, less respectful of authority, and tend to consider rewards more as rights than as privileges. Mature and aging organizations cannot supply the growth opportunities that the more ambitious employees seek. Locked into unfulfilling jobs with little future, countless millions of blue-collar and white-collar workers—and increasing numbers of professional and middle-management employees—are alienated from their work and often from themselves, their families, and society as well. Job frustration, lowered morale, and alienation produce *symptoms* familiar to every executive—absenteeism, tardiness, passive aggression (for example, dragging one's feet on the job), sickness including psychosomatic illness, vandalism, and sabotage and increasingly even terrorism. These symptoms cost business, industry, and government untold billions of dollars a year, and are a key reason for bringing behavioral science consultants into the organization.

Educational levels have increased greatly in recent years. There seems to be little doubt that more people are better educated now than in the past. However, having more years of education augments the effects of changing values and motivations. Management structure itself may be severely impacted. Most new graduates of business schools do not want to start at the bottom, working their way upward and thereby learning all levels of operations and control. The hottest jobs tend to be in the technical areas, in the staff advisory positions to top management, and in management consulting. Overall these trends indicate:

An increasing rationalization of the organization.

An increasing reluctance to accept intuitive or gut-feeling orientations—which in reality often represent creative subconscious problemsolving.

A decreasing understanding of human nature and human dynamics.

A decreasing understanding of the organization as a whole.

A decreasing capability of the organization for self-renewal from below.

Decreasing organizational adaptability.

Other *demographic* changes are also important. For example, *skill levels* need not increase. Organizations now employ large numbers of persons with few if any skills or with skills that have become obsolescent. Government regulations, an organization's desire to do social good, and the fact that previous types of workers will no longer accept the most odious jobs are the main reasons for these changes in employment patterns. Ethnic minorities, women starting in or returning to outside work after years spent working as housewives, and older workers whose skills have not kept up with technological change comprise the main categories of lower-skilled employees. Poor skill-to-job matches lower overall national productivity. Training programs to rectify the situation are often poorly designed or have actually become the creatures of corruption, graft, and fraud. Everybody pays the price for poor skill-to-job matches, and these costs are immense.

Sociopolitical changes in the external environment increasingly impact on the organization. The most obvious manifestation is *government regulation* and *control* of business and industry. Most executives and conservative political leaders believe that these regulations discourage investment, divert valuable resources into handling red tape, stifle innovation, increase costs, and lower productivity. However, the problem does not appear to be one of government against business. Public-opinion polls suggest an underlying lack of confidence in and hostility toward both business and government. Recent taxpayers' revolts and attempts to control government spending are probably analogous to attempts to control business through government.

Top management has long been attuned to changes in the economic world outside the organization, especially to *market* changes. However, this environment is now as turbulent as any. Businessmen have often overestimated their control over markets and have failed to heed early-warning signs about changes in consumer attitudes and purchasing behavior. Businessmen have often assumed erroneously that *fluctuations* are only temporary and that most things would soon return to normal—as indeed in the past they actually had. Markets that were thought to be tied down have proved to be very permeable to aggressive *foreign competition.* Traditional economics of every school has displayed failings, for example, in explanations of inflation, recession and depression, unemployment, and the ability to control *cycles* and *oscillations.*

The *natural environment* may prove in the long run to have the greatest impact on the organization. The most accessible nonrenewable *natural resources* have already been located and exploited, and it is necessary to go farther afield and deeper and to spend much more to discover and exploit new resources. Renewable resources also do not come cost-free, and the costs in many cases are subtle but severe longer-term ecological backlashes. In a politically differentiated, increasingly unstable world, the geographical distribution of natural resources has resulted in unexpected shifts in political and economic power. Well-endowed Third World nations guard their resources with pride and are reluctant to have their endowments quickly exhausted by seemingly greedy industrialized countries. Revolutions and changes in political alignment may mean that a previously reliable source of resources is now in the camp of the enemy or is made available to a more ideologically acceptable competitor.

Although, in hindsight, early-warning signals of the present and likely future world-system states clearly occurred in the 1950s and 1960s, it was of course the 1970s that provided the major lessons as to what the remaining years of this century are likely to be. Certainly of all these lessons the energy crisis and the rise in power of the petroleum-producing nations are among the foremost.

Finally, *logistics* and *temporal* limitations can impact on the organization. An obvious example is the breakdown of postal services and other communications and transportation systems.

MORE ON INTERNAL DYNAMICS

Changes in the internal dynamics of the organization also can affect the scale and state of the organization and lead it into crisis.

Not every organization passes through the sequence of stages described earlier. The failure rate of new organizations is high. The problems of getting an organization started and sustaining it are important. The founding of new organizations—and especially the design of alternative forms—is essential as replacements for older organizations that have foundered. New forms revitalize a society. Nevertheless, new organizations usually have not forged extensive links with other elements of society, and their demise does not have the repercussions that follow failure of an older, well-established organization.

There are a number of characteristics of aging, declining, or obsolescent organizations. Executives have long been familiar with the problem of appropriateness of *structure*. Some new organizations are born with obsolescent structure, a seemingly instantaneous bureaucratization. These organizations do not experience the growing pains—and learning—characteristic of organizations that pass through the evolutionary-revolutionary stages discussed above. As spinoffs of postmature organizations, such organizations come into being with staffs and ideas that may not be easily reconcilable with the purportedly new goals and bases for foundation. The problems of large government departments and regulatory agencies and of business-government interrelationships are more problems of organizational structure than of mission.

Structure becomes obsolescent when its different elements—communications, power, facilities, and so on—become incongruent. Communications often fail to keep up with the growth, diversification, and integration of organizations. Formal communications can atrophy, and new informal, dynamic media arise, when people begin to realize that the former impede rather than enhance getting the job done. In sick organizations employees and management subordinates actively try to sabotage formal communications. In more than one such case the organization began to operate by rumor, and the chief executive lost his job.

Management practices can rapidly become obsolescent. Executives can have an unfounded confidence in the persistence of a power structure, especially when this involves the external environment. Large corporations spend billions of dollars each year on advertising, polling consumer opinions, and sampling consumer behavior in attempts to influence and control consumer spending. Yet top management may overlook or ignore subtle nuances of consumer behavior, relegating them to a lunatic fringe. There are plentiful signs that the United States automobile industry, as it has existed for 60 years, is now obsolescent. Some of this obsolescence is due to several top executives' insistence on maintaining practices that had been highly successful in the past but were not suited to a changing natural-resource environment and a changing market environment.

Ingrownness can readily lead to obsolescent practices. Top management, in an attempt to consolidate and maintain power, may restrict both entry into its ranks and intercommunication with the rest of the organization and the outside world. The same people continue to set the same policies and make the same decisions, and each policy and decision is continually reinforced in what amounts to a closed system. To remain healthy organizations as well as people require occasional infusions of new ideas and opportunities for new experiences. Ingrownness appears to be a factor contributory to the demise of Detroit.

Old *technology* underlies many obsolescent organizations and industries. There are a number of reasons for this situation, including lack of necessity, lack of capital for investment, greed and a determination to milk a system for as long as possible, opposition of labor unions, poor design of the original plant and equipment, and lack of foresight and poor planning. The remarkable industrial success of Japan and West Germany in the past two decades, when compared with that of Britain and the United States, is often explained in terms of World War II destruction in the former countries and the consequent need to replace plant and equipment. However, this is a gross oversimplification like most single-cause explanations. Japanese and West German modernization were not one of a kind but were continual. For example, a large steel plant in the Tokyo area, rebuilt about 30 years ago, was completely redesigned a decade ago.

Some companies and industries may indeed lack the capital to invest in modernization, but often top management is reluctant to utilize new technologies that might disturb presently comfortable operations. Years ago Detroit *could* have retooled to make less expensive, fuel-efficient, reliable smaller cars. Detroit *could* have invested much more in R&D in order to discover viable alternatives to the internal combustion engine. American railroads *could* have invested more in upgrading the thousands of miles of badly deteriorated roadbed and rails. With regard to the last point, there has now arisen a sudden, if belated, public concern over America's deteriorated transportation infrastructure.

Scapegoating does not help the cause of an organization or industry in trouble. At the present time there are cries, from the automobile and steel industries for example, to loosen safety and pollution standards, provide tax and credit relief, and (paradoxically) more government support. Some leaders in these industries blame everybody and everything but themselves. And government bailouts like those of Lockheed and Chrysler impress many observers as rewards for mismanagement and incompetency, scarcely the rewards needed to revitalize national productivity.

If such bailouts are increased, there may be an increased proportion of (perhaps permanently) geriatric institutions. It is interesting to note again some American industries that display at least some symptoms of senescence:

Automobiles
Airlines
Steel
Textiles
Mass merchandising
Heavy machinery

Consumer electronics

Shipbuilding

Research and R&D

Banking and savings-and-loans

Real estate and construction

Health services

Education

Social services, including welfare and Social Security

Municipal transportation

Railroads

Postal services

This list is not meant to be exhaustive, and the specific problems differ of course from industry to industry. It should be noted that the list contains some industries like textiles and shipbuilding which are older than the Republic and other industries like some aspects of consumer electronics which are less than a decade old. In some cases it is not so much the age of the technology as an inability to utilize and manage technology. For example, some medical equipment is so complex that it cannot be used readily by physicians.

Obsolescent *skills* can limit the growth and success of organizations. The example often given is Detroit with its high preponderence of blue-collar workers over knowledge workers. However, increasing numbers of white-collar workers, managers, and professionals are becoming obsolete because of explosive social and technological change. Entire fields are changing almost overnight. Engineers who allow themselves to be lured into well-paying specialty jobs may find themselves obsolescent by age 30. Many organizations abet the obsolescence of their employees through featherbedding and abuses of seniority and tenure rights.

The *old goal structure* of an organization may have become fully saturated, so that the organization has lost its reason for existence but continues to coast along through momentum. The resources of the organization are utilized mainly to maintain the positions of the leaders. Several labor unions in the United States and in Britain are in this category. Periodically, old industrial management and old labor management, which have developed a symbiotic or mutually dependent relationship over the years, confront one another ritualistically to thrash out more of the same—increased wages, increased fringe benefits, guaranteed job security, restricted automation, and so forth. These unions may have lost contact with their constituency years before, with the younger workers motivated to achieve a better quality of working life, more control over their jobs, less rigid work rules, greater chance for advancement and personal growth, and less formal relationships with their superiors. It is little wonder that new organizational designs such as autonomous work groups and industrial democracy, in which workers deal directly with management rather than through unions, are seen as threats by the latter.

Just discussed has been a number of *symptoms* of troubled, especially aging or obsolescent organizations. Seldom do these symptoms occur in isolation; rather each is linked with others in a *pattern*. Each symptom reinforces others and in turn is reinforced through destructive positive-feedback loops. The pattern itself continues to grow in scope, progressively incorporating other system elements, and perhaps increasing in velocity and acceleration, until some threshold is exceeded and the system collapses. The antidote to such system pathology is obviously negative-feedback regulation and feedforward anticipatory planning. To reiterate some of the reasons whereby top management may neither understand nor be able to control the internal dynamics of the organization:

1. Subsystems are subtly losing congruence and cohesiveness, leading to the disintegration of the organization. For example, a traditional power subsystem may become increasingly incompatible with a social subsystem that has become greatly modified by values which reject any form of absolute authority.

2. Complexity, as defined in terms of the number of new linkages and interactions and the emergence of new forms, has far exceeded the information-gathering and communications capabilities of the organization. As a very straightforward example, some large companies are even unaware of the availability of spare parts needed for a new program.

3. The effects of policies are frequently counterintuitive (the opposite of what common sense would lead us to expect). Yet policymakers respond to the worsened situation with more of the same old policies which aggravates the situation even more.

4. Processes (dynamic changes in form and function) cross-cut structure (for example, facilities and equipment layout, organization chart, span of control, and centralization-decentralization) and function (for example, R&D, engineering, production, and marketing). Executives, by focusing on the latter, may not always recognize subtle, latent, or insidious changes in pressures, influence, communications, lags in getting things done, and so on. Structure and function have been well studied since Max Weber, Alfred P. Sloan, Jr., and Henri Fayol theorized in the early part of this century, but the forces and processes that operate within organizations and society are still relatively poorly understood. In the long run forces and processes are much more important to organizational and societal success or failure than are the structures and functions which are much more accessible both to observation and study and to management control.

5. The entire organizational or psychological climate can change because of the processes mentioned in Item 4 or because of the specific acts or deficiencies of given top managers. In these cases motivation and morale deteriorate throughout the organization. Employees lose confidence in the leadership. Aspirations and expectations fall, and the organization

collectively no longer has confidence in itself, no longer believes it can compete, achieve, succeed, and win. An aura of hopelessness and failure permeates the organization, the ability to learn rusts, and problemsolving and decisionmaking become more and more routinized, short-term, and shortsighted with an unhealthful element of every person for himself or every group for itself. Unhealthful, counterproductive conflicts abound. The organization responds sluggishly if at all to internal conflicts and tensions and stresses and to outside threats and opportunities.

6. Money commonly is not available either to start or to sustain the growth of a new organization or to maintain an organization at a stage of healthy maturity. This statement may seem to be so obvious as to have no place here; nevertheless, conscientious executives are not always aware of the uncanny ability of certain investment bankers to size up an entire organization, to determine product–market relationships quickly, and to sense that an organization is foundering.

7. Risks, especially conflicts between or among risks, are poorly assessed if they are assessed at all. This is notably true in bureaucratic, stagnant, and ingrown organizations.

SPECIAL FORMS OF ORGANIZATIONAL EVOLUTION AND ADAPTATION

Throughout Western history, some organizations have sought to grow, adapt, and survive. An early strategy was the brute-force attempt to control both the competition and the market. In a more polished form this is often still a good strategy. Another good strategy is to avoid having all one's eggs in one basket. Still another, and more recent strategy is to modify the internal structure of the organization. *Multinational organizations, conglomerates,* and efforts to *fine-tune bureaucracy* represent current applications of these strategies.

United States companies have long possessed sizable foreign assets. At one time single American companies dominated whole countries, for example, Honduras, almost the only export of which was bananas. The annual incomes of the first *Fortune* 500 companies still exceed the GNPs of many countries. Nevertheless, the rise and proliferation of American multinational companies appears to represent the exploitation of a one-time-only opportunity. The unique period of history involved extended from the rise of American economic, political, and military dominance at the end of World War II to the mid-1970s. By the latter period forces which had risen years earlier became powerful enough to restrict the growth and threaten the continued existence in many areas of American multinationals. The forces included the economic rebirth of Western Europe, particularly West Germany, and Japan, the intensification of nationalism, and the rise of economic—and sometimes accompanying political—power in the petroleum-producing nations, India and several developing countries in Eastern Asia.

There are several forms of multinational companies, and some forms are less vulnerable to foreign competition and attack than are others. Companies differ as to the amount of integration and centralized control over the subsidiaries or unit companies, type and number of products, market served, number of foreign nationals employed and (especially) in which capacities, percentage of foreign ownership, geographic area served, and type of technology.

For decades the growth in power of United States multinational companies has been greatly feared and resented, both in the United States and abroad. Yet these companies, like all others, are at the mercy of unanticipated or irresistible environmental changes. Two types of American multinationals are currently best able to weather the stresses of environmental change. These are the highly innovative, high-technology companies like IBM, Texas Instruments, and Xerox and the vertically integrated oil companies.[13] American companies that can integrate design, production, marketing, and servicing so as to turn out continually an array of products remain at an advantage over foreign competitors that excel, say, only at technology. However, Japanese and European companies are rapidly catching up with American companies in integrative capability, and petroleum-producing countries are developing their own expertise. All United States multinationals will have to anticipate and adapt rapidly. Companies whose technology and skill can be matched or exceeded, even by Third World countries, are already on the way out. Representative industries include beverages, tires, textiles and clothing, consumer electronics, and agricultural chemicals.

Another environmental threat to United States multinationals is legislation and changes in the tax structure in this country itself. A third or more of the earnings of some companies come from operations overseas. Reductions in or elimination of deferral in paying taxes and foreign-tax credits could greatly reduce the attractiveness of maintaining overseas operations.

Some companies seek not only internal growth but also external growth through acquisition of or merger with other companies. For example, a company can *vertically* acquire or merge with one or more of its suppliers or customers or can *horizontally* acquire or merge with another company in the same industry. A more interesting form is a conglomerate, which is made up of several unit companies in different fields of business or industry. Since the mid-1960s there has been a shift toward conglomeration.

Not all conglomerates succeed. Some have been overall so poorly planned and executed that they have had to be dissolved, or one or more of the new units have had to be sold. Conglomeration is almost always followed by *predictable* problems of reorganization and human relations. For example, if a *multidivisional* reorganization is made, the question will arise as to the centralization of R&D, legal affairs, public relations, financial planning, and the administration of insurance and pension plans. Managers and employees in the new unit will, even before acquisition, feel apprehensive and perhaps hostile. The organizational climate may change abruptly. Some managers and employees will lose their jobs or, feeling uncomfortable in the new environment, will leave. Acquisition or merger is one of the many ways of disturbing an organization that may call for behavioral science interventions. Also called for are improved public relations programs to assuage stockholders.

An important managerial strategy in many conglomerates is the suppression of information, so that it is lost to outsiders including the company's own stockholders as well as to potential or actual competitors and government regulators and antitrust agencies.[14] The summary reports on overall growth and profitability tell little about the details of operation within the company and may actually mask important, even critical, activities. Suppression, distortion, or aggregation of performance information may be an excellent short-term strategy but a poor long-range strategy for a diversified company. There are two main reasons for this statement. First, such practices reinforce the perceptions of an increasing segment of the population that believes business to be secretive, manipulative, inhuman, and generally untrustworthy. Second, absence of public information on large corporations and even entire industries seriously impedes both scientific research and practical understanding of the national economy as a whole. There are no easy answers to these problems.

Despite the many and obvious deficiencies of bureaucracies they have remained remarkably durable, and the process of bureaucraticization may actually be intensifying as things get worse. Critics in the 1960s expected bureaucracy to be replaced by more humanistic, freely organized forms. In Western Europe, particularly in Scandinavia, sociotechnical redesigns and industrial democracy have produced some results consistent with these expectations. In these cases the autonomous work groups, matrix organizations, and practices of industrial democracy are associated with fundamental underlying values—equality of people, an end to or at least a marked reduction in power and status hierarchy, and a democratization of work and organizations for its own sake.

In the United States, in spite of the dramatic changes in values and motivations, attempts to humanize and democratize large organizations lag far behind those of Western Europe. In addition it must be pointed out that the consensus-based feature of traditional Japanese culture, is closely associated with the remarkable success of Japanese business and industry.

The demise of bureaucracy as the dominant organizational form in the United States still may occur, but the reasons will be those inherent in large scale and complexity rather than failures to humanize or democratize to a sufficient degree in a sufficient time. Most executives are concerned about rigidity and slow response times, and many large firms routinely utilize ad hoc and project teams and matrix organizations. These designs are superimposed on the basic bureaucratic structure and can be seen as a fine-tuning of bureaucracy. Many so-called *alternative organizations* are of this type. Most of these efforts involve primarily the psychological and social subsystems of the organization. The technological subsystem must also be designed so as to enhance the anticipatory and learning capabilities of the organization and the rapidity and flexibility of its response.

ORGANIZATIONAL LIMITS AND FUTURES

The forces generated by human activities in given environmental contexts both inside and outside the organization eventually build up an autonomy and momentum that tax, and may well exceed, human understanding and control. Despite the best of intentions, rigid structure and incipient decay processes may be incompatible with the continued survival of most organizations. An organization comes into being at a given time and place as a function of a *total field of forces,* among which are included purposeful human actions. The organization and the field are congruent at that time and place. If the organization survives at all, the activities of its founders lead to predictable effects. But over time the organization and the field become decreasingly congruent because the initial common processes have diverged from one another. The relationships between organization and environments become increasingly undecipherable and out of control.

Over the years a number of speculations and predictions about the future of the organization have been made. Usually these are unidimensional rather than holistic. Most of these speculations and predictions fall into two categories—automation and human nature. Some brief interpretations follow:

1. Will the organization be managed by the computer, and will most work be automated, freeing the majority of the population for lives of leisure? No! The computer must and will become more active in problemsolving in the person–computer symbiotic sense. Thus the computer must become a more useful *partner* to management. But there are still formidable obstacles to organizing the impressive hardware capabilities and the not-so-impressive software capabilities of the computer. Even if there were no technological limitations, management would never willingly allow itself to be replaced or controlled by a machine. Further, automation will not in any simple or direct way free most people from having to work because the nature of work itself changes as a function of automation and social changes. And even if automation could free most people from having to work for a living, this would not be socially desirable because work itself or at least activity is a basic human need and many people lack the self-discipline to engage in productive activities. This statement in no way detracts from much current thinking that work should be as interesting, stimulating, self-controlled, and self-actualizing as possible. But for many of us the worksystem-environment must help guide our activities.

2. Will basic human nature change, and will the organization become more humanistic. Again, no! The basic driving forces of motivation and personality will remain much the same. Managers and employees and

outside critics and supporters will still aspire to status, power, security, and so on. People will continue to play games. Many will react to frustration and conflict with anger and aggression. Organizations will of necessity incorporate or internalize major value changes, but in most organizations humanization will be more lip service than real.

The future of the organization will be a function of past and present as well as future forces. These forces, and probably more importantly the conflicts and tensions involving them, are of course both internal and external to the organization. The large, complex modern organization which is of concern here, has its historical antecedents, and history from about 1800 to the present appears to have been marked more by continuity than by discontinuity. Now, it appears that a qualitatively different world in which interplay in the field of forces will produce *emergent* and unexpected *reconfigurations* will come to pass. Exponential and hyperbolic growth and their limits will suddenly give way to total world restructure.

Under these assumptions three future stages of societal and organizational evolution can be proposed:

1. *Stage of transformation.* This stage began about 1970; however, *early-warning signs* were evident to perspicacious observers years earlier. This stage will last probably 10 to 20 years more. It is a time of great interactions and reinforcements among forces. The world has become one vast hypersensitive, pulsating field in which actions in one part can trigger unexpected, seemingly instantaneous effects everywhere. It is time of *irreversibility* of major actions. It is a time of recognizable *limits to the manageability of interdependency and complexity.* Large numbers of organizations that are neither powerful nor adaptive enough will face problems of stagnation, decline, and imminent collapse. Because of population pressures, changes in the availability of natural resources, increased business and economic competition, decreased social and political stability, and so on, things will be tough all over. When crises threaten, the time-honored response is an authoritarian crackdown. Therefore democracy, in one of its forms at least, will suffer setbacks almost everywhere in the world. Humanistic and environmentally oriented practices will be constantly under attack. Many managers in business, industry, nonprofit organizations, and government will try to control crisis with more of the same obsolete methods. Unfortunately, control over a field of forces is not the same as control over people or over formal organizations, and most attempts at control are likely to resemble King Canute's order for the ocean waves to roll back.

2. *Stage of collision with limits.* Failure to understand the true dynamics of the world coupled with obsolete and failing methods of control will suddenly erupt into worldwide conflagration. Many nations in the Third World will have ceased to exist as integrated, functional entities. Ideological differences between other nations will be exacerbated by

uncontrollable internal conflicts and tensions. Even the largest and most powerful countries will feel increasingly threatened and isolated and will act in increasingly provocative and hostile manners. Large and small nations will fight for control of natural resources. World War III will break out, perhaps triggered by a small, local action that got out of control.

3. **Stage of darkness or of renaissance.**   World War III will not wipe out all humanity. What it will do is destroy the supersystem that is undergoing accelerated evolution today. The post-World War III epoch will be bleak, with exhausted resources, dead technological-support infrastructure, and scarred landscapes, all due more to the processes that led to the war than to military actions. Nevertheless, there will be a number of surviving subsystems. If these subsystems are dominated by the kind of thinking that is predominant today, it is likely that the world will retrogress into another dark age. If, on the other hand, a philosophy of equality, social justice, self-discipline and self-sacrifice, limitation of scale, and harmony with nature prevails, a new renaissance can emerge.

Is this scenario unrealistic? Not necessarily. Need this course of societal evolution and reconfiguration inevitably occur? No, but its avoidance will require a *massive* transformation of human thinking and action in congruence with the transformations in the world system. If this restructuring can be accomplished, the stages can be redefined follows:

1. *Stage of transformation and transition* or *interstage*
2. *Stage of renaissance*

At the level of the organization, innovative approaches of vastly new magnitudes will be required involving especially:

The philosophy of organization and management.

The utilization of all types of resources.

Technical and technological capabilities supportive of management.

The practices of corporate, strategic, and long-range planning.

Most important, the success or failure of an organization, and by extension the success or failure of the society of which the organization is a contributory element, will be a function of the organization's ability to assess its state and relations with its environments at critical points in time.

PRELIMINARY GUIDANCE TOWARD STEERING INTO THE FUTURE

As seen in the first three chapters, anticipating crises and managing the organization adaptively require a dynamic perspective. The organization is not limited to the here and now, and it is quite unlikely that what it is tomorrow will be just what it is today.

If a proper forecast can be developed and used, however, a crisis may be avoided altogether. In the past decade an appreciable body of knowledge has become available to the manager which enables him to evaluate possible future changes both inside and outside his organization. Methods applicable to the external environment have, however, received relatively greater attention. Here the usefulness and limitations of different types of futures research as relevant to surveillance, planning, and policymaking will be examined.[1] As also noted holistic or systemic approaches usually provide more explanatory power in today's tightly coupled world than do disciplinary orientations or interpretations which are based on single variables or subsystems or on isolated fragments of knowledge.

QUANTITATIVE FORECASTING METHODS APPLICABLE TO SINGLE UNRELATED OR A FEW LOOSELY RELATED VARIABLES

This section looks at single trends over time and the nature of and difficulty with the data necessary to establish these trends.

What *Is* a Trend?

For our purposes a trend is any continuous or continual connection between two or more points of data. The more points of data available, of course, the more realistic the trend. Mathematicians and statisticians have devoted much effort to refining the fit between data points.

Past or historical trends may be of great value in helping to explain organizational and environmental processes. However, concern here is with the *extrapolations* of historical data into the future. Extrapolation assumes that

111

future laws or forces will be like those of the past. Some future researchers speak of surprise-free futures. Surprises may come about from low-probability, high-impact events.

Trend extrapolation is not necessarily limited to a single variable. In econometric analysis it is the *correlation* between a dependent and various independent variables, which, once established, is assumed to apply in the future. Even complex systems dynamics models are basically extrapolative. The initial model *structure* which explained past behavior is expected also to explain future system behavior.

Pure trend extrapolation is most valuable in providing the manager or analyst with a first impression of a short-term planning situation. Many extrapolations are made in terms of low, medium, and high projections. The medium projection is often a base-line projection which continues the historical trend. For example, the World Bank's SIMLINK model makes projections of total Gross World Product in the year 2000 of $12.4, $14.7, and $17.4 trillion. Different growth rates were used before and after 1985. The U.S. Bureau of the Census projects world population in the year 2000 to be 5.9 billion, 6.4 billion, or 6.8 billion people. For purposes of long-range planning it is well to accept such single-variable, open-loop projections with extreme caution, even though the ranges of growth appear to be covered. The assumptions about underlying causality and the nature of the growth process may be fundamentally wrong, so that changing rates or other constants may produce a misleading picture of preciseness.

The Data Problem

A forecasting scheme requires two things: a formal framework and data. The formal framework may be a scientific theory or law, an established mathematical relationship, or a well-thought-out conceptual model. Data may be qualitative or quantitative, but must possess some degree of consistency. Neither logical framework nor data is complete without the other. Unfortunately, building logical frameworks and collection of data do not always advance in parallel. On the one hand, further refinements in the mathematical and statistical analysis of problems may be negated by the absence of usable data. On the other hand, vast stores of social indicators and other government-collected data may be of limited usefulness in the absence of integrative models. Ideally, concept development and data collection should go hand in hand. When dealing with complex systems, this is rarely the case.

Data may, therefore, be[2]

Entirely lacking

Sporadic

Used for purposes other than those dictating the original collection

Suitable to past systems but inappropriate to changing systems or vice versa

Downright wrong in spite of the best of intentions

Contradictory

Purposely biased

In the face of these deficiencies management effectiveness is greatly reduced, not merely because planning and decisionmaking may not take place, but also because the use of inappropriate data may lead to bad plans and decisions disguised within an aura of specificity and exactness.

Any number of reasons may underlie data deficiencies. Data may be *lacking* simply because the given area was at one time considered unimportant and nobody got around to collecting any data. More seriously, data may be entirely lacking because the problem requiring the data was not even anticipated, let alone defined properly. For example, there are poor concepts and essentially no methods of measurement and hence little usable data in the whole field of behavior-social *dynamics*. This area includes such important driving forces in society as value change, level of expectation, and alienation.

Data may be *sporadic* because of sloppy collection or recordkeeping or changes in the agencies responsible for collection. The most important obstacle facing the planner, however, is the absence of *longitudinal* data, especially in the behavioral-social sciences areas. Data in these sciences are usually cross-sectional, that is, they represent these situations at a certain time or, even worse, situations in which time is totally ignored. Past and present concentration on behavioral and social statics contribute major difficulties to the study and management of social systems. Further, even though data collection has accelerated in recent years, new needs for data are constantly being discovered. Rarely are longitudinal data available over even such a short period as a decade. The planner interested in changing values or attitudes toward work may find the problem unexpectedly difficult to grapple with.

A majority of the data available to planners and social science researchers have been collected by various government agencies. This paves the way for *uses of data for purposes other than those originally intended*. Government collects data largely for administrative purposes, sometimes quite routine purposes. The data may be poorly adaptable to testing models. United States Census data provide a prime example. A major effort, involving both the Census Bureau and the National Science Foundation, is now underway in an attempt to make census data directly usable by researchers from the time of collection.

Systems change makes it hard to generalize from past to present and from present to future. The same laws and forces do not necessarily operate at all points in time. New patterns *emerge*. In the absence of understanding either general laws and forces or different laws and forces applicable to different situations, misleading, even dangerous, interpretations can be made. An example is the *demographic transition* which holds that population growth invariably decreases as a function of standard of living and once decreased to some rate remains at that lower rate.

Some of the data deficiencies under discussion are esoteric and up to now have been largely the concern of the systems scientist. However, nearly everybody has had experience with data which are simply *wrong*, despite the best intentions of collectors and users. Consider the vast body of government-collected data. The final figure appears to be quite precise. But the data prepared for and utilized by the Federal and other branches of government have many sources, public as well as private, and have passed through many human *filters* in the tasks of collecting, editing, compressing, summarizing, and processing. Basic errors in measurement may be progressively distorted. There is tremendous formal and informal pressure to bend data so that they fit defined molds. Almost every type of business, economic, and social indicator fits into this category, even those which have been collected for decades. Population counts may be underrepresented by millions of ghetto dwellers and illegal immigrants. Employment and crime statistics depend heavily on shifting definitions. Are the unemployed only those actively seeking employment, or do the unemployed also include those who have given up in the futile search for jobs and those who never formally entered the workforce? What is the effect of pleabargaining on the different categories of crime reported? Correlational relationships, let alone causal relationships, between policies and effects of these policies are almost impossible to establish, given the widespread spuriousness of data. Yet it is on the basis of such data that the public and all too many in business and government make decisions.

A major problem in large-scale policymaking is that data are often *contradictory*. Contradictory data may be the nature of things in science, and that is how hypotheses and theories are refined and laws established. In the "soft" sciences contradictory data may be the rule rather than the exception. As seen before, the behavioral, social, organizational, and management sciences *as a whole* are soft, even though some constituent measurements, say, from engineering, may be hard. A current critical example is in the energy field. In spite of many years of questions and probes, it is possible to present any data one wants on sources, reserves, supplies at hand, demands, bottlenecks, and consumption.

Information is power and data are *biased* as part of the everyday course of affairs. The primary, even all-consuming objective of many organizations is immediate survival. The primary objective of many protagonists is the accumulation and maintenance of status and power. However, the organization that forgets that its own data are biased may be paving the way toward its own demise.

Finally, even an indicator as familiar to everybody as the Gross National Product, calculated continuously since 1929, reflects many of the deficiencies just discussed. Data come from many different sources, many judgments rather than hard facts enter into the calculations, and the quarterly revisions may already be out of date when released. Estimates of growth rate may vary as much as 50 percent, so that a preliminary estimate of, say, four percent in any given quarter may eventually be adjusted to anywhere between two and six percent. The statistical discrepancy between the product and income sides of the indicator, which as different measures of the same thing are supposed to match, exceeded $8 billion three times between the second quarter of 1974 and the first quarter of 1976. Policymakers are unwise in overreacting to apparently precise changes in GNP growth rate over short time periods.

Single Objective Indicators: Their Nature, Grouping, and Use

This category includes business, economic, demographic, and objective social indicators. At least the first three types are familiar to most people. However, because of their apparent straightforwardness, simplicity, and objectivity, these indicators are frequently misused.

Indicators are discrete measurements or estimates taken at selected time intervals, for example, once a year, once a quarter, or once a month. Sometimes, as in the case of measures of population and labor movements, the discrete intervals are so small that continuous mathematics like differential equations can be used.

Indicators are typically expressed in graphical form showing trends or percentages, as histograms, or in tabular form. Indicator data have been collected in developed countries, especially by governments, for decades or even centuries. For example, the U.S. Bureau of the Census has been collecting population data since 1790. The U.S. Department of Commerce, which oversees the Census Bureau, is a particularly prolific collector and disseminator of data. Most readers are familiar with the *Statistical Abstracts of the United States,* the *U.S. Industrial Outlooks with Projections,* the *Business Conditions Digest,* the *Handbook of Cyclical Indicators,* and more recently *Social Indicators* for given years. The U.S. Department of Labor's Bureau of Labor Statistics produces a wide variety of data on manpower and productivity.

A number of indicators are discussed throughout this book in specific planning contexts. Figures 4.1, 4.2, and 4.3, and Table 4.1 illustrate common ways of presenting single, objective indicators.

The wonder of it all though is not that such vast amounts of data are available—and are continuing to accumulate at exponential rates—but that the ability to use data has not kept up with these amounts. The problems are largely conceptual. They are not just problems of more data-processing and computers. The overriding problem, however, is the organization of data into useful knowledge, that is, one of building models. It can be reemphasized:

An apparently single objective indicator, like the familiar GNP discussed earlier, is often a composite of different sources, measures, and subjective guesses.

A single objective indicator is often a composite of other indicators.

A single indicator seldom has meaning outside a context.

A single indicator may be a good description, but of little analytic or causal explanatory value.

Although these points seem familiar and straightforward enough, they have

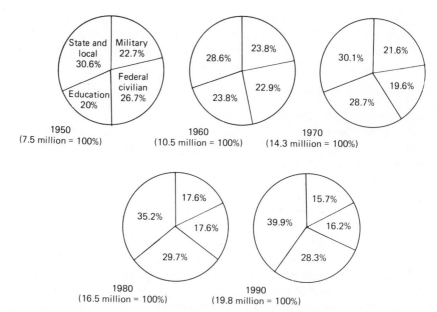

Figure 4.1 Pie graphs showing changes in government employment: 1950–1990. (From reference 29, p. 61.)

Table 4.1 Average Expected Years of Life and of Working Life of Working Males Ages 20 and 60: 1940–1970

Age and Year	Average Years of Life Remaining	Average Years of Working Life Remaining	Average Years of Nonworking Life Remaining	Working Life as a Percent of Life
Males aged				
20 years				
1940	46.8	41.1	5.7	87.8
1950	48.9	43.1	5.8	88.1
1960	49.8	42.6	7.2	85.5
1970	49.6	41.5	8.1	83.7
Males aged				
60 years				
1940	15.1	9.1	6.0	60.3
1950	15.7	9.8	5.9	62.4
1960	15.9	8.5	7.4	53.5
1970	16.1	7.4	8.7	46.0

Source. Modified from reference 25, p. 384.

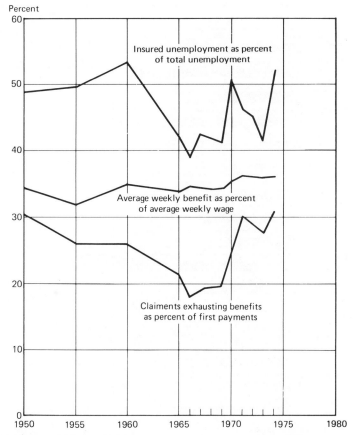

Figure 4.2 Trends of unemployment insurance ratios on coverage, claims, and benefits: 1950–1974. (From reference 25, p. 123.)

often enough been overlooked or ignored in organizational planning. As with Columbus and the egg,[3] things are often clearer in hindsight.

Most analysts and planners, however, do not rely on single isolated indicators. Relatively holistic patterns are utilized. Many banks, financial institutions, and consulting firms provide sophisticated analyses and interpretations of the economic environment of the firm. At the regional level, for example, the Security Pacific National Bank publishes a "Monthly Summary of Business Conditions, Southern California." A typical issue contains:

Recent trends in regional business activity summarized both verbally and as an overall graphical trend from, say, a base year like 1967 in which the index is set at 100, to the present year.

A more detailed analysis of a given industry, for example, the aerospace industry in terms of:

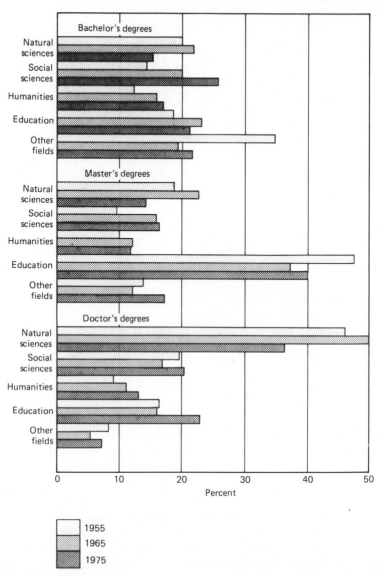

Figure 4.3 Histogram showing degrees earned by major field of study and level: 1955, 1965, and 1975. (Modified from reference 25, p. 277.)

Recent national trends and outlook

Industry activity in California

Outlook for the specific industry in California

Major projects in California of the given industry

Selected business statistics in Southern California, for example, month-by-month comparisons and percentage change from the latest month a year ago on trade, employment, industry, building, and real estate

Of value to both short-range and long-range planning are such quoted interpretations as:[4]

It is too early to assess the impact on the California economy of the long lines at service stations.

The existing backlog in the commercial aircraft, military, and space sectors is *expected* to result in continued growth in the state's aerospace activity over at least the next couple of years. *Assuming* that the airlines will be able to finance their aircraft purchases, the present level of firm orders *should* keep production high through at least 1980.

The upturn in overall aerospace industry, therefore, *could* continue well into the 1980s. That upswing, however, is likely to be followed by declines, as pronounced *cyclical* changes in aerospace activity are *expected* to persist in spite of diversification.

Such analyses, interpretations, and forecasts are, however, susceptible to shocks or surprises. The aerospace examples above come from the May 31, 1979 issue. On May 25, 1979 an American Airlines DC-10 crashed at O'Hare Airport in Chicago killing 271 persons. This single *event* will undoubtedly have at least some future impact throughout the system. It is the understanding, anticipation and management of this bigger picture that is of concern.

Subjective Social Indicators

The objectivity-subjectivity problem is a major one in science and also in management. Sometimes this problem is explicitly recognized as in psychology. Psychology has been defined as the science of (objective) behavior and (subjective) experience or mind. In studying perception, emotion, and personality, psychologists try to bridge or correlate the objective and subjective. People differ in their perceptions and interpretations of the same physical stimuli. Emotionally one may feel love or fear or rage, and physiologists can measure objectively the accompanying cardiovascular changes.[5]

We see the same types of problem in management when we try to relate supposedly objective working conditions to peoples' perceptions of these conditions, their attitudes and feelings about the job, their motivation to work, their morale, and their overall job satisfaction. Managers are increasingly concerned today with the *quality* of the worklife.

Subjective social indicators are based on people's answers to questionnaires and interviews. It is assumed that these answers express underlying feelings, attitudes, or beliefs. It is often further assumed that people will *act* on their stated attitudes and beliefs. Neither assumption may be necessarily true. In short, some of the reasons why attitude or opinion data cannot be completely relied on are the following:

Technical deficiencies in the measuring instruments.

Conscious or subconscious bias between the interviewer and interviewee, leading to overly positive or overly negative replies.

Peer pressure, bandwagon, and feedback effects.

Distortion effects due to dramatic events.

Oversaturation with polls and interviews, leading to cynical responses.

Fears of government prying and invasion of privacy.

Attitude measurement and public-opinion polling have been actively practiced for decades. Opinion polling has become institutionalized in the political process. Nevertheless, there are questions that still concern social scientiests. For example, what is the meaning of a nonresponse or a no opinion? Even a small pocket of ignorance could greatly distort the results of decisions based on peoples' supposed attitudes.

Subjective social indicators, like objective indicators, can be used in research. However, the overriding purpose of collecting these data is for planning, policy analysis, policymaking, and program analysis. Conceptually, both objective and subjective social indicators are direct descendants of economic indicators. Until recently economic indicators have been used with some reported success in managing or at least fine-tuning the economy. *Presumably,* according to advocates of the approach, the social system could also be managed effectively if only enough data were available. However, complex systems do not really operate in such a manner. The first social indicators were objective and, like the examples given in the last section tried to answer questions like: How well is the nation housed? educated? How much crime is there? How well is the nation protected from crime?

The first two questions are relatively straightforward. The third and fourth questions imply cause–effect relationships and are *not* easily answered. This illustrates a major problem in using social indicator data and indeed a serious problem in the evaluation of all social programs. Suppose so much crime in various categories is reported, and so many billions of dollars are spent annually on criminal justice systems. What is the relationship between the two?

Subjective social indicators are now widely available in the form of public perceptions about housing, health, public safety, education and training, work, income, leisure, and so on. Figure 4.4 illustrates such public perceptions.

Ideally, objective and subjective indicators could be interrelated within models variously used for forecasting, planning, policymaking, policyanalysis, and program evaluation. Such models would tie together, for example, incidence of crime in various categories, expenditures on various criminal justice programs, peoples' satisfactions with neighborhood safety, migration patterns, and urban stability.

Obvious versus Underlying Trends

Systems consist of hierarchies of subsystems. Each subsystem has its own reality or state. However, at any one time some levels of reality may be more

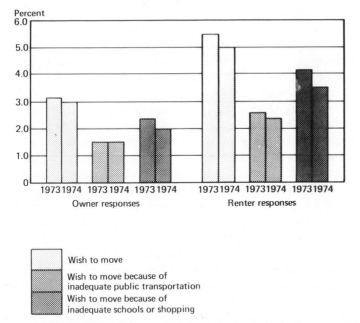

Figure 4.4 A subjective social indicator: Wish to move by major inadequate neighborhood services and by tenure: 1973 and 1974. (From reference 25, p. 86.)

accessible to observation and interpretation than are others. Thus, even if none of the deficiencies of indicators discussed are present, a trend may not provide the information that is really wanted.

First, consider again the case of subjective social indicators. We implied that, for a number of reasons, attitudes and beliefs are easily disturbed and easily changed. For purposes of planning we may be little interested in such unstable forms of behavior. What we want are deeper measures of behavior. Professor Milton Rokeach[6] believes that *values*, as he precisely defines them, are more profound, durable, and longer-lasting features of human behavior than are attitudes, opinions, or beliefs.. Values underlie the latter. What really should concern us most in the long term, therefore, are values and value change. Value changes can serve as early-warning indications of impending changes in attitudes, beliefs, and overt behaviors, much as radars and reconnaissance satellites give a nation early warning of an enemy military build-up.

Accepting Professor Rokeach's technical definitions, values further represent the intersection of the complex entity that is individual personality with sociotechnical changes in the outside world. Three important areas for the development of new values are growth, consumption, and the environment. For example, in the long run values about overconsumption, forced obsolescence, and the throw-away society are likely to be of more significance to planning than are attitudes about big or small cars. Changes in values about consumption can have profound influences on the world's way of doing business. Changes in attitudes about car size may indicate nothing more than how long one has to wait for gasoline this week.

A second situation involves knowing what variable is wanted but being unable to measure it. This often occurs in econometric modeling, in which case one indicator is substituted for another. One variable serves as a *proxy* for another. It is assumed that the two variables are closely correlated. For example, in looking at developing countries, literacy may serve as a proxy for degree of development. An egregious misuse of proxies is the substitution of material standard of living for the much more elusive quality of life.

A third situation is the most serious and can be associated with mistaking secondary trends for primary trends, without understanding the growing gap between trends, and with trends approaching thresholds. One instance which has received some study is the gap between level of expectation and level of achievement. Another is a collective cognitive dissonance; that is, different social perceptions and experiences do not add up to a psychologically consistent picture. We preach peace but prepare for and practice war. We stress education, but millions find themselves overqualified or misqualified for available jobs. Uncle Sam promises major socioeconomic reforms, but confidence in the policy continues to decline. Large institutions promise more but deliver less, and the trend appears to be decreasing confidence in formal organizations. Understanding such covert emerging trends will be absolutely indispensable to the anticipation and management of organizational crises.

The Necessity for Integrating Models

This section has discussed single trends and indicators or trends and indicators that are by implication loosely or informally related to one another. Classification of indicators into categories is one form of loose relationship. Correlating indicators ties them together a little more. These are tentative forms of models. Single indicators and loosely associated groupings of indicators are increasingly limited to preliminary or short-term applications.

Correlation and regression have a long history in behavioral and social science. The trouble with correlation is that in complex systems one can almost always find something to correlate with something else. The famous statistician Ronald A. Fisher supposedly found a high positive correlation between the apple crop and the baby crop in England just after World War II! Nevertheless, correlation and regression analysis have their strong advocates. The important school of econometric modeling relies heavily on these techniques.

An alternative and increasingly important approach to modeling is *causal* modeling. The Fisher correlation above could be reinterpreted as follows. Soldiers returning from the war went back to their regular duties as farmers and fathers and caused both the increased apple crop and the increased baby crop. Unfortunately, all correlations do not have underlying causal explanations which are evident and plausible.

Moreover, the art and science of modeling may have reached an impasse. Most of the large-scale models to be discussed later are severely deficient in the incorporation of noneconomic, nondemographic behavioral and social variables. How can we understand and predict the behavior of societal systems if we do not rely heavily on variables that depict peoples' perceptions, motivations, feelings, values, and attitudes? And know how people make comparisons and get into conflicts and how individual behavior aggregates into collective behavior? Ideally, the vast amounts of component information could be integrated into an overall model. This is called *bottom-up* modeling. In reality the opposite, *top-down* modeling, is almost always necessary. Qualitative, as opposed to quantitative, progress in modeling will be hindered in the short run because:

1. The vast amounts of indicator and other data briefly discussed in this section are more amenable to administrative use than modeling use, especially causal modeling use.

2. The economists and engineers who dominate the field of large-scale modeling usually lack experience in or a feel for psychology, sociology, and cultural anthropology.

3. Psychologists, sociologists, and cultural anthropologists, in decreasing order, have been concerned with small or local subsystems and their findings are poorly integrable.

4. Publish or perish requirements for survival in the universities and inertia and resistance to change in the research funding agencies appear to guarantee the continued fragmentation of knowledge into disciplines.

JUDGMENTAL METHODS

No human activity is completely objective, completely free from bias. Even in physical science judgements have to be made as to the nature of reality. Purely objective observations and interpretations are usually limited to two or three variables in combination. The theory of relativity has not yet been completely verified. There are several theories which attempt to explain the origin and nature of the universe. Opposing teams of engineers have testified on the safety of a dam—after it broke. The small mountain town of Wrightwood in southern California is threatened with annihilation by a landslide—or is it? Geologists from two different government agencies interpret the same landscape in diametrically opposite ways.

In the behavioral and social sciences—and *also in the systems sciences*—theory, laws, and methods of observation and data collection may be severely limited. As long as these deficiencies remain, it will be necessary to rely on both judgmental inputs and what appear to be loosely related lawlike regularities of relationships among variables.

A Fortiori Analysis

A fortiori analysis is one of several related methods developed or used by the Rand Corporation during the early history of systems analysis. These methods were utilized for eliminating alternative programs or contingencies when one alternative was not clearly dominant. *A fortiori* analysis involved specifying an alternative option and the contingency most favorable to that option in the most optimistic terms possible. If even under these favorable conditions it still performed poorly, it could be discarded.

A fortiori analysis is included here because of its use by futures researcher Herman Kahn and his colleagues at the Hudson Research Institute. Kahn is well known for his highly optimistic, surprise-free forecasts of the world in the year 2000, indeed, even during the next 200 years. As used by Kahn *a fortiori* analysis argues or debates an issue in terms of the strongest assumptions of the alternative to which one is opposed. One's own position is then argued by presenting the most moderate assumptions possible. If one's position even under such modest assumptions is still stronger or more forceful, the opposition's point of view can be eliminated. In Kahn's approach to futures research, *a fortiori* analysis is combined with extrapolating variables into the future independently of one another. This does *not* mean that the future will be a *straight* extrapolation of the past. Rather, the methodology presents a scenario Kahn would not be surprised to see develop—that is, a most probable future.

Futures researcher Kahn has, for example, applied his techniques to energy, food, and raw materials. He concludes that there is no real shortage in any of these areas in the intermediate or long-range future of the world. Although Kahn's approach may appear less scientific than are computer simulation models, it should be remembered that the latter are also based on many debatable assumptions. Kahn's work therefore provides a useful counterargument to the limits-to-growth position.

Delphi

Delphi was first introduced in 1959 by Olaf Helmer and Theodore Gordon, then at the Rand Corporation.[15] Delphi utilizes a specific set of experts to obtain group judgements. Both exploratory forecasts of the future and normative statements of what the future should be can be obtained from Delphi studies. Delphi is a communication device which through preserving the anonymity of individual responses attempts to minimize the well-known effects of peer pressure.

Advocates of Delphi believe that it utilizes the advantages of groups, while eliminating most of the disadvantages. As originally developed, and still stressed by most advocates, Delphi possesses these three main characteristics:

1. *Anonymity of responses.* Participants are not known to each other and interact only through questionnaires which are usually mailed back to a director. The effects of peer pressure, bandwagon effects, and dominant individuals are supposedly minimized and a person can change his mind without losing face.

2. *Iterative sessions using controlled feedback.* Each participant receives only

information on the current status of the collective opinion of the group, and pro and con arguments on each issue.

3. ***Statistical treatment of the group or panel response.***   Typically, for each question, the group response is presented as the median and the interquartile range. That is, the 50 percent of responses at the extremes, below the first quartile and above the third quartile, are excluded. Each opinion is reflected in the median and the spread of opinion is shown by the size of the interquartile range.

Delphi is a method of *steering consensus*. Delphi consists of several iterations or rounds, typically two to four. Costs, impositions on the time of busy experts, and reaching early consensus may reduce the number of rounds. A typical set of rounds of classical Delphi can be summarized as follows:

Preliminary arrangements.   Find a group of experts in the given area who are willing and have the time to serve, and explain the methodology to them.

Round one.   Present the expert panelists with a completely open-ended and unstructured questionnaire. The questionnaire asks the panelists to make forecasts about events and dates. It is unstructured so that all potentially important events may be included. Lack of structure, however, means that panelists' responses may be in a variety of forms which must be somewhat arbitrarily consolidated by the session director. Consolidation may be quite time consuming.

Round two.   Present the panelists with the consolidated list of events which is the output of the first round. Ask panelists (1) to estimate the dates by which the specific events will occur, and (2) to give reasons why these dates are correct. The session director then uses participant responses to prepare a consolidated statistical summary of the opinions as well as the pros and cons justifying why an event will come not sooner or later than a given date.

Round three.   Present the panelists with the output of the second round, which consists of (1) the list of events, (2) the panel median date and upper and lower quartile dates for each event, and (3) summaries of the arguments as to why an event should occur earlier or later. Ask the panelists to review the arguments and make new estimates of the dates. If the new estimates still fall earlier than the first quartile of dates or above the third quartile, that is, different from the other three-fourths of the panelists, ask the respondents to justify their views and to comment on views at the opposite extreme.

Round four.   Present the panelists with new medians, quartiles, and arguments. This round is essentially a further refinement of round three, and *could* be followed by subsequent rounds to a point of diminishing returns.

Over the years thousands of Delphi exercises have been performed and many modifications have been made to the basic methodology. For example, anonymity or feedback have been eliminated, different forms have been substituted, cluster analysis and multidimensional scaling utilized, and panelists have interacted through a computer. As with many of the other technologies discussed in this chapter, different Delphi exercises have produced inconsistent or contradictory results.

Delphi results can also be summarized in a pictorial method utilizing horizontally elongated polygons as illustrated in Figure 4.5.

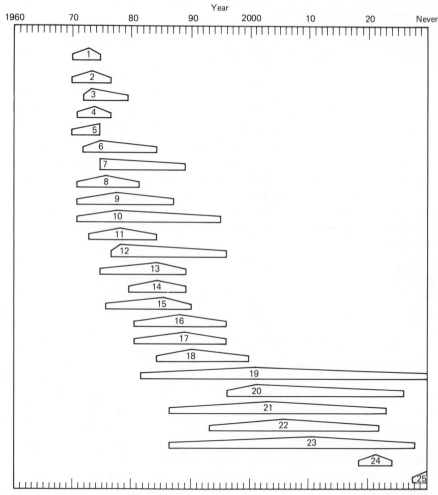

Figure 4.5 Delphi forecasts of the dates of occurrence of automation events showing the median and range of the middle 50 percent of expert respondents. (1) Increase by a factor of 10 in capital investment in computers used for automated process control, (2) air traffic control—positive and predictive track on all aircraft, (3) direct link from stores to banks to check credit and to record transactions, (4) widespread use of simple teaching machines, (5) automation of office work and services, leading to displacement of 25 percent of current work force, (6) education becoming a respectable leisure pastime, (7) widespread use of sophisticated teaching machines, (8) automatic libraries, looking up and reproducing copy, (9) automated looking up of legal information, (10) automatic language translator—correct grammar, (11) automated rapid transit, (12) widespread use of automatic decisonmaking at management level for industrial and national planning, (13)

   Delphi is most valuable for preliminary forecasts, plans, or evaluations or as an input to broader methodologies. Cross-impact analysis was originally developed in an attempt to overcome the problems Delphi respondents faced in considering interactions among events. Delphi will probably recede in popularity as more people turn their attention to cross-impact analysis.

Cross-Impact Analysis

Cross-impact analysis was first developed by Theodore Gordon in the late 1960s. Cross-impact analysis may be *correlational* or *causal*. The correlational form requires consistent estimates of the conditional probabilities of Event *A* given Event *B* and vice versa. Causal cross-impact analysis is based on the idea that the occurrence of one event might *cause* an increase or decrease in the probability of occurrence of other events. There are four basic types of impact:

Event-on-event

Event-on-trend

Trend-on-event

Trend-on-trend

An example of an event might be the introduction of a major new source of energy. A trend of interest might be world population. The inclusion of events provides a bridge to trends-only approaches such as most econometric models and systems dynamics.

   Pioneering futures researcher Olaf Helmer performs cross-impact analysis as follows.[8] It is often convenient to break down the entire planning horizon, which could range from years to decades, into subintervals called scenes. For long-range planning a scene might be of five years' duration. Inputs for the cross-impact model then include:

Probability estimates of the occurrence of each event in each scene.

Estimates of the value of each trend at the beginning of each scene.

Entries into the cells of the cross-impact *matrix* itself, that is, how the

---

electronic prosthesis (radar for the blind, servomechanical limbs, etc.), (14) automated interpretation of medical symptoms, (15) construction on a production line of computers with motivation by "education," (16) widespread use of robot services, for refuse collection, as household slaves, as sewer inspectors, and so on, (17) widespread use of computers in tax collection, with access to all business records—automatic single tax deductions, (18) availability of a machine which comprehends standard IQ tests and scores above 150 (where "comprehend" is to be interpreted behavioristically as the ability to respond to questions printed in English and possibly accompanied by diagrams), (19) evolution of a universal language from automated communication, (20) automated voting, in the sense of legislating through automated plebiscite, (21) automated highways and adaptive automobile autopilots, (22) remote facsimile newspapers and magazines, printed in home, (23) man-machine symbiosis, enabling man to extend his intelligence by direct electromechanical interaction between his brain and a computing machine, (24) international agreements which guarantee certain economic minima to the world's population as a result of high production from automation, (25) centralized (possibly random) wire tapping. (Modified from reference ix. Copyright © The Rand Corporation. Reproduced by courtesy of Professor Olaf Helmer.)

occurrence of an event or a deviation of a trend from its expected value in a given scene affects the probabilities of other events and values of other trends in the next scene.

A cross-impact on an event or trend causes the event probability or trend value in the next scene to be raised or lowered by some amount. Confining impacts to the next scene and making their sizes independent of time are of course oversimplications, which may be made more realistic by the introduction of carry-over effects. Certain transformations, internal to the model, may be necessary to prevent cumulative impacts from forcing the event probabilities or trend values out of bounds. Also the numbers entered into the cross-impact matrix should be as simple and intuitively comprehensible by managers as possible. A scale ranging from, say, -3 to $+3$ might be appropriate.

A single run of this type of cross-impact model involves:

1. Determining for Scene 1 which of the events occur, by using a standard Monte Carlo drawing of random numbers.
2. Adjusting the event probabilities and trend values for Scene 2 by using the values in the cross-impact matrix.
3. Adjusting the trend values in Scene 2 further by adding their random deviations drawn from an appropriate distribution associated with exogenous happenings outside the model boundary.
4. Repeating Steps 1 through 3 for Scenes 3, 4, and so on.

Before a cross-impact model can be used for actual planning, however, the team of designers and users together must be convinced that it gives as faithful a representation of real-world relationships as possible. Several iterations involving both the team and the computer program may be necessary to improve both the structure of the model and the inputs to the model. For example, the impact of one event on another may require that a third development has already taken place. Inputs can often be improved by confronting the experts with the explicit effects of their estimates.

The result of each basic computer run is a *scenario*, or a sequence of the occurrences of events by scenes and of adjustments to the values of trends (trend fluctuations). A number of scenarios are generated in order to give the planner an intuitive feel for a variety of contingencies.

Cross-impact analysis is usually limited to interactions among pairs of developments. Higher-order interactions place great demands for data and greatly increase computational complexity. Other refinements could also make computations so cumbersome as to exceed the point of diminishing returns. In this category, for example, would be an event's *non*occurrence raising or lowering the probability of its own occurrence at a later time.

As with the other methodologies discussed here, the original types of cross-impact analysis have been variously modified. There are different views as to the mathematical theory underlying cross-impact analysis. The computerization of the methodology has been simplified by new computer languages. One of the most familiar modifications is *KSIM* first developed by Julius Kane in 1972. KSIM is a causal cross-impact simulation methodology incorporating feedback, which can be quickly and easily used by a planning team to define and structure a set of variables in a complex system. A group of experts develops an interaction matrix and determines initial values of the elements. Each variable is assigned a value between 0 and 1, the lower and upper bounds. Interactions among the variables are dynamically modeled. A computer calculates and displays the changes in the variables over time, taking all the binary interconnections into account. The model is progressively refined through user interaction. The variables follow an S-shaped or logistic trajectory toward the upper or lower limits. KSIM does not employ traditional mathematical measures, but rather estimates of levels, amounts, weights, degrees, and so forth. Newer versions of KSIM, and related models like QSIM and GSIM, provide further improvements.

Trend Impact Analysis is a form of events-on-trends and events-on-events cross-impact analysis developed by Dr. Theodore J. Gordon and his colleagues at The Futures Group.[9] The methodology provides a forecast of the future values of time-series variables and an estimate of the uncertainty of the forecast. The technique involves these steps:

1. A computer extrapolates the past history of a trend in a surprise-free manner. The resulting baseline projection can variously be obtained through simple regression equations, computerized curve fitting, econometric modeling, simulation modeling, or scientific or engineering calculations. The projection is based on information about the past and assumptions about the future.

2. The users specify a set of potential and important future events (for example, the price of energy increases by more than 50 percent of inflation for a year) which could alter the baseline extrapolation. The probability of the occurrence of each event as a function of time is then estimated. Cross-impact analysis provides an estimate of the impacts of significant future events on one another.

3. The computer modifies the baseline trend extrapolation to reflect the impact on it of each event. The impacts are indicated in terms of five parameters:

   a. The time in years from the occurrence of the given event until the trend first begins to respond.

   b. The time in years from the occurrence of the event until the impact on the trend is largest.

   c. The magnitude as a percentage of the baseline curve of the greatest impact.

   d. The time in years from the occurrence of the event until its impact reaches a steady-state or final level.

   e. The magnitude as a percentage of the baseline curve of the final impact.

4. The computer calculates the expected impact-value of the combined events on the baseline extrapolation by summing the products of the probabilities of the events for each relevant year by the magnitudes of the impacts of the event. (The term *expected value* or *expectation* has a specific meaning in statistics to indicate the product of each possible value of a discrete random variable by the probability of that value and the summation of all these weighted values.) The computer calculation reflects the specific time lags. The computer also calculates the uncertainty of the forecast that stems from the uncertainty of the baseline and the uncertainty about the occurrence of each given event.

5. The users evaluate the adjusted extrapolation. If the output appears unreasonable, the users modify the computer input.

All forms of cross-impact analysis are limited, at least to some extent, by:

1. The lack of capability to incorporate the field-theoretic reconfigurational phenomena.

2. The psychological limitations of people in estimating states of the world and probabilities of occurrence or of being in a given state, and in coming up with new, innovative patterns of elements or variables that have not been biased by past experiences and perceptions.

3. The fact that events, seemingly insignificant at any given time, can reemerge with dangerous impacts at more distant *times and places*.

4. The fact that events can have impacts in various ways, not only gradually within what appears to be a reasonable time span, but also abruptly long after any impact would appear to be reasonably possible.

Finally, the various forms of cross-impact analysis, KSIM and its descendants, trend-impact analysis, and even systems dynamics, are often placed into a larger classification of models called *structural models*. Over 40 types of structural models have been identified.[10] The main objective of structural modeling is to capture form, geometry, or topology rather than to make calculations and to produce quantitative output. Some applications do involve arithmetic calculations and semiquantitative outputs; but the intent of even these applications is to give an overall picture and not to produce single precise answers, which, given the imprecision of the input data, would be an abuse of mathematics.

A structural model is usually started with a diagram (a signed digraph or directed graph), a network, or an equivalent matrix. The diagram consists of nodes and connections among nodes. Structural modeling is used when a number of people are working together on a problem defined in terms of previously determined system elements. Determining the elements is a prerequisite step, and any of the problemsolvers discussed in Chapter 8 can participate in drawing up a list of system elements or variables. Focus in the modeling effort itself is on determining the *interrelationships* among elements.

The causal diagrams we described in Chapter 2 for systems dynamics and the cross-impact matrices we just discussed provide examples of beginning model structures.

Structural modeling is a means of formalizing fuzzy or intuitive thought processes. It is a heuristic approach. Structural modeling thus may serve as a useful communications, problemsolving, and learning tool among people of different backgrounds, even in those cases where no final output is achieved.

Most forms of structural modeling, however, deal only with pairwise relationships among the elements. Such models must be viewed as only preliminary first cuts. This type of model is not equipped to handle complex interactions or emergence.

Multi-Attribute Utility Measurement

Decisions depend on human values which are highly subjective.[11] Decisions made for planning may variously be authoritarian and unilateral, the result of conflict and concession, or the result of a consensus. Multiattribute utility measurement (MAUM) is a rating-scale approach to aiding the last type of decisionmaking. MAUM attempts to develop an aggregation of individual values, especially when interpersonal or interorganizational disagreements are in degree rather than in kind.

Public, social, or administrative decisionmaking typically involves the values of different kinds of participants—decisionmakers, experts, pressure groups, members of the public, and others. MAUM attempts to spell out explicitly the values of each participant, show how much they differ, and thereby reduce the differences. Advocates argue that MAUM can be easily taught to and utilized by busy persons. MAUM has applications not only to planning, but to evaluation of continuing and completed projects. Advocates believe that MAUM can reduce the uncertainties of planning by providing a more systematic, less ad hoc treatment of the processes of advocacy and negotiation.

MAUM is still more academic than applied. Applications have been almost entirely to short-term decisional problems, but there seems to be no reason why the methodology could not also be applied to longer-range planning and policymaking for *normative* futures. Like the other methodologies discussed in this book, MAUM is based on certain assumptions. For example, assumptions about the independence of values may be violated, thus reducing or negating the relevance of MAUM. MAUM depends on the good will of participants. People frequently do not want to change their values or may feel it is against their best interests to do so.

The outcome of a human activity may have a value along one or more different dimensions. Multi-attribute utility measurement attempts to discover these values, one dimension at a time. The values are then aggregated across dimensions by using an aggregation rule and weighting procedure. The simplest, most widely used rule and procedure consist of taking a weighted linear average.

MAUM follows ten basic, usually iterative steps which may be elaborated on or modified in the most complex cases.[12] These steps are the following:

1. Identify the decisionmaking persons and organizations whose utilities are to be maximized. Such might be, say, a government agency. Utility is a function of the evaluator, what is being evaluated, and the purpose of the evaluation.

2. Identify the specific decisions relevant to these utilities.

3. Identify the object of evaluation, namely, the outcomes of possible decisions and actions. An object of evaluation could be a proposed research program, for example.

4. Identify the value dimensions, usually through face-to-face meeting. Often the result is a simple list or lists of goals important to the dissenting parties. Dimensions may be subjective, partly subjective, or objective. Generally eight dimensions are sufficient and 15 are too many.

5. Rank the dimensions in order of importance to the dissenting parties. This also is often by group process.

6. Rate the dimensions in terms of ratios of importance. Start with the least most important dimension and work upwards. A given dimension might end up, say, four times as important as another.

7. Sum the weights that indicate importance, divide each weight by the sum, and multiply by 100. The result is the normalized importance weight of a given dimension of value.

8. Measure the location of each action outcome on each dimension. A scale of zero to 100 is simplest to use. Zero is defined as the minimum plausible value and 100 as the maximum plausible value. The scale may later be expanded over the range 0–1000. Now draw a straight line connecting maximum plausible with minimum plausible values. The result of this step is the rescaled position of a given outcome on a given dimension.

9. Calculate aggregate utilities for the outcomes of possible decisions and actions using a weighted average formula.[13]

10. Decide. If a single outcome is to be chosen, simply maximize the aggregate utility for that outcome.

In practice some of the steps may be more critical, more difficult to implement than are others. Steps 1 and 3 may be especially tricky. In the first step on the first iteration, important decisionmaking parties may be overlooked. In the third step pinning down just what is to be evaluated is not always straightforward. For example, a government agency may initially find it difficult to discriminate among its own bureaucratic survival goals or dimensions, the goals of the populace served, and the goals of its own organizational superiors and evaluators.

An example of a value dimension or goal could be: The extent to which a recommended project is likely to produce tangible, short-term results. An importance weight of .167 might be given to this dimension. The weightings of the other, say, 10 to 12 dimensions might then range downwards to, say, .008. Final weightings might be the mean of the ratings of those participating in the exercise, or alternatively they could be assigned by a senior person who takes into consideration the individual weightings.

Suppose further that there are 10 value dimensions such as the above, 20 projects being considered and independently scaled on each dimension, and 10 raters. This would produce a total of 2000 judgments. If interjudge reliability is considered good, the average of the 10 judges can be considered to be the scale value for each project on each dimension. The projects should scatter over wide ranges on the 0-to-1000 scale for each dimension.

Like many types of systems analysis or evaluation, multi-attribute utility measurement may be of most use because:

It focuses attention on the problem, in this case the meaning of each value or goal, the relationships among values, the priorities of values, and the specific projects that might lead to goal accomplishment.

It brings the conflicting goals or values of contending parties into the open, encouraging recognition if not reconciliation of specific differences.

However, like other methodologies MAUM is susceptible to manipulation or domination by more powerful or persuasive individuals or groups.

If the earlier steps are performed well, the calculation of actual utilities may amount to the frosting on the cake.

TECHNOLOGICAL FORECASTING

The term technological forecasting was introduced in 1959 by Ralph C. Lenz, Jr., of the University of Dayton Research Institute. Technological forecasting is more an orientation or a philosophy than it is a specific technique. Dr. Joseph P. Martino, another pioneer in the field of technological forecasting, provides this definition: "A technological forecast is a prediction of the future characteristics of useful machines, procedures or techniques."[14]

The degree of precision of a forecast may vary from the very general to the quantitatively exact. Martino identifies four elements common to all technological forecasts:

The time period
The nature of the technology
The specific characteristics of the technology
The probability associated with these characteristics

In many practical cases, a fifth element, costs or other resources, must be added.

A technology does not spring from the air, but represents the culmination of many activities spread over a period of time. Many stages of technological development have been identified:

1. Scientific discovery of laws, physical properties, and so forth.
2. Laboratory demonstration of an operating model.
3. Development of a prototype capable of operating in its expected environment.
4. Introduction of production models to commercial, military, or other users.
5. Widespread adoption of the specific innovation or of the overall technology by the user population.
6. Diffusion to other user populations and/or to different applications.
7. Social, economic, and environmental impact of the innovation or technology.

These are idealized stages and any given innovation or even an entire technology need not pass through all the stages. Forecasting is easier within the middle stages than at the extremes. Technological development often is not specifiable and therefore far from perfectly manageable. The life history of an innovation often resembles a web reflecting the confluence of many ideas, discoveries, and technologies rather than a nicely defined sequence or chain of events. As a force technology appears more and more to have a life of its own, and the term *autonomous technology* has entered the language. And recently more and more attention has come to be paid to the impacts of technology.

Like the trend extrapolation discussed earlier, technological forecasting relies on incorporating within some logical framework reliable observations on and interpretations of the past and present. Nevertheless, quantitative forecasts may be made of probable attainable performances 20 years into the future within error ranges of 25 percent.

Ralph Lenz has pinpointed several things no method of technological forecasting can yet do well: [15]

Predicting the impact of new discoveries.

Predicting the rate of adoption of new technologies which have not yet realized a two-percent market penetration.

Predicting the date of occurrence of events critical to the initiation of a new technology.

Discovering and synthesizing the scatterings of research precursors to new discoveries.

Synthesizing the cumulative effects of discoveries in related fields.

Forecasting the cross-impact effects of technological and economic developments.

Forecasting rates of social and psychological change.

One of the themes of this book is that great change is occurring in both the external and internal environments of the organization and this change is not compartmentalized. Even more important than this change itself is the change in *relationships* between the organization and its environment and among the subsystems within the organization. In a labile world the applicability of past assumptions and methods must be questioned. The concept of exponential growth of technology may be one paradigm much in need of reevaluation. This paradigm has of course long been the type example for the explanation of increases in vehicular speed, engine power, computer power, and so on.

SCENARIOS

The word scenario is used in different ways by different researchers. Most basically, a scenario is a means of exploring *alternative* futures, a *synopsis* or *sketch* of one conceivable state of affairs based on given assumptions. Futures researcher Herman Kahn, perhaps the first person to use the term outside the field of drama, defined a scenario as "a *hypothetical* sequence of events constructed for the purpose of focusing attention on causal processes and decision points" (emphasis added).

For our purposes scenarios are particularly valuable techniques for environmental analysis and strategic and long-range planning because they integrate analyses of individual trends and potential events into a holistic picture of the future, that is, they provide a means of weaving the myriad threads into a *pattern*. Social, technological, ecological, economic, demographic, human-resource, and market trends and events can be combined into a multidimensional, dynamic field of flow. A scenario seeks to determine key branching points, factors that could lead to evolution from one branch rather than from another, and major consequences in a causal chain. Use of scenarios can greatly aid proactive or anticipatory organizational behavior in both internal and external adaptations.

Scenarios have been used in strategic planning in some large companies for a decade or more. A prime example is the program at General Electric Company. Ian Wilson of General Electric sees the objectives for using scenarios as being:[16]

1. Combine alternative environmental developments into an internally consistent and relevant framework.

2. Identify branching points, discontinuities, and contingencies which can provide early-warning signals and for which contingency plans can be made.

3. Develop a framework for translating environmental changes into economic terms and economic long-range forecasts.

4. Provide a basis for analyzing the range of possible outcomes resulting from interactions between the alternative environments on the one hand and varying industry and market growth and company policies on the other.

5. Test results of various company and competitor strategies in the alternative environments.

Scenarios can thus be used in planning to sort out environmental changes that are variously probable or possible and variously modifiable through strategic actions by the organization. Use of scenarios helps organizations to maximize the actions they *choose* while minimizing the *reactions* they are *forced* to take.

The development of scenarios involves three basic stages, which I have modified somewhat from Ian Wilson's list:

1. *Inputs.* Analysis of future trends and events in various separate areas, sectors, or environments, for example, the six major external environments emphasized in this book. For each area, sector, or environment, the following types of elaborations can be pursued.

    a. Historic review of the nature and momentum of present trends, say, over the last 10 to 25 years.

    b. Analysis of the most probable forces for change. This analysis can provide a benchmark or surprise-free forecast of the future.

    c. Identification and assessment of potential discontinuities or major inflection points in the probable trends.

    d. Identification of key strategic and policy implications of the trends for the company (in this case General Electric).

2. *Throughputs.* The first stage may produce too much information to be manageable, so the many trends, events, and discontinuities must be sorted and arranged by both probability of occurrence and impact on the company. Further, the results of the first stage do not show integrations. The main integrative methodology can be cross-impact analysis or computer simulation modeling or some combination of such methodologies.

3. *Outputs.* These are the scenarios themselves, derived from various combinations of trends, events, and discontinuities. Wilson believes that two scenarios are too few, and that users often characterize only two scenarios as the good and the bad. But six are too many, both in terms of cognitive complexity and in terms of ability to monitor changes in each scenario as it unravels and to follow through with such actions as may be necessary. Wilson recommends sets of three or four scenarios. Four scenarios for the next 10 years might be, for example, depicted as:

    a. A reference, benchmark, or surprise-free scenario.

    b. A scenario continuing the present trajectory.

    c. An extreme best-case scenario.

    d. An extreme worst-case scenario.

To summarize, in scenario writing, a great many inputs are integrated and synthesized to provide a manageable set of outputs.

The selection of scenarios to be used in planning, from among countless numbers of possible scenarios, should be based on such criteria as comprehensibility, believability or face validity, usability, relevance to the organization, interest and dramatic impact, and focus on major branching points. In terms of the last criterion, different scenarios could be based, for example, on the responses of business to given trends. Business responses—foot-dragging, hostile/aggressive, accommodating, that of assuming leadership—to the challenges and opportunities highlighted in this book may as much as anything contribute to the future societal acceptance of the company.

Depending on the audience, scenarios can be presented by an appropriate mixture of text and prose, charts, tables, graphs, computer printouts, or real-time (interactive) computer-generated displays. We shall consider further examples of scenarios in the next section.

COMPUTER SIMULATION MODELING OF COMPLEX SOCIETAL SYSTEMS

Computer models now play ineradicable roles in planning, policymaking, and decisionmaking. The computer has greatly aided in the formulations and calculations of most types of modeling, even those whose theoretical bases antecede the electronic computer. A large optimizing linear program may contain hundreds or even thousands of equations and be very costly in the use of computer time. However, such analytic programs are typically used repeatedly for things like annual investment allocations or for continuous adjustments of inventories or production processes, that is, for implementation of policies and ongoing decisionmaking *once* the system has been understood and policies formulated.

This section emphasizes those *simulation* models which developed because of and in conjunction with advances in digital computers. We are most concerned with long-range forecasts involving systems in which quite dramatic changes are possible.

Several schools of modeling have developed. These schools differ by overall world view; basic assumptions; use of underlying theory; structure; definition and use of data; concepts of fidelity, validity, and utility; and, indeed, as to ultimate purposes of modeling and the use to which the model should be put. There are even models strongly and explicitly imbued with political philosophy.

The arguments in favor of computer simulation modeling are convincing:

Managers make decisions on the basis of hunches, intuitions, and subjective feelings—in short, mental models—anyway, so it is better to make these mental models as precise and rigorous as possible.

A computer model can deal with vastly greater numbers of variables and interactions and amounts of data than can people.

A computer model is explicit and can be examined for inconsistency and error and revised accordingly.

A computer model is explicit and can be examined for assumptions underlying conclusions in a logical, error-free manner.

A computer model can easily be altered to represent different assumptions or test alternative policies.

The very process of model construction involving asking questions, stating new concepts, and searching for data, may enhance understanding of a problem so fully that formal computerization is no longer required.

The field of computer simulation modeling is characterized more by its diversity than by its solidarity. Protagonists advance and defend their own approaches with vigor, while attacking their opponents with rancor. Models will have increasingly important impacts on planning and policymaking. This introduces one of the most formidable problems in modern management. One can indeed envision future wars between the models. Particular attention is paid here to contrasting different modeling approaches.

Traditional Econometric Methods

Econometric methods have these primary characteristics:

They are at least nominally related to economic theory, which is unique in social science in its combination of long history and precision, and they at least nominally try to prove economic theory.

They go back to the work of Jan Tinbergen in the 1930s, and therefore antedate the electronic digital computer.

They typically but not always involve a small number of variables in correlational relationships.

They are structurally simple, that is, they do not usually employ feedback loops, time delays, hierarchical control, and so on.

They are heavily dependent on statistical data streams, that is, time-series data representing one value for each successive time period, for establishment of parameters or coefficients, and for model validation.

Econometric modeling usually involves formulating sets of simultaneous equations; that is, a variable is not usually defined in terms of just one equation. Like the equations in other simulation models, but unlike those of analytic models like many optimization models, the equations are difference equations. Such equations state how variables change from one discrete time period to the next. Econometric models contain variables which are both endogenous (internal to the model) and exogenous (imposed from outside the model). These simple statements disguise some major controversies within the modeling field to which we shall return later.

Consider the following simple example of an econometric forecast:[17]

$$Y = C + I \tag{1}$$
$$C = a + bY + cC_{-1} + \mu \tag{2}$$

where Y = National income
C = Total consumption
I = Total investment
C_{-1} = The previous time period of C
μ = A stochastic or random error term

The coefficients a, b, and c must be statistically estimated from historical data. Variables Y and C are endogenous; I is exogenous. Statistical estimation requires historical data on both types of variable. Inputs for the simulation are the initial value of C and values for I over the entire period being simulated.

Equations 1 and 2 can be rewritten using substitution to yield

$$Y = \frac{a}{1\text{-}b} + \left(\frac{1}{1\text{-}b}\right)I + \left(\frac{c}{1\text{-}b}\right)C_{-1} + \left(\frac{1}{1\text{-}b}\right)\mu \tag{3}$$

$$C = \frac{a}{1\text{-}b} + \left(\frac{b}{1\text{-}b}\right)I + \left(\frac{c}{1\text{-}b}\right)C_{-1} + \left(\frac{1}{1\text{-}b}\right)\mu \tag{4}$$

The purpose is to generate C and Y each time period. Suppose that statistical estimation based on historical data on Y and C has produced the following values of the coefficients: a = .3, b = .1, c = .8. Equations 3 and 4, neglecting the stochastic error term, become

$$Y = .33 + 1.11I + .89C_{-1}$$
$$C = .33 + .11I + .89C_{-1}$$

Suppose further that the value of C last year was measured to be $3 billion and I to be $1 billion and that I is expected to increase by 10 percent for the next several years. That is, $C_0 = 3.00, I = 1.00$, and $(I_1, I_2, \ldots) = (1.10, 1.21, \ldots)$.

Expected values for Y and C for the next several years can then be calculated as follows:

$$Y_1 = .33 + 1.11 \times 1.10 + .89 \times 3.00 = 4.22$$
$$C_1 = .33 + .11 \times 1.10 + .89 \times 3.00 = 3.12$$
$$Y_2 = .33 + 1.11 \times 1.21 + .89 \times 3.12 = 4.45$$
$$C_2 = .33 + .11 \times 1.21 + .89 \times 3.12 = 3.24$$

and so on over the calculated or simulated time period.

The conceptual format and arrangement of data contribute to the easy computerization of econometric models. The computer has permitted great expansion in the types, complexity, and scope of these models. However, model format or structure and validation remain largely inseparable from the existence of available statistical data. Econometricians attempt validation by statistical goodness-of-fit tests which compare model-generated data with real-world data. Like other modelers they also use intuitive and commonsense comparisons.

The method of estimating coefficients from time-series data is almost always a least-squares method, particularly regression analysis. The assumptions underlying such mathematical and statistical procedures may make for precise results but may also cause the model to depart from reality. This may produce the anomalous condition of a highly valid, low-fidelity model![18] For example, one requirement is that all coefficients (parameters) to be estimated enter the equations linearly. Another restriction is that the variation in one variable not be linearly dependent on the variation in any other variable and must be independent of the error term. Ordinary least-squares regression is theoretically not even appropriate for simultaneous equations. Most relationships in econometric models are therefore linear or log-linear, a situation that appears to depart more and more from the real world.

Econometric models can be used for large-scale or macroeconomic forecasting, for example, the total U.S. economy, and for policy analysis in the comparison of the effects of alternative policies on the economy. Their greatest value is in short-term predictions or analyses involving highly aggregated economic or economic-like (demographic, objective social indicator) data. Econometric methods seem to be particularly well suited to short-term planning in the firm.

No problemsolving methodology based on science or technology is completely objective, without bias, foolproof or eternal. Even the apparently most precise management sciences are based on philosophies of life, assumptions, and intuitions, can grow rigid and obsolete, and can be misused. Certain features of econometric analysis, for example, may have outlived their usefulness. It was pointed out above that ordinary least-squares is theoretically not appropriate for estimating coefficients for simultaneous equations. This recognized deficiency has led to refinements such as indirect least squares, two-stage least squares, three-stage least squares, and so forth. But these improvements increase the burden on the computer. Also these methods may lead to overfitting a model, that is, tying it so closely to historical data that it is actually *less* likely to forecast accurately. The wise planner will avoid both the lure of false precision and overcommitment to any specialized practice.

In response to the crises of those times, much of the economic theory and practice underlying econometric modeling was developed in the 1930s and shortly thereafter. Leading economists like Jan Tinbergen and Ragnar Frisch (the first recipients of the Nobel Prize in Economics), John Maynard Keynes, and Simon Kuznets (a father of the system of national income and product accounts) were concerned about the causes of the Great Depression and prevention of a recurrence. Economic modeling has for several decades depended heavily on modern Keynesian theory, which emphasizes the role of government fiscal policy in the maintenance of balance between aggregate levels of employment and production. Monetarist theory, which emphasizes the predominance of money supply, also infuses some models.

Especially since the early 1960s a number of small, intermediate, and large econometric models have been developed.[19] In parallel several large data banks have appeared. Most applications have been to national economies where the most data covering the longest time span exist. Some applications have also been made at the state and city levels. The government, universities, think tanks, and private consulting firms are involved in econometric modeling and provide competitive and often contradictory models. Every major U.S. corporation uses at least one commercial model linked to its own internal models. There is no one best and all-inclusive model. Comparisons of the predictive accuracy of different models and also comparisons between model outputs and judgmental forecasts by experts who do not rely primarily on formal models have produced no clear and consistent superiority of any one individual, approach, or model.

The importance of surprises, unforeseen events, discontinuities, and emergent phenomena has been stressed repeatedly. In 1974 the economics profession received a shock. Inflation and falls in production were severely underestimated and a predicted economic recovery failed to materialize. In a sense the post-World War II era had officially ended, even though some aspects of the 1976–1977 forecasts had improved.

At the present time both economic theory and econometric modeling are undergoing radical changes. Three major reasons for marked revisions in economic theory are the following:

The limits-to-growth concept.

The inclusion of ideas and variables that do not stem solely from the discipline of economics.

The specific marriage of economics and ecology as expressed, for example, by the work of Nicholas Georgescu-Roegen.

Econometric modeling is moving away from strictly macroeconomic models in rather opposite directions to:

Modeling much greater detail of business, industrial, market, service, and other microeconomic factors.

Constructing international megamodels which link together national models.

In turbulent environments planners cannot continue to rely for long on the same tools. It seems, unfortunately, that the users of econometric models have assumed a static environment, not only with regard to emergent phenomena but also with regard to the *impact* of their policies on the public. Because of what has come to be called the *rational expectations*[20] of people and because of their consequent behavior, the results of government policies are forestalled. Indeed, policies may be worse than useless. Favorite forms of government fine-tuning of the economy have included increasing or decreasing the money supply, reducing taxes, and deficit spending. The first time these interventions are attempted, they may produce the results desired by government. But people learn and anticipate. Suppose taxes are cut but that there is no parallel decrease in government spending. The first time people may invest or spend as desired and expected. But eventually taxes start to rise again. People observe that the government will have to borrow more to service the expanded debt. People become cynical. The next time a tax cut is made, people do not invest or spend as before. Sharp reversals from, say, Keynesian to monetarist policy do not in themselves obviate these difficulties.

How could a conscientious modeler get around such a problem? One way would be to: (1) treat the public as endogenous rather than exogenous factors; (2) formally incorporate aggregate learning, anticipations, and expectations into the model; and (3) build in feedback loops between policies and public behavior. The new model could very likely be a systems dynamics model.

The Systems Dynamics National Model

The basic features of systems dynamics have already been discussed in Chapters 2 and 3, tracing developments from the original industrial dynamics to urban dynamics and world dynamics. We stressed in particular the concept of structure derived from feedback loops, and the types of system behavior derived from structure. In this section we shall consider what is probably the most ambitious computer simulation project ever undertaken, a systems dynamics model which represents almost two decades' experience with the basic methodology.

Begun in 1973 the Systems Dynamics Model of the U.S. Socioeconomic System[21] consists of eight basic submodels called sectors: Production, Financial, Household, Demographic, Labor, Foreign Trade, Government, and, more recently added, Energy. The sectors describe important features of production, consumption, investment, prices, employment, government policy and similar activities and indices. The model also describes interrelationships between sectors such as labor and professional mobility and international monetary flows.

The *Standard Production Sector* was the first to be completed. By changing parameters the sector represents such varied production and distribution activities as consumer durable goods, consumer soft goods, capital equipment, building construction, transportation, knowledge generation, military operations, government service, service activities, agriculture, and resources. Within each production sector are such factors of production as capital, labor, professionals, knowledge for capital productivity, land, buildings, transportation, materials, and length of work week.

An *ordering function* is considered to be a particular strength of the Production Sector. It is considered to be more influential than the production functions of alternative national models. For each of the above factors of production the ordering function creates an order backlog in response to desired production rate, desired factor intensity, marginal productivity of the factor, product inventory and backlog, interest rate, growth expectations, financial pressures, price of the product, profitability, and factor delivery delay. Many similarities to the earlier industrial dynamics models can therefore be seen.

The DYNAMO III computer simulation language/compiler was developed for the National Model. DYNAMO III handles arrays of equations to permit the replication of the Production Sector and its parts. Thus, an equation for the ordering function is written once with array subscripts. This then identifies the ordering functions for each factor in each sector.

The structure of a standard production sector is like that of a single firm. Thus, there is an accounting subsector that generates accounts receivable and payable, saves, borrows money, and so on. Such detail permits communication directly with the real world which provides the wealth of information necessary to establish parameter values. A particularly valuable feature will be the interface between the individual firm and the model as a whole.

The *Financial Sector* is divided into commercial banking, savings institutions, and the monetary authority. This sector determines interest rates, buys and sells bonds, makes loans of different durations, and attempts to deal with intangibles like confidence in the banking system. The three elements of the Financial Sector perform the familiar expected functions. For example, the commercial banking system receives deposits and makes loans to households and businesses. The savings institutions allocate loans between businesses and households and monitor the debt levels and borrowing abilities of each business and household sector. The monetary authority controls discount rates and responds to unemployment and rates of inflation and interest.

The *Household Sectors* are divided into welfare, unemployed, labor, retired, and professional categories. Each household sector receives income, purchases goods and services, saves, borrows, and holds assets. Consumption demands respond to prices and availability of various goods and services. These sectors also determine the fraction of people actively seeking work as a function of such factors as demand for labor and standard of living.

The *Demographic Sector* determines population levels by controlling the flows of births, deaths, immigration, and aging. People are divided from childhood through retirement into age categories that describe their different roles in the economy. People are also divided into the two main categories of labor and professionals in response to wages, salaries, family background, capacity of the educational system, and demands of the production sectors.

The *Labor Sector* is usually expressed as a mobility network which describes the movement of labor and professionals between production sectors in response to changes in need, availability, and wages. The sector contains a general unemployment pool through which people can flow from sector to sector.

The *Foreign-Trade Sector* represents one or more aggregate trading partners of the single domestic economy simulated by the National Model. Equations coupling the domestic and foreign sectors generate exchange rates, flows of imports and exports, and balance of payments. A foreign manufacturing sector or resource sector can be derived through replicating a standard production sector. The Foreign-Trade Sector appears to represent an afterthought to which proper attention has not been devoted.

The *Government Sector* generates services, tax rates, expenditures, and sales of government bonds to finance the national debt. Government services are generated via a standard production sector.

The *Energy Sector* treats different sources of energy supply, the demands generated by population and industry, and cost and tradeoffs between energy variables and other social, economic, and environmental variables.

The Systems Dynamics National Model is used to examine the following kinds of problems:

The forces underlying *inflation*:

Major imbalances in the economy including overconcentration of employment in government, education, and the services.

Movement from a period of economic growth to a period of production output per capita limited by environmental constraints.

Continued population rise.

Overcommitment of space and resources, requiring increasing capital investment.

Government efforts to maintain a rising standard of living.

Masking of fundamental social and economic changes by monetary and fiscal means.

The nature of past and future *economic growth* associated with the interactions among population, resources, knowledge, technology, production, and environment.

The advantages and disadvantages of different types of *taxation*, especially if the flow of prices, wages, and money soon readjust to tax policies as we observed earlier.

Energy crises, especially the stresses generated on the internal economy, on international relations, and on the natural environment.

Life-cycle changes in *agriculture*, especially relations between:

Capital- and labor-intensiveness.

Output per man-hour.

Output of food calories per input of petroleum or other energy calories.

Migration from and reverse migration to agricultural areas.

Impacts of major changes in migration on housing, transportation, welfare, and other factors.

Education, viewed as a form of capital investment, as it reflects the interaction of productivity, consumption demands, technology, and an inventory of required skills, especially regarding the production of excess capacity.

Alternative economic theories and policies such as Keynesian, monetarist, growthist, nongrowthist, cyclic, noncyclic, and so on.

The National Model generates growth curves and fluctuations endogenously from the year 1850 to the year 2050. This modeling approach stresses generating typical historical behavior as a basis from which to anticipate the future. Forces and structures visible at any given time are considered to be dominant far into the future. Most major dynamic forces operating over the next several decades are thought to be detectable from careful scrutiny of the present system. However, this modeling philosophy requires qualification, and Chapter 5 examines the emergent phenomena which may vitiate the pure systems dynamics approach.

The National Model views economic stability in terms of the interplay between forces and constraints. The constraints describe system *modes* as follows:

1. From the beginning of the Industrial Revolution to the period immediately following World War II, there was available land and excess labor, but the restraint to excess growth was a *shortage of capital equipment.* Capital shortage determined the pace of economic development.
2. During the 1950s and 1960s, *labor* became the principal constraint. Hence, labor demands set the style and pace of the U.S. economy.
3. In the 1970s *environmental* constraints have become predominant and are expressed in terms of living space, crowding stresses, agricultural land, energy and other resources, capacity to dissipate pollution, and so forth.

The designers of the model hope it can help identify the nature of such mode *transitions.* Systems dynamicists pay particular attention to the dynamics around the ranges of transition. The ideas of societal transitions and reconfigurations are major ones in this book.

The most impressive demonstration so far of the usefulness of the National Model lies in its contribution to our knowledge about economic fluctuations and periodicities. Most planners are familiar with business cycles. The National Model has not only provided more insight into such short-term cycles, but has also clarified the existence of other cycles ranging in period up to 200 years. Systems dynamics interpretations may be controversial or at variance with those of other schools. Different systems dynamics processes can, however, explain cycles of different length. The four cycles of concern are:

The *business cycle,* lasting from three to seven years, which appears to stem from interactions between inventories and employment within production sectors.

The *Kuznets cycle,* lasting from 15 to 20 years.

The *Kondratieff cycle* or long wave, lasting about 40 to 60 years, which appears to be associated with the processes of accumulation of capital, buildings, and machinery, and with labor mobility.

The *life cycle of economic development,* occurring once in the history of a nation, culture, or civilization, and presently characterized in our own case by a stress-ridden transition period from growth to equilibrium.

Probabilistic Systems Dynamics

As seen at the beginning of this chapter, many techniques in futures research are basically extrapolative. These techniques assume that the future will be a simple extension of the past. Of course this will seldom be true because of the many reasons already cited throughout this book. Dr. Theodore J. Gordon and his colleagues have developed methods for incorporating information on potential forces and events into otherwise extrapolative procedures, a technique which is called *probabilistic systems dynamics.*[22]

Probabilistic systems dynamics employs cross-impact analysis to add the impacts of exogenous potential events to the closed systems dynamics model. Impacts of events on the basic trends in the model can be calculated, depending on the main purpose of the model, by one of two methods:

1. The *expected value method* can be used in cases involving large numbers of events specified at a much finer level of detail than are the model output variables. The value of the impact on the model variable, if the event occurs, is calculated and this impact is then discounted by the probability of occurrence. All events contribute to the overall model; that is, the probabilities of occurrence of the events are combined with their expected impacts. The impact of policies can be handled in the same way; that is, a policy can be regarded as an event.

2. The *occurrence/nonoccurrence* method, as the name suggests, involves the actual occurrence or lack thereof of given events. Occurrence is defined in terms of the time at which the cumulative probability of the event exceeds some previously defined arbitrary threshold, for example, .50. On occurrence the model is changed to reflect the full impact of the event. This method may be preferred when the user's main interest is in studying overall system behavior.

Development of the basic systems dynamics model and identification of elements in the cross-impact matrix are undertaken simultaneously. Time-dependent probabilities for each event are first estimated and expressed in familiar forms like the probability of occurrence of Event A by 1990 is .25. Second, the impact of events on events is described, a procedure that may modify the initial probability. Third, the impacts of events on the continuous trends of the systems dynamics model are described. As a result model structure may change or equations may be modified. Fourth, model trends may impact event probabilities.

The entire model is run employing the iterative interaction of the DYNAMO systems dynamics program and a cross-impact program written in FORTRAN. The model operates through these steps:

1. Using initial values for the systems dynamics variables, compute new values for the first solution interval in the usual manner of systems dynamics.

2. Transfer these new variables to the cross-impact matrix.

3. Determine new values of event probabilities from their original values and the impacts of trends in the model variables.

4. Determine impacts of events on events using the probabilities of the events and the occurrence or nonoccurrence of impacts.

5a. Transfer the probabilities from the cross-impact program back into the systems dynamics model;

  b. Calculate event impacts on the model trends; and

  c. Revise the systems dynamics model as appropriate.

6.   Calculate new values for the systems dynamics variables for the next solution interval using the revised model.

7.   Iterate Steps 2 through 6 for the duration of the time span being studied.

"Mankind at the Turning Point"/World Integrated Model

The "Mankind at the Turning Point" world model was developed under the direction of Professors Mihajlo D. Mesarovic of Case Western Reserve University and Eduard Pestel of Hannover University, West Germany[23] A second-generation model has considerably modified the original "Second Report to the Club of Rome." This model of global development is called the World Integrated Model (WIM). It divides the world into 12 regions: North America, Western Europe, the Developed Countries of the Pacific, the Rest of the Developed World, the Soviet Union and its allies in Eastern Europe, Latin America, the non-oil-producing Arab World, the Middle East oil-producing countries, Africa, South Asia, Southeast Asia, and China. A region may be broken down further into up to five national or subregional units.

Figure 4.6 illustrates the overall WIM model with its nine constituent submodels. Each submodel applies to each of the 12 regions. The WIM model itself is embedded in an Assessment-of-Policies Tool (APT) permitting scenario analysis.

The WIM model represents an evolutionary modification of the first-generation model. Modification reflects the experience of the modelers. Even

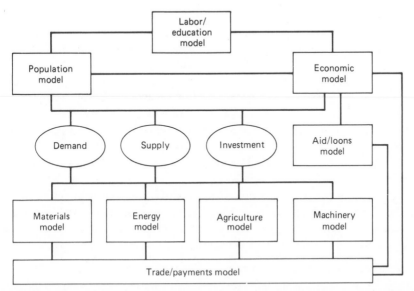

Figure 4.6 Block diagram of the Mesarovic-Pestel World Integrated Model showing interrelationships among constituent submodels. Note how the model reflects the underlying hierarchical, multilevel systems theory. Reprinted from *Futures*, Volume 10, Number 4, August 1978, pp. 267–282.

more important, modification reflects the incorporation of real-world occurrences which had not been foreseen in the earlier model-building effort. Mankind at the Turning Point, like the Systems Dynamics National Model, did not originally have a submodel devoted specifically to energy. The earlier model did not distinguish between the oil-producing and non-oil-producing Arab World. The tremendous impacts of the energy crises on world society, in all their ramifications, were not well anticipated or appreciated by most world modelers. Models generated as recently as 1975 were more preoccupied with the problems of world population and food supply, because these problems, also belatedly, had received such wide exposure during the 1960s. World modeling is still more *ex post facto* than it is anticipatory.

Table 4.2 shows the major submodels of WIM and what they represent.

Table 4.2. Major Submodels of the World Integrated Model and What They Represent

Submodel	What It Represents
Population	Regional total population and fertility and mortality distributions by 86 age categories
Economic	Production and capital formation in seven economic sectors: manufacturing, nonmanufacturing, industrial, agriculture, construction, wholesale/retail, and transportation, communications, and services
Agricultural	Five categories of food production: grain, nongrain industrial crops, fish, and livestock
Energy	Resources, production, demand, trade and pricing for five energy types: petroleum, coal, natural gas, hydroelectric, and nuclear
Materials	Resources, production, demand, trade and pricing for three metals: iron, aluminum, and copper
Labor/Education	Four educational levels: uneducated, primary education only, secondary education, and university or professional training
Machinery	Supply, demand and trade of various kinds of machinery
Trades/Payments	Integration of the Economic Model with the physical models, balancing global and regional supply and demand
Aid/Loans	Transfer of aid or loans via a pool or by fixed demand

Various kinds of open-loop, closed-loop, and combined-problems scenarios can be developed to produce curves to aid in analysis of problem areas. Typically the model runs from 1975 through 2025. One scenario could be based on the simultaneous combined occurrence of these three problems:

Stable annual global oil discoveries until the year 2000.

Reduction of agricultural yields by 20 percent by the year 2000, because of inclement weather and the use of marginal land.

No increase in indebtedness of the less-developed countries, because higher energy and food prices lower their ability to borrow.

As a result of the interaction among these worst-case developments, world economic growth is considerably reduced, agricultural production falls and prices increase, malnutrition and starvation deaths greatly increase, and all forms of energy production and consumption grow less rapidly.

One of the major emphases of this modeling approach, and one of its potential strengths, is the breakdown of the world into regions and subregions. This permits an assessment of the ability of each region to cope with stresses. Abilities of nations or regions to adapt obviously differ—and not always in the same or predictable manners.

In one study the open-loop economic, demographic, agriculture, and energy projections tended to agree with discipline-based projections of many governmental and private agencies.[24] More integrated analyses in which the connections between the strata or submodels were closed tended to produce much more conservative projections, that is, lower population growth, lower food production, and so forth. The combined-problems scenarios consistently led to the lowest level projections of all, whether or not the projected variables are to be considered normatively good or bad.

As in all world models the assumptions in WIM regarding causal interrelationships are open to question. For example, the relationships between an index of standard of living or national development on the one hand, say, income level, and birthrate or patterns of consumption on the other are at best correlational. The Mesarovic-Pestel Model in many ways resembles a large econometric model. However, there are two features of this model to which one might particularly object:

The underlying theory
The method of using scenarios

Model structure is greatly influenced by Professor Mesarovic's "Theory of Hierarchical, Multilevel Systems." Such systems are like the vertical chain-of-command structures in organizations. At the lowest level in the model is the environmental stratum. Successively superior are the technology, demo-economic, group, and individual strata. Man, the consumer, is on top. Level, layer, and stratum are used interchangeably. The environmental stratum is controlled by each successive superior stratum. The technology stratum is mainly an interface between the demo-economic stratum and the environmental stratum. It incorporates technologies which man has developed largely to manipulate and control the natural environment, mostly, if sometimes indirectly, for food production. The Mesarovic-Pestel Model perpetuates a world view of man the conqueror of nature, controlling and bending the environment to meet his ever-growing needs. Although the modelers recognize the existence of environmental constraints, ecological concepts appear to have had little influence on their thinking.

The causal model (the computer program) consists mainly of the three lower strata. The group and individual strata are represented mostly in the scenarios, although attempts are made to computerize certain norms, values, and decision processes. The scenarios are of the person–computer interactive type. Much use of the scenarios is apparently a measure of ignorance about the system and presumably preliminary and temporary. What is unknown about the system first is inserted exogenously using the scenarios. As more is learned, algorithms may be developed and incorporated into the causal model. Such endogenization is also called closing the loop. Scenarios will continue to be used as manual overrides of purely computer processes, for example, in policymaking. Unfortunately, the scenario process has been used as an excuse for not trying to understand human behavior better. The authors' view of human behavior is completely mechanistic.

Other Regional and World Models

Systems dynamics and econometrics are the dominant approaches today to the computer simulation modeling of complex societal systems. The Mesarovic-Pestel Model is also an influential model, although so far it is one of a kind. Its underlying theory, hierarchical multilevel systems theory, unlike those of systems dynamics and econometrics, has not spawned multiple models.

A number of other models of society have become available recently. Most of these are not based on new theory, nor do they provide basically new methodologies. Some, for example, are derivations of econometric or optimization modeling. Several were developed to examine specific problems or questions. One or two are admittedly normative or are counterresponses to other models. Examples of other interesting models include:

The University of California at Davis' SPECULATER/SAM

The Bariloche or Latin American World Model

The Dutch Model of International Relations in Agriculture (MOIRA), a model of the world food supply

The Japan Club of Rome Model, a world model of regional and sector changes in production

SPECULATER is an acronym for Simulation Program Examining Causalities Underlying Land, Agriculture, Transportation, and Energy Relationships. It was developed under the direction of ecology professor Kenneth E. F. Watt. Like systems dynamics it is a dynamic, mutually interactive, causal model in which cause–effect relationships between variables were developed from expert opinion. Like systems dynamics SPECULATER uses multiplier curves—linear, exponential, power, logistic, and so on—to express relationships between variables. Unlike systems dynamics the multiplier relationships apply to levels or state variables rather than to rates. Unlike systems dynamics but like econometrics, SPECULATER makes heavy use of exogenous variables and of historical time-series data to fit parameters in the equations. SPECULATER also uses a least-squares method. However, unlike the case in econometrics the statistical inferences of regression analysis are not valid. SPECULATER is written in FORTRAN and uses discrete-time simulation methodology.

SPECULATER is a U.S. national model which can be used as an input to a regional submodel, the Sacramento Area Model (SAM). SPECULATER consists of three sectors: Agriculture, Transportation, and National Level Oil. In addition, it has an exogenous National Population Submodel and a feature called the Composite Urban Area. The latter was obtained by averaging data from 101 individual American cities, all surrounded by prime agricultural land. The future is simulated through combinations of projections of exogenous variables which comprise alternative scenarios. Like the Mesarovic-Pestel Model SPECULATER makes heavy use of scenarios, although the term scenario is used differently.

Like most other models SPECULATER is closely related to the problems of the times and interprets the future largely in terms of a continuation of the interactions among recently past and present trends. That is, it does not address the problems of reconfiguration and emergence. In the early 1970s a favorite goal of then President Richard M. Nixon was called "Project Independence." SPECULATER examined the problem and determined that petroleum independence by the United States could be obtained by 1985, but only either at high social costs, for example, a severe recession, or by a combination of moderately expanded domestic oil production, slow economic growth, and increased efficiency of energy use.

Considering the recurrence of the energy crises and the major shock imposed on the world by constant changes in the availability and price of petroleum, SPECULATER has, I believe, anticipated energy and transportation problems better than have other models discussed. SPECULATER, although also a highly aggregated model, has also provided more detailed insight on the causal interactions of the subsystems modeled. In addition, SPECULATER like some other models provides refined understanding of evolutionary changes in the United States. For example, regarding exports, the United States has become like an underdeveloped nation with agricultural products becoming the major positive contributor to the trade balance.

SPECULATER examines such problems as:

The effect of export-induced scarcity on agricultural markets.

The effect of oil prices and scarcity on petroleum consumption and urban life styles in the United States.

The overall idea that agricultural exports will increase to offset the unfavorable trade balance caused by increased fuel imports.

Scenarios and simulations are developed in the following way. From three (low, medium, and high) to five or more trend projections for each exogenous variable are provided. A base-case simulation, consisting of all medium projections, is provided for comparative purposes. For example, six projections are provided for the exogenous variable "U.S. Oil Production" based on three prices of oil and "business as usual" and "accelerated development" relative to government policy on oil-field leasing. Simulation runs consist of combinations of exogenous variables. For example, the six scenario projections could be modified by showing the effects of economic conditions indicated by three versions of "U.S. Per Capita Disposable Income" (recession, slow growth, and fast growth). The result would be 18 different simulation runs (six projections of oil production times three variations in economic conditions).

Simulations are thus based on a varied set of input scenarios designed to reflect various assumptions, philosophies, or world views. SPECULATER functions as a tool for policy analysis or policymaking. As seen above, many input variables are subject to government influence.

For purposes of better intuitive understanding of the input scenarios, here are some examples of statements about exogenous variable projections from the base-case simulation:

Per capita disposable income increases after 1974 at the low rate of .5 percent per year.

Wheat yield increases linearly at approximately the historical rate.

Population growth rate increases from 1974–1983, then declines to a low value of .6 percent per year.

SPECULATER produced some invariant simulation outcomes regardless of the input scenarios used; for example:

Urban sprawl essentially comes to an end by 1985; land conversion rate per capita drops by a factor of 100 from the 1960 level.

Urban population densities are about one-third higher in the year 2000.

Some results were found in most but not all simulations, for example:

There will be much greater use of public transportation by the year 2000.

There will be a dramatic drop in energy consumption to less than half the present rate.

However, many simulated outcomes were sensitive to the scenarios used. That many input variables are subject to government influence has major implications for policymaking. Some of these results demonstrate interesting counterintuitive phenomena. For example, low oil costs could double the price of food. Lower oil prices would lower the cost of producing food, because costs of fertilizers, pesticides, transportation, and processing would be brought down. However, this improvement would be more than offset by the export of food to balance the trade deficit. Export of food would reduce its availability in the United States.

A desirable overall policy would be one of high energy prices and lowered population growth rates.[25]

The *Latin American World Model* is popularly known as the *Bariloche Model,* named indirectly after the small town of San Carlos de Bariloche in the southern lake district of Argentina.[26] The model consists of two models, an explicitly *normative* model and a mathematical model which attempts to show how the goals of the normative model *could* be met. The model is *not* a means of discovering what will happen if present trends continue. The modeling effort has this overall conceptual framework:

The desired type of future society—essentially socialist, egalitarian, fully participatory, and nonconsuming, yet liberated from underdevelopment, oppression, and misery.

The division of the world into the major regions of Latin America, Africa, Asia, and the developed world.

The concept of basic needs and their central role.

The use of a production function with substitition between capital and labor.

The criteria for treatment of the problems of energy, natural resources, and pollution.

The model is a *reaction* against the world view, which its authors hold to be particularly prevalent in developed countries, that the world's fundamental problems are due to *physical* limits. The Bariloche authors argue that the major problems facing world society are sociopolitical rather than physical. However, no modelers have been so naive as to believe that limits are merely physical. Professor Jay W. Forrester has stated from the beginning that the most important limits are social.

Yet the Bariloche authors deal with some world problems of increasing magnitude, problems which other modelers have largely ignored. These problems are based on the unequal distribution of power both between nations and within nations. The Bariloche authors emphasize that the results of such disparities are oppression and alienation, which stem from exploitation. A look at the world from the perspective of the historian or of the sociologist concerned with social comparisons tends to add weight to these arguments. Revolutions and wars have time and again arisen from real or perceived differences in peoples' power, status, rights, and access to resources.

The unequal distribution of power, wealth, and resources does indeed represent a powder keg. But the flow can go two ways, as today's massive shift of economic power to the OPEC nations demonstrates. National and regional power are transitory and many reconfigurations and perhaps collapses are likely in the next few years. Although of immense importance to planning, these factors are still incorporated poorly into present world models.

The Bariloche Model is not just an emotional diatribe against exploitive capitalists in the developed world, or a polemic for continued population and economic growth in the underdeveloped world. Much of its philosophy is well thought out and applicable to the world as a whole. For instance, degradation of the natural environment is not an inevitable consequence of human progress, but results from social organizations and individual practices based on destructive values.

To reach the Bariloche modelers' ideal society, radical changes in the world's social and international organization are deemed necessary. Two major modeling goals directed toward hastening these changes were established:

1. To determine that there are no physical environmental limits to attaining such a society. An analysis was undertaken of nonrenewable resources, energy, and pollution in an attempt to meet this goal.
2. To demonstrate that different countries and regions (even the poorest) could reach the normative society within a reasonable amount of time.

The mathematical model, basically an economic model, is devoted to the second goal. It has these assumptions and features:

1. A production system with the main purpose of satisfying certain defined basic human needs. As in the Mesarovic-Pestel Model, a Cobb-Douglas production function is utilized which allows substitutions between capital and labor. Improvements in productivity derived from technological change are also reflected.
2. Basic needs defined as nutrition, housing, education, and health.
3. Division of the production system into the five sectors of nutrition, housing, education, capital goods, and consumer goods and other services.
4. Generation of population size endogenously by relating demographic variables to sociopolitical variables. The assumption of demographic transition is evoked, as in the Mesarovic-Pestel Model, namely, that controlled population growth can be achieved by improving basic living conditions.
5. Mathematical functions which allocate capital and manpower among the five sectors in order to obtain an optimum distribution. Resources are assigned to each sector so that life expectancy at birth is maximized at each point during a run.

The model demonstrated that, if the proposed policies were implemented, all the world could attain an adequate standard of living after slightly more than one generation. These policies include:

Reduction in nonessential consumption.

Increased investment.

Elimination of political and social barriers that impede the rational use of land for food production and urban planning.

Equitable distribution of goods and services.

Elimination, in the developing countries, of deficits in international trade, for example, by fixing fair prices for the products of these countries.

Model runs ended in the year 2060. As with other models the Bariloche Model provides better understanding of counterintuitive phenomena. For example, present foreign aid from the developed countries contributes mainly to increased spending by privileged sectors and has little effect on the standard of living of the majority poor. Models thus make more explicit things that may not be fully understood by all parties. Understanding by the developed world and worldwide social change are two different things however. Historically over much of the world, bribery and graft have been expected social functions for otherwise underpaid bureaucrats.

In summary, the Bariloche Model probably is a harbinger of value-laden models to be used in international policymaking. Like other models it can be attacked on the basis of assumptions and on technical grounds. Examples are the demographic transition and the Cobb-Douglas production function. The model underestimates the severity of real physical limits, for example, of energy. The model is naive in the same sense as is the Mesarovic-Pestel Model, namely, that the provision of food, shelter, health services, and education is any guarantee of freedom from misery and exploitation. Indeed, it can be argued from the viewpoint of motivation theory that meeting peoples' basic needs simply releases higher level psychological needs that are much harder to realize. Another instance of repeated criticism of large-scale models failing to incorporate major behavioral and social variables is thus presented.

Interpreting Regional and World Models

Computer simulation models of regional and world societal systems may produce quite different results. This is to be expected, considering the myriad ways in which the elements of any one modeling approach differ from the elements of other approaches. Thus, the body of computer simulation models does not comprise one general-purpose scientific instrument for studying different real-world problems. The situation is more like that of a microscopist examining his realm through a variety of microscopes differing in construction, utilization of optical principles, magnification power, reliability, and so forth.

The manager who considers himself to be hardheaded, completely rational, and willing to accept only the facts, may be very uneasy with computer simulation modeling. Masked by a panoply of computer power, often sophisticated mathematics, and some of the world's wisest protagonists, the core of the model is basically soft. The core is soft because of:

The many scientific limitations to futures forecasting discussed elsewhere in this chapter and book.

Modeling paradigms may represent mutually incompatible world views.

Modelers are rooted in time and culture.

Results have a habit of reflecting preconceived norms, desires, hopes, and expectations.

There is, in short, no one perfect model or modeling approach, and the planner who would use modeling must learn to live with contradictory results.

Following the initial shock of the Limits-to-Growth Models, a great deal of effort was expended by systems analysts around the world in attempts to detect basic errors in these models. The concept of limits to growth must be viewed as one of the great revolutions in human thinking, a revolution with profound and probably not yet fully understood potential impacts on all facets of both organizational and societal management and daily living.

One of the most familiar sets of analyses of the Limits Models is that of the Science Policy Research Unit at the University of Sussex, England.[27] This interdisciplinary team dissected the major subsystems of the models, questioning assumptions and interpretations in great detail. Such critical analyses are fundamentally necessary to the continued improvement and evolution of computer simulation models. However, it would be a gross misunderstanding of the entire modeling field to believe that critiques such as that of the Sussex group could *prove* the systems dynamics models to be *wrong*. Rather, both the Sussex analyses and the Limits response, both incorporated with a laudable spirit of scientific honesty into the *Models of Doom* book, boil down to two opposing camps, each selecting findings to substantiate its world view. This rather typical situation is of immense importance to the role of models in the policy process.

That modeling approaches may represent mutually incompatible world views is not too surprising. Professor Donnella H. Meadows,[28] one of the authors of *The Limits to Growth* study, further contrasts her approach, systems dynamics, with econometric modeling. This is a succinct recapitulation of the points discussed earlier.

Systems dynamics stresses:

Long-term analysis of possible changes in historic trends.

Ambiguous, qualitative concepts of data.

Informationally closed systems.

Dynamic situations.

Procedures of structuring and validation that rely little if at all on statistics.

Nonlinear systems.

Search for internal structure-behavior causal relationships.

Situations in which human unpredictability allows only qualitative forecasts, even with the averaging out due to aggregation.

Little if any reliance on exogenous variables.

Long-term policy effects; the short term is already determined and hence unchangeable by policy; short-term gain often leads to long-term loss.

Interdisciplinary definitions of problems.

General problemsolving.

Asking questions about dynamic paths to system end-states.

Search for causes in feedback loops underlying the surficial[29] reality that can be directly observed.

Model structure over parameter identification; models mostly unresponsive to parameter changes.

Utility over validity.

Time lags.

Econometrics stresses:

Short-term precise prediction where the present situation does not differ from the historic.

Historic data bases continually updated; data are economic, demographic, and social statistics.

Systems which are not completely closed.

Generally static situations.

Situations in which formal statistical methods are indispensable to achieving model design and validation.

Linear systems.

Search for correlational relationships.

Situations in which great refinements in quantitiative estimations are possible.

Considerable reliance on exogenous variables.

Short-term policy effects.

Compartmentalization of problems, for example, economic versus ecological.

Specific problemsolving; specific responses to specific stimuli.

Asking questions about system end-states per se.

Observable reality, perhaps with underlying causal structure implied.

Parameter identification over model structure.

Validity as at least equal to utility.

It would appear at first glance that systems dynamics and econometrics are in many ways as complementary as contradictory. And indeed some attempts at marriage between the two approaches have been made; for example, some systems dynamicists actively seek reliable time-series statistical data and some econometricians include feedback and time lags in their models. However, for the most part rapprochement between the two camps is slight, and each appears to view the other as hopelessly naive if not with abject contempt and hostility. Unfortunately, the two approaches cannot be simply dichotomized as suitable for short-term planning and for long-term planning. In forecasting, planning, and making policies about the national socioeconomic system over the next two decades, both schools are actively involved. Without an understanding of the matters just discussed, the client is liable to suffer confusion as to what the right modeling approach is and right answers are.

Moreover, modelers, in spite of their worldly outlooks and future emphases, are still largely bound to particular times and cultures. This point is widely recognized by modelers, but is nevertheless a major basis for the acrimony and hostility existing between different groups of modelers. It is not only a mental model which becomes formalized as a policy-oriented computer model; it is also an *emotional* model. The world views underlying different models may be as different as any which have ever divided humanity. Modelers mount crusades with all the fervor of the great religious leaders of the past.

The Limits to Growth Modelers, for example, in their response to the analyses of the Sussex group, write:[30]

> One possible concept of man, the one that is held by the Sussex group, is that *Homo sapiens* is a very special creature whose unique brain gives him not only the capability but the right to exploit for his own short-term processes all other creatures and all resources the world has to offer. This is an age-old concept of man, one firmly rooted in Judeo-Christian tradition and newly strengthened by stunning technical achievements in the last few centuries.
>
> The opposite concept of man is also an ancient one, but it is more closely related to the Eastern religions than to the Western ones. It assumes that man is one species with all other species embedded in the intricate web of natural processes that sustains and constrains all forms of life.
>
> We see no objective way of resolving these very different views of man and his role in the world. It seems to be possible for either side to look at the same world and find support for its view.

At the obvious risk of oversimplification, then, we might characterize The Limits to Growth Models as Western civilizational models imbued with a strong essence of Malthusianism and modern environmentalism. The Latin American or Bariloche World Model discussed earlier gives a good impression of a sophisticated world view from the perspective of the underdeveloped world. In a sense then the Bariloche Model represents a reaction to the *Limits* Models. The model is explicitly normative. It does not try to discover what will happen if present trends continue, but rather tries to indicate a way of reaching a final goal. It does not *try* to be objective or value-free. The *goal* is to build a world liberated from underdevelopment and misery. World society would be egalitarian, socialistic, participatory, and nonconsuming, as opposed to its perceived basis in Western exploitation or at least condescending dominance and manipulation.

The rooting of models in time has been pointed out earlier. We mentioned the addition of energy sectors or subsystems, after the intial conceptualizations, to both the Systems Dynamics National Model and the Mesarovic-Pestel Model. Useful models can obviously not remain static or fixed, but must be modifiable with the accumulation of new knowledge and with the experience of application. Useful models require the constant dynamic interaction among the client, modeler, model, and new knowledge. Even so, it does appear that modelers have been unduly bound to the events and outlooks of the years immediately *preceding* the modeling effort. Problems of population, food production, and pollution, and values emphasizing equality were heavily emphasized in the 1960s and subsequently appeared in world models. Problems of energy, ongoing economic instability, and power shifting to the OPEC nations, to which widespread attention has been paid since 1973, now represent important design and policy features of present models. Unfortunately, the computer modeling field is much more *reactive* than *anticipatory,* a disconcerting but necessary commentary to make regarding the most sophisticated means of probing the future.

Finally, almost without exception the results of large-scale models have provided substantiation of their designers' preconceived norms and expectations, albeit with precision and forcefulness. It appears unlikely that, say, the Systems Dynamics National Model will prove the continued viability and desirability of past and present fiscal and demographic policies. It is unlikely that econometric models will offer conclusions as to the fragility of the natural environment. It is unlikely that the Mesarovic-Pestel and Bariloche Models will determine, in agreement with the familiar Maslow hierarchy of needs, that fulfilling needs for food, shelter, and education will release forces that make world society even more ungovernable than it is at present. Peter C. Roberts presents a further excellent summary of the relations among the theory, philosophy, modelers, and modeling of large systems.[31]

Experience with the Use of Models in the Policy Process

Recent years have witnessed a rapid expansion in the numbers and availability of computer models. More and more corporations and government agencies are developing or procuring such models. However, are computer models *really used* for planning, policymaking and policyanalysis? And, if so, how? These questions are not easy to answer and involve elaboration of several points.

First, many types of computer models, in the most general sense of the term, *are* used routinely, especially at the operations levels in industry and in lower levels of government. These include process-control models and optimization models in general, and models applied to manpower forecasts, solid-waste management, water-resource planning, bank management, investment policies, studies of the housing market, agricultural production and pricing, studies of health care, and educational enrollment forecasts—to give some indication of the variety of areas involved. Large-scale econometric models are widely and extensively used as we have seen and are continually updated to provide quarter-by-quarter forecasts of national business and industrial activities. Almost all large corporations routinely employ econometric models to predict strength of consumer markets, trends in wage rates, prices of materials, and so on.

However, it is often difficult to determine just what is meant by used, especially with regard to the policy process. There are different stages and types of uses. The stages follow:

1. Initial exposure, first familiarity, and (perhaps subconscious) diffusion of modeling philosophy, concepts, and findings into the thought processes of the manager.
2. Tacit, and eventually full acceptance of the importance of modeling accompanied by the intention to obtain a model some day. Peer and

outside pressures and bandwagon effects may begin to play a strong role at this stage. The manager may request testimony from modelers, for example, before Congressional committees.

3. Procurement or development of a model, used by modelmakers or analysts, but with no active management participation.
4. Active management use of a model developed by others.
5. Interactive development of a new model by management and a modeling team. This is of course the ideal situation.

The question as to the use and usefulness of models has no straightforward answer because the answer must be qualified in terms of these stages. As to the increased number, variety, and availability of computer models, there is no debate. However, there are myriad instances of models, developed or procured because of bandwagon pressures and persuasive sales pitches by model builders, which have seen little or no use. Many managers have been disappointed and disillusioned by the modeling field. It is likely that surveys accurately report the development and location of models but overestimate the use of models.[32]

Models can be used in many ways. They can be used for scientific study such as theory-building and hypothesis-testing. They can be used for policy evaluation, policy analysis, planning, and as weapons of advocacy. It is imperative to distinguish among these uses. The manager who expects computer simulation models to be new types of the scientific method applied to decisionmaking exposes himself to certain disappointment. The Limits to Growth was not merely an academic study or a model to sit around until somebody found a use for it. It was a powerful means of communication by the Club of Rome to alert people about dangerous economic and ecological trends and to move them out of their ingrained habits.

As pointed out earlier, an effective computer simulation modeling *system* involves the continuing interactions among perceptions and interpretations of the real world, the model of that world, the modeler or modeling team, and the client or user. Disjunction among any of these elements reduces the meaningfulness and acceptability of the model. If the model is not isomorphic (having similar structure) with the real world, the model lacks fidelity, validity, or utility.

A computer simulation model may never be used, in spite of great efforts on the part of the modeler to involve the policymaker, for any number of significant reasons:

1. The modeler and policymaker may come from such different worlds as to make communications nearly impossible. For example, the modeler may live in a world of science, rational analysis, and arcane language that sounds like jargon; the policymaker usually lives in a world of power, persuasion, and influence.
2. The modeler may be unable to provide the *exact* answers required or desired for specific immediate decisions.

3. The modeler and policymaker may have different values, goals, priorities, and senses of urgency.
4. The policymaker may believe that he needs great detail, but be unable either to comprehend or digest this detail when it is provided, say, by a computer printout.
5. The policymaker may be awed by the computer and complicated concepts and mathematics, and he may consciously or subconsciously feel he is patronized or preached to by the modeler. He may believe the modeler is trying to steal his thunder. In retaliation, he may adopt an attitude of "not invented here."
6. The model may be so badly designed externally, that is, so poorly human engineered that both its purposes and output are incomprehensible to the user.
7. Even if none of the above be true, the outputs of computer simulation models of society may be bad news, threatening the most basically held values and beliefs, threatening the maintenance of current organizational structure and corporate status and power, and threatening the short-term projects that could assure reelection of the politician.

Many of these difficulties will be improved with time. Large-scale computer simulation modeling represents another evolutionary step along the path pioneered by operations research, human factors, and systems analysis. All these are simply methods of bringing scientific and technical expertise to bear on management functions. This is the rational approach.

Finally, computer models promise to become even greater weapons in the advocacy process. This is the arational approach. If a policymaker does not like the results of a given model, he can hire an alternate team of modelers to build a model which will work backwards from the desired political results. This situation has recently occurred with regard to the regulation/deregulation of price controls on natural gas.

FUTURES RESEARCH IN THE PRACTICE OF CORPORATE PLANNING: GENERAL ELECTRIC'S FUTURSCAN

Many of the methodologies just discussed are now being put into practical everyday use *on an integrated basis* at General Electric Company. General Electric's corporate planners use an online, interactive, computer-based system called FUTURSCAN.[33] FUTURSCAN provides several levels of sophistication, tailor-made to the needs of the individual manager at any given time. Also the system as a whole can serve as an input to other planning models.

At the simplest level the system can provide a listing of events of potential future importance. Equivalently, the user can request one or more of about 20 naive or straightforward extrapolations of the historical trend lines of indicators. The user can select just one of the FUTURSCAN elements, or he can mobilize all of them as a system. He can supply his own data if he so desires.

At the highest level the user can request a complete Business Environment Report, specifically prepared in his field. This report contains:

1. A full set of *FUTURSPECS* data units.
2. *Scenarios,* which could characterize the business environment to the year 2000, and which are presented in order of their probabilities and planning importance.
3. An *executive summary*.
4. An *annual update* relating to key policies and strategies.

The General Electric system consists of five modules:

1. A data base called *FUTURCASTS*.
2. *Trend Impact Analysis,* a modification of trends by event-impacts which we discussed earlier.
3. *Cross-Impact Analysis,* in the event-on-event form, which was discussed earlier.
4. *FUTURSPECS,* a single consolidated data unit.
5. *Probabilistic System Dynamics,* discussed earlier, as a means to scenario development.

The *FUTURCASTS data base* consists of a concise listing of thousands of potential social, economic, technological, and economic events stated in measurable terms, so that both the probability of occurrence of an event and the future impact of that event can be specified. Each week several hundred *updatings* are made. By means of a computer terminal the user is provided with:

An exact statement of each potential event, including its impact on selected indicator trends.

The probability the event will occur.

The year of this probable occurrence.

The source of the forecast, that is, (1) a literature search based on a reader network and an automated index service and involving some 5000 publications, and (2) a worldwide Delphi process which makes possible the forecasting of the probability and impact of events.

Trend-Impact Analysis once again is a form of events-on-trends cross-impact analysis. Using it, the manager can correct the naive extrapolation of the historical trend of an indicator according to that indicator's sensitivity to various numbers of events over a period of up to 100 years. The Trend-Impact Analysis projection shows three possible continuations of the forecasted indicator following a given impact. This sophisticated extrapolation displays a median trend line and upper and lower boundary lines. In addition, the manager can request a rank order of events used to make the projection and can reorder these events by priority as appropriate to planning. Managers may also make projections from various other data bases.

FUTURSCAN's *Cross-Impact Analysis* is based on the idea that events can do more than move a trend line up or down. Events can also trigger other events, altering the total organizational environment. Some potential events carry others along with them, while other events in a cluster may cancel one another out. Cross-Impact Analysis uses a matrix to indicate how a number of events related within some category, for example, energy, alter the initial probabilities of occurrence in some future years of other events in the same or another category.

A summary of the first three elements of FUTURSCAN is provided. A comprehensive data unit called *FUTURSPECS*, designed for convenience and readability, makes available to the manager the following six key types of information on each indicator:

1. A graph showing the historical trend-line of the indicator and its modification by future events, expressed as a sophisticated extrapolation containing a median trend-line and upper and lower boundary lines.
2. A list of related indicators allowing comparison with the given indicator.
3. A table of potential events.
4. A narrative describing recent developments and how future events will impact the indicator.
5. A narrative describing corporate implications of the future behavior of the indicator.
6. A bibliography of data sources and defined terms applicable to the indicator and events and impacts.

Probabilistic System Dynamics utilizes the Systems Dynamics National Model, modified to handle the probabilistic impact of potential future events. (Of course the National Model is still not complete, so only certain concepts can presently be used.) This methodology allows the manager to enter a potential strategy into the model. The model responds in terms of the likely success or failure of that strategy. A strategy intervention is interpreted much as a potential event would be. Thus, by using Probabilistic System Dynamics the manager receives advance notice of the impacts of his alternative corporate strategies and policies on likely future environments of the organization.

As we have also seen, a prominent feature in planning for alternative futures is the use of scenarios which could characterize the organizational environment up through the year 2000 and which can be used for *contingency* planning. For example, part of the comprehensive "Business Environment Report" could be an "Energy Report," which indicates the likelihood, starting with the highest, of several scenarios which could characterize the energy future:

Economic and social dislocation brought on by sudden oil shortages.

Energy interdependence.

Energy independence.

Various wild-card futures, for example, a total nuclear moratorium or acceptance of a low-energy, no-growth economy.

A planning system must be dynamically updatable. These energy scenarios have already been modified. The probability of energy interdependence has fallen, while that of economic and social dislocation has risen since the energy scenarios were first derived. As a tentative planning exercise, you should compare these points made about the energy future with those provided by the SPECULATER model. How would you structure this comparison? Where would you find the answers? Which approach, if either, is right? How would you apply the results?

MAKING THE *RIGHT* CHOICES

In terms of knowledge, the problems of managing even the most complex corporate or government organization can be placed into either of two broad orientations:

We do not understand the basic forces of the world and tomorrow the organization will founder on the hidden Shoals of Crisis.

There is plenty of information and methodology around, but we have not selected and organized it properly into useful knowledge so that tomorrow we shall steer the organization right smack into the Island of Crisis.

In the first case hidden forces may combine to form a superforce, slowly growing subsystems may coalesce, tension within an existing system may reach a breaking point, or an unknown threshold may suddenly be exceeded. New patterns or systems with completely different and unexpected properties may then *emerge*. We have very little theory to help us understand emergent phenomena, processes, and forms. Most of the methods of futures research examined in this chapter are inapplicable to problems of emergence. Pending development of means of handling emergence, the best available technique would be a systems dynamics–cross-impact analysis hybrid (like General Electric's FUTURSCAN) greatly augmented by incorporation of psychological, sociological, and cultural variables. However, in the long run no institution can survive without an understanding of emergence.

Looking at the second area note that to a very great extent there is no scarcity of information and techniques that could be used to help management. But the pieces may not fit into a cohesive pattern of know-how and indeed may be downright contradictory.

This chapter saw the techniques of futures research fall to some extent into neat sequences. Trend extrapolation, Delphi, and econometric modeling, for example, can be very useful for preliminary overviews of complex planning situations or for shorter-range planning. Systems dynamics is the best general purpose methodology for long-range planning, because of its emphasis on ongoing structural dynamics rather than on past data. Nevertheless, what does the manager do when different models convincingly produce diametrically opposite results or—even worse—different modelers using the same methodology produce diametrically opposite results?

The answers to this and related questions would be the encouragement of a new career field.[34] These new supergeneralists in this field could be called "Systems Integrators." These new careerists will serve as interfaces and interpreters between the planning, policymaking, and control functions of top management on the one hand and the challenges, threats, opportunities, and methodologies associated with the external and internal environments of the organization on the other. But these new careerists will not simply advise an otherwise passive management. An important part of their role will be training—keeping management current on the knowledge and skills necessary to anticipate and manage crises as the organization evolves.

EMERGENCE

These days the word emergence is *IN* as in emergent problems, emerging nations, and so on. However, these usages, in which emergence appears to be interchangeable with development, do not convey the true richness of the term. Consider an example of an emergent phenomenon. Metallic sodium is a soft, slippery, beige substance that, if dropped into water, will displace hydrogen and lead to other chemical changes, producing an explosion. Elemental chlorine is a greenish-yellow toxic gas that, if inhaled, can lead to death. In fact, chlorine was used as a poison gas in World War I. When the ions of these elements are combined, however, the result is the white crystalline cubes called sodium chloride or common table salt. In rising from the atomic level to the molecular level involving two different elements, the *emergence of new properties* has been illustrated. This is the deep essence of the word emergence. The same ideas apply to movement between all the other adjacent levels of organization, even though myriad complex subsystems are involved rather than two simple chemical elements.

Another point must be stressed here, namely, the degree of *predictability* of the new properties emerging from the interaction of elements or subsystems. Generally, emergent phenomena have not been, a priori, predictable. However, this statement should be qualified. Prediction is enhanced if:

1. It is possible to *work back and forth* between or among levels of organization. This situation has been true to a considerable extent in science, especially in physical science. For example, we know a great deal about how atoms combine to form molecules because we have long been able to work at both the atomic and molecular levels and to deal with processes like ionization that operate between levels. However, had we been able to work only, say, with sodium chloride *or* only with elemental sodium and chlorine, it is highly unlikely that we should have been able to predict behavior at one level solely from knowledge of behavior at the other level. Thus as the history of chemistry successfully demonstrates, *analysis must be well integrated with synthesis.*

2. A faithful (high in fidelity) theory or model can be devised. A familiar example is the periodic law in chemistry. From a knowledge of the groups and periods in the periodic table of chemical elements, plus of course the underlying knowledge about atomic structure and quantum theory, it is possible to predict both the existence and general properties of elements before they are actually discovered.

The *forms* of interest in this book will emerge mostly in the future and will involve several levels of organization. Obviously one cannot easily work back and forth between or among loosely specified levels in combinations that do not yet exist. Therefore, we shall have to rely on theories and models of changes in form that appear to be equally applicable in the past, present, and future.

Before proceeding further, however, the points made or alluded to earlier about the new field theory of complex organizations will be briefly indicated. Field theory as emphasized here involves:

Much greater concern with forces and patterns or configurations than with individual trends.

Much greater concern with collectivities than with simple aggregates.

Thresholds.

Spontaneous behaviors, for example, fluctuations.

Discontinuities and sudden jumps.

Much greater concern with wholes than with parts.

Reconfiguration of structure or function with the emergence of new properties.

Irreversibility as well as reversibility of behavior.

Mutual causality.

Feedback dynamics.

Polarization, tension, conflict, divergence, and splitting in behavior.

Diffusion and contagion processes.

Critical points and ranges.

Morphogenesis or the creation *and* destruction of form.

Self-organizing behavior.

Behavior at points or under conditions far from equilibrium.

Universality of certain types of behavior.

Unification of laws explaining apparently quite different types of behavior.

Many of these points are interrelated. Given one point, a person may then seek other points. For the moment the above can serve as a checklist for organizations and environments amenable to the modern field-theoretic approach. Most of the terms and ideas may be quite different from those currently employed by executives. They are, however, part of the vocabulary of the next generation of top-management thinking.

FLUCTUATIONS, CRITICAL PHENOMENA, AND THE EMERGENCE OF COLLECTIVE BEHAVIOR

Physical Field Theory

No system and no environment is completely stable. Nor should they be. Nor should the systems of major concern seek over longer periods to return to the same equilibrium. *Fluctuations*—local instabilities or variations from the average—often enhanced by nonequilibrium conditions, are essential to certain changes in state and to evolution.

The main thrust here is behavior around *critical points or ranges,* above and below which the system exists in qualitatively different states or may even no longer exist as the same system. The levels of organization that will be considered first are the subatomic, the atomic, and the molecular. At all these levels the interest is in how simple behavior of the individual, say, particle leads to collective behavior with emergent new properties. Significantly, the relevant processes involve dissimilar physical and chemical substances. The changes in behavior of these substances are called *critical phenomena.*

In most cases temperature is a main or the main causal or independent variable. Therefore, this section and the next section can be considered to be extensions of the discussions on thermodynamics initiated in Chapter 1.

Critical phenomena have been known since the nineteenth century when deviations from Boyle's law relating the pressure and volume of a gas were observed. At a certain critical point (the gas-liquid phase transition point) the gaseous and liquid forms of a pure fluid can coexist. Boyle's law no longer applies and must be modified by van der Waals equation. Critical points also define temperatures above which metallic alloys lose the ordered arrangement among atoms, superconductors lose the property of superconductivity, and ferromagnets lose their magnetism.

Critical phenomena are due to strongly nonlinear interactions among atoms. They are also strongly associated with fluctuations. Until recently physicists did not have the conceptual and mathematical tools to deal with these complexities. The separate theories of superfluidity, ferromagnetism, and so on had been unified by L. D. Landau in 1937 into a mean field theory that ignored fluctuations. More recent and refined experimentation has shown mean field theory to be quantitatively wrong although qualitatively correct and has rectified many of the limitations of the earlier field theory.

The fluctuations in system state that develop near the critical points may take the form of volumes of greater density *embedded* in larger volumes of lesser density, which in turn are embedded in even larger volumes of greater density, and so on. Instead of density, the state may be the presence or absence of magnetization, the miscibility or immiscibility of liquids, or the presence or absence of the orderly arrangement of metal atoms in an alloy.

Well above a critical point, the system elements are arranged essentially randomly, and the system possesses only *short-range order.* As the critical point is reached from above, larger-scale order *begins to emerge.* At the critical value itself of, say, a temperature, disconnected patches representing order *abruptly expand* to infinite size. Even so, within the larger pattern, fluctuations at successively lesser scales persist.

A critical point thus represents a *discontinuity,* above and below which the system is *qualitatively different.* Below a critical temperature the particular property of the system may increase continuously in strength (for example, magnetization) or may fall off from the maximum observed at the critical point (for example, magnetic susceptibility, the change in magnetization for a given small change in an applied magnetic field).

This brief discussion of physical field theory and critical phenomena is included here to emphasize that general laws apply to physical, biological, and social systems. This should be evident later on. However, recognizing that most executives do not have the background or interest to pursue these theoretical matters further, additional discussion will be relegated to the Notes and References.[1]

Extension of Theory to Living Systems

The concepts of fluctuation, criticality, correlation across a field, and so on also apply to complex living systems, such as biological organization. For example, molecular biologists have studied the assembly of molecules into organized structures.[2]

Social systems have also been studied using these approaches. Throughout this book we have emphasized the *organization* of system elements and subsystems over their detailed study at given isolated levels. Individual behavior in the context of a higher organizational level may be either simple or greatly modified by virtue of incorporation into the greater whole. As in physics a higher statistical level containing concepts like entropy and order parameter may be defined independently of the particular properties at the individual level. Important qualitative insights at the higher level can often be obtained without having to specify the precise form of fundamental interactions.

Some social system behavior appears to be analogous to the phase transitions in physical and biological systems. Competitions between fluctuations and cooperative interactions produce similar macroscopic behavior above, at, and below some critical value. For example, there can be competition between independent behavior at the individual human level and cooperative interaction at a higher social or sociotechnical level. Indeed, economic thinking since Adam Smith has to a great extent centered on the questions of whether and to what degree competition of individual market forces yields a cooperative social product that benefits all.

As executives know it is often necessary to study complex systems probabilistically. In the systems under discussion only probabilistic predictions are made with regard to individual human behavior, individual fluctuations, individual mutations, and so forth. Such probabilistic behavior is of course a function of many direct and indirect interactions among individuals. Often in societal evolution a small, potentially influential, and largely self-contained group or subsystem will arise. Rock-music groups, groups with liberal sex and/or drug-use practices, the original members of the late 1960s' counterculture, certain cultists, and some communist and fascist groups provide some recent examples. The probabilistic behavior of each member of the small group, and the consequent large statistical fluctuations within this group, may *trigger* the statistical macroscopic behavior of the entire society. The fluctuations of the small group are transferred and enlarged into the collective behavior of the society as a whole. Whether or not any given fluctuations will have this effect or not at any given time is a function of the variety within and stability of society, the presence or absence of critical points and thresholds, and the ability of the society to damp the fluctuations. It is obvious, of course, that too much stability and too much damping can stifle desirable societal change.[3]

An interesting model of social behavior incorporating several of the ideas discussed in this section is described in *Collective Phenomena* by Professor D. F. Walls.[4] Walls uses the properties of a Markovian master equation to derive nonequilibrium phase transitions applicable to the conversion of members of a larger general population to the way of thinking or behaving of a small group of proselytizers.

The mathematical model utilizes some advanced forms of the Markov processes mentioned previously. Actually, because of lasting and indirect effects of earlier situations, societal evolution is in the long run strongly non-Markovian. The future state of society depends not only on the present state, but also on all past states that may still affect system behavior. However, by stretching the limits of the present state, the ahistoricity constraint of Markov processes can be relaxed. *The incipient, latent, and pretransitional processes must never be overlooked.* Nevertheless, many societal phenomena *appear* to happen suddenly, and a short-term or local approach assuming instantaneous interactions may be of value in developing further insights and workable constructs.

In Walls's model conversion to the way of thinking or behaving of the proselytizers is a function of a *social temperature.* Conversion can flow both ways, and indeed in real life social movements often build up, peak, and then wither away until they include only the diehard few. In the model there is a threshold above which an increasingly discontented population swings to the side of the proselytizers. Walls considers this analogous to a second-order phase transition—like the critical point of the gas-liquid transition.

Well below the critical-temperature threshold, the steady-state distribution follows a power-law probability distribution, but well above the threshold the steady-state distribution follows a Poisson probability form. Walls interprets this narrowing of the distribution above the threshold as the onset of collective behavior in the society. Below the threshold the distribution indicates independent behavior; above the threshold a sense of order is established. Alternatively, behavior below the critical point represents a maximum entropy for a mean number of proselytes. Above the threshold there is a relative decrease in entropy.

The mathematical model indicates, as a time-dependent Markovian master equation, the probability that at a given time a certain number of people will hold the beliefs of the proselytizers. Unfortunately, such equations are almost impossible to solve. They are approximated by another type of equation, called a Fokker-Planck equation. Once again note that most problems of complex living systems transcend quantitative solutions—it is in the qualitative aspects of mathematics that we may seek constructs or explanatory building blocks for models of complexity.

It should be noted that this model operates within a critical range. The highest physical or "social" temperatures would of course be associated with dissolution, breakdown, randomness, and increased entropy.

Another version of the Walls model deals with a first-order phase transition, like that shown by the ferromagnet discussed earlier. This model introduces several phenomena which will be of interest in our discussion of catastrophe theory later. In this (deterministic) version, relating to *three-body interactions,* the steady-state solution of the pertinent equation yields *two stable solutions* and an *intermediate unstable solution.* One of the stable solutions represents a small number of proselytizers and the other a large number of proselytizers. A plot of the number of proselytizers against the social temperature is shown in Figure 5.1.

This is a *hysteresis* (irreversible path) curve suggestive of a *fold catastrophe.* As the social temperature *(T)* gradually increases from near zero, the number of proselytizers *(X)* remains on the lower branch of the curve until *T* exceeds a critical value *(T₂)* beyond which the number of proselytes *suddenly* increases to a much higher value represented by the upper branch. However, if the social temperature subsequently decreases, the number of proselytes does not fall back to the lower branch until *T* falls to a value *(T₁)* below the original critical temperature.

In a stochastic extension of the deterministic model, Walls uses a Markovian master equation and its steady-state solution like that mentioned above. In a plot of the probability that a given number of people will hold the beliefs of the proselytizers against the total number of the latter for various social

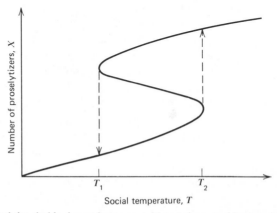

Figure 5.1 Critical thresholds, jumps between stable numbers, and hysteresis. (Modified from reference 26, page 128.) (Copyright Gordon & Breach Science publishers)

temperatures, a *bimodal* probability distribution occurs near the critical point. The two maxima represent metastable states and the minimum and unstable state. The two stable states remain so as long as fluctuations are below a critical size. Fluctuations above the critical size will drive the system into the other state.

DISSIPATIVE STRUCTURES AND SELF-ORGANIZATION FAR FROM EQUILIBRIUM

Many executives will already be familiar with the name and work of Professor Ludwig von Bertalanffy. Bertalanffy, a biologist, was a pioneering thinker in the area of open systems. He was also a founding father of the school of thinking called general systems theory. Bertalanffy argued forcefully that open systems did not operate in terms of the thermodynamic or chemical equilibrium characteristic of isolated and closed systems. Open systems operate far from equilibrium and consequently can do work.

Organizations and societies *are* open systems possessing certain properties as indicated in Chapter 1. However, until recently, the applications of thermodynamics and open systems concepts to organizations and societies appeared to have become exhausted. The application of the Entropy Law to economics and ecology, discussed earlier is one exciting new development. So is the concept of dissipative structures.

For executives, the advanced new ideas under discussion may just turn out to be the only ones of much value in interpreting the future evolution of organization-environment interrelationships.

The New Theory

Important new interpretations of thermodynamics and statistical mechanics, and of the behavior of open systems far from equilibrium have been made by Ilya Prigogine and his colleagues (the "Brussels school").[5] Some of this work earned Professor Prigogine a Nobel Prize in chemistry in 1977. Many of the underlying ideas and the supportive mathematics stem from problems in physical chemistry.

Nonequilibrium thermodynamics, and especially advances in fluctuation theory, provide improved tools for understanding the emergence and self-organization of new structures.

The older thermodynamics as applied to problems in physics and physical chemistry dealt mainly with equilibrium conditions. Readers may recall from a chemistry course the Gibb's phase rule dealing with equilibria between phases (like solid, liquid, or gas) of pure substances and the law of mass action. In the latter, say, two reagents yield two products in a *reversible* reaction. The equilibrium point can be shifted to the right or left by changing concentrations of reagents or products, but the system remains an equilibrium system. Crystals are familiar examples of equilibrium structures. And thermal engines operate according to equilibrium processes.

Thermodynamics can now be thought of as concerned with the processes of *evolution* of macroscopic systems consisting of large numbers of more microscopic elements.

The second law of thermodynamics deals largely with the difference between reversible and irreversible processes. The distinction is expressed quantitatively by the measurable property, entropy. Entropy production is always positive in isolated and closed systems and is due entirely to irreversible processes. But living systems are open systems and would seem at first glance to be far removed from the laws of physics. However, *specific nonlinear interactions under conditions far from thermodynamic equilibrium can lead to the emergence of a new order.* Professor Prigogine calls this "order through fluctuations" to contrast it with order in equilibrium systems.

Before continuing, the term nonlinear should be qualified. In Chapter 3, both in the text and graphically, linear and nonlinear growth and evolution were contrasted. For example, exponential and hyperbolic growth are nonlinear. But not much was said about the underlying equations. Most of the work discussed here is based on the solution or approximation of nonlinear differential equations. Consider the simple example,

$$\frac{dy}{dt} = ay^2 + by + c$$

The *dy* and *dt*, representing arbitrarily or instantaneously small quantities, are called differentials—hence, the name for the type of equation. The equation is nonlinear because of the term y^2. Squared, cubed, and other power terms, exponential terms, logarithmic terms, and so on indicate nonlinearity in an equation. Incidentally, one solution (integration) to the above equation yields the logistic function.

Nonlinear differential equations are notoriously difficult to solve—if indeed they can be solved—especially if they are also higher order (containing, say, an acceleration term), partial (dealing with two or more independent variables), have variable coefficients, and are parts of a set or system of equations. The strongly nonlinear interactions among atoms that underlie critical phenomena only recently became amenable to mathematical treatment. It may be that some of the advanced mathematics used in theoretical physics and cosmology will eventually prove applicable to organizations, societies, and ecosystems. However, progress in the latter fields is limited much more by the mundane problems of data and politics and by a dearth of innovative new ideas (except in ecology) than by the absence of the most sophisticated mathematical techniques.

Returning now to the main theme, biological and social structures can be considered to emerge both from interactions with the environment and from events occurring *spontaneously* in the open systems maintained far from equilibrium.

Open systems can variously present pictures of:

1. Thermodynamic equilibrium in which flows have eliminated concentration or temperature differences, entropy has increased, and uniformity exists.

2. Slight disequilibrium associated with small concentration or temperature differences. The Brussels school calls this "a state of linear equilibrium." The system is stable along the thermodynamic branch of system states unless some critical or bifurcation point is reached. Beyond this point alternately stable or unstable solutions to equations are possible. The thermodynamic solution permits of no new organization.

3. A state of being driven far from equilibrium. This situation, plus nonlinear interactions of system elements, can result in the spontaneous appearance of new organizations and structures—the so-called *dissipative structures*. ("Dissipative structure" is a somewhat unfortunate term because the popular uses of the term dissipation convey almost the opposite meaning to what Prigogine intends, namely, scattering, wastage, and even debauchery.) Albeit, dissipative structures can be further characterized as follows: They

    a. May, in contrast to equilibrium structures, show coherent behavior from the cooperation of many elements.

    b. Can appear as wholes with their dimensions due to their own underlying processes.

    c. Can arise at critical points in the state of the system at which stability changes into instability.

    d. Can arise when small perturbations or fluctuations, instead of dying out or remaining constant, are greatly amplified.

Other properties of dissipative structures will follow in the course of the discussion.

A laser is an example of a dissipative structure. Another simple physical example can be observed when a pan of liquid is heated evenly from below. At lower temperatures heat transfer is by conduction. At more intense heating to a critical temperature gradient, hexagonally-shaped convection cells *suddenly appear spontaneously*. The energy of thermal agitation is transferred to macroscopic convection currents showing an emergent molecular organization. In this case some small convection currents always occur as fluctuations from the average state, but below the critical value of the temperature gradient they are damped and disappear. Above the critical value selected fluctuations are amplified producing the macroscopic current and the new order. In one sense, therefore, a dissipative structure is viewed by the Brussels school as a huge fluctuation stabilized by matter-energy interchanges with the environment.

Work on chemical reactions (chemical kinetics) provided the basic models for Prigogine's generalizations to biological and social systems.[6] The terminology in this area is not standardized, therefore, some interpretations are offered. A *fluctuation* is a *seemingly* sudden, spontaneous, and often unexpected variation from the average in a variable describing the state of a system. A *perturbation* is a change in system structure or behavior imposed by an environmental stressor and associated with a weakening of linkages between subsystems. The small ongoing, random variations at any system level are usually referred to as *noise*. All these changes can of course reinforce one another, leading to a reconfiguration of the whole system field.

Because of these changes no system state will remain—or should remain—indefinitely stable. All open systems are continually being stressed by combinations of these changes, which sometimes ignite the field and produce massive reconfiguration.

Considering the many varieties of systems of interest to us, the types of fluctuations tend to be quite numerous. There can be fluctuations in physical variables like temperature, pressure, density, and concentration. There can be fluctuations in the biosphere and in the distribution of natural resources. Differentiation within a previously homogeneous organization can be a fluctuation. Mutations and innovations are other types of fluctuations.

The system itself or the interactions between system and environment prevents most small changes from being amplified, becoming interconnected, and causing the system to ignite. In chemical systems near equilibrium, for example, molecular motion produces local fluctuations in concentration. However, the system reacts in order to minimize the free energy, and this perpetuates the stability of the given state.

There appear to be qualitative as well as quantitative differences among fluctuations. Relatively few are selected to play a role in major system change. Only certain fluctuations attain a *coherence length*, an essential size under nonequilibrium conditions. Further, the probability distributions are very different for large and for small fluctuations.

A system driven further and further from equilibrium can progressively *branch* into many different solutions to the underlying equations. At the branches the mathematics of bifurcations and catastrophes (which will be discussed in the next section) can be applied.

Stability in the mathematical sense has certain definite meanings. The solution of some differential equations requires an intermediate equation called a characteristic equation. The more system elements in interaction, the higher the degree of the characteristic equation determining the characteristic frequencies of the system, the greater the chance of there being a positive root and therefore instability. With at least one positive root of a frequency the expression $e^{\omega t}$, where ω is a frequency and t is time, will tend to infinity and the system will explode. Stability occurs if the real parts of all the roots are negative or vanishing.

As emphasized earlier system growth and evolution are scarcely possible without a considerable amount of reinforcement. *Nucleations* represent such cooperative ventures that are important to the formation of dissipative structures. One type of nucleation results from seeding a chemical reaction, something you may recall from a chemistry course. A liquid drop in supersaturated vapor provides another example—below a critical size the droplet is unstable, while above the critical size the droplet grows and helps convert more vapor into liquid. The hydrocarbon micelles mentioned in the preceding section represent another type of nucleation, as do the groups of proselytizers discussed in that section.

All the field-theoretic phenomena described here variously involve competition, conflict, cooperation, and cohesion or the four Cs. The same is true of the size of nucleations. Two types of antagonistic forces are involved. Instabilities associated with interactions inside the system tend to amplify certain fluctuations. But the outside environment acts as a *mean field* (qualitative approximation in the absence of precise quantitative tools) that more or less damps the fluctuations through interactions at the system boundary. For small fluctuations the boundary effects predominate, and the fluctuations regress. However, in the case of large fluctuations, the boundary effects are negligible. The actual size of a nucleation is a function of processes at the two extremes.

The importance of transitions, transformations, and evolution-revolution has been repeatedly emphasized. In the evolution and reconfiguration of systems generally, deterministic processes appear to predominate during some periods and probabilistic or stochastic processes during others. Although in the evolution of living systems deterministic and probabilistic periods alternate, this situation should by no means be thought of as simple periodicity with eventual returns to former system states. Movement of the system through time produces qualitative and irreversible changes.

The continuing cooperation between deterministic and stochastic processes leads to evolving systems. In the deterministic periods averages or simple aggregates may represent accurately the state of the system. Stochastic processes are of significance during periods of instability and bifurcation points. *Critical events*, for example, the appearance of discoveries, inventions, and great people, are particularly characteristic of points of instability.

It is not possible to predict a priori the appearance of a given fluctuation at a given time or whether any given fluctuation will be selected for amplification. However, in the nonlinear systems far from equilibrium, the fluctuation that comes first and grows fastest may drive the system to a new stable state. Once a fluctuation, of stochastic origin, has caught on, deterministic processes then take over to produce macroscopic order—once again, order through fluctuations.

It is difficult to say exactly just how much stability a system or system-environment interrelationship *should* have at any given time. In person-related systems the normative values of those having vested interests are obviously important. Yet the natural evolution of these systems may run quite counter to the desires and expectations of the stakeholders.

Two more terms should be defined. A *metastable* system is somewhat less than stable under the given conditions. This term has long been used in physical chemistry. An *ultrastable* system is somewhat greater than stable under given conditions that include both the known and unknown or unpredicted. The term was designed by cybernetician, W. Ross Ashby, to deal with problems of homeostatic regulation. Both these concepts are extremely important to the design of adaptive systems. Together they offer another instance of the *complementarity* of evolutionary/morphogenetic and regulatory/cybernetic processes.

Professor Prigogine and his colleagues regard sufficiently complex systems as usually being in a metastable state. The threshold for metastability is, once again, a function of competition between growth and the damping effects on the boundary between system and environment. This situation may place some limits on complexity, a topic introduced earlier. Complexity of a given system at a given time is limited by stability, which is in turn limited by the strength of the system-environment coupling. A very tight coupling between system and environment may perpetuate a stability for a long time beyond what otherwise would have been possible. But if the environment suddenly changes, this coupling will most likely be broken, with the system facing imminent collapse. This is a fundamental theme of this book. The large-scale bureaucratic organizations discussed in Chapter 3 appear to illustrate the type systems we are considering here.

Prigogine points out that no ecological—and I add societal—equations can be structurally stable to all possible mutations and innovations. Thus there is bound to be continuous diversification and expansion into areas of unused freedom.

Although individual organisms and organizations may reach the limit to complexity and become extinct, the course of evolution as a whole has been toward increased complexity. Whether or not contemporary human organizations are now rapidly approaching the limits to their own complexity in the present stage of the evolution of living systems is a concern we raised in the first pages of this book.

It is important to note again that the question of limits to systems growth and complexity has been raised from a number of different perspectives. With regard to approaches discussed in this book, greatest concern has also been expressed by cyberneticians, systems dynamicists, hyperbolic growth theorists, and scholars at Stanford Research International.

In conclusion, the basic ideas of the Brussels school can be summarized as follows: *Nonequilibrium conditions lead to exceeding a threshold, which increases instability through structural fluctuation, which in turn leads to the production of dissipative structures. The last, in a feedback loop, modifies the threshold. Such evolutionary feedback results in evolution through a succession of transitions.*

These dynamics can be shown as follows:[7]

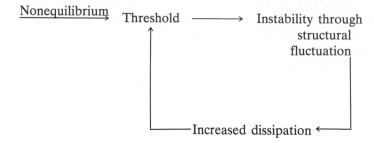

Further Applications of Theory to Living Systems

The theory developed by the Brussels school can be applied to a wide variety of threshold and saturation behavior, qualitative-quantitative differences in behavior, critical phenomena, collective phenomena, and emergent phenomena in living systems.[8]

Earlier Walls's model of the increase of proselytes as a function of social temperature was discussed. In a somewhat similar vein Prigogine describes oscillations between autocratic and democratic social structures among the Kachin tribes of northern Burma.[9] When the prestige of a new chief is greater than dissatisfaction with ascension, the autocratic regime remains stable. On the other hand, if dissatisfaction is greater than prestige, the introduction into the system of a few rebellious persons drives the system into a revolutionary state as the number of rebels increases explosively.

Certain previous theory and findings in cultural anthropology and in sociology have proved to fit well with the work of the Brussels school.

Back in the 1860s and 1870s the biologist, evolutionist, and sociologist, Herbert Spencer, distinguished between *growth* and *development* in evolution. Growth and development alternated—beyond a critical point there could be no further growth without further organization.

Spencer's ideas have been greatly extended by Dr. Robert L. Carneiro, an anthropologist at the American Museum of Natural History.[10] In further differentiating between growth and development, Carneiro notes that growth:

Consists of an increase in substance.

Is usually manifested by a proliferation of structures *already present*.

Is essentially *quantitative*.

Can proceed, in the absence of new structures, only up to a point; beyond this point existing structure cannot support further growth, and growth declines or ceases.

Development on the other hand:

Consists of an increase in structure.

Is characterized by the *emergence of new* structural forms.

Is essentially *qualitative*.

Is a response by the growing system to an increase in scale.

Dr. Carneiro writes—in a statement that excellently summarizes some major themes of this book:[11]

> But while growth tends to be continuous . . . development is generally *discontinuous* and *abrupt*. It proceeds by a series of *jumps*, however small, *from one level of organization to the next* . . . change in natural phenomena proceeds by the *accumulation* of relatively small quantitative increments, which, every so often, results in a *sudden transformation* and the *emergence of something new and qualitatively different*. (emphasis added)

Dr. Carneiro is one of the relatively few social scientists to have conducted extensive *longitudinal* studies. He has examined the evolution of cultures worldwide, particularly with reference to the *cumulative* development of traits. Examples of traits are special religious practitioners (found in almost every society), markets, census taken, and empire (characteristic of relatively few societies).

Carneiro selected Anglo-Saxon England (449–1087) for a special study of evolutionary sequence. Fitting his data, he found two straight lines and two linear regression equations (Figure 5.2). But these lines had notably different slopes, and the year 650 appeared to be an inflection point. Carneiro interpreted this point not as a slowing down of growth but as a discontinuity. That is, cultural change between 450 and 650 represented mainly development, and change from 650 to 1087 indicated mainly growth. The second period represented a consolidation and spread of innovations made or obtained during the first period. Stochastic processes operated more in the first less stable period and deterministic processes more in the second period.

In conclusion, the processes discussed in this section will continue to operate—but at an accelerated rate! The succession of structural instabilities will continue as a function of explosive sociotechnical change. Efforts to reestablish equilibrium will collide with limits because the entire world-system field is rapidly reconfiguring. Most existing societal institutions will find it ever harder to cope with increasingly greater perturbations. Sociotechnical advances will continue to lead to an ever-expanding exploitation of natural resources. Entropy production per individual person and/or worldwide will continue to increase, at least in the thermodynamic sense if not in the

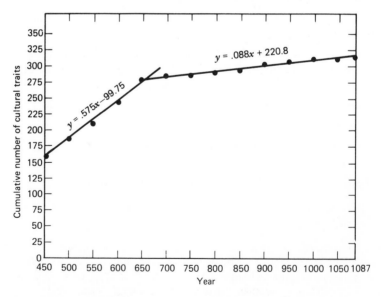

Figure 5.2. Linear regression lines suggesting development, discontinuity, and growth in Anglo-Saxon England. (Adapted from reference 6, page 1019). Copyright New York Academy of Sciences. Courtesy of Dr. Robert L. Carneiro

informational sense. A mighty force with essentially irreversible effects has been unleashed.

The adaptive organization will be the organization that can think in terms of fields of forces, that can anticipate likely alternative reconfigurations, and that can elaborate a structure characterized as much by self-organization as by self-regulation.

CATASTROPHE THEORY

In a number of places such terms as discontinuity, sudden jump, abrupt change, divergence, splitting, stability, bifurcation, criticality, hysteresis, and qualitative have been used. Catastrophe theory is an exciting and very controversial recent outgrowth of the abstruse mathematical specialties of topology, structural stability theory, and bifurcation theory that deals with the concepts embodied by these terms.

To understand and use catastrophe theory, one has to have a bit of patience and good faith. One has to make several rather far-reaching basic assumptions; a new vocabulary is needed; and historical, field, and experimental validation still have a long way to go. Catastrophe theory, nevertheless, is an invaluable means of conceptualizing the field-theoretic, reconfigurational, and emergent behavior of complex systems. These are the interrelationships:

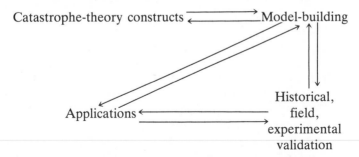

In brief catastrophe theory can provide invaluable insights toward further theory- and model-building, its own validation, and applications. But applying catastrophe theory now need not depend on validation in the traditional sense—which quantitatively may never be done in the systems of interest here.

The Basic Theory

Catastrophe theory is the discovery of French topologist René Thom. The terms in the title of his book, *Structural Stability and Morphogenesis,* reveal something about what catastrophe theory is trying to do.[12] However, Thom's approach is by itself rather hard to understand and to apply. The modifications and interpretations of British mathematician E. Christopher Zeeman are more concrete and form the basis for much of the following discussion.[13]

A basic feature of catastrophe theory is *Thom's Classification Theorem* as modified by Zeeman. Although the proof of this theorem is formidable, the results are held to be straightforward and relatively easy to apply. In the catastrophe-theory literature the depth and generality of the theorem are often stressed. The theorem can be summarized as follows: *For every situation representable by up to five* independent, causal, or control *variables and one or more* dependent, effect, or behavior *variables, there is a set of* potential functions *such that*

1.   *A line or three-to many-dimensional surface called a* manifold *can be conceptualized.*
2.   *Each* singularity (breakoff point, line, or surface) *is locally equivalent to one of a finite number of* elementary catastrophes.
3.   *The situation is structurally stable at each point of the manifold with regard to small perturbations of the potential function.*
4.   *Because of the qualitative equivalency of topological maps and graphs, a* canonical *form of the potential function can be substituted for the actual potential function, which may never be known.*

With large numbers of control and behavior variables and therefore dimensions, an infinite number of catastrophe types could be conceived. At least 25 have been identified. However, only some 7 to 11 (up to four or five control variables) have received much study, and of these only three are of immediate interest.

The first four of the elementary catastrophes are the *fold*, the *cusp*, the *swallowtail*, and the *butterfly*. The next higher-level catastrophes are called *umbilicals*. In this book only the fold, cusp, and butterfly catastrophes are considered. Following Professor Zeeman, note that only these catastrophes can be easily relatable to probability distributions—respectively, the monomodal, bimodal, and trimodal distributions.

Catastrophe theory is based on certain assumptions. One assumption is that the potential function, once acknowledged, is *smooth*, that is, infinitely differentiable to all orders (first derivative, second derivative, and so on in the language of the calculus). One "very obvious catastrophe," the liquid–gas phase transition—the most familiar critical phenomenon discussed here—does not behave like a cusp catastrophe because at the critical point there is a discontinuity in a second derivative.

Much more tenuous is the assumption of the existence of a potential function at all. The term potential has been extended from its familiar use in classical mechanics, for example, in potential energy. The potential function is expressed in terms of the control and behavior variable. Basically the system tries to minimize the potential function in response to some change or perturbation involving the control variable. Mathematically, *gradient dynamics* are said to apply to the system.

The potential function is alternatively called an *energy function*, an *entropy* function, a *cost function,* or a *probability* (distribution) *function.* In some cases, particularly those involving probability distributions, a function is maximized rather than minimized.

The idea that the true nature of the potential function does not have to be known but only its canonical equivalent is nevertheless appealing and is consistent with observations of many phenomena and processes in organizations and society. These include motivational dynamics, value change, political power and influence, conflict, economic stability and instability, perceptual shifts, and others we shall consider later.

One other feature here of the system's search for a stable minimum or maximum should be mentioned. In some cases a system seeks a *local* value and is said to follow the Delay Rule—it delays until the last moment in making a catastrophic jump. In other cases the system jumps immediately to the *global* value and is said to follow Maxwell's Rule.

With this introduction a catastrophe can now be defined. *Whenever a continuously changing force yields an abruptly changing effect, the phenomenon can be described as a catastrophe.* A small change in stimuli or initial conditions can produce a major change in behavior or system state. A slight quantitative change in the continuous processes potentially describable by a differential equation can produce the sudden emergence of a qualitatively different kind of behavior. In short catastrophe theory is a means of explaining how discontinuities arise from continuously changing causal factors.

A catastrophe is shown on a graph or diagram by the sudden jump or fall to another level or surface as the system passes a critical point or region, the singularity. In the literature as a whole, the terms catastrophe, discontinuity, singularity, and sudden jump are roughly synonynous.

A rich attribute of catastrophe theory is its embodiment of several otherwise apparently unrelated phenomena and processes. Some of these have been met before, and catastrophe theory suggests that when one is present the others should be searched for. These five properties suggest use of the *cusp* catastrophe, for example:

1. *Bimodality* of behavior in at least part of its range. For example, a population, continuously distributed, could show two statistical modes or peaks or high points rather far removed from one another. The two modes could represent qualitatively very different values, attitudes, beliefs, motivations, consumer-brand preferences, or voting behaviors. The trough between the two modes would represent the least likely or least probable behavior. It should be noted that in this case the potential function would be a probability distribution and we would be dealing with stable maxima rather than with stable minima. The minimum would represent unstable behavior. The well-known probability functions like the normal, gamma, and exponential do not deal with bimodality.

2. An *inaccessible region* representing least likely behavior. If the potential function is to be maximized, the minimum would represent an

intermediate unstable and therefore inaccessible region. If the potential function is to be minimized, the opposite would apply. On control-behavior graphs of the cusp catastrophe, the inaccessible region is usually displayed by a middle sheet *over which* behavior jumps.

3.   The *catastrophes themselves,* that is, the discontinuities or sudden jumps from one mode of behavior to another.

4.   *Hysteresis,* a lag in behavioral response due to inertia in the system. Hysteresis can also be interpreted as path irreversibility because the jump from the top sheet of the behavior surface does not occur at the same place as the jump from the bottom sheet. Thus behavior will follow one path when a control variable increases and another path when the variable decreases.

5.   *Divergence* of two pathways on the behavior surface on either side of the pleat formed by folding the surface. Divergence represents behavior, starting with nearly identical conditions, which evolves into very different final states.

Let's also mention here several other attributes of catastrophe theory in general:

1.   *Sequences of catastrophes.* There are two ways to look at this situation:
     a.   Higher-dimension catastrophes also incorporate lower-dimension catastrophes or portions thereof. Thus, according to the Classification Theorem, in the cusp catastrophe, which contains only two control variables, the only singularities are fold *curves* and cusp *points*. In the butterfly catastrophe, which has four control variables, the only *complete* singularities of the manifold are cusp *surfaces* and butterfly *points*. The butterfly catastrophe also incorporates fold *solids* and swallowtail *curves*. The fold catastrophe, having only one control variable, of course, shows singularities only at the fold *points*.
     b.   The elementary catastrophes are held to represent local rather than global phenomena. Of course what is local and what is global are often arbitrarily determined. In mathematics the terms often apply to the relative sizes and locations of maxima or minima. In our applications of catastrophe theory to real-world situations, all the phenomena are considered to be global and to represent concatenations of the elementary catastrophes.

2.   The behavior surface or manifold is an *equilibrium* surface. It is made up of a very large number of fixed points. The surface corresponds to the great many local maxima or minima of the potential function or rather its canonical, topological, and qualitative equivalent. The behavior surface is the graph of all the points at which the appropriate first ordinary or partial derivative equals zero. For each coordinate point on the control-variable surface, there is at least one point that can be placed directly above and at a height consistent with the magnitude of the behavior.

As seen in the preceding section, many of the most interesting—and perhaps most important—forms of emergent new structure arise far from equilibrium. Catastrophe theory may be of limited usefulness in nonequilibrium systems and under conditions far from equilibrium. The underlying assumptions may have to be bent to make it fit the more complex situations.

3. The *exact values* of the control and behavior variables, very fortunately, *need not be known.* Indeed, they may be *ordinal-level* variables, that is variables expressed only as greater than, lesser than, increasing, or decreasing.

4. Catastrophe theory is basically *deterministic.* Given the appropriate values of the control variables and the exceeding of a threshold (singularity), a catastrophic change invariably occurs. As already seen, combinations or sequences of stochastic or probabilistic behaviors usually apply to real-world systems.

Before examining some catastrophe models in more detail, certain definitions must be qualified further. What I have called control variables are also frequently called control parameters or control factors. In keeping with both a field-theoretic orientation and the large scales often involved in organizational, societal, and ecological situations, these causal factors may be referred to as forces. Indeed, they can be viewed as vectors in the old sense of the term meaning lines with direction and magnitude. Catastrophes thus are one type of outcome emergent from the dynamics of a field of forces.

The term *attractor* is often applied to the stable equilibrium positions and the term *repellor* to the unstable or inaccessible regions.

The hardest thing about trying to understand and to use catastrophe theory is knowing where to start. When entering this field it is hard to determine just what are the basics and the givens and what are the derivations. Understanding is not limited only by new terminology and sometimes esoteric mathematics. It is limited as much, or more so, by the intrusion of seemingly extraneous material, by fuzzy descriptions, and by frequent disconnected jumps (!) between theory and examples and between causal and affected factors.

Three catastrophe models—the fold, the cusp, and the butterfly—shall now be considered in more detail. However, because the cusp catastrophe is the simplest that can be depicted wholly or in part using three dimensions, we shall concentrate on it in further explaining the properties of catastrophe theory in general.

The fold catastrophe is the simplest of the seven or eleven so-called elementary catastrophes. It involves one control variable and one behavior variable and therefore can be drawn on a familiar two-axis graph. It is illustrated in Figure 5.3.

We have drawn the fold catastrophe as an S-shaped curve. Sometimes it is depicted as half of this curve, that is, as U-shaped or like a parabola. The graph

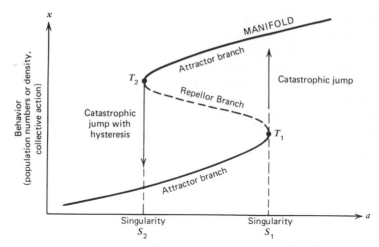

Control variable as normal factor (environment: temperature, carrying capacity, threat, etc.)

Figure 5.3. Fold catastrophe.

as a whole is called a manifold, and it represents a set of equilibrium points that in turn represent the set of points at which the first derivative of the potential function or canonical equivalent equals zero. Note that the curve has three main branches—a stable upper branch, a stable lower branch, and an intermediate unstable branch. The stable branches are called attractors, and the middle branch is called a repellor. Here the stable branches represent maxima, and the unstable branch represents a minimum.

As the control variable, here considered a normal factor, increases, behavior also increases along some scale. We can visualize movement up and to the right on the lower branch until a critical point or threshold, T_1, or fold point is reached. At the fold point the graph folds over continuously into the unstable repellor branch, and behavior catastrophically jumps to the upper attractor branch. If the control variable is subsequently decreased, behavior does not immediately drop to the lower attractor branch. Rather, it can be thought of as moving along the top branch downward and to the left until another critical point or threshold, T_2, or fold point is reached, when it suddenly and catastrophically falls to the lower attractor branch. The lags or delays before the catastrophic jumps, coupled with path irreversibility, represent hysteresis. The projection of the fold points down to the control-variable axis represent the singularities of the system, S_1 and S_2.

You might wonder how an ordinary S-shaped curve evolves into the curve shown in Figure 5.3. Implied is the existence of another control variable, the splitting factor, which is held constant but at different levels. The higher the value of this constant factor, the more accentuated is the graph, and the greater is the tendency for the graph to rupture into the separate branches.

Finally, we have presented a picture of dynamic system movement.

However, some authors would prefer to view these changes simply as a sequence of equilibrium levels, which follow in a 1:1 manner a sequence of settings of the control parameter.

The cusp catastrophe is illustrated in Figure 5.4. Before describing its geometry, let's look briefly at some of the mathematics involved. The canonical model of the potential function is given by the algebraically simplest polynomial equation. For the cusp catastrophe, this equation is

$$f(a, b, x) = \left(\frac{1}{4}\right) x^4 - ax - \left(\frac{1}{2}\right) bx^2$$

where a and b are the two control variables, and the fractions are just conveniences for the process of differentiation. The first derivative is

$$\frac{\partial f}{\partial x} = x^3 - a - bx$$

which, when set is zero, is the equation for the behavior surface or manifold. This surface consists of course of a great many individual points, each representing an equilibrium value.

The *fold curves* occur where vertical lines are tangent to the surface, and their equation is produced by further differentiation to give

$$3x^2 - b = 0$$

The projection of the two fold curves *down* to the horizontal control surface produces the *bifurcation set*. Its formula is

$$27a^2 = 4b^3$$

obtained by eliminating x from the last two equations. The bifurcation set has a cusp at the origin, hence the name of the catastrophe.

To summarize the qualitative features of what we have just presented:

1. The fold curve separates the *behavior manifold* into three sheets above the bifurcation set. The *behavior surface*, consisting of the upper and lower sheets (equivalent to the two modes of behavior in a bimodal probability distribution), is single-sheeted outside the cusp and double-sheeted inside the cusp. The middle sheet is an inaccessible region, which represents the trough between the two modes of a bimodal probability distribution. The behavior surface is an attractor of behavior; the middle sheet is a repellor of behavior.

2. The bifurcation set is the set of a,b-coordinates or control points over which behavior qualitatively changes or bifurcates. It should be noted that behavioral change must be traced *both* on the behavior surface and on the *control surface* that consists of all the a,b-control points. change in the a control variable to the *right* in Figure 5.4 will pass *through* the bifurcation set to the *right* edge where, looking up now to the behavior surface, a catastrophic jump from the lower to the upper sheet will occur. Change to the *left* will pass *through* the bifurcation set to the *left* edge, where a catastrophic fall from the upper to the lower sheet will take place.

3.   The *b*-control variable or parameter is called a *splitting factor* and is defined to be the direction, at the cusp point, of the axis of the cusp. The *a*-control variable is called a *normal factor* and is defined to be any direction transverse to *b* and oriented towards *a* greater than zero. At the back of the behavior surface where *b* is less than zero, transverse or left-to-right movement will be smooth. More toward the front, where *b* is greater than zero, behavior will split. If one imagines movement starting near the origin on the behavior surface and coming forward, then this movement will show, on either side of the pleat produced by folding, the *divergence* mentioned earlier. In trying to understand catastrophe theory, the learner is often in a chicken-and-egg or which-came-first situation. Splitting is considered to cause the fold curve to appear and therefore the catastrophes. It produces a progressively larger separation between the top and bottom sheets. However, it is convenient to think of splitting as applying to the control surface and divergence to the behavior surface.

In some situations the splitting factor is not used, but rather two *conflicting* factors are employed. The conflicting factors form a right angle bisected by the splitting factor. That is,

$$\alpha = b + a, \beta = b - a.$$

The control variable α tends to push behavior onto the upper sheet; β tends to push it onto the lower. Inside the bifurcation set the two factors conflict. Some of the critical phenomena discussed earlier fit this situation. For example, pressure and temperature are conflicting factors affecting the density of a fluid.

The butterfly catastrophe is illustrated in Figure 5.5 to follow. The butterfly catastrophe involves four control variables and often is associated with a trimodal probability distribution. The butterfly catastrophe is an extension or generalization of the cusp catastrophe. As such it can be expressed by *a* as a normal factor and *b* as a splitting factor. The new factors are *c*, a *bias factor*, and *d*, a *butterfly factor*. Five dimensions are involved, which cannot be depicted in a drawing. Even the bifurcation set is four-dimensional; it is usually shown as two-dimensional sections. Some of these sections look a little like a butterfly, hence the name. Figure 5.5 shows the normal and splitting factors, with the bias and butterfly factors assumed to remain constant.

The canonical form of the potential function is

$$f(a,b,c,d,x) = \frac{1}{6}x^6 - ax - \frac{1}{2}bx^2 - \frac{1}{3}cx^3 - \frac{1}{4}dx^4$$

and the associated four-dimensional manifold is

$$\frac{\partial f}{\partial x} = x^5 - a - bx - x^2c - dx^3 = 0$$

The partial derivatives indicated by the ∂ symbol (an archaic "d") indicate that the potential function was differentiated using the calculus only with respect to the behavior variable, x, and that the four control variables were held constant.

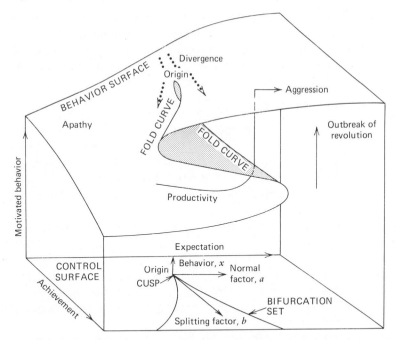

Figure 5.4. Basic features of the cusp catastrophe. When a society can no longer produce opportunities for achievement proportional to the expectations of people, frustration may suddenly lead to the violent outbreak of revolution. (Modified from reference 11.)

The bias factor biases the position of the cusp in the positive direction of the normal factor (positive bias) or in the negative direction (negative bias). The bias factor also raises or lowers the behavior surface, intensifying or diminishing behavior.

The butterfly factor bifurcates the cusp into three cusps. This can result, when bias equals zero, in the emergence of pockets of compromise on the control and behavior surfaces and of a stable third sheet on the behavior surface. Time is the butterfly factor in many applications—as time progresses, the pockets of compromise grow.

Finally, catastrophe theory models are usually thought of as involving *gradient dynamic systems*. Rates of change are in the direction of maximizing or minimizing the potential function. In a physical system change might be in the direction of minimizing potential energy. In a social system change might be in the direction of maximizing, say, public support of a political administration. The following differential equation expresses these dynamics

$$\frac{dx}{dt} = \frac{\partial f}{\partial x}$$

That is, the rate of change of behavior is in the direction of increasing potential (maximizing popular support, perceptual meaning, social structure, degree of organization, value change, utility, and so forth) and proportional to the gradient or slope of the potential field. In the case of minimization (of physical free energy, entropy, personal or social conflict, cognitive dissonance, incongruence of organizational structure, and so on), a minus sign must be placed on the right side of the equation.

Applications to Living Systems

Most applications of catastrophe theory to living beings, organizations, societies, and ecosystems have involved the cusp and butterfly catastrophes. Only these two will be considered in any further detail. However, the fold catastrophe should be considered briefly. The swallowtail catastrophe is seldom used, and the umbilic catastrophes, also seldom applied so far, are beyond the scope of this book.

The fold catastrophe is illustrated in Figure 5.3. The control variable, a, here viewed as a normal factor, can be, for example, an environmental variable like temperature, carrying capacity, or threat from another organization, nation, or species. The behavior variable, x, can be, for example, numbers or density of a population or a collective action. Referring back to Figure 5.1, social temperature could be viewed as a control variable and number of proselytizers as a behavior variable.

The cusp catastrophe is illustrated in Figure 5.4. This example incorporates features of a number of theories from behavioral and social science, including the theories of levels of aspiration and expectancy, frustration-aggression, ego-defense mechanisms, hierarchy of motives, social comparison, and revolution. These theories are widely incorporated into the literature of dynamic behavioral and social science. Collectively, they contribute to our understanding of the *motivational dynamics* of an organization or society.

In considering the societal dynamics underlying Figure 5.4, it is, however, always well to remember the observations of the astute French social scientist, Alexis de Tocqueville. Tocqueville noted in the early nineteenth century that people will tolerate extremes of deprivation, misery, and oppression—until things appear to be getting better. Once improvements are underway, even the slightest reversal toward conditions that previously were accepted with equanimity, can trigger the most violent of outbreaks. This situation is yet another example of the essential irreversibility of societal evolution.

Much collective violence like urban riots, insurrections, and national revolutions, therefore, can be explained by the emergence of an intolerable gap between expected need satisfaction and actual need satisfaction or achievement. When expectation and achievement are both low, people are apathetic. When achievement and expectation are both high, and achievement approximates or exceeds expectation, people are productive and society is harmonious. But when achievement falls off greatly compared to expectation, pent-up frustrations and disappointments are released suddenly in the violent outbreak of rioting or revolution. In this model expectation is a unifying or normal factor or control variable, and differential achievement is a splitting factor or control variable, influencing *type of* motivated behavior. In modern technological societies, until very recently, nearly everybody expected to have a better life than did their parents and to have a future better than their present. Recent socioeconomic reversals may augur ominously for societal dissolution and even for war.[14]

Suppose now that the societal dynamics change and expectations decrease somewhat. If reversal does occur, it will not take place immediately or along the same path. It will follow a lag. Such lags in attitudes and feelings following rectification of a wrong can indeed be observed in social systems. This is the hysteresis effect discussed earlier. It is associated with the control factors (a,b) moving right to left through the bifurcation set.

Two types of smooth, that is, noncatastrophic behavior should also be mentioned. The first of these involves roughly left-to-right or right-to-left behavior at the back of the behavior surface. This behavior could occur, for example, when expectations and achievement are both lowered, followed by a rise in achievements to produce once again a harmoniously productive society.

The second type of smooth behavior, involving back-to-front paths and shown in Figure 5.4 by dotted lines, is the divergence mentioned earlier. Divergence is a common and important phenomenon in the evolution of species, organizations, and societies. In the model we are considering, divergence could occur within or between organizations or societies. Evolution in the direction of high achievements consistent with expectations is obviously the preferable condition.

There are many more applications of the cusp catastrophe important to the management of complex organizations. There are applications to the behavior of individuals, groups, organizations, consumers, economies, and ecosystems. Some representative examples follow:

Force strength of an existing value as a normal factor and force strength of dissonant ideas as a splitting factor influencing value change.

Excess demand for stock as a normal factor and the ratio of the amount of the market held by speculators to that held by investors as a splitting factor influencing the rate of change of the price index in stock market crashes.

Price of a given consumer-product brand relative to the average price as a normal factor and features of the product (for example, durability, maintainability, or tasteful design) as a splitting factor influencing loyalty to the brand.

The butterfly catastrophe is illustrated in Figure 5.5 This deals with a sociotechnical systems field of great contemporary, and probably ongoing, significance—the economic and sociopolitical situation in Iran (and by extension in many other Near East and Middle East countries). Many field-theoretic concepts and constructs—precursor and latent processes, diffusion, seemingly spontaneous and instantaneous change, the integrating role of communications nets, the formation of collectivities, critical thresholds, discontinuities, emergence—can be identified in this setting.

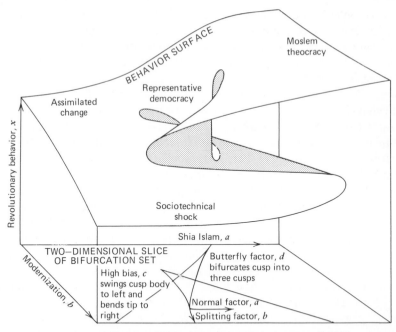

Figure 5.5 Butterfly catastrophe rendition of the sociotechnical systems field of contemporary Iran. High stick/carrot ratio biases behavior in favor of Shia Islam, makes revolutionary behavior more aggressive, and may eliminate productive communications. Effective communications may open up a third mode and a third sheet representing less extreme conditions.

Figure 5.5 depicts a butterfly catastrophe model of prerevolutionary Iran in which a number of factors have been integrated into four basic forces. Shia Islam is a *normal factor* in that it tends to unify peoples' conservative, anti-Western, anti-Shah feelings. Shia Islam represents traditional beliefs and practices going back hundreds of years, a source of knowledge and authority, and a perceived sanctuary for the oppressed. Modernization is a *splitting* factor. Modernization represents a massive attempt, especially by the late Shah Mohamed Reza Pahlavi, to utilize Western technology to raise the standard of living and increase economic and military power to levels approaching those of the West. This program alienated many conservative and religious elements, and raised peoples' expectations, while at the same time there were not enough new goods and services immediately available to everybody.

Stick/carrot ratio is a *bias factor*. The carrot-and-stick management philosophy promised land reforms, more consumer goods, and so on, but at the same time the secret police (SAVAK) and other government agencies were quick to crack down on dissenters. And the more the socioeconomic system eroded, the more people saw the stick rather than the carrot, the more people thought of the Shah and his regime as the focus of all their frustrations and conflicts. Bias also tended to make revolutionary behavior more aggressive by raising the behavior surface. Thus, the more the repression by the Imperial government, the more the shift in favor of the Moslem clergy, the more the aggressiveness of revolutionary behavior.

Communications is a *butterfly factor* that bifurcates the slice of the bifurcation set shown on the control surface, yielding three cusps. Communications includes the original broadcasts of the Ayatollah Ruhollah Khomeini from Neauphle-le-Château, France to Qum, Iran and the almost instantaneous rebroadcast mosque-to-mosque all over Iran. (This is analogous to the spread, neighbor-to-neighbor, of electron-spin alignments in the magnet models in field theory in physics that we considered earlier.) Communications also express the cohesiveness of present feeling.

The butterfly factor may eventually force the emergence of a third stable sheet reflecting the middle mode of a trimodal probability distribution, as is shown in Figure 5.5 Only when the bias factor equals zero, however, can the diamond-shaped pockets on the bifurcation-set slice and the corresponding third sheet emerge. Therefore, continuing bias (for example, highly focused anti-Western feeling) can destroy effective communications and all possibility of compromise.

With time, however, communications may become less all-or-none, and compromise may become more resistant to increasingly larger perturbations.

Revolutionary behavior includes the values, attitudes, practices, zeal and anti-Western, pro-Ayatollah Khomeini focus characteristic of the revolution and the period following. Because this is a dynamic unstable configuration, further reconfiguration associated with shifting forces can be predicted. One likely event is a split (a further catastrophe) in the apparently monolithic ethnic Iranian, Shi'ite support for Khomeini.[15]

In a stock market or real estate application of the butterfly catastrophe, consumer demand can be a normal factor, speculative content a splitting factor, interest rate a bias factor, and time a butterfly factor influencing rate of change of prices.

Finally, catastrophe theory models not only aid understanding of basic forces inside and outside the organization but also help one to select appropriate variables to be brought under management control. Control over interest rates, market speculation, and features of consumer products exemplifies such situations.

COLLECTIVE BEHAVIOR—SOCIAL AND SOCIOTECHNICAL SYSTEMS INTERPRETATIONS

The major theme of this chapter is the emergence of qualitatively new properties when the elements or bodies of a system interact. Such many-body problems, basic to the notion of field theory, have a long history going back to the ancient Greeks. For over 2000 years these problems have been among the most difficult in all science. In the first part of this chapter we sought *constructs* or basic building blocks for theories and models and *heuristics* or hints, guidance, or rules-of-thumb for problemsolving in developments that are pushing the state of the art in physical science and mathematics.

If top management is really to understand the nature of change in the organization and in its environments, then it is of the utmost importance that management be provided with an infusion of constantly new concepts and methods.

Many types of collective behavior are important to assessing the state of the organization and to assessing environmental changes. Collective behavior is necessary both for maintaining the stability of the organization or society and for healthy organizational and social change. Collective behavior includes both relatively unstructured forms like crowds, mobs, masses, riots, publics, and panics and fads and more structured forms like social movements, revolutions, informal networks in the organization, lobbies, unofficial organizations, and formal organizations. Almost all these forms can critically impact on the success or failure of the organization. Consider, for example, fads in consumer buying, antibusiness or antigovernment voting behavior, gold or silver or stockmarket panics, the rise of powerful environmentalist organizations and lobbies, and rumor mills operating in the organization. We discussed some of the dynamics of revolutionary behavior in the preceding section of this chapter.[16]

Many collectivities are ephemeral and one of a kind. Others rise and crest, then wither away after having contributed some of their characteristics to a changed organization or society at large. Still others explode into massive reconfigurations of an organization or society. Consider the following sequence of activities that can be identified in the evolution of a successful new collectivity:

1. Social, technological, and sociotechnical change, especially with regard to fluctuations and perturbations, that produce uncertainty, frustration, and conflict leading to a large number of grievances or general dissatisfaction with the status quo.

2. Individuals or small pockets of people who are particularly well attuned to fluctuations and to possibly emerging new order.

3. Strain within the organization or society generated by the rapid change and characterized by cognitive dissonance (the pieces do not fit together mentally), perceived injustices resulting from social comparison, tension, and conflict.

4. Regulation and control mechanisms of the organization or society weakened so as to be unable to contain or resolve the strain.

5. Overt and covert behaviors characteristic of organizations and societies undergoing strain, and that reinforce decay and dissolution—terrorism, sabotage, vandalism, crime, loss of faith in old practices and institutions, disintegration of basic building blocks, widespread alienation, search for and persecution of scapegoats, blaming others for one's own deficiencies, perceived exploitation of one group by another, and so forth.

6. Concentration and focusing of perceptions and beliefs about the reasons for frustration, injustice, and so on by a leader and associated symbols, and contagious spread of beliefs abetted by modern telecommunications and transportation technologies.
7. Mobilization of the constituency for action, for example, through propaganda, by the formation of local cells or chapters, and by providing weapons and training.
8. Possible triggering events—the sparks that ignite—a natural disaster, a technological failure, an economic setback, the arrest of a minority group member, or the burning of a mosque that lead to exceeding the critical point or level of the field *now prepared* for reconfiguration.

Collective Behavior Following Technological Failures or Natural Disasters

Technological failures, such as those of electric power, communications, and transportation systems and natural disasters, such as earthquakes, dam breaks, severe storms, and wildfires, can perturb a social system leading to collective and emergent behavior. Depending on the situation, collective behavior may be short-lived and even violent as is often the case with urban rioting and looting, or it can persist long after the triggering event and be associated with the emergence of new leaders and new, viable organizational forms. Analysis of these situations is quite important to the understanding of organizational reactions to disaster and crisis and therefore to future planning. Some social scientists specialize in *disaster research* and *crisis research*. Unfortunately, large-scale failures continue, and understanding is better in retrospect than in anticipation.

New York City electrical power failure followed by blackout looting.[17] This is a quite instructive example both in terms of the inherent weaknesses of large person-machine systems and in terms of the close interdependency of the social and technological subsystems of society.

On the evening of July 13, 1977 separate bolts of lightning (a rare event) hit two transmission towers, of the Consolidated Edison utility, near New York City. About 8 million people lost electrical power, and total losses from loss of power and looting were estimated at more than $310 million. The lightning strikes triggered a chain of events—short circuits, circuit-breaker openings, loss of transmission lines and generators—which soon led to the decomposition of the system. A concatenation of human and machine errors amplified what might have been a recoverable perturbation into a massive system failure.

Major top management and human factors deficiencies contributed to the failure. There was inadequate total system and contingency planning. The control room was poorly human engineered in design. Equipment was not kept in good operating condition. Operators were poorly trained, especially for emergencies. Overall, system reliability was not high. As one might have expected, the utility blamed "legislative, regulatory, and environmental opposition" to its building plans for the failure.

Looting broke out spontaneously and generally in all five New York boroughs and also almost instantaneously, that is, within 10 to 30 minutes of the power failure. Looting progressed through three stages, dominated, respectively, by professional criminals, unemployed and alienated youth, and more or less respectable people caught in the mass hysteria. In contrast, almost no looting had followed the huge northeast United States–eastern Canada electrical blackout of November 9, 1965. That blackout had, indeed, been associated with a neighborly cohesiveness. But in the 12 years between blackouts the field of forces had changed; the urban system was no longer the same.

Three Mile Island nuclear reactor failure.   Like the power system failures just discussed, it illustrates the *fragility* of complex person–machine systems and the approach to the *limits to complexity* of human designs. Most importantly, it symbolizes a change in thinking with regard to the reliability and safety of large-scale systems and perhaps the beginning of the end for the nuclear-power industry in the United States. For several years advocates of nuclear power had cited the "Rasmussen report," the consensus of a study by some 60 scientists headed by MIT professor Norman Rasmussen. This study produced estimates of the probability of a serious nuclear accident to be about the same—one in a million—as that of a meteor striking a large city!

Early in the morning of March 28, 1979 a pump failed in the secondary loop that carried hot water from the reactor to the turbines that drove the electric generators. Auxiliary pumps were set up for failure by human error during routine test and maintenance two weeks previously. As in the cases just discussed, a minor perturbation from which the system was potentially recoverable triggered a series of human and equipment failures that soon led to a near meltdown. Had the reactor melted its container, it could have dropped into the cooling water beneath or even into the ground, triggering a steam explosion that could have blasted radioactive material widely into the surroundings. As it was, about 600,000 gallons of dangerously radioactive water were spilled onto the floor of the containment building and about 425,000 gallons onto the floor of one of the auxiliary buildings.

At the time of this writing the Metropolitan Edison facility in the Susquehanna River near Harrisburg, Pennsylvania is still shut down. Removing the contaminated water and other repair costs alone may exceed $400 million.

In social systems terms the main lessons to be learned from this technological failure are the refusal of many planners and policymakers to acknowledge the limitations of complex systems, including the fact that interactions within the system of supposedly known parts can yield the emergence of a barely comprehended whole, and the lack of planning for crisis. The near meltdown led to considerable confusion and lack of coordination among utility, Nuclear Regulatory Commission, local, and state personnel. There was, for example, no comprehensive evacuation plan.

Tax Revolt: California Proposition 13 Property-Tax Relief

In a stable democracy revolution is fortunately a very rare occurrence. Further, in a healthy and adaptable democracy, people can express their disillusionments and grievances, even though current practices may have reached a point of diseconomies of scale and the usual channels of expression become clogged through misuse.

Complaints against taxes are of course nothing new. But by the late 1970s resentment of California property owners, particularly homeowners, against rapidly increasing property taxes had reached a critical level. Large numbers of people perceived that continued high taxation would lead to the loss of their homes. People whose incomes did not keep pace with inflation, for example, the elderly, actually did lose their homes. Inflation put people into higher brackets, which automatically led to larger and larger tax increases. People also perceived the recipients of their tax dollars to include not only the legitimately needy but also a large number of freeloaders. Finally, people perceived widespread inefficiency and waste in government and arbitrary and arrogant uses of government power.

What was needed was someone to catalyze the feelings of the voters. Catalysis came particularly in the person of 75-year-old Howard Jarvis, who with his associates was able to gather enough signatures to place Proposition 13 on the June 1978 California ballot as a voter initiative, thus bypassing the state legislature.

The Howard Jarvis-Paul Gann measure attracted voters from all socioeconomic levels, ethnic groups, ages, and areas of residence. It passed by a ratio of about two to one. Property taxes of the large numbers of qualified persons were cut about 57 percent. The total tax cut from Proposition 13 was $6.4 billion, and another $1 billion was subsequently cut in state income taxes.

Proposition 13 of course met a lot of opposition, accompanied by dire predictions of massive layoffs and cutbacks in education, fire-protection, police-protection, and other services. These did not occur. The loss of about 100,000 jobs in local government was apparently compensated by an increase in jobs spurred by an improved economy. And education, for example, did not collapse. Retrenchment was expressed mainly in terms of things people can accept in an era of increasing austerity, such as somewhat shorter school days and fewer summer sessions.

Because perceived unfair taxation is not limited to California, Proposition 13 has generated considerable attention elsewhere in the United States and abroad. Tax-cut proposals have been triggered elsewhere in the societal field. In California the success of Proposition 13 stimulated further voter initiatives to cut other taxes and to limit government spending. Although far more signatures than necessary were obtained to place a new initiative on the ballot, the measure failed in a November 1979 special election by a margin of about two to one, the same margin by which Proposition 13 had passed. The field of forces had changed. More people were worried about unemployment, for example. And Proposition 13 had apparently catastrophically discharged enough pent-up potential energy such that further large-scale collective demand for reform would not be possible for a while.

CONFLUENCE AND COALESCENCE OF FORCES

Field-theoretic phenomena can be interpreted in terms of the interactions of aggregated forces as well as in terms of the collective behavior of a great many individuals. The distinction may be arbitrary in the treatment of any given phenomenon. In the physical science/mathematical modeling approaches considered in the first part of this chapter, physical field theory and self-organization far from equilibrium were expressed more in terms of collective phenomena and catastrophe theory more in terms of cooperation or conflict among forces. But as seen, a critical phenomenon could be viewed either way.

Societal and natural forces are with us all the time, but most people are not trained to think in terms of them or to observe them. In retrospect, the countercultural revolution and the opposition to the Southeast Asia war of the late 1960s-early 1970s were probably inevitable. The main forces were education, patterns of child-rearing, values, and material standard of living. More highly educated young people questioned established traditions and practices and were markedly less tolerant of absolutes imposed by others. At the same time permissive child-rearing had prepared young people to expect little impediment to having their own way and to reject authority even more than would have been the case because of the disintegration of the family, church, and so forth. Values were changing rapidly, partly because of higher education and partly because communications and transportation provided a greater variety of experiences and opportunities to compare what is with what ought to be. Finally, greater affluence and general improvements in material standard of living led to satisfaction of more basic needs while higher needs for self-worth and self-fulfillment remained frustrated.

This particular interpretation is of course meaningful only in terms of the period and circumstances covered. Future generations of Western youth may be conformist and warlike. A period of history represents a particular, perhaps unique *configuration* of forces, structures, and system states. Field theory is a powerful and useful way of thinking, which helps greatly in understanding the evolutionary changes in organizations, societies, and ecosystems. But one must be careful to distinguish between the fundamental ideas and any specific interpretation. In attempts to forecast the future, it is important always to remember that the particular forces almost always differ in the past, present, and future, but that the force laws and constructs remain the same.

Science and technology are forces of paramount importance. Executives and corporate planners in advanced modern companies are especially concerned with the source, rate, and utility of discovery and innovation. Here are several case studies.

The Battelle-Columbus Laboratories performed historical analyses of eight major innovations in terms of antecedent decisive events.[17] The innovations were the following:

1. The cardiac pacemaker.
2. Hybrid grains and the so-called Green Revolution (hybrid maize, hybrid small grains, and Green Revolution wheats).
3. Electrophotography.
4. Input-output economic analysis.
5. Organophosphorus insecticides.
6. Oral contraceptives.
7. Magnetic ferrites.
8. Videotape recorder.

Decisive events were those events that provided major and essential impetus to the innovation. They tended to occur at the convergence of several sequences of activity. In the absence of a decisive event, the innovation would not have taken place or would have been greatly delayed. For example, invention of the transistor was a decisive event for the development of the cardiac pacemaker. The isolation and determination of the structural formula of the hormone progesterone was a decisive event in the development of oral contraceptives.

Twenty-one factors of importance to the rate and direction of the innovative process were rated as to specific importance to each of the decisive events of the eight innovations. One factor, confluence of technology, is particularly relevant to the present discussion.

Unplanned confluence of technology was important to the development of Green Revolution wheat, electrophotography, input-output economic analysis, oral contraceptives, magnetic ferrites, and the videotape recorder. Confluence of technology, involving some degree of planning—for example, for interdisciplinary research—was important to the other developments as well.

Although the process of innovation can be aided by management—for example, by providing the proper organizational environment, encouraging the motivations of technical entrepreneurs and others, and structuring the appropriate perceptions of need and opportunity—it can by no means be completely planned, preprogrammed, and controlled. This is especially true for basic or nonmission-oriented research.

It is interesting to note that, according to these studies, the period from first conception to first realization is not growing shorter. The periods ranged from six to 32 years, with an average of about 19 years. Two of the most recent innovations, the cardiac pacemaker and input-output economic analysis, involved the longest periods. As systems become more complex, rapid scientific discovery, invention, and technological change do not necessarily result in better use of these developments.

EMERGING PROBLEMS—THE MORE POPULAR INTERPRETATION

So far emergence has been treated in terms of rather definite or abrupt reconfigurations of fields and qualitatively distinct properties. Emergence is more popularly thought of as a gradual coming out of hiding through slow but continuous change. From this perspective, qualitative change may result from the sheer might of quantitative change. The two approaches are not at all exclusive. The popular interpretation provides a far richer system description, but the field-theoretic approach offers much greater explanatory power.

Stanford Research International has assessed a number of future national and international problem areas.[18] Many of today's serious world problems were, in hindsight, predictable—had people had the correct orientations and tools.

The main goal of the Stanford Research International team was to assist government decisionmakers by providing appropriate *early-warning* techniques for the *anticipation* of *future* problems so that these problems can be handled *before* they become serious or intractable. Some 1000 problems were sequentially sorted and aggregated according to various selection criteria. Eventually 41 major problems were identified, and six of these were subjected to detailed analysis.

The problems were not what most people would think of offhand. The problems tended to be global, interdisciplinary, systemic, and even diffuse. Problem definition was not very amenable to existing rigorous analytic techniques. Obviously, there were few data to help define such problems. Overall, the problems tended to emerge as the results of continuing past trends interacting in new ways and reaching a limit.

The six problems that received detailed analysis were these:

1. Chronic underemployment and unemployment.
2. Growing conflict between central control and personal freedom.
3. Barriers to achieving large-scale technological projects.
4. Limits to the management of large, complex systems.
5. Potential use and misuse of consciousness technologies.
6. Effects of stress on individuals and societies.

We considered the fourth problem in some detail in Chapter 3. We shall consider some of the other problems in subsequent chapters.

PREDICTING CORPORATE FAILURE AND COLLAPSE

The constructs and heuristics regarding growth, evolution, structure, reconfiguration, and transformation developed up to now have a direct and unavoidable bearing on the most critical, most catastrophic states in the life history of an organization—failure or collapse.

The focus of most organizational and management thinking up to now has been on growth and success, not on anticipating and warding off failure or collapse. We regard *failure* as a general condition of an organization's not achieving its goals. *Collapse* is a plunge from a previous level of achievement that eventually ends in a terminal financial or legal event such as merger, retrenchment in size, bankruptcy, receivership, or liquidation. Collapse often involves two or more stages separated by plateaus which may span months or years. Some companies can be saved from complete collapse by quick and drastic changes in organization and management. However, deciding on *the* correct steps is seldom easy. Many attempts to rectify patterns of organizational failure have actually exacerbated the situation.

British corporate consultant John Argenti has estimated that in any average year in Britain and America about 10 percent of companies are in failure states or have collapsed.[19] However, in the past several years the world environment has become even more turbulent, and both the frequency and magnitude of failures and collapses are increasing. The frequency may level off or decrease, but this should not be seen as a signal for optimism. A large number of failures occurs among new companies, which barely get off the ground. Present hard times may mean the demise of many small companies, say, one to eight years old, and a cutback in the start of new and vulnerable small companies. Even in the group of larger organizations that have survived the first tumultuous years, the frequency and magnitude of failures and collapses are increasing.

Predicting corporate failure and collapse is still a rare specialty. Even rarer are attempts to make systemic and dynamic predictions. Thus, regressional-econometric models, typically deal with *apparently* linear or otherwise simply monotonic periods, say, 1950–1974, in recent societal evolution. The mixed economic picture, energy crisis, and so on have not been, and probably cannot be, usefully incorporated into these models.

This chapter has stressed the overriding importance of latent and precursory processes, critical thresholds, stable and unstable equilibria, and subtle followed by sudden and catastrophic changes in organization. Much remains to be done in devising predictive models of corporate and other organizational failure and collapse. However, there is now a theoretical framework into which more empirical studies can be fit.

John Argenti has developed a holistic, dynamic, evolutionary, qualitative model of corporate collapse. The model is a synthesis of Argenti's literature review, interview of experts (accountants, financiers, and others), consideration of one regressional-econometric predictive model, and detailed examination of the Rolls-Royce and Penn-Central collapses. Argenti came up with 12 main *causes* and *symptoms* and a number of subitems extending the main factors. He also developed three main types of failure trajectory.

Briefly, if a company has poor *management*, especially associated with one-person rule, it will tend to make two major errors of ommission and three of commission. The errors of omission are the neglect of (accountancy) *information systems* and, even worse, the failure to respond to long-term *changes in the environment.* The three errors of commission are the tendency to *overtrade,* to launch a *big project* that is beyond the company's capabilities, and to allow *borrowing* to increase, such that even *normal business hazards* or perturbations and fluctuations offer a constant threat. Companies, even well-managed ones, can be damaged by various imposed *constraints.* These eight factors are the chief *causes.* As the company deteriorates, the following four *symptoms* appear—certain *financial ratios* will decrease, top managers (usually the first to be aware of the decaying situation) will begin *creative accounting* (conscious or subconscious fudging, manipulating the books, and financial obfuscation due to reasons ranging from wishful thinking and self-delusion to fraud), *nonfinancial symptoms* will become more important as the financial ratios' predictive value erodes, and finally the company will enter the characteristic period of its *last few months.*

These 12 and their ancillary *indicators* can be evident to the trained and acute observer for months or even years before failure or actual collapse. They represent the latent or precursory processes mentioned above. Corporate collapse often appears to occur suddenly, dramatically, catastrophically, a surprise even to people close to the scene such as creditors, board members, and top management (who may have known something was wrong but not what or that calamity was near). The field-theoretic framework and Argenti's model now *bring us much closer to the anticipation and management of crisis in complex organizations.*

The failure trajectory of Type 1 organizations never rises above the *poor* level of performance. The curve resembles an inverted saucer and covers a period of about two to eight years. This type of performance curve applies only to small, newly-formed organizations.

The failure trajectory of Argenti's Type 2 organizations rises, apparently hyperbolically, to the *fantastic* level of performance and then collapses suddenly from the sharp peak. The curve covers a period of about four to 14 years. Type 2 organizations are founded and run by entrepreneurs who are flamboyant supersalesmen.

Type 3 failures happen to mature organizations that have been operating successfully for years or decades. Performance has consistently been at the *good* to *excellent* level, but some critical events occur that drive performance down to a *poor* level. The curve covers a period of two to 20 years, and the plateau representing poor performance may last weeks or years. Large, older companies usually have considerable, even vast resources. This explains the plateau and why these organizations do not collapse immediately into extinction. Fortunately, the plateau—which can be interpreted to be the temporarily stable equilibrium of a catastrophe surface—provides the opportunity to save the company if the top management is willing.

Refer back to Figures 3.1 and 3.3 The three types of trajectories roughly resemble the performance curves in Figure 3.3. Argenti also provides a nonfailure trajectory—the S-shaped curve.

Examining again Figures 3.1 and 3.5, it is noted that growth and decline can be considered to be roughly symmetrical. Both overall growth and overall decline result from a succession of S-curves. There are platforms of temporary stability on the way up and platforms of temporary stability on the way down. Examining Figures 5.1, 5.3, and 5.4 and comparing them with the logistic curves in Figure 3.1, and imagining the S-curves and the fold curves evolved from them to be reversed to indicate decline instead of growth, one can then understand the situation displayed by Argenti's Type 3 trajectories. A platform of more or less stable equilibrium at the performance level of good to excellent is terminated by a critical event, plunging performance to a lower level (the poor level) of stability. Weeks or years later, following another critical event, the organization collapses into extinction. Before each plunge, a critical threshold is exceeded.

Argenti indicates 17 points on his Type 3 trajectory. Here are the *critical points*. Because of the *preexisting* deficiences of poor management, poor information systems, and failure to monitor the external environments mentioned above, the organization has become *vulnerable to environmental fluctuations and perturbations*. These may take the form of normal business hazards or externally imposed constraints. Also the weakened, strained, overextended organization may overtrade (overbuy and oversell) and/or launch a big project like a merger, a diversification, or the introduction of a major new product in a compensatory attempt to maintain the slowly eroding equilibrium. At Point 5, a critical threshold, these stressful forces converge or coalesce, and overall corporate performance plunges to the lower equilibrium level.

At Point 11, the first point on the new, lower plateau, the corporation has become waterlogged, that is, the company has *both* borrowed so much that a large part of its profits must go into paying interest rather than being available for investment in the future *and* has lost its competitive edge. It has lost contact with its customers and its market. Although performance is now on a new equilibrium level, the domain or range of stability is not large. Threatened organizations usually tighten up, reducing variability. The internal innovations or fluctuations, the necessary creative problemsolving, are damped when they are most needed for survival. Consider again the discussion in Chapter 3 of the qualitative and quantitative features of aging organizations. On the lower plateau the organization has such little adaptive capability that almost any perturbation will sink it.

At Point 13 the managers, perhaps aided by the banks and government, may attempt a new big venture in a desperate attempt to save the company. This may indeed produce a slight—*and very misleading*—trend upward at Point 14. But all such efforts are doomed to failure because the resilience, the resources, the overall adaptive capability just are not there. Point 15 is thus a repetition of Point 5. At Point 16 the crisis has become intensified, and the drama of the last several months begins. At Point 17 the organization has gone into receivership or has otherwise become extinct in its present form.

The Type 3 failure trajectory and associated significant and critical *indicator*

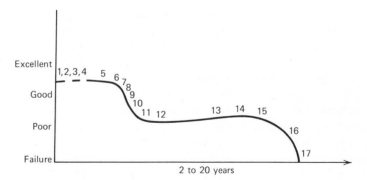

points are shown in Figure 5.6.

Once again it should be emphasized that major changes in the perceptions, orientations, frames of reference, and strategies of top management will be absolutely mandatory if certain corporations are to survive. A strategy for adaptivity, high achievement, and survival will require loosening up, not tightening up; encouraging internal variety and fluctuation, not developing and enforcing strict controls to damp spontaneity and variety; and enhancing resilience and the domain of stability, not trying to maintain equilibrium at a level just above the threshold of extinction.

As stressed throughout, the design of adaptive organizations capable of anticipating and managing crisis requires first and foremost a means of monitoring and responding to changes in the external and internal environments.

THE SIX MAJOR EXTERNAL ENVIRONMENTS

Understanding the external environment and the interrelationships between the organization and the external environment is a requirement, unsurpassed in importance, in the design and continued success of an adaptive organization. Chapter 1 stressed the importance of the concept of external environment and introduced the six important dimensions of that environment. Chapter 3 began a discussion of the dynamics of the external environment; Chapter 5 continued this discussion using some advanced theories. Both Chapters 4 and 5 provided the means of attempting to forecast future environments. Chapter 5 also noted that failure to monitor and interpret correctly the changes in the external environment is a primary cause of corporate failure.

The division of the external environment into six environments is, of course, a matter of convenience in analysis and discussion and also provides a focus. In reality, as repeatedly emphasized, the world is one turbulent field of forces in which all elements are interlinked and increasingly tightly coupled. The basic dynamics of the field are the same for each of the six environments. However, at a given time differential attention to the environments is usually required because of qualitatively and quantitatively different patterns and configurations.

Several approaches to the classification of environments will be considered next, then followed by focus on the turbulent-field environment of the organization in which certain salient features of the six environments will be discussed. The chapter will conclude with a look at how best to utilize knowledge and experts in each area.

CLASSIFICATIONS OF ORGANIZATIONAL ENVIRONMENTS

A number of approaches and associated criteria can be used in the classification of the external environments of an organization. These include classification:

By physical, chemical, biological, or behavioral/social properties, or, in a related sense, by specialist study areas.

By static versus dynamic nature; by nature and rate of change.

By age, for example, young, mature, or senescent.

In terms of richness or exhaustion of resources.

In terms of degree of complexity.

In terms of heterogeneity or homogeneity; in terms of variety and diversity.

In terms of evolution toward a more encompassing whole, or, contrariwise, toward fragmentation.

By amount of interaction with the given organization; by organizational impact.

By degree of comprehension and predictability; by certainty or uncertainty.

By degree of controllability by the organization.

All these dimensions have not been used in formal classifications of organizational environments. In the most holistic sense, insights about environments and their salient phenomena and processes come from cosmology, astronomy, geology, paleontology, biology, behavioral and social science, and history. This book has stressed throughout the essential unity of humankind, human organizations, and nature. A number of natural laws and apparently universal constructs have been discussed. It should be reemphasized here only that *ecology* is the study of the interrelationships between organisms and their environments. *Social ecology* can be thought of as the study of interactions between human social structures, including organizations, and their social environments. Many of the advances being made in ecology today may prove to have a profound effect on organizational success or failure.

The Classification of Emery and Trist

Sociotechnical systems pioneers Fred Emery and Eric Trist have provided a seminal contribution to the literature on organizations, especially because of the orientations toward emergence, field theory, and evoluion intrinsic to their classification.[1] The classification begins with four types of lawful connections: (1) within the system or the internal environment, (2) from the system out to the environment, (3) from the goals, opportunities, challenges, and threats provided by the environment which flow as information to the system, and (4) within the environment itself independent of the attempted impositions or manipulations of human organizations. The fourth situation is called the *causal texture of the environment.*

   Human organizations may impact on the external environment in such a way that forces are generated that assume an independent life of their own. The external environmental *field* is continuously evolving in ways that greatly tax human understanding and efforts at control. Organizational success or failure are at least as dependent on the happenings in the external environments as on those within the organization.

   Emery and Trist's classification involves a progressive increase in causal texturing. Four types of environments are presented:

1. *Random, placid environments.* In this static type of environment the opportunities and threats associated with the system's survival are randomly distributed. What will occur next and when and where cannot be known. Except perhaps as laboratory abstractions or brain-washing sessions, such environments do not exist. Real wildernesses, for example, possess—as every nature lover and survival school graduate knows—distinct *patterns* of fauna, flora, and inorganic resources that are dependent on geology, drainage, slope, soil type, temperature, sunlight, and so forth.

2. *Clustered, placid environments.* In this type of environment, also static, opportunities and threats cluster in lawful ways. Planning seeks maximum access to opportunities and minimum exposure to threats.

3. *Disturbed, reactive environments.* This type of environment has become dynamic because of the competition and games of strategy and tactics between two or more systems of the same kind. Problemsolving is of the nature of chess playing, syllogistic reasoning, and much of decision theory and game theory. Until recently these environments were the principal environments of organizations and nations. To cope with competition, conflict, and environmental stress in general, human designs are *variety-reducing. Fail–safe,* implemented in terms of redundancy of parts, standardization of parts, interchangeability of parts, and concentration of power at the top of a hierarchy, is the dominant design criterion. Unfortunately, all too many planners, policymakers, and decisionmakers still think of this type of environment as the real world.

4. *Turbulent-field environments.* The dynamic processes in this type of environment arise not just because of the interactions among systems but also from activities triggered in the environment itself.

The concept of the turbulent-field environment has been extended beyond the original authors' framework to include the theories and constructs emphasized in Chapters 3 and especially 5. Before continuing with this topic, some other classifications should be reviewed briefly.

Organization-Theoretic Classifications

Several other classifications of organizational environments were produced during the period of major flowering of organization theory. Three of these are mentioned here.

Professor James D. Thompson classified environments as:

Homogeneous, stable

Homogeneous, shifting

Heterogeneous, stable

Heterogeneous, shifting

Professors Paul Lawrence and Jay Lorsch saw organizational environments to be:

Low diversity, not dynamic

Low diversity, highly dynamic

High diversity, not dynamic

High diversity, dynamic

Ray Jurkovich[2] has integrated the ideas of Emery and Trist, Thompson, Lawrence and Lorsch, and other theorists into a potentially expandable taxonomy of 64 mutually exclusive environments. The taxonomy can be depicted in matrix form, but the several dimensions are shown in outline form as follows:

I. Movement (rows in a matrix)
    A. Low change rate
        1. Stable
        2. Unstable
    B. High change rate
        Stable and unstable
II. General characteristics (columns in a matrix)
    A. Noncomplex
        1. Routineness of problems and opportunities
            a. Organized elements in the environmental field
                i. Direct relation between the organization and these elements.
    B. Complex
        Routine/nonroutine, organized/unorganized, direct/indirect

There is of course a great deal of intuition, subjective judgment, and perceptual bias involved in using these classifications. They should be thought of as useful points of departure and heuristic guides to problem recognition and identification rather than as rigid means for pigeonholing any given organization. Concepts like complexity and stability have taxed serious thinkers for a long time. Determining the configurations and reconfigurations of the environmental field and how emerging new order in the field is related to the organization is severely pushing the state of the art.

In dealing with the above or other dimensions of the external environment, the traditional methods of behavioral and social science may be inadequate. The use of questionnaires, rating scales, and so on may produce a false impression of preciseness. For example, Professors Henry Tosi, Ramon Aldag, and Ronald Storey[3], employing correlation methods and behavioral–social concepts of validity and reliability, found deficiencies in the Lawrence and Lorsch Environmental Uncertainty Subscale.

This book concentrates on external environments that, in Jurkovich's nomenclature, show high rates of change, are unstable, are complex, present nonroutine problems and opportunities, and are characterized by poorly known order or lack thereof and poorly known relationship to the organization. Organizations in these environments totter on the edge of chaos.

Planning tends to be general and even diffuse. Boundary-spanning and executive roles tend to fuse, but in an unstable manner. At a certain level of environmental stress, the organization may be paralyzed into doing nothing, or it may try to cope through demonstrably unsuccessful, repetitive, standardized behavior. Decisionmakers fall back on their own subjective, biased models of the situation, and differences in perception and interpretation generate serious conflict. Problemsolving is replaced by problemcoping. Organizational methods become more complex but not more certain.

In brief these organizations:

Possess serious information problems.

Possess abstract, tentative sets of strategies and tactics that cannot be implemented without major alterations.

Generate loose coalitions that change unpredictably.

Must constantly redesign, or provide exceptions to, programs for decision-making.

These ideas of course provide just one more way of expressing the arguments made throughout this text. The design in Chapter 8 is intended to overcome these and other deficiencies of organizations in turbulent environments.

Shirley Terreberry has presented a historically interesting interpretation of the evolution of organizational environments.[4] Her study was based both on Darwin and on the Emery and Trist classification. Over a decade ago she found strong evidence for the increasing turbulence of these environments, for an increasing ratio of externally induced change to internally induced change, and increasingly unpredictable input–output transactions with the external environments. She also stressed that other formal organizations increasingly comprise the elements of the external environment of any given organization. In responding to environmental evolution, organizations were seen to go through three stages: (1) from systems within the unorganized clustered, placid environment, (2) through an intermediate bureaucratic stage, to (3) subsystems of a larger social system. Organizational success is thus vitally dependent on a continuing ability to learn and to perform as a function of changing environmental *contingencies.*

Ecologists, whose science deals with the interactions among organisms and environments, have long made the most valuable contributions of any regarding dynamically changing environments.

THE ECOLOGICAL PERSPECTIVE

Attempting to convey the importance of ecology to an audience of top management executives and planners is sometimes difficult because of popular misconceptions. Until the late 1960s there were few professional ecologists, and departments and institutes of ecology were rare indeed. The same period saw the rise of the counterculture, and many businessmen have come to associate ecology with flower children, ecofreaks, and bleeding-heart obstructionists—just as the opposition often has seen in business only exploitation of people, rape of the environment, and obscene profits. Actually, both business and ecology are far too important to be reduced to such polemics. And indeed businessmen and environmentalists have been quietly cooperating on a number of projects for a long while.

Ecology is a serious branch of science and, in dealing with complex systems, has much in common with and much to offer to economics and societal science. More specifically, there are several reasons why CEOs and long-range planners would want to know more about ecology:

1. To learn more about the dynamics of organizational environments as a whole.
2. To develop better understanding of specific environments.
3. To obtain new principles of designing organizations that can adapt to turbulent environments.
4. To anticipate possible reconfigurations in the economic and social environments, inferred from the responses over geological history to natural perturbations and responses more recently to increasing human perturbations.
5. To learn more about the management of complexity.
6. To provide greater variety and depth to management through exposure to novel problems and the development of new types of case histories.

Embellishing these points collectively, it can be noted that ecologists study many of the same things that concern executives and planners in business and government, for example:

Variety and diversity

Competition and conflict

Processing of energy, matter, and information

Fluctuations in numbers, scales, and magnitudes

Regulation and control

Combinations and interactions

Connections

Complexity

Resource availability and utilization

Growth patterns, rates, and laws

Equilibrium and steady-state and their opposites

Carrying capacity

Niche size and characteristics

This book has stressed throughout a continuity with nature and the development and utilization of natural laws. Again it is emphasized that, in viewing environments, one's concern should be with *systemic* properties and properties *emergent* at the level of a *field of forces,* not with the behavior of individual people, fishes, trees, or machines. It is often difficult to get this point across to some people—especially to discipline-biased scientists—who dismiss comparative systems studies as being at best analogy and at worst metaphor. Fortunately, the climate of thought is changing, and more and more investigators are seeing a unity of human and natural systems.

The assessment and management of ecological and environmental problems and projects provides many parallels with the development of weapons systems. In both cases some elements are sensitive to management control and some are not. In both cases it is imperative to involve a variety of experts and managers and users from the very beginning of conceptualization and to incorporate in the development process at that time all the critical forces, variables, and linkages. Both cases involve ranges of alternative goals and objectives, key policies, key indicators, information handling, modeling, evaluation, and interactions and communications among participants.

Total systems planning is imperative for both approaches. At the same time both approaches share the types of data problems discussed here, the necessity to select the proper methodological tools from among a repertory that includes many irrelevant, obsolescent, or inappropriate tools, the tendency to want to measure everything, and the proclivity to concentrate on the static and cross-sectional as opposed to the dynamic and longitudinal and the obviously measurable as opposed to the obviously important but hard to measure. These comparisons refer to systems-level behaviors, not to the recognizably precise aerodynamic or ballistic measurements that may characterize the behavior of some elements of the system.

Most of these factors apply also to the conceptualization, development, design, evaluation, and management of other categories of systems—economic, sociotechnical, urban, transportation—as arbitrarily defined at any given time and place. Nevertheless, the person familiar with the weapons system development process experiences a feeling of *déjà vu* when first attempting to tackle environmental problems.

Ecosystems, like other complex systems, introduce problems of uncertainty. Handling uncertainty requires special techniques for dealing with processes that are only partially known and requires designs that are less sensitive to the unexpected. These designs must be anticipatory rather than reactive. Adaptive management is *not* just the better mobilization of the obvious and of known information. The new theories and techniques presented in Chapter 5 provide key means for succinctly representing the most important environmental forces and factors.

Good design in the face of ecological uncertainty dictates a number of considerations. Most importantly, the uncertain and the unknown cannot ever be completely eliminated, nor should the attempt be made to try to eliminate all uncertainty. Design should be *for* uncertainty and in full recognition of the system-testing value of a moderate degree of environmental surprise and shock. Completely protected or shielded systems tend to lose their adaptability and to forget how to respond when crisis finally does reappear. Attempts at tighter monitoring, regulation, and control produce only the dangerous illusion of being in control.

Further, good designs should lead to obtaining benefits from the unexpected. Good designs should encourage learning, but not the blind trial and error that characterized peoples' interaction with nature through most of human history. Good ecological designs can be the most parsimonious designs in that they avoid the intrinsically irreversible as well as the irreversible due to investments of funds and prestige. Post hoc repairs and patch-ups of faulty designs are notoriously costly.

Still further, good designs do recognize that impacts often occur far removed in space and time from the original source. Present decisions may lead to future consequences that produce even more severe problems. What a complex ecosystem is doing now may offer no clue as to what it might do under changing conditions. Surveys can be prohibitively expensive, while producing little insight into important causal linkages. Good designs work with rather than against the flow and rhythm of interrelated ecological, economic, and social forces. And finally, research should be focused through policy and other management needs, not through scientific orientations which tend to be narrow and parochial.

Classifications and Principles

Professor Crawford S. Holling and his colleagues, an international team of environmental scientists, have contributed greatly to changing ecology from an interesting but remote academic subject to a professional field that is squarely confronting human and management problems of the utmost importance.[6]

Just as management has received a lot of misleading guidance on the handling of uncertainty, so have policymakers as well as people in general been misled as to the meaning and value of equilibrium and stability. Chapter 5 noted that living systems usually function far from equilibrium, that perturbations often modify the equilibrium positions, and that these systems often flip back and forth between or among equilibrium positions. It was also noted that stability is a relative thing and that under certain conditions stability can stifle evolution and other necessary change. A primary design goal should be to learn from change rather than try to ensure stability under all conditions.

Professor Holling and his colleagues have developed a great deal of new expertise in systems management as a result of applying catastrophe theory and other systems theories and methodologies to several real-world environmental problems. In-depth environmental assessments were made of the spruce budworm–coniferous forest management problem of northeastern Canada; the management of Pacific salmon; resort development at Obergurgl in the Alps of Austria; regional development in the Orinoco River basin of Venezuela; and wildlife impacted by oil-shale mining in the western United States. These case histories have yielded both a much better understanding of the applications of the new theories and new insights into the design of adaptive systems.

The stability properties of a system help determine how it will respond to human and natural, planned and unplanned perturbations. Holling and his colleagues present four views of nature, listed in order of increasing relevance to today's problems (compare these with the classifications of organizational environments discussed earlier):

1. **Benign nature.** Bigness of scale is not only allowed but necessary. Any trial and error is possible. No matter how large the perturbation or disturbance, the ecosystem will return to stability once the perturbation is removed.

2. **Ephemeral nature.** Small is beautiful. The ecosystem is basically highly unstable, fragile, and diverse, and tampering with it easily leads to irreversible effects such as species extinctions.

3. **Mischievous nature** or **nature, the practical joker.** A combination of the first two categories of properties. There is more than one stable mode of behavior, and catastrophic flips may suddenly and unexpectedly follow small incremental changes.

4. **Resilient nature.** The different distinct behavior modes are maintained because of, not in spite of, diversity and variability. Not only do variables like sizes, numbers, and ages shift, but so do entire boundaries between regions of stability. Therefore, the success of a management strategy in maximizing the distance from a supposedly dangerous boundary of stability (for example, setting certain standards of safety, health, and reliability in both engineering design and government regulation) may precipitate system collapse because the boundary retracts or implodes to meet the restricted variability. *Resilience*—the ability of a system to absorb, utilize, and benefit from shocks and other changes—emerges as a main design criterion for adaptive systems. No system is infinitely resilient, however, as can be witnessed by the sudden death or eutrophication of lakes.

Ecologists have developed a number of important principles, highly relevant to the management of ecosystems and problems in the natural environment per se, but space limits consideration to those principles and properties most applicable to organizations and organization–environment interactions.[7] Holling and his colleagues provided four major properties describing reaction to change and relevant to both ecosystems and human institutions:

1. **Organization of connections among parts.** Elements are organized in selective ways to form subassemblies. Connections are tight within the subassemblies but loose between them. Failures may therefore have a limited effect. This design idea of course originated with social scientist, Herbert Simon, in the 1960s, and was expressed as hierarchical design in

his famous *architecture of complexity*. It is gratifying to see successful application of the concept to ecological problems. Nevertheless, considerable evidence points to increasing coupling among the world's subassemblies, and the principle may be more valuable to organizational design than to the interpretation of environmental phenomena.

2. *Spatial heterogeneity.*   Impacts of human activities are not limited to the initial area or time. A pipeline, for example, may have an immediate and recognized local impact and also a more subtle generation of boomtowns rather far removed from the pipeline site. Pollutants do not gradually dissipate over time but often combine as photochemical smog or return to earth as acid rain. Economic perturbations are not necessarily damped by the myriad transactions in the socioeconomic system.

3. *Stability and resilience.*   The system may not recover from disturbances once these perturbations are removed. Instead, the system may respond in unexpected ways involving different paths ranging from stable and static equilibrium paths through the sustained oscillation of dynamic equilibrium to instability leading to extinctions and catastrophic reconfigurations.[8]

4. *Dynamic variability.*   Dynamic change determines in part the structure, diversity, and variability of the system. The greater the ongoing change and stress, within limits, the greater the chances of survival of the system. Reduction of variability leads to gradual loss of resilience through relaxation of selective pressures. Constancy produces fragility. Unless reminded by change, the system becomes rigid. Resilience is dependent on continual testing of the system, even though the tester appears to be undesirable or even obnoxious. For example, the spruce budworm has been found to be necessary for softwood forest renewal and survival. Spraying with insecticide, a seemingly rational policy, turns out to be counterproductive.

Let's now look at some examples in a little more detail.[9] A striking case involves the Great Lakes fisheries, on which data on the seven most important commercial species in all five lakes go back as far as 1880. For a number of years there was a large and sustained yield with modest fluctuations. Then, in only two to three years, some species became extinct and others plummeted to very low numbers. Even when the pressures from both fishing and predators were removed, the fish populations did not spring back to their higher equilibrium level. A catastrophic reconfiguration had taken place in a system with at least two equilibria. Populations fluctuated around each equilibrium, but when exogenous stress became too great the fish populations suddenly fell to the lower or lowest equilibrium and remained there. The lowest equilibria are often around the threshold for extinction.

Such dynamics apply widely throughout complex systems. Many other examples could be provided of predator–prey, herbivore–plant, pest–host, and disease–organism interrelationships of immense importance in the management of wildlife, preserved natural areas, forests, fisheries, agriculture, and public health. In Chapter 5 we noted that many organizations appear to operate on at least two equilibrium levels of performance. Many chronic problems of modern societies, such as unemployment and underemployment, lowered productivity, alienation, and crime, can be better explained by stability and catastrophe theories. These ideas will be expanded later in this chapter and in the next chapter.

Another example involves the conversion from sugar cane to cotton as a main crop in some river valleys in western Peru in the 1920s. Seven native insects became major pests. In 1949 chlorinated hydrocarbon insecticides were first applied. Initially there was a great decline in numbers of pests and a 50 percent increase in the cotton yield. However, within two or three years, six new species of insects emerged as serious pests because their predators and parasites had been greatly reduced by the spraying. Just a few years later the original insect pests had developed immunity to the insecticide, and crop damage increased. In spite of increasing the rate and concentration of spraying and the substitution of organophosphates for the chlorinated hydrocarbons, the cotton yield dropped and the agricultural economy approached bankruptcy. Then chemical control was minimized, the food web allowed to reestablish itself, and cotton production rose to the highest level in the history of the effort.

This case provides yet another example of what, as discussed earlier, Professor Jay W. Forrester has called the counterintuitive behavior of complex systems. The moral is, once again, that the most obvious, seemingly most rational management policies may turn out to be the worst ones.

Numerous other examples of the mismanagement of ecosystems could be mentioned. These include the failure of a massive bureaucratic program to halt the spread of the fire ant in the southeast United States through spraying, the biomagnification of DDT in the food web, the salinization of agricultural land in the Central Valley of California, the conversion of forest and savanna into desert in large areas of Africa and Latin America, the spread of debilitating disease (schistosomiasis) and decline of Mediterranean fisheries off Egypt following construction of the Aswan Dam (widespread water pollution in the sea didn't help either!), the destruction of recreation areas and the death of rivers and lakes worldwide through pollution, and the extinction or near extinction of myriad species of animals and plants.

The instances of ecosystem mismanagement are too many, too huge, too varied, too long-lasting, too serious, and too well documented to be scoffed at and perfunctorily dismissed. Even if executives should decide that environmental problems are not important (and many do not feel that way), the issue of environmentalism and conservation as a major social movement must be dealt with. And even more importantly, the lessons learned from nature apply also to socioeconomic systems.

Briefly, societal systems possess multiple-stability regions, so that sudden catastrophic jumps can precipitate crises. Systems that have evolved toward maximization of stability, minimization of perturbations, and minimization of risk (for example, the large, aging bureaucracies discussed in Chapter 3) tend to *react* to challenges and opportunities as crises. The adaptive responses of these systems gradually erode, and they try to reduce undesirable perturbations even further by means by rigidly repetitive, stereotyped, and decreasingly productive behavior. This clearly calls for changes in both organizational design and in legislative practice. Holling et al. suggest that flexible and adaptive behavior can be designed into organizations through alternating periods of innovation and consolidation. This suggestion accords nicely with the theory of sociotechnical evolution of world society as a whole, as expressed by families of successive S-curves in Chapter 3.

The purpose of this section has been to enrich the concept of organizational external environments, particularly of the turbulent-field environment, using principles, applications, and examples from ecology and environmental science and benefitting from the experience of professional ecologists. The *practical* applicability of the new field theories in the context of ecosystems is particularly gratifying.

Environmental Selection and Fit of Organizations

A strong evolutionary theme runs through this book. To survive, at least at desired performance levels, organizations must adapt to turbulent environmental change by acquiring and maintaining fit to the given environmental situation. Organizational structure *and* function are very closely related to environmental structure and behavior and to the particular form of organization–environmental interactions. This is the contingency and open-systems approach to organizational design, which was introduced in Chapter 1. Then Chapter 3 discussed a number of reasons, particularly associated with aging, grossness of scale, and misunderstanding of the environments, whereby organizations can lose their adaptive capability and hence their fit to the environments and thereby have their continued survival threatened.

But what about selective pressures exerted by the environments? Are there limits to adaptability? To survivability? Obviously the environments do select in favor of some organizations and against others, and the evidence is against infinite adaptability. The attrition rate of new and small organizations is appreciable. And, as was discussed in Chapters 1 and 5, the number of organizations that either fail or collapse, continue to survive after shocks but at lowered levels of expectancy and performance, or suffer periodic crises is large.

Environmental selection of organizations for or against survival at a desired performance level can operate in several different ways. These operations are complexly interrelated, but for convenience we can present them as follows: (1) selection of a single organization in the absence of competitors, (2) selection of an organization from among a population of organizations, and (3) protection of a given organization. Both the apparently blind and relentless, or at least poorly understood, field of forces and purposeful human actions contribute to these operational processes.

An individual organization can succeed or fail because of its intrinsic capabilities or limitations, such as has been already discussed in detail, and fit or lack of fit to a particular broad or narrow ecological niche. For example, an organization can offer a product or service or such a variety of products or services as to make the organization essentially unique. Sometimes an individual organization becomes so powerful that it can overwhelm environmental pressures toward selecting against it. These situations are, however, always ephemeral. Eventually, in capitalist countries, competitors spontaneously arise or are encouraged to arise, and no organization has the power to control *all* environments over prolonged periods.

In capitalist countries similar and competitive organizations comprise, in the short range, the most important elements of the external environments of corporations. In the longer range, social, economic, and ecological *forces*, at least partially generated or triggered by competition among organizations and nations, are the most important environmental features. In dealing with multiple organizations, populations of organizations can be spoken of and the principles of population ecology can be brought to bear.

The third situation, protection of an organization, has unfortunately become a dominant way of doing things these days. Government organizations, government-controlled organizations, and even entire nations are protected from real competition and shock by even more encompassing organizations. As seen in the last section, these organizations are freed from the need to learn and adapt through continual testing by the environment, and they eventually lose their resilience. This results in passing the needs to adapt and maintain resilience up to the protecting body.

The government bailouts of Lockheed and, particularly Chrysler, do not make good ecosense for several reasons. First, executives of other large corporations see rewards for failure, and, therefore, some executives may become demotivated or may change their motivations in the wrong direction. Second, the little person sees capriciousness and injustice in the fact that some large corporations, having exceeded a magic threshold, are not allowed to fail, while the neighborhood hardware store, say, is. These perceptions further erode faith in the capitalist system. Third, the perpetuation of weak links in a tightly coupled system renders the existence of that system even more precarious.

This is a situation of general systems importance. For completeness, many other weak units such as the welfare system, the criminal justice system, the health services system, some labor unions, and other large social and sociotechnical systems must share the contribution to macrosystem fragility. Lockheed and Chrysler, by themselves, are only symbols and between themselves are not strictly comparable. Lockheed made poor financial, scheduling, contract, and technological decisions with regard to the L-1011, C5A, and Cheyenne helicopter, but the company was part of a highly viable industry, important to national defense, basically competitive, and possessed a successful unit in Lockheed Missiles and Space Company. Lockheed has since repaid the $250 million loan advanced in 1971.

Chrysler is part of an old industry that for decades has witnessed the demise of the smaller automakers. For years Chrysler has been losing its market share and its competitive capital capability compared to that of Ford and especially of General Motors. Thus, Chrysler has intrinsic problems superimposed on those faced by all American automakers.

Evolutionists, ecologists, and many organization scientists stress the importance of diversity and variability among individuals, species, and populations. But what happens when the individuals of the species or population become more and more alike? Because of common, simplified environments in almost every respect, many industries and companies have moved toward decreased diversity and variability. These environments are simplified in the sense that government regulations, common labor unions and workforces, common markets, and so on have shielded or protected the companies from the true turbulence. Consider the U.S. automakers again. They are much more similar than different. Although differing in capital, market share, and to some extent relative investments in R&D, GM, Ford, Chrysler, and American Motors are remarkably similar or even identical in terms of the sociotechnical production system, the labor force, the relatively small amount of successful diversification outside the auto industry, the small percentages of knowledge workers, the approach to advertising, and—perhaps most important—the world outlook. In 1980 Chrysler lost $1.7097 billion (the second year in a row of large losses), Ford lost $1.5433 billion, GM lost $762.5 million, and American Motors lost $197.525 million. Firestone Tire and Rubber, in a dependent industry with similar problems, lost $105.9 million.

The moral is that if the units of a system show little variability, share common weaknesses, and are highly interrelated, the chances of overall system failure are high. The most vulnerable is merely the first to fail.

To return now to some points raised at the beginning of this section, obviously no organization and no system—except perhaps the entire universe—is infinitely adaptable. Adaptability can be increased greatly, perhaps even optimized against some criterion, and it is the purpose of this book to provide guidance in so improving organizational adaptability.

One of the main adaptive goals of an organization is to avoid being selected out by the environments. Professors Michael Hannan and John Freeman have studied, from an ecological perspective, such selecting out or loss of organizations.[10] To assess the magnitude of loss, they compared the *Fortune* 500 list of 1955 with that of 1975. They found that, adjusting for mere name changes, of the large industrial corporations listed in 1955 268 (53.6 percent) were still listed in 1975, 122 companies had disappeared from the list through merger, 109 companies had slipped in rank, and one company has been liquidated.

Hannan and Freeman suggest that the differences among organizations are due mainly to selection and that structural inertia seriously limits adaptation. Structural inertia emanates from both inside and outside the organization and includes sunk capital investments, information limitations, resistance to change, conflicts in the rationality of decisionmaking, historical precedent, legal constraints, and reality biased by the perceptions of specialists. These factors can indeed be serious impediments to building adaptive organizations. However, all are remediable, given time and especially the active desires for change and support of top management.

A further look at selection is, nevertheless, warranted. One approach is to examine the ecological niches into which competitive organizations might fit. Hannan and Freeman employed the familiar Lotka-Volterra model. This model was developed about 1925 as a description of predator–prey interrelationships. However, it can be applied to any two competing species or populations. Basically, it involves the logistic equation, which has been discussed, modified in terms of a pair of coupled differential equations to include the effects of competition on carrying capacity.

Hannan and Freeman determined that the greater the similarity of two resource-limited competitors, the less likely a given environment can support both in equilibrium. Therefore, the population that is less fit with regard to some characteristic necessary for survival will perish. Of course this is a closed-system model, but many organizations do in effect operate in relatively closed environments. For example, markets for given products cannot be expanded indefinitely. Also, if consumer disposable income decreases greatly, products and services seen as luxuries will lose out in competition with the necessities.

In time the number of medium-sized organizations declines as larger organizations enter the competitive field. In fact there is an ecological principle that states that mature systems exploit immature systems. However, there is a threshold below which larger organizations do not deign to compete. For a long time IBM ignored the market in small computers. Thus, there is opportunity for new, small, and viable organizations, but once these babies grow to a certain size, the giants are usually ready to take them on.

The stability or instability of the environment helps determine the relative advantage of a specialist as opposed to a generalist design strategy. In a stable environment a specialist design that can exploit the resources of a given niche is preferable. Under stable conditions, specialists will outcompete generalists in the specialists' optimum environment. Even under some unstable environmental conditions, some specialist organizations may be robust enough to ride through the hard times.

Hannan and Freeman point out that generalist organizations either rely simultaneously on a variety of resources or maintain excess capacity. At any given time, generalist organizations may appear to have a great deal of waste. Specialist organizations appear to be more efficient because they have less excess capacity (often called slack or redundancy). However, too little excess capacity in changing environments leads to being selected out of existence.

Note how designs, "efficient" in the short range, threaten long-term survival.

FOCUS ON THE TURBULENT-FIELD ENVIRONMENT

Early in this book the term turbulent environment was introduced; at the beginning of this chapter the term was defined more fully. The world environmental *field* is becoming ever more turbulent. Adaptive-system design is contingent on, and should be isomorphic to, the turbulence in the external environmental field. Then in Chapters 3 and 5 and the early part of this chapter detailed arguments for increasing turbulence and descriptions of processes within the turbulent environment were presented. Also discussed in detail was why organizations can, and many organizations do, lose fit with their rapidly changing environments.

Most of these discussions have been strongly flavored by the rich ideas about dynamic growth and evolution of organizations as one form of sociotechnical system, of sociotechnical systems themselves, and of environments themselves. The highest-level integrating concept is field theory, and the latest thinking in physical science and qualitative mathematics has been used as a source of new building blocks for a construction of explanations of what organizations and environments are doing in these critical times. A number of applications of the new field theory to social, ecological, economic, and other complex systems also have been offered.

Science, and fortunately the humanities too, are becoming more interdisciplinary, multidisciplinary, and—even better—nondisciplinary. This salutary evolutionary change is especially important in the management and organizational sciences, which must necessarily deal with plans, policies, and decisions that affect the future welfare of the entire planet.

Chapter 2 summarized a number of approaches that in some instances maintain local, subsystem value or utility *when incorporated into a holistic program* but that in other cases are obsolete, worn out. Organizations waste immense amounts of time, effort, and money on programs that on the one hand are only of local value and are most likely swallowed up in the maelstrom of the system as a whole and on the other hand are no longer appropriate or even wrong. Chapter 4 stressed the importance of trying to forecast future environmental and organizational–environmental configurations, particularly through the use of simulation modeling. It was noted, however, that a number of deficiencies were apparent in these models in terms of theoretical underpinnings, basic constructs or building blocks, basic assumptions, and incorporation of behavioral and social factors.

Emphasis has been on the discontinuities, transitions, and transformations that seem most to characterize the world of today and tomorrow. If this world view be granted, what are the theories, models, techniques, types of information, designs, and decisions most appropriate to such a turbulent world? They must stem from the most viable parts of systems theory and practice, nourished and sustained by the continually important concept of human continuity with nature, and invigorated by the vibrant new ideas of field theory that are so rapidly advancing the state of the art.

The idea of periods of innovation alternating with periods of consolidation has cropped up a number of times. Earlier generations of executives and planners were faced with the requirement to develop new perceptions, insights, and orientations and to learn new vocabularies and methods of doing things. A look at history shows that the new philosophies, theories, and techniques were often viewed as being shockingly radical. But eventually the strange new concepts and methods are incorporated into the general body of executive thinking, are exploited, and with age are modified or replaced by even more novel ideas and disappear.

In the 1960s CEOs were exposed to heavy doses of operations research, behavioral science, and data-processing, which they were able to survive and use. And they will survive—and learn to benefit from—hyperbolic growth theory, the Entropy Law, dissipative structures, symbiosis, tighter coupling, emergence, computer simulation models of complex systems, ecological principles, and catastrophe theory, which initially might appear to be bizarre and rather removed from the workaday business of organization design and top management function.

To return to the more specific topic of the turbulent-field environment, it will be seen that the term is an especially felicitous one because turbulence in nature is very complex and has baffled physicists, astronomers, and meteorologists for centuries.

The turbulent-field environment can be viewed in terms of (1) the causative or generating forces and (2) the processes in the field itself. Emery and Trist say a great deal more about the first than about the second. Further, they say a lot about social processes but very little about natural processes. Emery and Trist emphasize the field behavior of the turbulent environment as triggered by the activities of human organizations. The concept of the turbulent-field environment has been extended by (1) adding greater mathematical precision to the description of processes in the field itself through catastrophe theory, for example; (2) emphasizing the fundamental oneness of natural, economic, and sociotechnical systems; (3) introducing a long-term evolutionary framework and the concept of major societal transformations as expressed partially by the theory of successive S-shaped growth or change stages enveloped by a hyperbolic curve; and (4) suggesting that turbulent environments are an intrinsic attribute of nature, and that they have arisen, for example, in the geological past at the time of the origin of life and at the times of the great extinctions of species.

This section will conclude with a brief look at the human causative or generative forces that are making the environmental field of the organization more turbulent. Professor Emery proposes five major trends.[11]

1. The immense growth in organizational size and concentration of power. In the disturbed, reactive environment, maximization of power is the basic adaptive strategy. But beyond a critical point of diminishing returns or diseconomy of scale, the concentration of power is no longer able to reduce

uncertainty. The continued exercise of great power triggers the generation of processes in the environment that both have lives of their own and are dangerous to all.

2. The growing interdependence among all parts of society. Part of this ensues from greater affluence and education and from technological changes in transportation, communications, and trade, but more important has been the transformation of man-as-a-tool to man-as-a-citizen. This will be much less reversible.

3. The harnessing of scientific R&D to augment competitive organizational power.

4. The revolution in communications, transportation, and information. This trend has augmented the growth of organizations and the emergence of multinational organizations. However, the great increase in information has not reduced relevant uncertainty, but rather has generated problems of information overload and a false sense of knowing and confidence that have often led to precipitous decisions and actions.

5. Increasing bureaucratization in every walk of life.

In examining the bureaucratic contribution to turbulence, Professor Emery provides some insights that are remarkably similar to interpretations offered earlier. Emery analyzed a graph taken from *Fortune,* which depicted the annual number of mergers and acquisitions of U.S. manufacturing and mining companies between 1895 and 1972. These longitudinal data indicated three major peaks, around 1898–1900, around 1928–1930, and around 1967–1969, which Emery interpreted as the crests of waves. These waves look like the Kondratieff long waves, which the systems dynamicists are studying and which were discussed in Chapter 4. Emery made primarily a sociotechnical and organizational analysis rather than an economic analysis and did not comment on the coincidence of the collapse of the second wave and the stock market crash of 1929.

Emery believes that the 1895–1900 wave was unique in Western history because of the marriage of the bureaucratic organization, the scientific management of Taylor, and others, and the capability to harness vast amounts of energy. This marked the emergence of the disturbed, reactive environment. In turn, the period 1967–1969 introduced the turbulent environment. To Emery the "bureaucratic solution" has both led to the instability of the turbulent field and sapped our ability to solve problems and to plan for and implement constructive futures.

In commenting on the entire time series, Emery writes:

> . . . these peaks have occurred with *dramatic suddenness* and lasted about two–three years. This strongly suggests that the existing system absorbs the strain of technological change, without adequate piece-meal adaptation, until, *on some stimulus, radical restructuring occurs—unplanned and unpredicted.*[5] (emphasis added)

Sound familiar? Sounds like periodic catastrophes to me.

Even more significantly, the third wave is qualitatively different from the other waves in many ways. It should be emphasized that the dynamics of the evolution far transcend the single indicator, acquisitions and mergers.

THE NATURAL ENVIRONMENT

This section serves as an introduction to the specific environments as a whole. Most of the crises that top management must anticipate will be in one way or another associated with the environments. There are of course vast amounts of data about each environment, but, as usual, these data may be inconsistent, contradictory, and available outside an integrating framework.

Information and knowledge—organized, integrated, combinable, selectable by category and priority—are indispensable for planning. The external and internal environments are of course complexly intertwined and are in no way independent of one another. However, it is convenient for purposes of problem identification, priority determination, and the construction of subsystems in theories and models to treat the environments, in an *interim* fashion, as if they were independent. People have thought in terms of disciplines and specialties for a very long time, and most data, trends, projections, and predictions are organized accordingly, even though the real world does not operate that way.

As emphasized especially in Chapters 2 and 4, one of the greatest impediments to even understanding the behavior of the organization, let alone planning, is the deficiency of integrated, causal theory and models. This should continually be borne in mind as the events, trends, projections, symptoms, and problems that follow are examined. These limited pages can offer only key interpretations, principles, warnings, and alerts of greatest value to top management in anticipating critical changes. Once key factors have been recognized, and executives have developed a holistic understanding of the system, top management may wish to consult further with specialists, who can pursue each lead more fully.

The natural environment is *the most important* external environment. Most simply, that is where food, water, oxygen, and energy are obtained. The natural environment is the base of the pyramid of human needs. Although humankind could conceivably thrive without elaborate economic, technological, social, and political systems, it cannot survive the continuous and catastrophic degradation of the natural environment. And this is what is happening to the natural environment. The evidence is vast and varied and cannot be questioned.

If the crumbling of the very base of all human institutions is well under way, what does this mean to the executive? It means that all facets of business—finance, production, importing, exporting, general trade, relation to law and legislation, and so on—will become increasingly more precarious. One likely outcome in long-range planning for many a company will be the demise of the company.

Organizations differ of course in the *directness* of their relationships with the natural environment. Companies and industries that are heavily involved in agriculture, food production, mining, forestry, and energy production have close interfaces with the natural environment. So do industries like chemicals and steel whose effluents may pollute the environment. However, the indirect relationships may be just as critical or more so. For example, almost all companies will be affected by the increasing chaos in the Third World. The operation of conglomerates and multinationals, the lending practices of international, national, and private organizations, and the nature of trade and markets will shift suddenly and greatly as combined population pressures and nearly irreversible environmental destruction take further toll among remaining stable social and political structures.

Another indirect effect stems from the perceptions of people about business and the environment. At the present time millions of people are antibusiness, antigovernment, and antibigness. Environmentalism and conservation are one of several strong social movements, which represent large-scale changes in values and attitudes. Whether these movements will greatly expand or contract during the coming years of intensified stress for all requires much further thought by executives.

A number of early warnings about increasing environmental degradation have been provided in the past two decades or so, perhaps starting with Rachel Carson's indictment of the misuse of pesticides in *Silent Spring*. These warnings were amplified by several of the policy-directed computer simulation models which were discussed in some detail in Chapter 4. In May 1977 President Jimmy Carter requested a study of the long-term implications of present world trends in population, the natural environment, and natural resources and of the United States government's capabilities for long-range planning in these areas. The result of the three-year study is *The Global 2000 Report to the President.*[12]

The *Global 2000* study is important and valuable, not only because it is a rich compendium of data, trends, projections, and interpretations, but also because it provides further evidence on the strengths and weaknesses of modelling for policymaking. Perhaps most important, it illustrates an increasing systems sophistication and realism on the part of government.

The *Global 2000* study states:

> Our conclusions . . . are disturbing. They indicate the potential for global problems of alarming proportions by the year 2000. Environmental, resource, and population stresses are *intensifying* and will *increasingly* determine the quality of human life on our planet. These stresses are *already severe enough* to deny many millions of people basic needs for food, shelter, health, and jobs, or any hope for betterment. At the same time, the earth's carrying capacity—the ability of biological systems to provide resources for human needs—is eroding. The trends reflected in the . . . study suggest strongly a *progressive degradation and impoverishment* of the earth's resource base.
>
> If these trends are to be altered and the problems diminished, *vigorous, determined new initiatives* will be required worldwide to meet human needs while

protecting and restoring the earth's capacity to support life. Basic natural resources—farmlands, fisheries, forests, minerals, energy, air, and water—must be conserved and better managed. Changes in public policy are needed around the world *before problems worsen and options for effective action are reduced* (emphasis added).

And further:

If present trends continue, the world in 2000 will be more crowded, more polluted, less stable ecologically, and more vulnerable to disruption than the world we live in now. Serious stresses involving population, resources, and environment are clearly visible ahead. Despite greater material output, the world's people will be poorer in many ways than they are today.

The *Global 2000* study reports the following principal findings:

1. Population growth rates for the world as a whole will have barely decreased at all—from 1.8 percent a year to 1.7 percent. In terms of sheer numbers population growth in 2000 will be greater than it is today. Total world population will have increased by over 50 percent from the 1975 level—from 4 billion to 6.35 billion.

2. The large present gap, in wealth and standard of living, between rich and poor nations will widen.

3. World food production is projected to increase 90 percent over the 1970 level. However, real prices for food are expected to double. And the overall increases will amount to less than 15 percent when averaged worldwide. Most of the improvements will be in countries with already high per capita consumptions. The food situation in many countries will scarcely improve and in others will actually decline below present inadequacy.

4. The amount of arable land will increase only four percent. Hence increases in food must come from far greater yields, aided by better fertilizers and pesticides and power for irrigation and machinery—all heavily dependent on oil and gas.

5. Energy availability will continue to be a major problem with differential impacts. Collectively, the finite fuel resources—oil, gas, coal, tar sands, oil shales, uranium—should be sufficient for centuries. However, these are differentially distributed and pose unknown or unsolved problems of exploitation, environmental impact, economic feasibility, transportation, and use. During the 1990s world oil production should approach maximum capacity. The richer industrialized nations should have no difficulty meeting their growing energy requirements through 1990. The one-fourth of humankind that depends on firewood and animal dung will find themselves in an increasingly dire position.

6. Regional water shortages will become more severe. Deforestation will make supplies even more erratic. Development of new supplies will be more costly.

7. Serious losses of forests will continue in keeping with mounting demands for forest products and firewood. The amount of commercial-size timber is projected to decline 50 percent per capita.

8. Serious deterioration of cropland and rangeland will continue worldwide because of erosion, leaching, loss of organic matter, desertification, alkalinization, acidification, lateritization (conversion of tropical rain-forest soil to brick), salinization, and waterlogging.

9. Concentrations of carbon dioxide and ozone-depleting chemicals in the atmosphere are expected to increase at rates which could significantly alter the world's climate and upper atmosphere by 2050 or *sooner.*

10. Perhaps 20 percent of all remaining plant and animal species, important for retaining genetic diversity even if one ignores esthetic and humane considerations, will have irretrievably vanished as their habitats are destroyed and they become increasingly vulnerable to human destructive activities.

The *Global 2000 Report* is a relatively optimistic scenario! It is relatively optimistic for several reasons, some of which its authors identify and some of which are identified here.

First, the study was based on three major underlying assumptions: (1) the continuation worldwide of present types of policies, (2) the continued rapid rates of technological development and adoption, with neither revolutionary breakthroughs nor disastrous setbacks, and the continued market regulation of demand and price, and (3) the absence of major disruptions in international trade and the economy due to war or political upheavals. The *Report,* however, does recognize the increasing dangers of international conflict and stress to the international financial system.

Second, the study was not a *systems* study. Rather it represented analyses and projections from a number of independent or sequentially (output-to-input) related modules for which data had been routinely collected for a number of years. The models and data banks of the various participating agencies had been created at different times, for different reasons, and using different methods. These components had not been designed or intended to be used together in an interactive and consistent fashion. This important problem of top–down versus bottom–up modeling was discussed in Chapter 4.

The result of the lack of causal feedback and other linkages was to overstate the availability of resources and the earth's continuing ability to provide ever increasing amounts of resources and to understate greatly the mutually reinforcing stresses of the interacting forces.

The *Global 2000* study was compared with several of the world models discussed in Chapter 4. Findings were generally consistent. When the linkages were cut in the World 3 *Limits to Growth* model and in the Mesarovic-Pestel *World Integrated Model,* in order to approximate better the *Global 2000* projections, the outputs of the former became much more optimistic.

Third, the *Global 2000* study, in not being based on systems theory and sophisticated systems modeling methodology, did not produce the dramatic oscillations and collapses of a systems dynamics model, let alone the structural reconfigurations and discontinuous, catastrophic, and irreversible changes stressed in the form of field theory. Further, the population and other projections in *Global 2000* were based on customary, not hyperbolic, rates of increase.

Several overall conclusions of *The Global 2000 Report* coincide well with the thrust here:

1. The United States must greatly improve its ability to identify *emerging* problems and assess alternative responses (emphasis added).
2. The world in 2000 will be more vulnerable both to natural disasters and to disruptions stemming from human ignorance, desperation, and malice.
3. There will be no quick fixes—technological, political, economic, or social.

It is becoming increasingly evident that many hopes of the past have turned out to be pipedreams if not nightmares. Consider resource substitution. Major resource substitution is extremely complex and not a straightforward function of relative prices as some economists hold. Long lead times are required for scientific discovery or invention, innovation, and diffusion or market penetration. And the results, under *some* criteria, can turn out to be steps backward. Thus, the widespread substitution of petroleum for coal forced the industrialized West far out onto a limb, far from a maintainable stable equilibrium. This is true because of the greater scarcity of petroleum and because of the differential geographic distribution of petroleum, which increasingly perturbs the past type of economic and political stability of the world. Likewise, the substitution of aluminum for iron has markedly increased the dependence on electricity.

Many businessmen misinterpret the nature of environmental issues, the forces operating on the environment, and the magnitude and near irreversibility of environmental change. Businessmen often get themselves trapped in polemics such as jobs versus pollution and trees versus people and locked-up resources versus resources developed to expand the good life. But the inexorable and relentless worldwide destruction of farm, field, pasture, forest, and recreation area attracts far less attention. Yet the more widespread and intense the conversion to desert, the irreparable damage to soils, and the eradication of at first local life-sustaining qualities, the fewer and less varied the options for future business. One reason is that large devastated areas such as the African Sahel and parts of south Asia, as well as smaller areas like Haiti, simply will be unattractive to business. Another reason is that nations threatened with internal chaos and collapse will begin to fight over things like water rights, and this instability will not be conducive to good business practices. Still another reason is that national or regional instability will trigger political upheavals, which are almost always associated with a search for scapegoats. The new governments will most likely be anti-Western and the scapegoats will be Americans and things American (the United States is the perennial ogre!), and this situation won't be very good for business either. And just one more reason is that at least some of the disgruntled nations will have nuclear weapons.

To close this section, several warnings that apply to dealings with the natural environment are listed:

1. In competition with humankind, nature is sly, tough, and adaptable. Although living parts will be sacrificed (for example, soils, forests, and species), nature will eventually wear humankind down. The results are not always pleasant—penicillin-resistant gonococci, drug-resistant malaria parasites, and poison-resistant insects and rodents. Problem: inasmuch as about a quarter of the world's stored grain is estimated to be destroyed annually by rodents, what should be done? Answer: develop a more powerful rodenticide and a program to apply it. Wrong—get a cat or perhaps a snake.

2. In competition with humankind, nature matches strategy for strategy. Problem: Southern California is thirsty. Solution: use up your own water and then grab as much water from afar as possible. Nature's partial response: deposit salts in the newly irrigated western San Joaquin Valley and force salt water from San Francisco Bay into somebody else's farms in the Sacramento-San Joaquin Delta.

3. In competition with humankind, nature is patient for a long time but then strikes back suddenly in force. Problem and solution: wildfires are bad, so put them out as soon as possible. Nature's response: wait until the brush and forest understory really builds up, then burn the whole area to the ground.

4. In dealing with humankind, nature giveth and nature taketh away. Nature's offer: here are some gifts (fertile soil, redwoods, whales, passenger pigeons, clean air and water). Humankind's response: we want these, but there are lots more of us now, and we want more—and more. Nature's reply: fine, I'll take these gifts away now.

5. In dealing with humankind, nature presents several faces. If you don't like me green and blue, how about brown and grey? If you don't like this side of me, how about my flip side?

THE TECHNOLOGICAL ENVIRONMENT

For a very long time human technology has provided many of the wonders as well as many of the woes of the world. The technological environment is linked to the natural environment in terms of the extraction of resources and the by-products, such as pollution, of processes. Most importantly, technology functions as a multiplier, greatly amplifying the effects of human numbers and activities. Technology, once initiated, appears to be autonomous, that is, to have self-organizing properties and to assume a life of its own. For example, demands to open up a wilderness area for exploitation of petroleum, mineral, and forest resources may lead to the building of roads. Villages may then grow up to service the geologists, miners, drillers, and others. But villages need services—electricity, water, schools, and so forth. Roads should then be paved, and all these activities provide jobs for local people. The new roads bring hunters, fishermen, campers, and sightseers, and by now it is time to build a large ski development. With the beginnings of luxury, large numbers of condominiums are constructed. Speculators have moved in, and land prices have gone sky high. And so on—each technological or sociotechnical step leads to an expanded next step. Overall, the process is irreversible.

The technological environment has significant multiplier effects and impacts on the other environments as well. Technology is an important underlying factor in economic strength and growth. Technology can be the basis of new products for entering new markets and increasing market share. Technology provides a means of concentrating political power. New technologies require a continual updating of education and skills. An increasingly technological world has alienated millions. Millions of others have willingly or unwillingly become the servants of machines rather than vice versa.

Mentioning these linkages among environments reminds us again that the external environments of the organization consist of one turbulent field with closely coupled components. The organization and environment are continuously—and discontinuously—evolving both within themselves and in relation to each other. The longitudinal, historical, evolutionary approach to analysis, design, and management will continue to be stressed in this section. Anticipation, long-range planning, adaptation, and survival are dependent on this approach.

Technology can be viewed at three levels:

1. Inside the organization in terms of:
    a. Its *generation,* say, by those companies that produce capital goods, consumer goods, or information technologies.
    b. Its *impact,* say, on those service organizations that receive their technology from the outside.
2. Outside the organization in terms of major opportunities and challenges that call for appropriate adaptive strategies.
3. As a major component force in the evolution of sociotechnical macrosystems.

Invention, Innovation, Strategy, and Risk

Turning first to the second area, the fundamental question might be asked: how can top management anticipate new technologies, and maximally exploit both new and extant technologies, while minimizing undesirable, harmful, or dangerous side effects and impacts? Experience shows that there are no hard-and-fast answers to this question. However, considerable guidance on the formulation of strategies, plans, and policies can be offered.

The development of a new core technology depends on historical, evolutionary, and field-dynamic processes. Lead times are on the order of two decades on the average, and, as noted in Chapter 5, are not getting any shorter. Total development over time can be thought of as consisting of a sequence of activities, although this simple representation is in reality complicated by numerous feedback loops. The sequence incorporates: (1) basic scientific theory and discovery and invention—which are not identities; (2) applied scientific demonstration that the basic idea or discovery can be implemented in a practical and practicable manner; (3) innovation (following economist J. A. Schumpeter) or the commercial introduction and exploitation of a discovery or innovation; and (4) the diffusion and acceptance of the resulting product or process throughout some relevant area of society.

Scientific theory and basic discovery and invention are functions of a dynamic field of forces that, as emphasized in great detail in this book, is not yet well understood and is certainly not easily susceptible to direct management control. These creative human endeavors can be encouraged by the right culture or climate in an organization or nation; they can be discouraged by the wrong culture or climate. There is a widely prevalent belief among journalists and bureaucrats and some scientists and technologists that there is a direct relationship between money spent on basic research and R&D on the one hand and quality of output on the other. Quality of output is a function of, among other things, the age and scale of an organization (or society), that is, the evolutionary cultural phenomena such as those discussed in Chapter 3. Thus, countless billions of dollars could be poured down a research hole with the cumulative result of countless reinventions of the wheel, production of so much useless data and information as to render the search for useful knowledge an increasingly formidable job, and critical impairment of the long-term research capability through the mistaking of priorities and the misallocation of resources and support.

These matters deserve a closer examination. Traditionally there have been two rather oversimplified theories—perhaps two types of theories is more correct because different advocates have stressed different things—that attempt to explain scientific discovery or invention or innovation or all three. These theories tend to be polarized. One theory emphasizes historical factors and the accumulated body of human knowledge—when the time is ripe a discovery will emerge. More sophisticated versions of this theory are probabilistic rather than deterministic. One advocate of historical determinism has been a sociologist of science, S. C. Gilfillan. One version of this type of theory is called the science- or technology-*push* theory. All in all, this orientation emphasizes processes internal to he field.

The opposite theory emphasizes exogenous processes. J. A. Schumpeter stressed the role of entrepreneurs, and J. Schmookler wrote of the importance of the *pull* of market demand (hence demand-pull theory).

These theories have analogies in the time-is-ripe and great-man theories in history and in the cost-push and demand-pull theories of inflation in economics. Of course there are elements of truth in all these theories, but they must be better integrated causally and individually softened through incorporation into a higher systems structure. The theoretical frameworks provided in Chapters 3 and 5 offer just such a structure.

In trying to clarify these issues, the groundwork of Schumpeter and Schmookler, and the more recent analyses and interpretations of their work, are invaluable. The theoretical and empirical studies of long-range technological and economic change provide a point of departure for envisioning future reconfigurations. Schmookler very patiently collected *patent* statistics, *as an indicator of invention,* covering approximately the years 1840–1950 (for the United States). His data covered principally the railroad, petroleum-refining, agricultural machinery, and paper-making industries, but he also collected data on other existing industries as well. Schmookler believed that his comprehensive study validated the demand-pull theory, but that is not a major concern here.

An important point to make here is that longitudinal or time-series data, collected for routine accounting or administrative purposes, *are* sometimes both fairly complete and valuable for research on trends and patterns. Schmookler's patent data have been used, sometimes in sophisticated mathematical and statistical analyses, to yield indices of relative or absolute growth or decline in creativity in industries and in nations. Evidence indicates that industries and firms are differentially sensitive to the impact of science. Also there may be no causal relationship between invention and innovation.[13]

Director Christopher Freeman of the Science Policy Research Unit in Sussex, England has continued and extended Schmookler's work.[14] Freeman used statistical time-series of the publication of scientific papers as well as patent statistics in the United States, United Kingdom and West Germany. He concentrated on the science- or technology-intensive chemical industry. Scientific papers, patents, investment, and production provided the sequential bases for studying longitudinal *waves*. One type of indicator could be viewed as an early warning of subsequent activities. For example, successive waves of scientific papers, patents, and new investment might corroborate the science-push theory. Of course these studies, using aggregate statistics, are subject to the limitations discussed in Chapter 4. Maybe the most important scientific discoveries are not always published, and the most important inventions are not necessarily patented.

Freeman's main findings accord with the evolutionary and environmental-fit emphases. In a given branch of the chemical industry, for example, drugs or plastics, an earlier science-push stage, lasting several decades, may later give way to a demand-pull stage. Such evolution is also characterized by a shift from product to process inventions.

In general, executives in young organizations and industries should keep a close eye on science and technology, both inside and outside their organizations. Executives in mature organizations, assuming they have taken advantage of the new opportunities for investment and production, would want to emphasize process improvements and market expansion. This sounds straightforward and obvious, but CEOs often—perhaps because of the reasons discussed in Chapter 1—misjudge the stage of their organization's evolution.

Scientific, sociotechnical, and socioeconomic change will, for a long time at least, continue to present problems of unknowability, undecidability, and uncertainty. Outmoded ways of thinking and outmoded designs, based on linearity, incrementalism, continuity, extrapolation, and isolated trends and events rather than emergent clusters will render organizational growth and survival more subject to chance than many executives would want to admit.

Processes and occurrences that are variously random, selective, and mutually reinforcing contribute to long-term societal change. Technology is a major contributor to hyperbolic growth (Chapter 3), socioeconomic cycles (Chapter 4), and the emergence of self-organizing systems (Chapter 5). Schumpeter interpreted the genesis of the Kondratieff long wave in terms of the appearance of radically new clusters of innovations or technologies. In the rising leg, new technology is followed or accompanied by rising investment, rapid growth, and lower levels of unemployment. In the declining leg of the curve, the opposite is true, even during the upswings of the shorter cycles, for example, the business cycle.

Society is now well into a quarter-century-long period of general intellectual exhaustion, slow growth, stagflation, and chronic unemployment and underemployment, assuming only the Kondratieff cycle. However, as pointed out previously, because of the reconfigurational nature of complex systems, it is highly unlikely that a simple cyclic swing back to the "normalcy" of the 1950s and 1960s will ever occur again.

These matters are among the most critical in human history, not only to business and industrial executives but to policymakers in general. Part of an overall survival strategy will be to select appropriate technologies, technologies that will help stimulate recovery and improvement without triggering a terminal collapse.

These choices must necessarily be part of the long-range planning of businesses, industries, and nations. However, there are interim considerations of almost equally critical significance. These have to do with the competitiveness and survival of individual firms, industries, and countries.

Countries can be compared and classified with regard to their abilities to respond quickly and effectively to challenges, opportunities, and competitive threats. The situation is dynamic, and nations with hitherto lower levels of technological development and competitiveness are constantly snapping at the heels of the more technologically advanced countries. Such a state of flux is of course often as much due to the rising costs of labor in the advanced countries as to the acquisition of new technology by the developing countries. At the present time Brazil, Mexico, South Korea, and Taiwan are moving into such areas as steel production and ship building. These industries have become decreasingly profitable in such countries as West Germany, Sweden, the United States, and even Japan.

The future competitive potential of a country can be partially estimated using the types of indicators of scientific productivity, inventiveness, and innovation discussed above. For example, the number of U.S. patents taken out by *foreigners* has increased greatly from the early 1960s. Increases of 50 percent or more have been shown by Belgium, France, and West Germany. Sweden, and especially Switzerland, increased already high levels. Japan showed a tenfold or greater increase of U.S. patents per capita!

Increasing the competitive—and survival—capability of any nation will *not* be a matter of applying simple formulas of giving more money to R&D or providing more training programs. Rather complete evaluations, and attendent imaginative policies, will be required with regard to the total fabric of society including education, attitudes toward work, distributions of possible skill levels, mobilization toward goals, and other factors to which the discussion will return later in this chapter.

Such total systems approaches will not bear fruit overnight. In complex organizations and in nations decay is often covert and may take years or even decades to manifest itself. The organization or nation may first fall to a lower level of performance equilibrium as discussed in Chapter 5 and earlier in this chapter. Once the full extent of decay, or even crisis, is evident, redesigns themselves may take years or, especially in the case of nations, decades.

An important case in point is Britain. It is unknown exactly when and why Britain began to decline relative to certain other nations. It may have been as long ago as the mid-nineteenth century. World Wars I and II and the loss of the colonial empire drained Britain even further. And post-World War II management and labor difficulties and nationalizations have certainly exacerbated Britain's woes. By themselves, the return to conservative government (of Prime Minister Margaret Thatcher), the North Sea oil and gas bonanza, and the investment of pounds in R&D are unlikely to reverse trends set off by deep-seated changes in values, work substitutions, class rivalries, and widespread national malaise.

There are obviously many parallels between Britain and the United States. Of overwhelming concern these days is the increasing socioeconomic decay of the United States.

A primary danger to organization and nation alike is the search for and reliance on simple rules and explanations—the profit-maximizing entrepreneur, the return to good times through sleight-of-hand manipulations of the economy, or the clarity of market signals and the alacrity of the ensuing response. Whatever the complex systems approach taken, imagination, innovation, and flexibility must play a major part in it.

The present and growing inequality among nations and within nations must, for the foreseeable future, be accepted as an unfortunate given. The reasons for these disparities are many and include factors emphasized in this book such as lack of understanding of phenomena and processes in the world-system field and associated bad policies and actions. The competitive advantages of nations and organizations within nations are functions of fieldlike infrastructures—

motivation, morale, alienation, education and skill levels, group conflict, and other features of the social environment to which we shall return shortly. But given the functional integrity of this infrastructure, purposive strategies for mobilizing sociotechnical resources can bring one nation into the first rank, often at the expense of others. Germany compared to Great Britain from about 1880–1914 and Germany compared to the rest of the world later on provides one excellent example. Japan today compared to the rest of the world, but perhaps the United States especially, may provide an even better example.

Japanese industriousness and productivity and the Japanese economy have been marvels of adaptive success. Social factors will be considered in the following chapter. Here the concern is with technological strategies and support for these strategies.

Japanese penetration of world markets has been based largely on Japanese *innovative* improvements on scientific discoveries or inventions made elsewhere. Consider the quartz movement for watches. This was a Swiss invention, but the Swiss failed to capitalize on it. The Swiss lost most of their former market and retreated to the position of limited manufacture of luxury watches. The Japanese captured a large part of the market for lower- and medium-priced watches and are now moving upward to try to capture as much as possible of the world market for luxury watches.

As every CEO knows, the situation in electronics is even more dramatic. The Japanese started with the humble miniaturized, portable transistor radio. The transistor was an American invention, as has been most invention in solid-state electronics since the 1950s. By 1962 Japanese imports made up 68 percent of the U.S. transistor radio market. Japanese success in the manufacture and sales of black-and-white and color television were soon to follow.

Until recently the U.S. position in microelectronics, computer chips, and large computers seemed secure. As of this writing the Japanese have captured over 40 percent of the U.S. market for 16,000-bit random-access memories, which are key computer components. The Japanese are moving successfully into the manufacture of large, mainframe computers.

The present great economic success of the Japanese, like the success or failure of other nations, cannot be dissected out of historical and cultural patterns. This means that the Japanese model cannot be transferred 1:1 to other situations. Japanese success is due to a constellation of factors. Japan is a homogeneous country. Even centuries ago, the Japanese had a saying that went something like this, "Chinese invention, Japanese discipline." Since the World War II defeat, the Japanese have seen technological and economic growth and external competition as national goals, indispensable for survival. Japanese government policies encourage cooperation among Japanese companies in advancing the technological base. Quality control and reliability of products is high, and Japanese goods are generally well made and of superior quality. Productivity has been enhanced by heavy investments in automation, including the new robotics.

Japan is, however, very dependent on the importation of fossil fuels. Values are changing there as well as elsewhere. Productivity increases in the 1970s did not meet levels projected at the beginning of the decade. Rising labor costs are helping to drive some industries out of the market, increasing competition from developing countries. This spurs a determination to automate just about anything that can be automated at home and to transfer labor-intensive industries elsewhere. And one must wonder just what Japan, or any other country, will do with millions of highly educated persons whose skills are no longer needed in production and service industries that are both highly automated.

Not all national strategies are as integrated as the Japanese, nor do corporate strategies fall into line as a function of national strategy in other countries as in Japan.

Corporate technology or technology-related strategies should obviously be functions of the evolution of the company, the product, and the market. For example, assuming basic discovery or invention, a company whose capabilities span the life histories of products or services should successively emphasize product or process improvement, market and sales expansion, and cost minimization.

Although such advice may seem run of the mill, it is not always heeded by top management. Some of the most serious organizational difficulties can often be traced back to simple errors of omission or commission. A perusal of any current issue of *Business Week, Forbes, Fortune,* or *Wall Street Journal* will reveal instances of seemingly poor top management decisions. For example, the December 22, 1980 issue of *Forbes* has two sequential stories on top management choices relative to technology:

TRW Inc. in the mid-1960s anticipated the decline of the auto industry and shortages of locally produced oil. So in its diversification moves, it acquired small companies that would subsequently produce components for small cars and would enable secondary or tertiary recovery of oil from wells the most accessible petroleum of which had been exhausted.

Prime Computer, in a five-year period, shifted from being a technology-oriented company producing a superior piece of equipment, but lacking a proper market, to a market-oriented company selling a product that has lost some of its competitive edge. Perhaps this was a premature shift, and strategy should have been that of expanding the technological superiority and depth of a range of products.

Innovation, as noted earlier, has come to mean the commercial introduction and exploitation of a discovery or invention. Thus, executives are often required to make strategic assessments of radically new inventions with regard to both further technical and sales and marketing potentials. Vice President George R. White of Xerox Corporation has proposed four strategic criteria for such assessments.[15] These criteria are defined using the subsonic, commercial-aircraft jet engine as an illustration. They are:

1. Inventive merit—provided major power, speed, and fuel-economy advantages over previous aircraft engines.

2. Embodiment merit—permitted the construction of large aircraft with sharply swept wings, which could exploit the full potential of long ranges, large numbers of passengers, and full subsonic speeds.

3. Operational merit—design and manufacturing, and reliability and maintenance, had been greatly aided by previous military work with the Boeing-designed B-52 and KC-135.

4. Market merit—provided speed, comfort, and safety advantages to passengers, which in turn reduced the competitiveness of piston-engine and turboprop aircraft.

White does not see good future prospects for supersonic transports when similar assessments are made.

Single strategic choices about a revolutionary, discontinuous technology often appear, in historical retrospect, to have set an irreversible course for a company. The power of such choices, for good or bad, can be illustrated by a further look at the commercial aircraft industry. When it seemed certain in the 1950s that the piston-engine era was coming to an end, Boeing, Douglas, and Lockheed were faced with the critical choice as to which technological direction to take next. Boeing and Douglas chose the path summarized above. Lockheed chose the less radical turboprop engine.

The choice of Lockheed to build the Electra aircraft may have been a symptom of a poor organizational climate for decisionmaking. This choice may have paved the way for further bad choices. The Electra was not commercially competitive and did not have a very long history of use by the major airlines. Several Electras crashed when engine nacelles tore loose, frightening away passengers. Later attempts to introduce the wide-bodied L-1011 and develop certain military aircraft, together with the association with Rolls-Royce, led to the large-scale failure and government bailout which was discussed earlier. Then in the late 1970s Lockheed was caught up in bribery scandals involving the Dutch and Japanese governments. These scandals hurt Lockheed, cost the Japanese prime minister his job, and threatened the Dutch monarchy.

At the time of the introduction of the jet aircraft, Boeing had not previously been a successful manufacturer of commercial aircraft. But by 1980 Boeing had built well over half of the world's commercial jets. In 1980 McDonnell-Douglas had about 20 percent of market share, Lockheed about five percent, and the European Airbus about eight percent. The next several years may well witness the almost complete retreat of McDonnell Douglas and Lockheed from the world of manufacturing new commercial aircraft. Boeing will probably end up with about 70 percent of market share and Airbus with about 20 percent by the late 1980s—if no catastrophic reconfigurations occur first.

There are a number of factors contributing to the competitive advantage of Boeing. Being first on the scene with a successful wide-bodied jet, the 747, a good safety record, and a more organic organizational structure come first to mind. The three-engine DC-10 and L-1011 may be technological dead ends. Among other things the recently deregulated commercial airlines are fighting for survival, and there is an increased emphasis on greater pilot productivity. One way to increase productivity is to eliminate the third pilot, a feat easier to accomplish on short-haul aircraft if the new aircraft has two rather than three engines.

The Airbus will be increasingly successful because of a mixture of technical quality, politics, and European pride and business acumen. Look for further erosion of another of America's once seemingly impregnable industries.

One of the most important abilities CEOs can develop is an appreciation and insight about the history and evolution of their companies. Yesterday did not *determine* today, nor does today *determine* tomorrow. Nevertheless, an awareness of historical continuity and discontinuity provides much needed know-how about the strengths and weaknesses of a company. Corporate memory is weakened by departures of the early founders, by the regular processes of aging such as those discussed in Chapter 3, and by high executive turnover. But developing a historical and evolutionary perspective is well worth any extra effort on the part of top management.

Some examples of technological choice in which bold decisions led to strong positive results, and cautious or conservative, even timid, decisions led to loss of market share and perhaps elimination from an industry have been noted. What about situations in which bold or incautious decisions lead to long-festering troubles or to calamities?

Corporate decisions have become a lot more risky these days because actions by corporations spread rapidly and widely throughout the turbulent field and often trigger secondary and tertiary reactions. Lawsuits and government regulations have become increasingly the consequences of organizational practices. Edward W. Lawless and his colleagues analyzed 45 technological shocks to society; they also synopsized 55 other cases.[16] The cases covered about a 25-year period following World War II. The study was concluded in the early 1970s, so more recent dramatic happenings were not included and the dangers of the misuse of technology consequently understated. Nevertheless, Lawless and his associates found that in about half of the 45 main cases, early-warning information was available but was ignored, a technology with recognized problems was allowed to grow, or the technology had been irresponsibly utilized.

The sheer complexity and *autonomy* of technology, and the increasingly sharp recognition of deleterious side effects of technology on society and on the natural environment, coupled with the sharpened determination to obviate these side effects, render technological choice and decision more and more difficult. In the past decade or so a number of techniques have arisen that purport to handle *technology assessment, technological impact, environmental impact, appropriate technology, decision analysis,* and *risk analysis*. Most of these methods are sorely deficient for the reasons discussed in Chapters 2 and 4 and in the earlier part of this chapter. Most are subsystem-limited or closed-system limited, do not adequately incorporate behavioral–social or ecological factors, or consist of elaborate probabilistic analyses overlaid onto some rather shaky subjective foundations. There has been considerable disillusionment with these approaches from the perspectives of both doers and users. The assessment of technology and its impacts should be as holistically sophisticated as the better computer simulation models discussed in Chapter 4.[17]

Making a technological choice is not only often quite difficult, but the internally and externally generated *conflicts* arising out of the decision to develop or utilize a new technology add greatly to the psychological, social, and financial costs. There may be no practical way to assess risks at the level of the individual firm.

The Macrosystem

Technological risk can, however, be roughly bounded and estimated at the societal level if one's criteria are what people collectively seem willing to accept. Dr. Chauncey Starr has elaborated on this theme.[18] The upper bound is the average disease mortality rate. The lower bound is the mortality rate for natural hazards. Both are for involuntary exposures. If risk in death rate per year per million people is indicated by the ordinate of a linear scale, and the relative value of benefits is indicated along the abscissa, a gently sloping S-curve results. The asymptotes are the two horizontal bounds. To the left of the curve lies an unacceptable region of relatively high risks and low benefits. To the right of the S-curve lies an acceptable region of relatively high benefits and low risks.

Models like this should be used only as a rough first approach to technological risk assessment. Risk cannot be reduced simply to loss of life or limb—there are fates worse than death. Further, the benefits of technologies are becoming increasingly controversial and difficult to identify, measure, and quantify. Finally, determining the probabilities of failure of large person–machine and sociotechnical systems, so that these probabilities can be compared with the upper and lower rate-bounds, is an increasingly formidable task. Remember that the probability of failure of a nuclear reactor—like that at Three Mile Island—was once estimated by an august body of *hardware-oriented* scientists to be about the same as that of a city's being hit by a large meteorite!

Another major sociotechnical consideration is *automation,* including the presently growing *robotization.* People have been concerned with the effects of mechanization and automation on jobs and on society at least since the Luddites went about smashing machines at the beginning of the first Industrial Revolution.

Throughout this book we have stressed the importance of searching for and heeding early-warning signals—to a considerable extent that is what anticipation is all about. Early-warning signals were mentioned in the discussion of the natural environment. In the mid-1960s there was major concern with the effects of automation and technological change on employment and on the economy. A National Commission on Technology, Automation, and Economic Progress was set up. In 1966 a report in several volumes was released. The report was thorough, but the conclusions and recommendations were meek. Keynesian thinking seemed to dominate the effort. Thus, most of the problems of unemployment could apparently be eliminated through expansion of the economy. The report did not lead to appropriate further study. Concern with the deleterious effects of mechanization and computerization largely disappeared at the policy level, even though isolated scholars continued to worry. Even the great economic, energy, and employment crises beginning in the early 1970s, and the world models that purport to deal with these and other major threats, have stimulated little if any further concern. Most people do not know, or do not believe, that automation and technological change, unharnessed, augur direly for world society.

New automation technologies, particularly those based on or highly dependent on microprocessors, are already having impacts on both production and information-processing industries. The magnitudes of these impacts will accelerate. Acceleration will be partly the result of direct conscious effort to increase productivity, but partly it will be due to the further stimulation of an autonomous technology in a turbulent field.

It is now popular to say that we are in the midst of a robot revolution. There are strict definitions of just what constitutes a robot, but it is convenient to think of robots as part of a larger family of devices that increasingly take over tasks and functions previously performed by human beings. This family of machines includes "smart" or "intelligent" sensors, instruments, and terminals, word processors, appliance-embedded computers, and simple and "intelligent" robots.

Linking together these and other computer-related devices, it is theoretically possible to build a factory of the future in which microprocessors control individual pieces of equipment; minicomputers sample, collect, and process data and information from the microprocessors; and large central computers integrate data and information into an overall display or report of factory performance. A sociotechnically trouble-free factory of the future may be another story.

Robots are being rapidly put to work on automobile and other assembly lines. However, their applications are not limited to the larger-scale operations. This versatility will bring more and more smaller industries under potential robotization. Robots will increasingly aid the handicapped. And robots are being built that can in turn build other robots.

Robotization is most advanced in Japan at present, with the United States, Western Europe, and parts of Eastern Europe following. U.S. companies started making robots as long ago as 1960. Some of the earliest customers were the Japanese, who now have plunged actively into the robot-making business. Robotization is in the countries mentioned projected to be a high-growth industry. Most of these technological changes so far have involved simple robots, which are, in factories, basically *manipulators*. However, studies in pattern perception and artificial intelligence, coupled with further advances in computer chip and sensor manufacture, could lead to the introduction of more intelligent robots.

All this promises to have a sociotechnical impact perhaps greater than that of the first Industrial Revolution. *Unless understood and managed properly,* this revolution could produce long-term costs that far outweigh short-term productivity gains.

The words understood and managed are critical. Technology, coupled with the other forces in organizations and societies, introduces not only the popularly acknowledged complexity and uncertainty, but perhaps also a fundamental *unknowability*. There are many arguments for an *autonomous technology,* of which several will be considered in conclusion of this section.[19]

First, in most corporations and government organizations there is a separation between technologists and top managers. Engineers and scientists function better as entrepreneurs than as executives of large organizations. To a considerable extent, engineers and scientists are thing-oriented rather than people-oriented, and necessarily so. Further, as a company grows or evolves, there is both an increasing emphasis on sales, marketing, and finance and increasing competition from specialists in these fields and in law for the top management jobs. Even if a technologist does become or remain a top manager, the demands of his job usually result in his losing contact with a rapidly changing field. Thus, within and between large organizations, there is an increasing isolation of key decisionmakers from the technological base.

Second, technology is rarely if ever a one-shot affair. Large numbers of people who come and go contribute to the development of products and systems. Improvements, modifications, retrofits, and patch-ups are added to the original design. Equipment and systems drift with use. In computer systems, layers of software are superimposed onto one another. Cumulatively, these changes contribute to the evolution of a new system that no single person or group of people can ever know.

Third, technology and sociotechnology have developed such a momentum as to be essentially out of control and beyond manageability. The effects of massive technological change are, given existing circumstances, irreversible. Attempts at reversal or better management in, say, old industries could trigger unemployment across the nation. As the first energy crisis demonstrated, few people are capable of tracing the impacts of a perturbation throughout the system-field. Few executives are aware of the complex linkages binding together vendors, suppliers, producers, users, and providers of support services.

Fourth, the spontaneity of scientific discoveries and inventions, and simultaneous but independent discoveries and inventions, are indicators of activity in an underlying but poorly understood field of forces. The nature of fluctuations, amplification of fluctuations, and the confluence of science or technology were discussed in Chapter 5.

THE HUMAN RESOURCES ENVIRONMENT

The human resources environment is the source of workers and skills at all levels for the organization. In a sense the human resources environment is a way station between the larger social and technological environments and the organization. In this section some of the factors affecting the numbers, types, and skills of workers available to the organization will be considered. Chapter 7 will discuss what happens to these workers, and what impacts they have, once they are inside the organization.

Like most other things discussed in this book, the supply and skills of personnel is not, in any simple way, predictable. The *behavior* of personnel has often been quite unpredictable. Rapid social and technological change—and, increasingly, political activity and government regulations—are greatly modifying the type of employee top management might expect.

A number of agencies in the U.S. Departments of Labor, Education, and elsewhere produce detailed manpower analyses and projections. However, these analyses and projections are based on present understandings and assumptions of future continuity. In addition, the quantitative indicators, for example, level of education in a given employment area, are increasingly but crude approximations of quality that, even more seriously, tell us little or nothing about behavior.

There are several important reasons why CEOs can expect continued uncertainty regarding future employees. First, education and skill mixes are changing, but not in a necessarily desirable way. Although more people are completing more education, the quality of this education appears on average to have been lowered through grade inflation and through the continual passing of students and granting of diplomas and degrees whether these students have met appropriate criteria or not. Thus, there are frequently cases where a high school diploma or even a bachelor's degree is essentially worthless. At the same time, completion of more education is perceived by the holders of diplomas and degrees as an entitlement to better, or at least better-paying, jobs.

Second, rapid social and technological change exacerbate the aging process. Even people under 30 years of age often find themselves technologically obsolescent. And just at the age when people used to settle down to a lifetime occupation or job, they now find that they must change their way of thinking, learn demanding new skills, and adapt to different circumstances. For people who are middle-aged or older, these required changes can be quite stressful, and cases of midlife crises, even among executives, are increasing. The demographic aging of the population, as the baby-boomers grow older, will further aggravate the problem of the aging and technologically obsolescent worker.

Third, the relation between education and employment is essentially open-loop. Educational institutions, many of which are only diploma mills, crank out larger and larger numbers of graduates whether there are appropriate jobs waiting for these graduates or not. If there are not enough suitable jobs, students eventually get the word and most change options. At the same time, industry does not, and usually cannot, feed back to the educational institutions the kinds of jobs it anticipates five or more years in the future. One reason why it is difficult to determine future job needs is that future social and technological interactions and reconfigurations are difficult to conceive. The result is an unstable or badly oscillating macrosystem of the systems dynamics type. There is either feast or famine. Outputs of graduates and inputs of employees needed are not well synchronized.[20]

In the systems and organizations of today and tomorrow, utilization of human resources far transcends any simple description of jobs or positions in terms of numbers of personnel skills and tasks. Personnel departments in business and industry and government employment offices are candidates for a much needed and long delayed critical evaluation and restructure.

Fourth, at the present stage of evolution of the sociotechnical macrosystem, it is probable that both unemployment and underemployment are chronic and structural. In catastrophe-theory terms, there are at least two levels of temporary equilibrium. Employment activities, or lack thereof, fluctuate slightly about these equilibria. The behavioral mechanisms involved in these fluctuations need much more precise study, but some of them are fairly obvious—hope or hopelessness, need satisfaction or frustration, independence or dependence, having needed and valued abilities and skills or not having them. It is likely that automation and technological change will precipitate increasingly greater numbers of people onto the lower levels of temporary equilibrium. But therein lies salvation in a rather perverted sense. For as in the ecological models discussed earlier, when population numbers reach a certain critical threshold, the whole system can be expected to flip.

There *are* individual differences—between apples and oranges, between cats and dogs, and among people. These differences are examples of the fluctuations discussed in detail in Chapter 5. These differences are part of nature. Unfortunately, in modern societies there are increasing numbers of persons whose cognitive or personality limitations place them outside the realm of the needed, in the pragmatic and mechanistic use of the term. The evolution of world society both among and within nations is moving in the direction of increasing divergence between the Haves and Have Nots.

The overly educated may also feel undervalued and unneeded. A college education and even more so a graduate degree may at the same time produce a questioning mind, an expectation and longing for better things and a better quality of life, a deficiency in the specific skills needed by business and industry, and a dissatisfaction with the rather pedestrian jobs that are often the only ones available.

Fifth, society's attempts to rectify deficiencies, inequalities, and injustices often have neutral to critically negative effects. Social welfare programs appear to have institutionalized hopelessness, helplessness, resentment, and poverty. Minimum-wage laws mean no work for many Americans, but a magnet drawing millions of job-seeking poor people from Latin America and elsewhere. In fact, migration to the United States is now seen as a *right* in some foreign countries.

The Social Security program for transferring payments between generations is on the brink of foundering. Massive expenditures at the level of federal departments, which are threatening to break even the most affluent nations, trickle down through layers of bureaucratic inefficiency and even corruption and graft to produce negligible benefits for the needy. More than one job-training program has enriched local administrators. More generally, over a decade ago, Jay W. Forrester in his *Urban Dynamics* identified the counterintuitive nature of many job-training programs.

Equal employment opportunity and affirmative action legislation have helped many people. Some people have suggested, however, that not all the newly hired women and minority-group members have the abilities, attributes, or skills that business and industry may urgently need at a given moment. This situation applied, for example, to the Electric Boat Division of General Dynamics, the difficulties of which were mentioned in Chapter 1. Some critics have contended that recent declines in U.S. productivity are at least partially due to decreased skill levels associated with government pressures to hire.

A predominant reason why many government employment programs have been failures is that they rose out of recognizably severe problems of the Great Depression and civil injustices. But these programs just grew without evaluation and redirection. Today they show the signs of enormity of scale and over-age discussed in Chapter 3. And like the autonomous technology, these social programs have taken on a life of their own. They cannot easily be brought under control. Businessmen should be leery of promises of conservative politicians to bring such institutions under control.

Finally, perhaps the most serious shock to executives is the change in values and attitudes toward work. Employees at all levels, including managers, seem to feel that they are entitled to an increasing variety and level of benefits, while at the same time they are eschewing any risk and abdicating more and more responsibilities. To countless millions work is at best a means of passing time while benefits, little if at all related to productivity, are accrued. Millions of others are not just indifferent to work, but are passively alienated or actively hostile and aggressive. Changing values and attitudes toward work are functions of historical forces and circumstances, including trends toward greater socioeconomic welfare for everybody, the affluent, mostly worry-free period in which younger workers grew up, and perceptions of the fulfillment value of jobs in a populace with changing motivations.

The discussion of work will be continued in the next chapter.

THE POLITICAL ENVIRONMENT

The political environment has begun to affect the way corporations operate at least as much as does the market environment. An important part of corporate capital-investment decisions are now based on factors other than profits or the interests of the employees and shareholders. These trends have a historical origin and are likely to continue and even to intensify.

This section will consider the political environment both internal and external to the United States. The factors are broadly the same in each case—rising feelings of entitlement; increases in numbers of special-interest groups or stakeholders; alienation from or resentment or criticism of the status quo; rapid sociotechnical change; and at least two-body competition and conflict. The specifics of course may differ greatly from country to country. In the United States, for example, the three bodies are business and industry, government, and the people.

A great deal of confusion exists in America today. Many opinion polls show that respondents are about equally disenchanted with business and industry and government—in short, with bigness. Yet polls show that at the same time people want fewer and lower taxes and less government spending, they also want government to provide more services. A continued labile situation and large fluctuations in behavior can be expected.

There is some serious concern that conflict among business, government, and the workers is leading the United States down the path to becoming another Britain or Italy. Although those two countries are not strictly comparable, both are characterized by declining economies and lowered productivity, severe labor–management inefficiency and conflict, and almost cradle-to-grave welfare and job-security programs. Such programs are of course also prominent in Scandinavia and West Germany and other partly socialist countries, but in these countries productivity is still high enough to offset the huge costs of these programs. However, the socioeconomic situation is deteriorating in these countries too.

Neither businesspeople nor politicans should underestimate the inertia of the societal system changes that have accumulated over the past 100 years. Such anathemas to many executives and conservative politicians as massive government spending, government regulation of just about everything, and high taxation are largely irreversible—outside world war, ecosystem collapse, revolution, or a dictatorial effort to restructure society. For one thing, Americans lack common goals or purposes, at least those that would motivate them to sacrifice for the overall well-being. The me attitude goes right up to the corporate penthouse and boardroom. For another thing, symbiotic interrelationships have evolved among business and industry, government, and labor over the decades. Not all executives would want the government to get off their backs. Ask the top management at Lockheed, Chrysler, and the now deregulated airlines and banks which will not be around several years from now.

The games played and the strategies implemented must therefore be selective, with considerable attention to whose oxen are being gored. However, blatant hypocrisy in political maneuvering and in advertising will have the effect of further alienating an increasingly enlightened and cynical public.

As discussed in the early chapters, many current problems, especially those of work-system design, arose in the first Industrial Revolution. The hostility between business and government also arose at that time. Large enterprises such as the railroads and steel industries often were insensitive to the needs of local communities or were seen as exploiters of the workers and consumers. Government antitrust action was of course one result.

More important than specific business or government terminal activities (price wars, monopoly formation, antitrust suits), however, were the psychological dynamics involving owners, managers, workers, and customers—involving in many cases Haves and Have Nots. Millions of rural or newly urbanized, but poorer native Americans as well as immigrants saw the doors to power, privilege, and dignity closed to them. Companies were often oblivious to hardship or suffering, discriminatory, and arrogant. But education provided the avenue to having or sharing power, prestige, and wealth. Government often provided newly educated but still bitter people a better opportunity to acquire power, prestige, and wealth—and increasingly security—than did business and industry. A strong anti-business feeling arose in government and has grown to this day.

Unfortunately, neither business nor government has always acted responsibly. Further, with societal evolution, many different groups of people have come to realize that they have *direct* interests in the actions of both business and government. Activist *stakeholders* now include local communities, conservationists and environmentalists, consumer and product-safety advocates, occupational safety and health advocates, consumers at large, and senior citizens, as well as employees, government regulators, stockholders, and managers. Each organized group has its legal war chest, its litigation, its lobbies in Washington and in the state capitals, and its vote power. Each group has its wins and its losses.

Even more unfortunately, the solutions and countersolutions to perceived problems often intensify the underlying difficulties. Heavily bureaucratized institutions, especially those dealing with social welfare, education, health, criminal justice, housing, and urban and regional problems, can certainly be faulted. Government regulations add immense amounts of paper work, demand unnecessary levels and details of accountability, and, ironically, often conflict with one another (consider, for example, certain Occupational Safety and Health Act and Department of Agriculture regulations). On the other hand, the cries of some businesspeople and political conservatives to abolish pollution standards and open up the remaining wild lands for exploitation and development ring hollow. One might ask rhetorically: is Appalachia something to be proud of? the old, decaying cities of the East? what good is more energy if there is nowhere decent to go for recreation in an increasingly despoiled and crowded environment? what good if the main benefits consist of variations on products and jobs the occupants of which are as alienated as ever?

Obviously there are serious paradoxes in American society today. But differences in needs, perceptions, and goals and conflicts and confrontations can be resolved in win-win-win manners if each party tries to understand the total system and is willing to make concessions. However, if management, labor, and the workers cannot get together to build better worksystems, it is very probable that productivity will continue to decline and socioeconomic decay to increase in the United States. If executives are thought to be mostly maximizing their own incumbencies and associated perquisites, oblivious even to the eventual fates of their organizations, this may be the death knell of many organizations as we know them. One often hears that corporations must necessarily be self-serving and short-range in their thinking and actions. Executives must take the lead—these are not matters to be delegated to public relations or simple irritations to be overcome through advertising campaigns. The issues also transcend adding some courses on "business and society," "business and the environment," and "business accountability" to business school curricula. There must also be significant changes in organizational structure.

Executives should rely neither on the continuity of political thinking nor the ability or willingness of politicians to aid business causes. New groups of stakeholders continually arise. Coalitions form, only to fall apart again. At the present time there is a resurgence of far-right and far-left groups, as well as continued strength in groups that are not ideological in the traditional sense. Where should business turn for support? A far-right group helped defeat the reelection of several important liberal congressmen in 1980. Another or overlapping group is trying to clean up TV by boycotting the products of companies sponsoring some of the most popular shows.

President Ronald Reagan started out before the 1980 election talking like an archconservative and offering few but simplistic solutions to complex problems. But just before and just after the election, reality was forced upon him. On second thought, Chrysler and New York City *did* deserve their bailouts—there were lots of blue-collar and minority-group votes out there. Nor were ultraconservatives appointed to most key cabinet and other posts to their disgruntlement.

Nor should the support for President Reagan be overestimated. One of the most important features of the 1980 election, and of almost all other American elections in recent years, was a combination of voter apathy and voter negativity. About 51 percent of the electorate turned out, and about 52 percent voted for Reagan. Reagan was elected by about 27 percent of the possible voters—scarcely the landslide the media claimed, scarcely a rational reason for the Dow-Jones to shoot past 1000, and scarcely a rational reason to feel bullish about America. The people who did vote for Ronald Reagan were fairly representative of the country at large, and only about 26 percent considered themselves to be conservative.

Businesspeople should also remember that government spending, regulation, and bureaucracy did not perceptibly decrease under former conservative Presidents Nixon and Ford.

In short, the types of dynamic forces stressed throughout this book operate in the political field as well as in the other environmental fields. The very existence of these forces, prerequisite to understanding and attempts at control, is presently beyond the ken of most top policymakers and decisionmakers. Thus, even if a top elected or appointed manager wants to do right for a cause or for a constituency, he is likely to find the system outside his control and his well-intended actions counterproductive.

Much of the problem is once again of evolutionary origin. Both capitalism and Marxism were reactions to eighteenth and nineteenth century societal situations. Each has influenced the other to a considerable extent in many countries. Each has led to a mammoth bureaucratic apparatus with the attendant characteristics of aging and scale as discussed in Chapter 3. Neither apparatus is, in the absence of catastrophe, reversible. Both are threatened along a number of dimensions. Neither offers an ideological or pragmatic solution to today's intersecting crises.

We should all remember the evolution of the American work ethic away from the visions of the Founding Fathers—the intrinsic worth of work itself, discipline, thrift, and savings for investment. Today capitalism, free enterprise, and market forces have much different meanings from the original. Today they are very often identified with overconsumption, waste, throwing things away, and debt. Business and government have symbiotically interacted over the two centuries to help bring about the paradoxes we face today.[21] There may be a radical shift in the goals and purposes of business in the next few years.

The types of societal dynamics that have been stressed here can be illustrated by the 1980 presidential election. There was apparently a last-minute catastrophic jump, by about 8 million voters in 48 hours, to Ronald Reagan. The triggering event may well have been the Carter–Reagan TV debate that preceded the election by a few days. Carter had nothing to gain; he was no mystery; his record was clear. But the debate conveyed the impression that Reagan was rather like plain folks and not a wild-eyed warmonger. The jump to Reagan appears to be a classical example of the application of the Delay Rule in catastrophe theory and of the dove-to-hawk (or hawk-to-dove) jumps in support for an administration as studied by Professors Isnard and Zeeman and mentioned in Chapter 5. In the 1980 election the unifying or normal factor could be considered to be anti-Carter feeling or fed-up-and-need-any-change feeling. The ephemeral grouping of Reagan voters does not, as discussed above, augur well for President Reagan. At the time of this writing, the Reagan Administration appears to be misjudging the permanency of support for it, the lability of human behavior, and the depth and resistance to beneficial change of the underlying problems of U.S. and world society.

Further, the failure of the pollsters in the 1980 election was just one more indication of the exhaustion of concepts and tools that had served well until the present epoch of critical transformation.

Finally, the foreign political environment is even more precarious to U.S. interests than is the domestic environment. Revolutionary changes in catastrophe-theory terms were discussed in Chapter 5 and illustrated in Figures

5.3 and 5.4 and with reference to Iran in Figure 5.5. As discussed earlier in this chapter, ecosystem destruction will continuously erode the very basis for subsistence in many parts of the world. The spread of higher education and continued technological change in communications and transportation will intensify social comparison processes and feelings of relative deprivation, envy, injustice, and resentment.

Even in the leading Western European countries, the signs of significant change and even reconfiguration are evident. In Britain the socioenonomic problems have intensified both because of and in spite of the policies of conservative Prime Minister Margaret Thatcher. The North Sea oil and gas bonanza, while stabilizing the pound and improving the balance of payments, has had little if any positive impact on the *underlying structural* problems. The Labour Party has fallen apart, with the emergence of a new far-left and aggressive group. In France in the Spring 1981 presidential elections, voters rejected conservative Valery Giscard d'Estaing for socialist François Mitterand. France's socioeconomic position had continued to improve under Giscard's presidency, but many voters resented his aloofness and apparently felt that change was required for change's sake. In West Germany the popularity of Chancellor Helmut Schmidt has decreased, and it seems likely that his center-left coalition will fragment into radical left and center factions. In all these countries, the social temperature appears to be increasing. Once again, material standards of living and affluence are insufficient to meet human needs, a point that must not be ignored by political and business planners.

THE SOCIAL OR SOCIOECONOMIC ENVIRONMENT

This section will consider certain dangers of misjudging economic indicators, some views of value change, and some critical indicators of deteriorating social environments.

That the economy has become much more complex and unpredictable is no secret to executives. However, few executives—or anyone else—are familiar with the many interacting dimensions of change. Some of the economic factors considered elsewhere in this book include: (1) the nature and limitations of econometric models, (2) the systems dynamics National Model, (3) the rational expectations school of thinking, (4) the business, Kuznets, and Kondratieff cycles, (5) the ecological base of the economy including the Entropy Law interpretation, (6) the interactions between technological change and the economy, (7) systems dynamics and catastrophe-theory interpretations of stock market and real estate crashes, and (8) some limitations of orthodox approaches, whether they be Keynesian, monetarist, market-capitalist, or Marxist.

In short, just about any of the traditional, *nonsystems,* attempts to manipulate, control, or fine-tune the economy are likely to be wrong. Yet executives and policymakers often make critical decisions on rather flimsy information. Here are two examples.

Federal agencies and policymakers, interest rates, the performance of certain (interest-sensitive) industries like automobile production, housing and construction, and overall stock market performance are now showing behaviors that *look familiar* but in reality may reflect deeper and much different underlying phenomena and processes. Many executives, investors, and others have become used to looking at one or more essentially independent trends over short periods of one month to several quarters. The antirecession and anti-inflation policies and swings of 1980 provide an example.

On April 2, 1980 the prime interest rate had risen to 20 percent per year, a consequence of President Carter's anti-inflation drive. The Federal Reserve Board then shifted from anti-inflation to antirecession tactics, among other things removing credit restrictions that had been imposed only in March. On July 25, 1980 the prime rate fell to 11 percent. There were some increases in consumer spending, probably triggered mostly by the greater availability of credit. These changes were interpreted by many executives, investors, and economic experts as signals that the recession was over. Many companies, *overly quickly,* made plans to expand and began to borrow money again. But these decisions were made at a time when fluctuations in money and bank accounts were more violent than in any other year in over 20 years. On December 10, 1980 the prime interest rate had once again risen to 20 percent per year. Some companies are having to sell assets, postpone or abandon capital spending, or reduce dividends. For companies that cannot reduce their debt load, the likelihood of bankruptcy is high.

The second example deals with energy modeling and energy policy. Policies may be based on a *single* variable or parameter such as the price elasticity of demand. In turn, this parameter is usually dependent (in econometric models) on historic time series. Back in 1974 the Nixon-Ford Administration, reacting to the first energy crisis, was strong on Project Independence (of imported foreign oil). The government's model, the validity of which was strongly tied to assumptions about the value of the elasticity of demand, led to politically critical but almost opposite interpretations. Thus, the United States could reduce imports of foreign petroleum by removing controls and letting the marketplace operate so as to increase the price of crude oil or by adding more controls in the form of rationing or taxation. The Administration of course chose the first option. However, choice of either or both simplicity-based options would probably have led to a worsening situation. The U.S. dependence on foreign oil is of course much greater now than it was in 1973. The results of earlier poor thinking, poor planning, and poor judgments, not only about energy but in most other areas as well, may be war in the Near East and Middle East and certainly the massive despoliation of the environment and quality of life in the mountain states of the American West.

The essentially discontinuous jumps in the price per barrel of OPEC (Organization of Petroleum Exporting Countries) crude oil have represented reequilibrations of countries and a world that had lived for a long time dangerously far from a stable equilibrium. The first discontinuity, unexpected and unpredicted by most of the experts, occurred within a few weeks in 1973 and 1974 when OPEC raised the price of a barrel of crude oil from $2.41 to $10.95. The second discontinuity covered most of 1979 and 1980 when crude oil prices in a series of brief increments jumped from about $12 per barrel to over $30. There will of course be no easy solutions to these problems.

The 1960s and early 1970s represented one of the most important recent historical periods of rapid value change. Change greatly affected the family, the church, the institutions of education at all levels, work, sex, appearance and clothing, music, the use of drugs, lifestyles in general, women, minorities, technology, the environment, perceptions of other countries, war, patriotism, concepts of the self, concepts of authority and dominance-submission, consumption, materialism, and the roles of business and government. For many people it was a period of affluence, freedom, personal expression, independence, hope, and optimism. Youth, the minority groups, the intellectuals, and the increasingly educated were the main contributors to rapid value change. Some behaviors that appeared to represent fundamental value change turned out to be merely fads. Other radical value change was eventually absorbed into the culture at large. Some value change may be reversed as things get even tougher, but most values of today will remain and will be the basis of increasing confrontations in the future. Significantly, large numbers of people still adhere to the older values, and in a world of diminished options there will be less tolerance for different views.

Finally, as major social dynamics there will be increased split, polarization, and strain both within and among nations. Some of the most disturbing signs are crime and violence everywhere and a drift toward World War III. Apparently random and senseless crimes like mass murders as well as politically motivated kidnappings, murders, and terrorism will increase as individual hopelessness and social strain reach the breaking points. Prominent people in all areas, including executives, will find themselves perceptual foci—and targets—of the disaffected, deranged, and disgruntled. At the time of this writing Beatle (rock musician) John Lennon has been assassinated, and assassination attempts have been made against President Ronald Reagan and Pope John Paul II.

The problem is essentially one of a Frankensteinian sociotechnical monster unleashed. As with most of the other critical situations discussed in this book, quick fixes will aggravate matters. The purchase of James Bond-type automobiles and the increased militarization of offices, factories, and stores may appear to be a sensible response—or it may just take place with little or no conscious attempt on anybody's part—in the face of increasing societal entropy. But such actions will simply add to the schisms within society. A remote and isolated set of leaders, managers, and celebrities will most certainly lose their followings or markets.

Nor are tough responses usually successful for any prolonged period in releasing the monster. A few years back the Federal government launched Operation Intercept to try to cut down on the amount of marijuana smuggled into the United States. The program was associated with a switch to the greater use of hard drugs, and the quiet internalization of marijuana use into most segments of American culture continued unabated.

Employing more police or national guardsmen often triggers more crime and violence, especially in minority-group neighborhoods. Militarizing airports has cut down the number of, but not eliminated, skyjackings. Many of these skyjackings appear to have been fads anyway. The goals of the skyjackers were to gain attention, to gain ransom, or to gain some political concession like the release of prisoners. But the goal was not primarily terrorism. Terrorism might some day be expressed by blowing airliners out of the sky with heat-seeking missiles or rockets launched from small, portable equipment, as was the case with two Rhodesian Viscounts a couple of years back. The point is that responding to the *actions* of individuals or groups, without *major* attention to the *structure of the system,* is liable to be counterproductive.

The drift toward a major war is even more ominous. Isolated occurrences seem to be early-warning signs of things to come. There is increased discussion of and publication about the inevitability of World War III. One hears of increasing talk among NCOs and officers on U.S. military bases that a little war or a little bit of war might be quite good for the morale of the demoralized, often poorly performing American military. Soviet-American relationships continue to deteriorate. The problems in the Near East and Middle East have no easy solution and will most certainly get worse. Continued war is highly likely in southern Africa. Guerrilla actions and civil war will spread in Latin America.

The most ominous portent, however, is a gradual change in collective consciousness rather than any one or more specific events. This change is illustrated by the attitudes and behavior of some members of Solidarity, the federation of new, independent trade unions in Poland. Many of these workers continue to intensify their demands and threaten nationwide strikes, continuing to tweak the nose of the Russian bear quite unmindful of the inevitability of a repeat of Afghanistan, Czechoslovakia, and Hungary. The point once again is that there is a system under severe strain, with many people feeling that they cannot take it anymore, come hell or high water.

Recently, I wrote:

> The order parameter of collective consciousness represents a level emergent from the contributory forces of near instantaneous communications, rapid travel, and rapid diffusion of new ideas and practices. It is likely that popular thinking will soon enter a new phase with regard to a World War III. The power and influence of the older generations, exposed to the horrors of World War II or to the shock that came with realization of the vast destructive power of nuclear weapons, will soon die out. Most people alive today have grown up with "the bomb." Like all people they discount those things that are remote in space or time. One has only to witness the history of Spain in the last half-decade compared with the three and one-half decades following the civil war of

1936–1939 to realize that world stability cannot be based on indirect perceptions of events long past. In this sense the world system is indeed Markovian.

Further, the persistence and frequent success of terrorist and insurgent movements in recent decades demonstrate continually how many people place their particular values ahead of safety and comfort. As other solutions fail, it is likely that the world by a common, perhaps unconscious consensus will have agreed, as on the eve of World War I, that the time for World War III has arrived.[22]

At the present time, especially with the stepped-up emphasis in the United States by the Reagan Administration on military spending, the race between the United States and the Soviet Union is strongly reminiscent of the military and economic race between Imperial Germany and Great Britain that preceded World War I by three decades. Concern for these great dangers has led me and several colleagues to launch a major effort to study war and peace as systems.[23] Currently, the nations of the world are spending about $450 billion on defense. The amount spent on defense since the end of World War II has been astronomical. But very little has been spent on peace research. This is an area to which corporations—if they want a future operating environment—can contribute a great deal.

THE MARKET ENVIRONMENT

The market environment is probably the external environment that is best know to CEOs. Nevertheless, there are subtle nuances and surprises to be expected in this environment too. For example, as seen earlier, market share can be lost because of delivery delays following asynchrony among production, inventory, and sales.

Another common difficulty is that much more effort is expended, through advertising, in trying to control target markets than is spent, say, through improved market research, in trying to understand these populations. Much advertising is both offensive and misdirected. For example, advertisers apparently assume that most people cannot distinguish between quantity and quality—more pain reliever rather than a higher quality drug or more automobile engine power when the speed limit is 55 miles per hour and the costs of repairs keep going up.

The loss of market share is often insidious and occurs over many years. Executives are not always aware of the subtle changes in peoples' perceptions and preferences or of the role of isolated events. Children form impressions that may last their entire lives. People put themselves in the roles of victims of faulty advertising or shoddy products. Hostility breeds hostility. Consider the following:

A large, old airline with which customers had consistent experiences with surly stewardesses in dirty uniforms, poor food, and indifference to slipped schedules and disrupted itineraries (arranged by that airline).

A large retail chain that hounded people who complained of shoddy merchandise and refused to pay for it, until they lost their homes.

One of the world's largest banks that repeatedly made errors in customer accounts, leading to the imposition of penalties on the depositors, but which refused to apologize for or rectify the errors.

A large utility and one of the world's largest financial and travel agencies that apparently assumed that all customers were ne'er-do-wells and that threatened customers whose payments were late or misdirected, even though the fault lay in frequent errors by the companies themselves.

A large government agency all the personnel of which are either indifferent or hostile to the customers.

Enough people have had enough bad experiences of this nature, such as not only to reduce the market share of specific companies but also to reduce collectively Americans' confidence in business and government.

Looking once again at the difficulties facing the Chrysler Corporation, one might ask exactly when Chrysler's market share began to drop. It was quite a whole back. Indeed, Chrysler's recent history strongly suggests the pattern of failing organizations discussed toward the end of Chapter 5.

One might also ask if more of the same is the solution to Chrysler's woes. Assuming Chrysler should and could be saved, was Lee Iacocca the person to do the job? Was the answer really another Mustang? Mr. Iacocca built up a well-deserved reputation at Ford. But Detroit has long been criticized as being highly ingrown. Did not Chrysler really need an imaginative and broadly based chief executive from outside the automobile industry, a person who could redirect Chrysler away from major dependence on yesterday's product? The unimaginative crash effort to sell the K-cars failed, and Chrysler is worse off than ever.

And, in passing, one might also ask why call new cars J-cars, K-cars, and X-cars? Is this supposed to indicate cars so new that they have not even received proper names yet? Are they supposed to be like experimental aircraft or missiles? Isn't such silliness a legacy of yesterday?

Consider once again the success of the Japanese and the Germans. After World War II these countries had everything on the surface going against them. The Japanese were the folks who had "stabbed us in the back with a dirty sneak attack" on "a day that would live in infamy." "Made in Japan" meant cheap, imitative, flimsy, and unreliable. The Germans were the folks who had "started" three major wars against innocent and unprepared democracies in less than 70 years. The first Volkswagens *were* bizarre automobiles—small, funny-looking, and almost powerless. But the funny little foreign cars chugged away, up and down hill, for a hundred-thousand miles or more, using little gas, going a long way without repairs, and eventually costing relatively little to repair. They had good resale values, while American behemoths piled up in junkyards.

The American automobile industry looked to the past, showed a great deal of arrogance, refused to heed the handwriting on the wall, and misused corporate power in a futile attempt to stifle opposition and needed change.

CEOs should assume neither expanding markets nor constant and loyal markets. Entry into new markets may also be unexpectedly perilous, especially if these markets are international. The USSR and China might appear to be promising new markets. But these countries are historically xenophobic, and Westerners who have tried to negotiate trade agreements with these huge countries have found that the Russians and Chinese are slow, cautious, and tough bargainers. Blanket sales of grain and other commodities are one thing, sales of technologies needed by these countries something else, and mass sales of consumer goods something else again. Selling to foreigners is an intricate, often exotic business that many American companies still have to learn from scratch.

In addition, American companies will face increasing competition from Japanese and Western European companies that not only can market products that are just as good as, or better than, American products but also may have a lot more experience in the field.

Further, many of the consumer goods wanted or needed by the developing countries are things Americans no longer manufacture efficiently or in large scale—such as bicycles, sewing machines, radios and televisions, manually operated or energy-efficient equipment and appliances for home, field, and factory, and textiles, clothing, and shoes. Even buses, streetcars, locomotives, tractors, ships, and steel-making plants are increasingly provided by countries other than the United States.

Thus, even the market environment will be increasingly turbulent in the years ahead. This turbulence involves issues that have scarcely been identified as yet. For example, what actually *is* a product or a service? From perhaps 1880 to 1930 new products really did satisfy important needs. Without cooling, food would usually spoil (of course drying and smoking had been known since prehistoric times), and the new refrigerators were certainly more convenient than the cumbersome old ice boxes. Washing machines did reduce greatly the drudgery of the housewife. The automobile, airplane, radio, and television did (or potentially could) bring people closer together and provide much readier sources of knowledge. But somewhere along the way the idea of a basic and needed product became adulterated, and substituted was the idea of product built-in obsolescence, throw away, and incessant moving upward to more and more expensive grades of products. Although this idea has caught on just about everywhere, it is a basically American concept that now appears to be running out of steam. The world can no longer afford such extravagance and waste.

For a number of years, scholars wrote of a postindustrial society. Production-oriented society was supposed to evolve smoothly into service-oriented society. For the reasons discussed throughout this book, this smooth change will not occur. Service-industries have most of the problems of production-industries and suffer from the same shocks. Both types of industries suffer problems of automation and technological change, unemployment and underemployment, alienation, and overexpansion. Although the industries are not strictly comparable, banking, savings and loan, insurance, real estate, and travel all are overexpanded both in numbers and in sizes of organizations. Some major retrenchments, even crashes, in these industries can be expected.

DESIGN, MANNING, AND STRATEGY

This chapter has focused on multidimensional turbulent-field environments. A number of forces, factors, events, and examples in the treatments of the various specific environments of the organization have been considered and, some linkages among various forces and environments have been indicated. However, the chapter is mainly an open-loop model of the collective external environment. If loops were closed, many of the forces would undoubtedly appear in intensified forms, and many of the forecast situations would be worse.

All systems and all organizations, by definition, have *boundaries*, even if these boundaries are diffuse regions. Boundaries separate the system from its environment, governing the interchange of matter, energy, and information. Boundaries, even those like the plasma membranes of cells, have specialized structures and functions. In complex organisms and organizations, these structures and functions can be highly elaborate. They include various sensors and means of grappling with the external environment. In living systems theory, the direct interfaces with the external environment are called *input* and *output transducers*. Applied to organizations the structures, equipment, personnel, techniques, functions, plans, and actions that handle organization–environment interactions are referred to as *boundary-spanners*.

In *positively* adaptive and survival-oriented organizations, there must obviously be great congruence among the present and anticipated environments, the internal organizational structure, and the organizational actions intended to come to grips with environmental threat, challenge, and opportunity. Unfortunately, when dealing with multiple turbulent environments, such congruence is rare.

Most organizations will require major redesigns of both the boundary-spanning structures and functions and the central information-processing capability that ties together the input and output activities. CEOs now spend a large part, if not most, of their time on external affairs and planning. The present types of support framework are entirely inadequate, especially since demands on executives' time in these areas will most certainly increase.

Several areas of improvement can be indicated. First, considering the great variety of environments, configurations of forces, and types of change, organizations will have to rely on emerging new types of experts and techniques. However, specialist experts tend to be narrow in outlook. Many of the experts will necessarily be academics, who are often inward-looking, driven by pressures to do pure research and publish in archival journals, impractical, and contemptuous of the business and political worlds. Severe communications problems among disciplinary specialists and between academicians or staff experts and managers impede the application of innovative new ideas.

Therefore, a new, *explicitly* recognized and designed corporate-level function will be required. The new top management position will report directly to the CEO, who himself must become much more actively involved—not just concerned or worried—with environmental problems in the broadest sense of the term as used in this chapter. The position of Systems Integrator was first introduced in Chapter 4. This person should have an extremely broad base of knowledge and associated breadth of experiences. Knowledge should include systems theory and applications, the specifics of several of the environments, and organizational practices. Knowledge of a specific business or industry or governmental area will also be valuable, but the otherwise qualified generalist can easily pick up this knowledge along the way. The ability to manage a team of experts in the disciplines and interdisciplines will be important. Smaller organizations will want to rely on consulting firms for these services, but almost all organizations should reorient themselves.

The use of new types of experts and the systems integration of capabilities apply, for example, to the assessment of competitors and of international business risks. In many parts of the world, American companies need the services of area experts, who might be anthropologists, sociologists, political scientists, or long-term residents. Some of these fields are far removed from the usual education and experience of executives, and executives might not ordinarily think of using their specialists' services. But in the absence of current and detailed information on local cultures, customs, and conditions, many an otherwise promising business deal will fall apart. Foreign cultures often have quite different practices from ours with regard to women, drinking, dress, language forms, and even body language. A hand gesture that means A-OK, to your health, victory, or may I hitch a ride in the United States may mean something degrading or scatological in other parts of the world.

Another way in which the design and function of the boundary-spanning or input-output-transducer activities can be improved is to introduce environmental dimensions at the very beginning of the planning, policymaking, or development scheme. Environmental considerations must not be neglected, only to crop up later as embarrassing afterthoughts.

Boundary-spanner design requires major new thinking and rethinking. It is not something that can be effected by small, incremental changes to existing functions like market research or public relations. Boundary-spanning activities include not only the information acquisition and processing and long-range planning that have so far received great emphasis in this book but also negotiation with an increasing variety of stakeholders.

Finally, the nature of strategy formulation and strategic planning is obviously changing greatly in the face of environmental turbulence. Corporations will in many cases want to design and implement preemptive strategies. However, it is highly important that strategies be adaptive and not maladaptive. Adaptive strategies will lead positively to organizational learning and growth, improved fit to the environment, and an overall improvement in quality of life. Maladaptive strategies, perhaps initially successful, will lead inexorably to diminished fit with the environment, generation of increasingly powerful opposition, and a general worsening of conditions. Adaptive strategies will lead to the resolution of crises. Maladaptive strategies will trigger and amplify ever greater crises. Adaptive strategies will recognize the limits to power. Maladaptive strategies will try to overpower.

Chapter 8 will have a lot more to say about adaptive design and strategy. Here are some self-evident, maladaptive strategies:

Pretend *they* don't exist.

Don't look under the rug.

Don't rock the boat.

Look only at the elephant's tusks.

Jobs versus pollution.

Grind the SOBs down ("illigitimi carborundum").

Go down with the ship.

7

THE INTERNAL
ENVIRONMENT

This chapter stresses internal forces and dynamic processes, the continuing changes which must be monitored. Whereas many of these factors originate in the external environments, they assume new meaning and problem status when incorporated into existing organizational structures and functions.

Chapter 1 discussed the basic features of organizational structure, function, and design, and that chapter also introduced the four organizational subsystems, social, technological, psychological, and political. It is the interactions of structures and processes within and between these subsystems that most contribute to the characteristics of the internal environment. The nature and dimensions of the four subsystems and of the total interacting field of forces are by no means usually evident at first inspection, however. Chapter 2 discussed many specialist or disciplinary approaches to solving organizational problems. Most of these approaches assume, erroneously, that part-problems can easily be dissected out of the dynamic whole. Chapter 3 emphasized the dynamic behavior of organizations in terms of its stages of evolution and growth.

Problems of the internal environment also can severely tax the abilities, skills, and available time of the CEO. The many people problems come immediately to mind. This chapter is concerned primarily with some new looks at the people and sociotechnical problems of organizations and with the forces shaping new looks at organizational goals and performance.

MORE THAN PRODUCTIVITY AND PROFITS—FORCES MOVING ORGANIZATIONS TO NEW GOALS AND OUTPUTS

Almost all CEOs now recognize that their organizations are changing, and that the type and magnitude of change all too often do not represent planned change. As pointed out in the previous chapter, most organizational change can be traced to factors—new motivations, new values, new technologies—that originate in the external environments. The turbulent external environment can produce changes in organizations that are unwanted by, and even unknown to, top management. In many ways the internal environment itself mirrors the external turbulence and becomes increasingly uncertain and unmanageable, increasingly demands different types of managers and techniques, and requires focus on performance goals other than the traditional high productivity and profits.

The Changing Nature of the Workforce

Longitudinal studies over periods ranging from 10 to 25 years indicate unequivocally that there have been fundamental and disturbing changes in the values, attitudes, and motivations of the workforce in U.S. companies. These changes require new perspectives and new policies by top management.

One of the most convincing studies was performed at Opinion Research Corporation.[1] Using written questionnaires that assessed 64 key employee attitudes, some 175,000 hourly employees, clerical employees, and managers in 159 small to very large companies had been studied since 1950. The research reports results on 13 critical attitudes carefully selected from the 64 and is summarized as follows.

With regard to attitudes toward the company and the job, several salient findings were discovered. One highly consistent finding was a *hierarchy gap,* that is, as one goes from managers to clerical workers to hourly employees, one finds fewer and fewer satisfied persons. The gap applied both to the company as a whole and to a given department. Another important finding was that managers, as well as clerical and hourly employees, indicated that the company had become a worse place in which to work. In fact, this particular rating was at an all-time low, in spite of apparently improved management practices and personnel policies through the years. A third major finding was the decreasing job satisfaction among hourly and clerical employees and the apparently increasing identification of personnel in these categories with one another. In other words, white-collar workers have begun to see things the way only blue-collar workers once did. These findings are of course consistent with the job enrichment and sociotechnical systems research discussed in Chapter 2.

Attitudes toward extrinsic rewards or sources of these rewards such as security, pay, supervision, and management also showed some important changes and some inconsistencies. Most of the employees in all three categories felt secure in their jobs (it is doubtful that this would be true today, only a few years later than 1977, the last year of reported results). People in all three employment categories reported satisfaction with pay; in fact, satisfaction with pay had greatly increased in recent years. However, the increased satisfaction of hourly and clerical workers with pay was accompanied by decreased satisfaction with their jobs. Increasingly, every category of employee is demanding something more from a job than just adequate security and pay. Further, if the question about satisfaction with pay were rephrased today to include the features of inflation and cost-of-living increases, it is probable that the levels of satisfaction with pay would drop precipitously. Satisfaction with top management and with supervision showed increases over the years. That these two ratings, at about 75 percent favorable by managers, 50 percent by clerical workers, and 40 percent by hourly workers, were considered high by the researchers emphasizes the generally unfavorable attitudes most employees have of their companies.

It will be recalled that Abraham Maslow's famous *hierarchy of motives* postulated the following levels from most to least basic: physiological needs; safety, security, or survival needs; love or social needs; esteem or ego needs; and self-fulfillment or self-actualization needs. As more basic needs are met, motivation jumps to higher levels. The study discussed above produced some rather dismal findings with regard to perceived gratification of esteem needs. Opportunities for advancement had always been low as rated by all three categories of employees, and ratings fell even lower in recent years. Another critical finding was that the majority of neither clerical nor hourly employees felt that they were treated with respect as individuals. Nor did these groups feel that the opportunities to communicate upward were particularly good. Further, few of these employees rated their companies highly in terms of doing something positive about problems and complaints once identified. At the same time, employees' expectations for positive action have greatly increased. Feelings of being treated fairly (playing no favorites) by the companies were also essentially negative. Even in the case of managers, only 45 percent believed that employees were treated fairly, a drop from over 80 percent in the 1950s.

Declines in the perceived meeting of esteem needs, rather than declines in satisfaction with security and pay, thus underlie the recent deterioration in overall job satisfaction. In most modern organizations there are, to put it most simply, severe disincentives to doing a good job. Changes in workforce values, attitudes, motives, perceptions, and behaviors are thoroughly ingrained in the culture, are pervasive, and essentially irreversible.

Whether these changes in a given organization are due mostly to an infusion of new ideas and behavior from the external environments or to an internally induced deterioration of organizational climate following years of disillusionment, exhaustion of hope, and the contempt that comes with familiarity, top management will have to develop new strategies and tactics to deal with the internal environment. More of the same, such as only pay increases and human relations programs, just will not work.

Another indicative study involved 98,000 blue- and white-collar, supervisory and nonsupervisory employees at 132 branches of Sears, Roebuck and Company.[2] Employees completed a questionnaire during three intervals from 1963 through 1972. Once again, a general downward trend in job satisfaction was revealed. Deterioration involved both higher-level and lower-level employees as in the study just discussed.

To the results of these formal longitudinal studies, most CEOs can add personal observations about quantitative and qualitative changes in people problems and sociotechnical problems in their organizations. Most of the old weather vanes such as blue-collar absenteeism and extensive use of sick leave are still around. But the passive and active expressions of underlying discontent appear to be increasing in number and in variety, to be shifting in favor of more active over more passive response, and to include almost all levels of the organization.

Whereas in the past people just hoped, grinned, and bore it, or perhaps dragged their feet on the job, today they are much more likely to articulate their demands for greater participation, greater sharing, and more intrinsically rewarding jobs. In the absence of satisfaction, they may act aggressively rather than talk. White-collar crime, ranging from pilferage to sophisticated computer-based embezzlement and swindling, has increased. Employee attitudes toward property have changed greatly at the same time that loyalty to the organization has greatly diminished. Vandalism is epidemic. Sabotage and even terrorism have become acceptable ways of handling grievances. The CEO should not be misled by the still relatively low incidences of computer crime, sabotage, and terrorism. As times get tougher along many personal, social, technological, and economic dimensions, a catastrophic jump in these frequencies might be expected. Top management must never ignore possibly critical early-warning signs.

Many factors can of course be held responsible—waves of layoffs and hirings, the shift to civil problems, the Vietnam War and its aftermath, the all-volunteer military, loss of perquisites, new types of personnel, decline in discipline, the cynicism of the newest generation of workers, and overall societal entropy. Clearly the picture is that of a spread of alienation to almost every level of the organization and society.

That problems once considered inherent to the blue-collar worker or to the poor are now the concern of most people is further attested to by the rapid increase in collective bargaining among white-collar and professional people. Airline pilots, air-traffic controllers, nurses, physicians, lawyers, public school teachers, and university professors are among the many groups to join the ranks of the unionized. So far as is known there are no large unions of computer programmers, but most certainly such unions could bring even the most powerful corporations to a halt. Companies are particularly vulnerable here because, unlike the cases of strikes of supermarket workers or even by air-traffic controllers, management cannot easily assume the tasks and the amount of work usually discharged by programmers. This sociotechnical Achilles' heel is likely to keep a great many top managers, especially in the information-processing industries, tossing and turning at night.

Another change in the nature of the workforce, which may be noted here, is the demand for privacy and the consequent increase in legislation to protect privacy. This change has a great impact on the way business is done in general, but it has been especially great on the design and use of information systems. With the Reagan Administration there are proposals to curtail the scope of such legislation.

Responsibilities Toward and New Demands by Society

New employee expectations, demands, and behavior are not the only pressures forcing top management to consider goals and strategies in addition or alternative to the traditional maximization of productivity and profits. A number of changes in the social environment in which management must function are now requiring changes in the nature of management. Collectively, the changes in society and the accompanying management changes are known by the terms corporate social responsibility, corporate social performance, and business and society.

To review: changes in the external environment that impact on the organization can be roughly divided into two categories, those more or less within the scope of management understanding and control and those not so. Most CEOs have had considerable experience with problems involving the first category of changes. Nevertheless, considerable improvements in performance can be made in this area simply through changes in perceptions and orientations. The second category of changes are those we have called field-theoretic, reconfigurational, and catastrophic. As emphasized throughout this book, development of effective adaptive strategies to cope with these problems requires major rethinking.

Corporate social responsibility is one important area in which improvements in organizational structure and management can be made. CEOs should not be misled—or mislead themselves—into believing that demands for product reliability, release of full information on products, occupational safety and health, concern for the local community, and overall corporate accountability are fads that will soon go away. These demands are features of overall massive societal change that can be neither easily reversed nor easily overcome. Greatly increased educational levels, which have led to more and more people being able to question, to compare, and to think, provide one key explanation of this situation. Rolling with powerful environmental forces, rather than attempting to overcome them, is usually the best long-term corporate strategy. It is better for management to anticipate societal pressures and to design actively to maintain fit with the environment than to stall or to waste resources in enormous but out-of-date onslaughts of advertising until an alienated public forces changes through more government regulation. Presently the Reagan Administration is attempting to cut back on government regulation; public response may then be both increased apathy and violence.

Many CEOs of course have long since come to these same conclusions. Nevertheless, quite a few organizations still show a resistance to changes in thinking and practice. In keeping with the evolutionary emphasis of this book, several stages in the change in thought and practice might be envisioned.

Professor S. Prakash Sethi describes three such stages:[3]

1. *Social obligation.* This is a proscriptive stage in which corporate legitimacy is defined only in terms of economic and legal criteria. This stage was more appropriate to a society in which scarcities predominated and increases in production were a major societal concern. Adaptive strategy is defensive.

2. *Social responsibility.* This is a prescriptive stage in which corporate

legitimacy involves not only economic and legal criteria but also the development of congruency with prevailing values, social norms, and social expectations of performance. Adaptive strategy is reactive. However, this stage does not require a revolutionary departure from customary corporate practices. It is simply adaptation before the changing social expectations are codified into legal requirements. By adapting before legally forced to, the corporation can better choose its own responses and achieve legitimacy at lower institutional and societal costs.

3. *Social responsiveness.* This is an anticipatory and preventive stage in which emphasis is on the corporation's long-term role in a dynamic environment. Adaptive strategy is proactive. The corporation assumes an active role in bettering itself and the external environments. Top management initiates policies and programs that minimize externalities or adverse side effects of present and future practices before these externalities take on crisis proportions and trigger further waves of antibusiness feeling and protest.

In fact, corporate social responsibility is usually associated with good management and business practices as a whole. Professors Edward H. Bowman and Mason Haire have studied these relationships.[4] They measured corporate social responsibility in terms of lines, organization, and content of prose devoted to the topic in the annual report. Independent measures were obtained for responsibility. Responsible and neutral firms were then compared. It was found that the firms that performed responsibly reflected this behavior in their annual reports. Further, corporate social responsibility was not associated with less profit.

In the Bowman and Haire study an inverted-U or parabolic curve (somewhat like the one in Figure 3.5), was repeatedly obtained, for example, when corporate responsibility was plotted against profits. That is medium corporate responsibility was more clearly associated with high profitability than were either too little or too much activity. Once again, we see a law of economies and diseconomies of scale in operation.

The parabolic relationship was interpreted as follows. Corporate social responsibility is an indicator of a style of management that extends broadly across the entire business domain and leads to more profitable operations. It is diagnostic of a strategic posture appropriate to dealing with the turbulent environments as discussed here.

One indication of this posture is the makeup of the board of directors. Firms with high debt/equity ratio, which need strong boundary-spanning relationships with capital markets, tend to have more representatives of financial organizations on their boards. Enterprises in industries that are more or less regulated tend to have more lawyers on the board. In general, companies that must confront a challenging or threatening external environment tend to have fewer inside directors. In the case of firms with higher levels of corporate responsibility, the board members that bring connections with powerful forces that could constrain the firm's activities tend to be college presidents, newspaper editors, foundation officials, and representatives of more or less organized groups in society.

High corporate responsibility is indicative of managerial sensitivity to the myriad intangible, uncertain, and even inchoate factors in the external environments. Sensitivity is closely associated with flexibility and responsiveness. The effective CEO must now "not only buy well, convert efficiently, and sell well, but he must also sense well and adapt well to a variety of almost nameless pressures" in the external environments.

Professors Bowman and Haire stress:

> . . . it is exactly this ability to sense, adapt, negotiate with, and cope with these forces that is—in addition to the internal management—the sign of managerial excellence and hence profitability. Some demonstrated concern for corporate responsibility is a sign of that sensitivity.

Changing Relationships with the Natural Environment

As in the last section, the concern here is only with those factors potentially understandable and controllable. Once again "control" implies adaptation to, not overwhelming of, the environmental forces.

The environmental movement is also not a fad that will gradually peter out. Large numbers of Americans are convinced that conservation and protection of the natural environment in its many dimensions are essential for human survival and the survival of a truly habitable planet. Most environmentalist organizations have continued to grow. There has been no great backlash against environmental protection. Park-bond issues passed in California in the 1980 general elections. At least three states—Illinois, Montana, and Washington—took measures to prevent the dumping of nuclear wastes in their states. It seems unlikely that the nuclear power industry will be rejuvenated soon, if ever.

Grass-roots support for environmentalist issues appears to be as strong as ever. The decade ending in 1980 ended with more conservationist victories than defeats. Perhaps the culminating event was the passage of the Alaska National Interest Lands Conservation Act of 1980, which added almost 104 million acres as national parks and monuments, national wildlife refuges, national wild and scenic rivers, and wilderness areas. This act alone essentially doubled the amount of land under such protection. And, ironically, the appointment of development-oriented James G. Watt as Secretary of the Interior by President Reagan has triggered a spurt in memberships in and donations to environmentalist organizations. Millions are demanding Watt's recall.

In the past 10 years the values and attitudes of Americans toward health, fitness, and exercise have also changed greatly, and in a way that reinforces appreciation of the natural environment.

Collectively, environmentalist organizations and environmental activism continue to be powerful forces in the external environment. Further, more and more people are seeing social, economic, and ecological problems as features of the same massive and systemic wave of revolutionary change. This contributes to the irreversibility of values and attitudes in any specific area. Some polls show strong support for boycotting corporations that are not environmentally and socially responsible.

The matter of value change involves not only workers and consumers and citizens in general but also corporate executives. The previous chapter noted the change from the frugal capitalism of the Founding Fathers to the hedonistic consumption of recent years. With an increasingly well educated and evaluating public and with environmental (in all senses of the term) crisis now imminent, there will not be again a return to the kinds of consumption that characterized the 1950s, 1960s, and early 1970s. And more and more corporate executives will find that running a company can be just as important a job and just as much fun when one of the major performance outputs is improving the quality of the natural environment.

Other Pressures for Corporate Change

In addition to pressures on corporations to reevaluate goals and performance outputs, which stem from changes in the workforce, society at large, and the natural environment, there are pressures that stem from the debilitation of long-standing government and corporate practices. Pressures on pension plans, retirement plans, and related worker-incentive packages are particularly critical.

As one would expect, the difficulties and any possible solutions are systemic in nature. Basically good ideas simply wore out in the face of inflation, the counterproductive activities of the Internal Revenue Service, and demographic changes and worker behavioral changes that produced higher retiree/worker ratios, earlier retirement, and longer life spans. In addition, labor unions were unable or unwilling to see that corporations and society as a whole do not possess inexhaustible resources.

The near collapse of the federal Social Security system is familiar to most readers. But company-sponsored plans are also in serious trouble for many of the same reasons. Depending on the method of calculation, corporate pension-fund contributions may have increased 100 to 200 percent or more in the past decade. In many companies the dollar amount of yearly pension liabilities may approach the amount of operational assets. In some companies appreciable amounts of the pension liabilities remain unfunded.

Federal regulations require that the obligations of most private pension plans be met. However, it remains to be seen whether most companies will be able to meet these obligations. It seems certain that the nature of these plans must change. However, it is not easy to reverse peoples' expectations and established demands. A further schism between labor and management, perhaps like that long prevailing in Britain, is likely. Adaptive strategies will require radical new looks at worker incentives and the contracts between employees and management.

ORGANIZATIONAL CLIMATE AND COGNITIVE STYLE

In the first part of this chapter, direct impacts of the external environments on the organization were considered. Now the discussion turns to more internally generated phenomena and processes.

One of the most interesting concepts is *organizational climate*. There is considerable confusion in the literature as to the exact meaning of the term. Following the field theory discussed in Chapter 5, organizational climate is an *order parameter*, that is, an emergent, qualitatively distinct and holistic characteristic of the internal environment of an organization, which results from the interactions of many different elements at a more micro level. Although considerable insight can be developed as to the nature of the elements and their interactions, the holistic *Gestalt* is not amenable to reduction into neat categories of organizational analysis.

Organizational climate is usually sensed, felt, or perceived before any attempt is made to analyze it. Almost all of us—executives, consultants, and laymen—have had experiences of going into an organization or one of its parts and sensing a bad or good climate. Surly personnel, sloppiness and disorder, delays in getting things done, an air crackling with hostility, plant and equipment allowed to run down, rumors, officiousness and rigid interpretations of rules and regulations against customers, cold formality, and perfunctory discharge of duties can be indicators of bad organizational climates.

Organizational climate is an end product of many actions, designs, feedbacks, interactions, and subtle, discontinuous jumps or reconfigurations that may evolve over many months or years. A good climate is hard to build; a bad climate may be nearly irreversible. Bad organizational climate is a key factor underlying organizational declines in performance and productivity. And organizational climates have parallels in the external environments in cultural climates and social climates. Until the emergent, holistic nature of these climates is understood, as is scarcely the case today, attempts to increase morale and job satisfaction and productivity will produce limited or even negative results.

Unless one thinks in terms of mutual causality and field theory, the origin and evolution of organizational climate are difficult to understand and explain. Organizational structure and technology play roles, but not in any invariable and strictly deterministic sense. Yet poor organizational design and poor use of technology, coupled with a management deficient along several dimensions, are good places to look for initially causal factors.

A particularly critical feature is *human individual adaptability,* which often runs quite counter to overall and long-term organizational adaptability. Incongruence between a given design or set of practices and what the design or practices actually should be is usually signalled by adaptive individual or group behaviors. I shall mention three examples:

Rumors typically indicate faulty communications system design. Poor design may be due to technological defects or misuse of technology; incompleteness, for example, one-way, top–down only; implied potential threats against communicating freely and openly; and so on.

Kludges or ad hoc person-machine designs indicate the absence of or faulty human engineering.

Inadvertent counterintuitive effects of management policies and programs, for example, cost-accounting systems, can result from designs that encourage or force employees to try to maximize their own individual or group performance behavior while suboptimizing overall corporate behavior. Thus, cost centers or profit centers appear rationally to be good design ideas, but in actuality these centers minimize their own costs by externalizing them or passing them along to other centers. Designs intended to stimulate healthy competition may induce self-serving behavior instead. Overdetail or rigidity in a cost-center design may indicate to people or groups exactly what they should do rationally to better themselves at the expense of the company.

Although individual structures, technologies, designs, and practices may contribute differentially to organizational climate in organizations, in general one can expect climate to deteriorate as a function of extremes of scale in the manner discussed in Chapter 3.

Another feature contributing to the evolution of organizational climate, for better or worse, is the tendency of like to beget like. It is natural for people to try to surround themselves with other people with whom they feel comfortable or with people who complement their own capabilities. Executives usually prefer employees who fit into the existing organization. But this cloning tendency can often be carried too far in that valuable capabilities—variety, diversity, and variability—necessary for long-term adaptability and survival may be irretrievably lost. Thus, another indication of a bad organizational climate may be too much blandness, sameness, and standardization. Closer investigation often reveals a pressure-cooker climate ready to explode or a management lacking in confidence or a history of unimaginative and unproductive ventures.

The concept of *cognitive style* overlaps that of organizational climate. Organizational climate refers to the intuitive, perhaps subconscious *perception* of the internal environment as a whole by employees including managers, customers, and visitors. Cognitive style, also a holistic concept, describes the overall way of thinking or approach to problemsolving of the organization. Cognitive style also has a number of dimensions, discussed elsewhere, such as degree of creativity, spontaneity, or innovativeness, systems or part approach, subjective versus objective approach, degree of flexibility or rigidity, synthetic versus purely analytic, reductionistic approach, role of intuition, and significance attributed to rationality.

"The myth of the rational decisionmaker" has been referred to previously and some further consideration is warranted with regard to the collapse of models of human rationality, in the most restricted use of the term rational.

For example, the classical theory of the firm holds that the business organization behaves so as to maximize its profits in the context of prices, schedules, and production costs.[5] However, empirical evidence on the actual decisionmaking behavior of executives largely contradicts this notion. Thus, the theory has had to be modified to describe business firms as unwitting or incidental profit maximizers, with profit maximization sort of a by-product of competition for capital and other resources and therefore of survival of the fittest. The fittest can have Lamarckian or acquired as well as Darwinian characteristics.

Classical theory is also limited by virtue of being part of equilibrium economics. Chapter 5 pointed out that many complex systems operate far from equilibrium, and that what equilibria do exist may be local or temporary with catastrophic jumps or flips between or among several stable levels. Businesses do not seem describable as simple profit-maximizers, because this implies a static equilibrium rather than the dynamic steady state of living systems.

The idea that human behavior is, or should be, rational is alluring to executives. Often businesspersons feel or believe that business is rational but environmentalism and worker safety, say, are irrational. Or executives are disappointed when employees seem to be thinking only of themselves. Actually, there is no such thing as rational behavior, if rational means nonemotional. Laboratory exercises in behavioral decision theory and game theory cannot demonstrate the existence of such rationality.

Further, studies of motivation and personality demonstrate the interlocked nature of needs, emotions, thoughts, and decisions. Therefore, the concept of rationality is now usually included under the larger rubrics of adaptiveness or goal direction. Rationality becomes relative, and irrational behavior becomes definable in terms of deviations from what is the best adaptive strategy of the individual or group or organization or society. Even neurotic and psychotic behavior can be rational in that they protect the person from something even worse. Often there are conflicts between the perfectly rational behaviors at different levels. Recall again the behavior at the level of the company cost-centers discussed before.

As mentioned in Chapters 2 and 4, too strict adherence to rational models of human behavior in the restricted sense of the term may be serious departures from reality. Unfortunately, as with many optimizing operations research techniques, models like the Subjective Expected Utility (SEU) model may be exploited and applied in situations far transcending their capabilities. Human abilities to judge easily and realistically features such as all the relevant states of the world or of the system and the probabilities of states, actions, and effects is, by the evidence, very limited.

Most organizational thinking and problemsolving must therefore by necessity maintain a significant ingredient of intuition. This statement is not so unscientific as it might appear at first. A field of forces operates in the brain and in the mind just as it does in the external environment. In fact Gestalt psychological and field-theoretic interpretations of cognition and learning have been around for many decades. Almost everyone has had the experience of seemingly sudden and spontaneous insights or answers to problems following a period of worry or dither (unconscious incubation). The purpose of refined data, information, and models is to provide better and more up-to-date inputs to the conscious and unconscious mental processes of integration and synthesis. But the means should not be mistaken for the ends.

Almost all experienced executives recognize the value of a hunch, or an array of impressions that may be scarcely articulatable, and intuition. Experience shows that in some people these mental processes provide much better assessments and forecasts than do analytic, quantitative techniques. Some investment bankers are remarkably astute in sizing up people and companies that request loans. Studies of retrospective technological forecasting show that holistic thinkers like Jules Verne and H. G. Wells made more accurate forecasts than did such pragmatic individuals as Henry Ford.

Most CEOs recognize the roles of intuition and holistic thinking, but middle managers fresh with MBAs and inculcated with the miracles of quantitative business administration may want at first to rely heavily on analytic and rationalized techniques.

NEW FINDINGS IN MOTIVATIONAL AND ENVIRONMENTAL PSYCHOLOGY

Executives have long been familiar with motivational theory and with attempts to implement motivational programs in organizations. One familiar name is Frederick Herzberg, whose studies of job enrichment were summarized in Chapter 2. Another familiar name is Abraham Maslow, whose hierarchy of motives has greatly influenced organizational and management thinking.

Students of human motivation can be divided into two categories, those who take a holistic orientation augmented by real-world clinical and organizational observations, by intuition, and by common sense, and those who insist on what they consider to be rigorous, analytic experimental or psychometric methodologies.[6] These distinctions and associated problems were discussed in Chapters 2 and 4. Recall, for example, the contrasting of systems dynamics and econometrics. Recall also the difficulties associated with validation. The usual statistical techniques of establishing validity and reliability in experimental psychology and in psychometrics, for example, paper-and-pencil techniques, internal consistency, and repeat reliability, are far removed from the dynamic and systemic world of organizations and management.

Put another way, there is increasing feeling among behavioral and social scientists that these disciplines have been slaves of a philosophy of science, called *logical positivism,* that can account only for the simplest physical, mechanical, and reductionistic features of human behavior.[7]

Other familiar names from the literature on management and organizational psychology are David McClelland, John W. Atkinson, and V. H. Vroom. The works of the first two theorists are examples of more generalized but real-world approaches. Vroom has provided a more rigorous, testable theory along the lines of traditional laboratory models. Both approaches have stimulated much further study, some of which is summarized below.

The value of a theory in systems science is not related in any simple manner to its validation using existing concepts and methods. That is, a global theory or model of the types widely discussed in this book, which can easily or realistically neither be validated nor falsified, but which stimulate much further thought and application, is far more valuable than a small theory or model, abstracted from the real world, which satisfies present criteria for validation or falsification, but which remains an academic curiosity.

The research of David McClelland is particularly interesting because McClelland defines several types of motives and relates them to managerial behavior, leadership, and career and historical trends.[8] Briefly McClelland identifies the following types of motivation:

1. *Need to Achieve* is the need to do something better than it was done before. Like all motives, this need is meaningless and useless outside the context of a supportive or encouraging environment. The need to achieve is a key to entrepreneurial behavior and economic growth. People high in this need may be capable owner-managers or individual salespersons. They are not dependent on the judgments of others and try to improve their own performance according to their own criteria. Their actions may be one-person efforts that minimally involve other people; hence, they are seldom leaders of other people.

2. *Need for Power* is the need to have an impact on, or to control or influence other persons or groups. This need is closely related to managerial, social, and political leadership.

3. *Need for Affiliation* is the need to make friends, receive love, show concern for others, and belong to organizations.

Societies can be high or low in any of these motives, and the types of needs can change over time in history paralleling periods of economic growth, wars, religious revivals, and so on. For example, McClelland correlates the highs and lows of the three motives in the history of England from 1500 to 1800 and in the history of the United States from 1780 to 1970. Relevant to historical trends, McClelland identifies three patterns of people, all of whom are high in the Need for Power:

1. *Personal enclave.* High levels of both power and affiliation motivation.

2. *Imperial motivation.* High level of power motivation, low level of affiliation motivation, and high level of inhibition.

3. *Conquistador.* High level of power motivation, low level of affiliation motivation, and low level of inhibition.

These power patterns have contemporary as well as historical value in the sense that they can be used as tests of the amount of congruence between a manager or leader and his organization in the manner discussed in Chapter 1. To McClelland's classification can be added Michael Maccoby's taxonomy of corporate leaders as the craftsman, the jungle-fighter, the company man, and the gamesman.[9] For example, the craftsman appears to be a person high in the Need for Achievement, and the company man a person fairly high in the Need for Affiliation. Both McClelland's and Maccoby's approaches are holistic or phenomenological with strong psychoanalytic, clinical psychological, and projective-technique (Thematic Apperception Test and Rorschach) flavorings. That is why these approaches are rejected by behaviorists and other reductionists.

Before proceeding to the most recent ideas, here is a brief summary of a familiar example of a rigorous model which is strongly influenced by cognitive psychology. W. H. Vroom's *expectancy theory* can be succinctly stated:

$$\text{Motivation} = \text{expectancy} \times \text{valence}$$

The model holds that people *consciously* make choices based on the *valence* or *attractiveness* of *outcomes* to result from a given action *and* the *expectancy* that this action will produce the *desired* outcomes. Neither expectancy nor valence alone is sufficient to predict motivated behavior; hence, the relationship is multiplicative. The model assumes that people will be motivated toward pleasant outcomes and will avoid painful outcomes, and that their behavior rationally will attempt to maximize the former and/or minimize the latter. Proponents maintain that the model predicts job satisfaction, performance levels, and occupational choice fairly well.

Returning to achievement motivation, it should be noted that recent advances are mostly associated with the work of John W. Atkinson and his colleagues.[10] These advances fit well with the evolutionary, long-range, longitudinal emphases of this text. Theoretical explanations of achievement motivation have become increasingly broad, especially in terms of its use to predict career and historical trends as functions of configurations of several underlying motives.

Motivated action is now seen as a continuous, long-term stream, not as discrete responses taken one at a time. This view is more consistent with systems dynamics modeling, and the new concept of motivation may be one answer to the problem of deficiency in the treatment of behavioral and social variables in large computer simulation models which was identified in Chapter 4.

Motivated action is now seen more holistically to be a function of motives or underlying internal driving forces, incentives toward an immediate task, consummation, success or failure probabilities on present tasks as related to success and failure on past tasks, future orientation to tasks and goals as related to present successes and failures, ability, and self-value or self-importance. Such multidimensional, holistic theory extends and enriches both the older achievement motivation theory and the older expectancy theory.

This discussion may have an academic ring to the many CEOs faced right now with increasing numbers of unmotivated employees—70 percent of chief executive officers of 434 major U.S. corporations believe, according to one *Forbes* survey (December 22, 1980, p. 8), that changing attitudes or motivations toward work are the main factor underlying productivity declines. Sixty-two percent believe that salary increases do not yield sustained productivity gains.

Today's theory can, however, be tomorrow's practical program. The idea that motivation is a continuous action stream is of great explanatory value when one searches for subtle changes in a career, in entrepreneurial behavior, and in the history of an organization or a society. In brief: success begets success and failure begets more failure. Thus it is often asked why people as varied as American Indians, Australian aborigines, Eskimos, big-city ghetto dwellers, rural poor, parolees from penitentiaries, and the mentally ill do not take more immediate and positive actions to correct their plights. The answer of course is a history of repeated failure, low self-esteem, and very low estimates of the probabilities of future success. Research shows that, when a future path is thought to be difficult, even successful people tend to become discouraged.

As with other dynamic behaviors discussed here, motivated behavior may experience a threshold beyond which an individual or a people simply give up trying at the same level, reduce their effort to a lower level of performance, or adapt dysfunctional strategies such as apathy or hostility. Much of the productivity decline and national malaise affecting many countries in recent years is due to the cumulative effects of myriad small shocks and readjustments of motivational levels. A major shock may set back a predisposed person or people almost irreversibly. The historical record provides many examples of natural crises or military defeats that appear to have precipitated a previously successful or invincible nation onto a downward spiral of decline. The Vietnam War, the energy crisis, and the decline of the dollar may be examples of such shocks in the case of the United States today. It is doubtful that the Reagan Administration, through changes in the priority of spending and taxation, can correct problems that have become deep-seated and structural. And if this Administration's promises fail, the likelihood is for *accelerated* decline.

When the strength of motivation is plotted on the x-axis against level of performance of the y-axis, our old friend, the upside-down U, or parabolic curve, results. In motivation theory this relationship is called the Yerkes-Dodson Law. It has been substantiated by computer simulation and could serve as a multiplier in a systems dynamics or other large-scale computer simulation model of societal systems. The law shows that there can be *overmotivation*. Refer again to Figure 3.5, and note the effects of extremes of effort or scale. Whereas some effort and moderate effort are associated with breadth, flexibility, and increasingly desirable results, extremes of effort are associated with the narrowing of options by concentrating too much on one thing, rigidity, and diseconomies of scale.

Again, more of the same policies or programs very often leads to counterintuitive and counterproductive results. Pay as an incentive, and many overall incentive plans in organizations, represent ideas now requiring reevaluation.

As noted earlier, power motivation as well as achievement motivation is expressed in fundamental longitudinal changes. Reasonable control over one's self, one's life, and one's destiny is one of the most important needs, but it is a need that is seldom specifically identified. Perhaps it is tacitly thought of as the inverse of power motivation or part of self-actualization. Longitudinally, people may react at first to the realization that things are uncontrollable by increased attempts at control. Performance may even improve. But eventually people may give up in the manner described above. There then may develop what Professor Martin Seligman has called *learned helplessness*.[11] Learned helplessness is powerlessness or lack of control over things. There is a great deal of clinical and experimental evidence for learned helplessness. In the face of continuing overcontrol in many bureaucratic and scientific management-based organizations, learned helplessness may be a major contributor to alienation, a deteriorated organizational climate, and lowered productivity. At the individual level, the most common symptoms of learned helplessness are depression, apathy, and psychosomatic conditions.

One of the most important advances in our understanding of motivated behavior is our increased recognition of the role of *intrinsic* motivation vis-à-vis the role of *extrinsic* motivation. Although job-enrichment theory, hierarchy-of-motives theory, and sociotechnical systems theory at least tacitly acknowledge the importance of intrinsic motivation, almost all motivation programs in business, industry, and government are based on extrinsic-reward schemes. Redesigning organizations to reflect the importance of intrinsic motivation is one of the most pressing jobs confronting top management.

Design for intrinsic motivation is a more humanistic design. But this argument will fail to impress many hardheaded businessmen and government bureaucrats. More important, top management's insistence on its own perceived reward plans for its employees may elicit the very decreases in morale and productivity that the plans were intended to prevent.

Evidence shows that extrinsic rewards can actually *undermine* intrinsic motivation. External rewards communicate *other peoples'* concern over one's own activities and therefore greater control and hence may provoke greater anxiety. As mentioned earlier pay by itself is rarely if ever a sufficient motivator. Social welfare, awards like "employee of the month," and company retirement plans may "turn off" peoples' motivation to do the immediate job well. Regulative factors like surveillance by closed-circuit television, overmonitoring, and deadlines cause people to lose interest in jobs that were intrinsically motivating.

Professor Mihaly Csikszentmihalyi points out that *enjoyment* is an indispensable feature of both work and play.[12] For a total involvement in work or play—and the two should reinforce one another—task difficulty should slightly exceed competence. Large disparities between competence and task difficulty, a common characteristic of jobs in today's large organizations, produce anxiety or boredom. Implementation of these ideas about enjoyment could greatly improve the quality of life. It is very important that a person perceive control over his immediate environment without self-conscious direction. Csikszentmihalyi showed that when people are deprived of doing such apparently unnecessary things as daydreaming, whistling, and humming, they become irritable, less creative, depressed, develop psychosomatic problems, and enjoy their jobs less. Thus, an intrinsic sense of enjoyment is more important in work-system and total-life planning and design than are extrinsically imposed rewards.

Unfortunately, many institutional designs and practices are more devoted to imposing power over people than to anticipating and precluding alienation and counter-power ploys. Today nobody has a complete monopoly on power, and redistributions of power will be important aspects in the maintenance of adaptive organizations.

Although vulnerable to being redirected or "turned off" by teachers, school administrators, supervisors, and other persons perceived as, or attributed to, holding controlling power over the individual, intrinsic motivation is probably less readily satiable and therefore of greater long-term survival value to the organization. The redundancy, smallness, and lack of imagination of much research and R&D may be due to a shift in emphasis on getting grants, contracts, and bonuses. This hypothesis is of course counter to the customary wisdom that American industrial productivity and research output have declined because of reductions in expenditures on research and development.

In conclusion, some recent findings from environmental psychology should be noted.[13] First, crowding, a function of facilities and task design, may be one source of a person's perception of loss of control over his immediate environment. In turn, this can lead to a reduction in job satisfaction and a deterioration of overall organizational climate. Although there are cultural differences, people do have needs for privacy and for an unviolated personal space.

Second, the *behavior setting*, the basic unit of analysis in ecological psychology, has certain attributes that bear on staffing requirements. A behavior setting is a recurrent pattern of human activity that takes place within specific time and space boundaries. This concept originated with Roger Barker, a follower of field theorist, Kurt Lewin. A certain number of participants is required to maintain a behavior setting at an optimum level. This number is referred to as adequate manning.

A behavior setting such as a game, a work situation, or a community can also be undermanned or overmanned. Members of overmanned settings tend to feel less needed, less important, and less inclined to help others than do members of adequately manned and undermanned groups. There is evidence that undermanning of organizations may actually increase efficiency and productivity. But this finding would have to be applied judiciously. Under certain conditions, undermanning can lead to the breakdown of people. Military air crews and air-traffic controllers come immediately to mind. Also, undermanning is counter to the idea of organizational slack, usually considered to be an important feature of adaptive organizations. Once again, design ideas should be tailored to the size, age, functions, and other aspects of the total configuration of the organization.

MANAGING NEW TECHNOLOGIES

The impact of technology on the organization and the interactions among technological, social, and economic factors are among the most widely studied areas of the many considered in this book. Chapter 2 discussed problems of classical sociotechnical systems and worksystem design, especially in industrial-production settings. Problems of management-information systems and of the computerization approach were also discussed. Chapter 6 discussed several dimensions of technology, including interrelationships among innovation and economic and social opportunity, technological strategies, technological risks, and advances in automation, especially in the new field of industrial robotics. This section will concentrate on the impacts of the most recent and projected computer and communications technologies on organizational structure, function, and the internal environment in general. Most of the emphasis will be on white-collar, professional, and management functions and tasks.

There will continue to be, at least for a while, strong pressures to increase greatly the degree and variety of mechanization and automation of clerical, professional, and managerial work. These elements are usually considered to be the most unproductive of U.S. workers. Between 1972 and 1977 blue-collar productivity is estimated to have increased at a rate of over two percent per year, while white-collar productivity increase was about four-tenths of one percent per year.

Attempts to improve productivity through the introduction of new automated equipment are greatly abetted by decreasing unit costs of equipment systems, modules, and components. The rapid technological change and markedly declining costs in the area of microprocessing were reviewed in Chapter 2. Increasing capabilities and reliabilities and decreasing costs also apply to computer peripherals, large computer mainframes, advanced typewriters such as word processors, copying machines, and customary communications equipment. Advances in communications satellites, fiber-optic-based ground communications, and cable television are also now or expected to be cost-effective. Equally important pressures to automate include rapid worker wage increases, changing skill levels, actions of trade unions, and markedly changing attitudes toward work itself. In addition, the information explosion feeds on itself, creating needs for more immediately available and accurate information.

Surprisingly, most of the perspectives on automation and technological change represented today are about the same as those expressed 10–20 years ago. Except for the concepts discussed in Chapters 3 and 5, there appears to have been little or no revolutionary thinking in this area. There have long been diverse viewpoints among technologists, organization theorists, sociotechnical systems theorists, economists, and cognitive scientists. But within each school, thinking does not appear to have changed much, although some protagonists in each group may have become somewhat sobered by reality. Some of the facts today, compared to the forecasts of a decade or two ago, include:

The long-term question as to the effects of computer-related automation and technological change on unemployment is about as far from an answer as ever. There is some isolated evidence, for example, involving switching jobs in the telephone industry, that automation does lower the number of jobs. The factors of jobs lost, new jobs created, skill levels, demographic changes, and economic push and growth are too complex to consider here.

Artificial intelligence, aside from applications to robotics and some specialized programs in science, mathematics, and medicine, has not lived up to its apparent early promise. Heuristic nonalgorithmic computer programming and programs to play chess and checkers, compose music, and invest in the stock market (without making their designers rich!) were introduced in the 1960s.

Person–computer symbiosis, the deep merging of person and computer into one entity for purposes of solving complex problems, has progressed little. Even in the 1960s computer graphics allowed design engineers to enlarge, contract, and rotate displays of proposed automobiles and ships and allowed chemists to do the same things in the study of complex protein molecules. Present graphics can do some things that people might not ever be able to do, for example, display the various surfaces and sections of the more complicated catastrophe theory manifolds. The results of laboratory studies of problem-solving have not been widely applied to real-world situations.

The computer has had little effect on higher management functions.

Technologists still promise wonders and ignore side effects as if people do not exist. The sociotechnical consequences of poorly planned implementations of new technologies are about as prevalent as ever.

In the previous chapter the long lead times involved between scientific discovery or invention and innovation and between the first conceptualization and the first realization of an innovation were discussed. This book has also stressed that much sociotechnical change is latent, just waiting for some event to trigger reconfiguration. It now seems likely that the promise and threat of computer-communications-based automation and technological change are nearly upon us.

Evolution, Hierarchy, and Impact in the Implementation of New Computer-Communications Technologies

The implementation of a new technology is seldom an isolated, one-of-a-kind event. Usually in large organizations the following evolutionary sequence of five steps applies:

Manual operations.

Formalization of manual methods through block diagramming, flow charting, preparing algorithms, and writing computer programs. Often this step alone is the most revolutionary, most difficult, or even the most costly. Elements of many different jobs may be combined and the manual records validated. Seldom is there a 1:1 translation of manual tasks, formats, and procedures into computerized forms. The computer may do things that were never before done by people. Often this second step is the most disruptive.

Mechanization, for example, using new copying machines and telephone switching techniques.

Automation in spots, for example, using batch data-processing in an otherwise mostly manual or partially mechanized office.

Large-scale automation using computer terminals hooked to a large central computer, small local computers, word processors, microforms, computer graphics, and teleconferencing.

If one considers that office automation began with the typewriter, telephone, and copying machine, then large-scale office automation will have taken more than a century. The pace has increased greatly recently, but over much of the period steps were small, incremental, costly, and often disruptive.

We can consider automation of white-collar functions at four levels:

1. *Clerical.* There has been rapid expansion at this level, with great improvements in accuracy, in error detection, in the capability to manipulate and edit text, and in the general provision of much information very rapidly. The greatest effects have been on offices hiring dozens of clerks doing homogeneous, routine, repetitive work. In fact, automating many clerical functions and tasks is so far under way that not much further improvement may be possible. Devices are now available that can translate much dictation into typed pages. The easiest applications are well under way using computer videodisplay terminals and computer-to-computer electronic communication. Neverthless, the longer-range impacts of the automation of clerical operations are far from certain. Clerks do perform myriad tasks including oral communications and exception–detection that may not be susceptible to parsimonious automation. The costs of displaced clerks must be compensated for by the costs of analysts, programmers, and maintenance personnel. Changes in skill levels, up or down, between, say, the older, more generalized clerk/typist job and the more specialized word-processor job, remain moot. Although the long lines of desks appear to be disappearing, many of the new word-processing centers look suspiciously like the old typing pools. The overall effects on unemployment, after-job transfers and attrition ("silent firings") is not known. The silliest idea is that of a paperless office. Legal requirements, the increasingly evident vulnerability of both batch and interactive computer systems to interference and sabotage, and personal preferences and fears would not permit such a thing.

2. *Supervisory and middle management.*   Much routine checking, comparing, searching, looking up, asking, and following up is being automated at these levels. Elimination or partial automation of jobs at the clerical level changes the nature of jobs of supervisors and middle managers. Should offices ever be automated to the extent of many refineries, chemical-processing plants, machine-tooled operations, or even robotized assembly lines, the need for so many supervisors and middle managers could be greatly reduced, and the jobs of many of the remaining persons limited mostly to monitoring and exception–detection. However, some middle managers would always be needed as buffers between persons and problems at the operational level and top management, and as resource persons, perhaps equipped with specialized information systems, when top managers ask questions about the external and internal environments, questions that involve working with highly esoteric areas or with specialists or experts in these areas. Early forecasters predicted a much greater impact of computers on middle management than has actually taken place.

3. *Scientists and other professionals.*   The impact of automation and new technology has been the greatest in this area. Advances in sensors, computers, control devices, and communications devices have been impressive if not wondrous. Miniaturization, packaging, and increased reliability have been particularly impressive. Unmanned space technology, represented by the probes and landers that have explored Mercury, Venus, Mars, Jupiter, and Saturn and their moons, as appropriate, appears to have been quite cost/effective as programs compared with many social, military, and commercial programs. The Voyager spacecrafts to Jupiter and Saturn represent an acme of technological progress. However, a number of less well-known developments are benefitting scientists and engineers in many different organizations. Some of these developments have already been translated into high-technology products. Several large artificial intelligence programs—MATHLAB, DENDRAL (chemistry), DOCTOR, ELIZA, and INTERNIST (medicine and psychiatry)—show or appear to show strong analytic or diagnostic capabilities through being programmed to mimic human activities, some rather profound but others dangerously superficial and silly. Proponents argue that these programs approach the performance level of a PhD or MD. Many of such programs take years to develop and are tailored to the analytic thought patterns of individual scientists or physicians. Experience with ELIZA, which simulated not the deep insights of psychiatric analysis but only superficial questions and answers, but which even sophisticated persons began to take seriously, cautions one to remember that most work involving higher-level problemsolving and decisionmaking is still in the R&D stage.[14]

4. *Top management.*   There has been rather slow progress at this level. This book is largely devoted to the development of an information system and problemsolving and decisionmaking capabilities for top management. Executives must be able to evaluate different alternatives, construct

scenarios, interact with computer simulations, detect early-warning signs and emerging patterns, anticipate crises, and evaluate and select among different courses of action. They need to be able to ask the right questions of specialists, especially in regard to the dynamics of the external environment. There has been little formalization of top management functions, and these may never be automated.

The most important impacts on organizational structure and function of the automation of white-collar, professional, and executive work will include:

Greater integration of functions or departments such as sales, orders, and inventory. Closer monitoring of errors, misdirections, and thefts are by-products. The Universal Product Code system in supermarkets and large discount chains provides an example. The now familiar dark-on-light, varying width, parallel lines found on most products in these businesses are scanned by a laser sensor. A computer records the sale, adds up the customer's bill, prints a sales slip describing each item tallied, deducts the item from inventory, and reorders.

Continued misguided attempts to break jobs down to their smallest components or create new jobs from fragments of many old jobs and *then* fit people to these jobs—classical sociotechnical systems misdesign.

Much greater rationalization of the corporation.

Much greater rigidification of the corporation in general, unless handled very carefully, and much greater vulnerability of the corporation to collapse in the face of events like power failures, sabotage, and sheer, unknowable complexity.

Much greater concentration of power.

Greater opportunities for tradeoffs between centralization and decentralization, between highly centralized computer processing and distributed processing.

Little practical overall effect on bureaucratic structure.

Greater opportunities to make tradeoffs between travel and communications. Advances in telecommunications and teleconferencing are among the most exciting. The new technologies include blends of computers, television, satellites, electronic blackboards, ground lines, and telephones. Informatic Communication, developed in Sweden, allows a large television screen to be split into up to 16 frames, with each frame representing an individual or small group at different remote sites. Each group can see itself as well as all other groups, providing effective visual, auditory, and body-language communications and interactions.[15] Other systems involve ordinary television screens and electronic blackboards from which writing can be transmitted to remote sites. Computer conferencing allows people to see and hear one another and to interact also through a computer. Although the more sophisticated approaches have not yet been widely implemented, some companies expect soon to be able to save $50–100 million in annual travel costs.

Large-scale electronic information transfer between companies and between companies and their subsidiaries. Preparation of paper documentation in both person-readable and machine-readable form will accompany this trend in many cases.

Greater flexibility of operations in the field through mobile sites and communication via satellite.

Some of these impacts may contradict one another or cancel one another out. Others may have deleterious side effects. Once again, in dealing with sociotechnical systems it is the way the technology is implemented that counts for good or bad.

Problems and Caveats

Consider two examples of present problems of design and operations. The first involves the so-called office of the future. In many cases the arrangement and use of word processors and computer terminals resembles the assembly line or factory of the past. Work is repetitive, boring, and stressful. As usual the computer is a hard taskmaster, and the computer paces the person rather than serving the person. As soon as one portion of work, displayed on the terminal screen, is completed, up pops another and then still another. After the novelty of the new equipment wears off, workers are little motivated to pursue the fragmented, isolated-by-specialty jobs. Job redefinition is often associated with lower status and lower pay. Many jobs are further impoverished by designers' having turned over most decisions to the computer, so that people merely provide inputs on demand. Some companies report little or no work improvement from designs that make high production demands coupled with boring, repetitious tasks.

The second example involves the Universal Product Code system described above. The attempt to automate supermarkets has met both consumer and union resistance. For moment-to-moment shopping, the system provides customers with *less* information. Person-readable price information no longer appears on each item. Prices indicated on the shelves are subject to error or vandalism. The system results in eliminating jobs, especially those of the people who formerly stamped prices on items. Net profits are fairly low in the supermarket business, and managers promise to pass along cost savings in the form of smaller price increases. However, it appears to be a law of human nature that things—land, money, or other people—once in the hands of an individual, organization, or nation, are rarely given up voluntarily. The cumulative effect of myriad vignettes like this one is probably the further augmentation of polarization and schism within our society.

Nor are other aspects of computer-communications systems at all clear. For one thing the government has already moved to prevent further concentration of power through consolidation in already powerful industries. American Telephone and Telegraph Company's new computer-communications subsidiary will be wholly independent. And the near monopoly of the telephone industry, which AT&T held for decades, may be broken through partial or total deregulation. The field promises to become increasingly competitive, which may drive some prices down, but may increase interface difficulties.

More importantly, there is too much technological "gee-whiz" about both office and home information-systems. Sociotechnical and human factors considerations have scarcely been recognized, and few if any comprehensive studies performed. Problems range from deep and irreversible societal disruptions to small and remediable irritations. Consider just a few points from among myriad potential problem areas.

Even after the experience of more than three decades, the lasting impacts of television on society are still not understood well. Numerous studies have been performed, including that of the Surgeon General. Nevertheless, television has probably contributed through repeated exposure to almost *any* stimulus to feelings of overall emotional remoteness and detachment, which contribute in turn an increased shallowness, demand for immediate gratification, lack of profound interests, and lack of self-restraint. What would be the effect of increasing the isolation of people through home/office information systems?

Completely decentralized work systems will probably never come about because managers will not permit this to happen. Most managers have strong needs for power and status, which would be greatly frustrated by the widespread dispersal of workers. The persistent viability of bureaucracy is neither accidental nor incidental. In addition, boring, repetitive work is even more repulsive at home to most people than it is in an organization where many social needs can be met.

As emphasized in Chapter 2, advances in software still lag far behind those in hardware. Further, almost all complex computer-communications systems have interface problems among the constituent subsystems. Faults and errors are often difficult to pinpoint within any particular subsystem. Systems are often patchworks of the old and the new. Software packages, for example, may represent the inputs and superimpositions of many different and unassociated contributors.

Many systems have human engineering deficiencies. Some of these are straightforward, although annoying, like flicker, glare, poor contrast between image and background, and poor design of characters. Other deficiencies are more profound and stem from failure to ask questions about what people really need and what people do best in comparison to what machines do best. For example, why should entire texts of newspapers be displayed on a screen? What provisions are there for assigning priorities to and combining, compressing, or selecting from information? Some designs are 1:1 attempts to automate present types of information sources.

New Technologies and Productivity

Productivity of computer and communications technologies can be examined in terms both of making and using these technologies. Most of the emphasis in this section has been on the latter. Continuing in this vein, it remains to be demonstrated whether the new technologies will improve *real* productivity. A major limitation is the long-standing problem of defining and measuring white-collar, professional, and managerial productivity. Certainly the technological capability to process much more information faster, store and process more text, turn out more copies, and so on cannot be questioned. But the distinction must be made between quality and quantity. Most of the great works of humankind were done manually—with pen, ink, brush, paper, and canvas. Technology greatly improves precision, control, the ability to deal with the very small and the very large, and the ability to sense and gather a great variety and amount of data. But here some people can be misled. The jobs of professionals and managers, and most other workers for that matter, are or should be holistic. Health, for example, must be a holistic concept. To devise machines that automatically read X-rays, ECGs, EEGs, and so forth and to conclude that these advances now greatly increase the productivity of physicians is to mistake the nature of the physician's job, perhaps the most important element of which is the encouragement, support, and problemsolving help provided patients.

Major generators of paperwork have been bureaucracies—usually viewed as notoriously inefficient—and company advertising. A sizable portion of newspapers, magazines, and the mails consists of advertising. The past performance of management-information systems in improving the quality while reducing the quantity of unneeded information has been less than impressive. Commercial television, by definition, consists of a sizable amount of time devoted to advertising. There is little precedent for reducing quantity in going from one technology or medium to another. Quality is an elusive concept. Measuring worker output in automated offices in terms of keystrokes or lines per minute may yield a spurious picture of improved productivity. A report by the General Accounting Office failed to show that word processors were cost/effective or had increased productivity, despite investments of several hundred-million dollars between fiscal years 1977 and 1982 by the Federal government.

It is often observed that the capital investment in equipment per worker is about $25,000 per factory worker, about $50,000 per farm worker, but only $2000–5000 per office worker. Therefore, one should increase capitalization per office worker. However, at times of societal instability like the present, this may be advice of uncertain value. Social and economic pressures may dictate a return to labor-intensive workforces.

Finally, as emphasized throughout this book, the abilities to organize technology in institutional and societal contexts lag far behind the abilities to develop new technologies.

Turning to the production and marketing of new information technologies, barring massive societal trauma, the forecast should be quite an optimistic picture. Sales in 1980 were about $30 billion per year. They are forecast to exceed $100 billion per year by 1990 and $500 billion by the turn of the century. Smaller companies like Wang Laboratories, Digital Equipment Corporation, and now Apple Computer (the stocks of which were committed even before it went public in the fall of 1980) are expected to prosper even more. Large corporations are either diversifying or entering the market. These include AT&T, IBM, Xerox, Honeywell, and even Exxon. The information-systems industry should continue to expand very rapidly to become one of the biggest in the world.

Finally, mention should be made of another possible new growth industry, namely, that based on genetic technology. Genentech, one of the first companies based on this technology, went public in the fall of 1980, with stock market response startlingly like that associated with Apple Computer. In fact, both these companies appear to be classical examples of the entrepreneurial founding of new companies in areas which could be expected to experience rapid growth. However, genetic technology is much less firmly established than is microcomputer technology. And living systems are much more complex than are nonliving ones. Thus, splicing a single mammalian gene that may regulate the production of a hormone onto bacterial chromosomal material may soon lead to factories to produce that hormone. But it must be remembered that there are long lead times between scientific discovery and innovation and between innovation and widespread production and use. Revolutionary changes in agriculture, food production, fuel production, and elimination of genetic deficiencies and disease are likely to be a long way off.

FURTHER THOUGHTS ON PRODUCTIVITY

Productivity, and economic growth and decline in general, present a very complex problem, a systems problem of the nature emphasized in Chapters 3, 4, and 5. In spite of a multitude of rather local theories and practices, overall knowledge is still scant. The current productivity slump, along with inflation and recession or depression, appear to be according to natural law involving the reconfigurational dynamics of societal evolution. Thus, these factors are presently beyond easy and direct control toward desired results. Control has dealt largely with secondary processes, but even so has yielded unexpected, contradictory, or undesirable effects.

The U.S. economy today is displaying some startling oscillations and fluctuations indicative of deep-lying instability. Some of the recent quarterly fluctuations have been among the most severe in recorded history. In addition, the economy may be increasingly vulnerable to exogenous perturbations. The gold and silver panics of early 1980 provide one type of example.

A second example of economic vulnerability to external perturbations illustrates the power of one person, who on January 6, 1981 sent a "sell" message to about 3000 of his clients. Within two days the Dow-Jones industrial average had fallen from about 1005 to about 965.

The economy appears now to be an autonomous system in which the pattern-wise undesirable forces of inflation, recession, unemployment, very high interest rates, low productivity, and low growth reinforce themselves through positive-feedback loops. Put another way, the economy is perhaps a dissipative structure, emergent from the long strains of operating under nonlinear, far-from-equilibrium conditions and tampering (regulation, fine-tuning) that assumed a linear or monotonic and equilibrium world. Put still another way, to the extent that we can think in equilibrium terms, it is probable that we are dealing, not with *an* equilibrium, but with multiple equilibria of differing degrees of stability, and that catastrophic reconfiguration is imminent. A societal price will have to be paid now for policies of trying to manipulate either demand or supply, in this simple supply–demand model, and assuming that the other will automatically rise or fall.

At the present time both the frequencies and the amplitudes of the oscillations or fluctuations within the economy appear to be changing in a manner indicating imminent reconfiguration. For example, the periods between recessions appear to be narrowing. Of course part of this pattern is due to the conscious attempt of the Federal Reserve Board to control the money supply (including effects on lending rates) in order to damp either inflationary or recessional tendencies. Nevertheless, one gets two impressions: (1) that, based on the increasing amplitudes, the cybernetic system is out of control, and (2) that, based on the increasing frequencies, a merger of adjacent fluctuations into a giant fluctuation, with qualitatively different characteristics from earlier great depressions and hyperinflations, is about to occur. An associated early-warning sign is the increases in bankruptcies in 1980 over those of 1979—from about 7800 to about 11,800 according to Dun and Bradstreet. These failures may represent increasing correlation lengths within a field of forces in the vicinity of a critical threshold.

Following this review of the state of the macrosystem, the somewhat more restricted topic of productivity will be discussed. Although the discussion is generalized but still rather macroeconomic, most points have a direct bearing on strategic planning and the internal environment of the organization. Facts, suggested causes, interpretations, and alternative models will be presented.

Facts on Productivity

The highest-level measure of productivity is called *total factor productivity,* defined as output per unit of input. This measure is difficult to specify precisely. It includes labor, capital (plant and equipment), and natural resources. It is increasingly important to make tradeoffs among these factors. The more familiar measure of productivity is *output per person-hour*. Both measures have shown an accelerating downward trend in recent years. The average annual percentage rate of growth of total factor productivity between 1916 and 1966 was estimated at 2.2 percent, but has declined since. The changes in average annual rates of growth in output per person-hour were: 1946–1966, 3.2 percent (4.1 percent during a post-World War II boom between 1947 and 1953); 1967–1977, accompanied by some fluctuations, declines to about 0.7 percent; 1978, 0.4 percent; 1979, negative growth.

Sectors, industries, and individual organizations of course differ in productivity. New and high-technology and some service industries usually have the highest rates of growth. Over the years, air transportation, gas and electric utilities, chemicals, refineries, computers, and tourism have variously had the highest average annual growth rates. The high-growth information industry was discussed in the previous section. Old industries like steel and shoes tend to show the least growth. Many service industries tend to have lower *measurable* outputs per person-hour, and the shift from production workers to service workers in the past three decades undoubtedly contributed to the decline in measured productivity.

The relationship between education and skill levels and productivity is far from clear. Increases in educational levels have tended to parallel declines in productivity. Most people with higher educations have entered white-collar work, which, as has been noted in some detail, does not yield to easy measures of productivity. Skill levels for jobs may not have increased in recent years—by one estimate some 80 percent of college graduates are underemployed. The combination of oversupply in some sectors of the job market, underemployment on many jobs, and skill levels in general which are potentially amenable to automation suggests serious misdesigns that do not augur well for future organizational and societal stability. This combination also explains much of the job dissatisfaction today.

Much of the concern over productivity has centered on ways to increase labor productivity or mechanize or automate manual jobs. Recently, energy has replaced labor as the high-cost factor. As mentioned before, a return to labor-intensive jobs in many areas seems likely.

Finally, socioeconomic woes, including the productivity plunge and stagflation, are worldwide. Almost all developed countries have failed to live up to the very optimistic projections made at the beginning of the 1971–1980 decade.

Summary of Suggested Causes for the Productivity Slump

Systems people must of course think in terms of mutual causality and dynamic feedback systems. Some of the ingredients of the system are:

Changes in labor-force mix to include more minority-group members, women, and youths, who may temporarily possess lower levels of skills.*

Accelerating inflation.

Major decline in R&D expenditures as a fraction of GNP, from 3 percent in 1964 to 2.2 percent in 1978, and major decline in technological progress.*

Lack of national purpose or will, widespread antiestablishment feelings, widespread alienation, and resultant behavior (absenteeism, turnover, strikes, and so forth).

Increased government intervention in and regulation of the economy.

Featherbedding.

High prices for social, environmental, safety, and health programs.*

Energy crisis and generally poor use of natural resources.*

Insufficient capital investment for modernizing plants and equipment.*

Major deficiencies in job design.*

*These items are those that could be most readily brought under the control of top management in the individual corporate organization. However, any one of the indicated areas may be necessary but insufficient. Top management should do some serious *re*thinking about all these areas. However, resources are often limited. If I were to single out the *one* area that would, I believe, bring about the best overall results, it would be the redesign of worksystems according to sociotechnical systems principles.

Interpretations

Productivity decline is a natural phenomenon, which was to be expected. Western societies are overripe and characterized by saturation or exhaustion along many dimensions. Although individual pockets of improvement can be made as indicated previously, dealing with aging, overly large and complex business and government organizations is another matter. Among the many symptoms discussed in Chapter 3, the following can be reiterated as conducive to declining productivity and declining performance in general:

Reduced capability to comprehend the system as a whole and its deteriorating function.

Disproportionate expenditures on *internal* regulation and control, with minuscule legitimate returns, that is, decline in total quality and even quantity of output.

Increased rigidity indicated, for example, by reliance on rules and procedures.

Decreased willingness to take risks.

R&D coupled with decreased variety of discovery and innovation.

Tendency to coast on past discovery and innovation—reinventing the wheel.

Reward for compliancy and predictability—old-boy networks.

Maximization of realization of individual versus collective goals.

Emphasis on short-term solutions and neglect of long-range planning.

The productivity system as a whole can be thought of in terms of the families of S-curves like those shown in Figure 3.1. There is some evidence that it is far harder to invent new processes and products that are demonstrably superior.[16] Improvements in the past were often of a once-in-the-lifetime-of-an-industry nature. For example, the shift from making house calls to seeing many patients concentrated in an office, clinic, or hospital could be thought of as having increased the productivity of physicians. Shifts from electromechanical to electronic processes greatly increased the productivity of the chemical and refinery industries. Mechanization of agriculture after World War II greatly improved productivity.

In some instances changes appear to have surpassed points of diminishing returns as illustrated in Figure 3.5. Levels appear to have been reached or exceeded for effective speeds of transportation, scale of machines and bureaucratic organizations, and efficiency of energy conversion. After over 30 years in development and the expenditure of billions of dollars, atomic energy is still a minor source of power. As more machines and people are connected in large systems, problems of reliability increase. In the health field massive expenditures have been more associated with rising costs of care than with increases in life expectancy.

As stressed throughout this book, the world appears to be on the verge of a major transition or transformation. Most of the ideas generated around the time of World War II and just afterward have reached the limits of their exploitation. Many of the newer ideas focus on complexity, unknowability, and improving the quality of life. The new information technologies, in application, do not lend themselves to easy measures of productivity. The time has really come for companies to rethink their fundamental goals and purposes.

The Japanese Model

No CEO is unaware of the amazing Japanese successes in productivity growth, product improvement, and market penetration. From 1960 the average annual growth in output per person-hour for all manufacturing of Japan exceeded that of the United States by over 200 percent. Of course the Japanese started from a lower base and in several areas have already reached saturation, and in the absolute sense overall U.S. productivity is still ahead of that of the Japanese. It is likely that the economic woes of the rest of the developed world will soon catch up with the Japanese, and in the longer term the Japanese are in a precarious position in terms of natural resources.

Nevertheless, U.S. companies have a lot to learn from the Japanese. One lesson teaches the design of a well-thought-out long-range strategy to this effect: start low, get a foot in the door, work hard to do better than the competition, sacrifice short-term profits, up the grade of the products, and finally take over the whole market. This strategy was discussed briefly in Chapter 6. The strategy has been successfully applied to textiles and clothing, steel, motorcycles, automobiles, ball bearings, ships, transistor radios and tape recorders, cameras, television, copying machines, and—increasingly—computers and microelectronics.

Competitive and viable Japanese companies usually receive much more support and backing from their government than do American companies. Japanese companies also take a much broader world view than do American companies. Japanese industry is well integrated into long-range national goals. However, Japanese successes have often been as much due to United States weaknesses as to any strength of the overall Japanese model. United States companies often held the competitive advantage even in Japan, but then lost it because of unimaginative and sluggish reactions on the part of American executives.

The Japanese way of doing things is obviously not transferrable in any 1:1 manner to the United States or to any other country. However, American companies could greatly improve both productivity and quality-of-work life by adapting from the Japanese such features as group harmony, consensus in decisionmaking, nonconfrontation, shared feeling of ownership, and mutual loyalty.

At the present time there are many books and articles that attempt to explain Japanese organization, management, productivity, and marketing. Much of this literature is superficial because (1) it fails to fit present Japanese methods into the complex milieu of Japanese culture, and (2) it fails to recognize that some "new" Japanese practices are really either feedbacks of American management concepts, or, even more seriously, are equivalent to what sociotechnical systems designers have been proposing for years. CEOs had best start becoming familiar with the Japanese way by reading anthropologist Ruth Benedict's *The Chrysanthemum and the Sword*, published back in 1946.

MONITORING

Organization–environment interrelations are major themes of this book. That fields of force and processes operate and phenomena and events occur in the many environments of the organization cannot be questioned. However, the rich variety of the environment is just now being appreciated. Merely being aware that many things are happening in the environment is not enough though. A much better understanding of the *what, when, why,* and *how* of these happenings must be developed. This requires theories and models which, ideally, would provide the basis for monitoring, sensing, and measuring the individual events and continuous and discontinuous changes of environmental factors. But to deal with immense complexity and uncertainty, the monitoring and sensing and measuring functions must go hand-in-hand with theory and model-building.

Adaptive organizations will be those that have been designed or redesigned to provide for a strong monitoring capability. Organizations will need relatively more information about the external environments than about the internal environment. So far there has been little thought about how to design a monitoring capability. Certainly the capability will involve a mixture of physical devices and measures, computers, informal human sources, social and economic indicators, and human experts and interpreters. Putting together this package will require considerable expertise. The organization itself will monitor for and acquire some information. However, even the largest corporations lack the ability to monitor all aspects of the environments and will have to rely on other sources and interpretations. Assessing the reliability of these primary sources and tailoring the information to specific organizational needs will also require an expertise not widely available today.

This topic will be pursued further in the following chapter. In the remainder of this chapter, monitoring the internal environment will be discussed.

No full-fledged program for monitoring the internal environment of the organization exists. However, elements of such a program are available. It has been pointed out in earlier chapters that even large, successful, competitive organizations often lack basic *at-hand* information on stocks, inventories, spare parts, orders, and so forth. Apparently, in such cases nobody knew that certain questions should be asked or how to ask the right questions. Simply doing these things and implementing a simple manual or computerized system could greatly improve knowledge of the internal environment of many organizations. But if an executive does not know what questions to ask and how to ask them, all the computers in the world cannot help him. Once again, this is why most MISs until now have been of limited value.

Behavioral-monitoring systems, such as that discussed at the beginning of this chapter that led to new knowledge about longitudinal changes in job satisfaction, are increasingly available. Most of these systems are based on questionnaire information. Many federal agencies and large companies now have data banks or have access to data banks that contain the results of hundreds of thousands of questionnaires taken over many years. Through these information systems, executives can become aware of long-term changes in some features of society as a whole and in their own companies. The systems also allow executives to make cross-company comparisons. For example, CEOs might want to ask, is job satisfaction higher or lower than average in my company? Or, why is job dissatisfaction so low in Subsidiary B?

Of course terms like average, higher, and lower must not be given a preciseness that does not and cannot exist. Once again, it is the qualitative features of systems and the qualitative nature of change that are usually most important in providing insight for executives. Remember again that highly advanced mathematics is often qualitative, as was emphasized in Chapter 5. Elaborate calculations may be necessary in the development of theories and models, but the myriad deficiencies in data and great difficulty in establishing causal interrelationships militate against great quantitative accuracy for societal systems. Lord help the executive who gets caught up in or bogged down by ideas such as statistically significant deviations from the mean!

In addition to information on job satisfaction, behavioral monitoring and inventory systems can provide executives with information on jobs, tasks, composition of the workforce, skills, turnover, vandalism, accidents, errors, health, losses of supplies and tools, and so on. These systems, however, should be used as a means of diagnosing problems in the solution of which everybody can participate. These problems are *organizational* problems, not assembly-line problems, clerical problems, middle-management problems, or even top-management problems. Recall from the earlier discussion in this chapter that surveillance and overcontrol can *de*motivate people. Monitoring the internal environment to catch people in the act or to attempt even greater one-way control over the workforce is very likely to backfire, bringing about or aggravating the undesirable behaviors the system was designed to obviate. Systems that are critically necessary to the adaptability and survival of the organization may collapse unless handled carefully. Any use of questionnaires or other information-gathering techniques must be in the context of *two-way communication* and in the context of *mutual problemsolving*.

Finally, the system to display the information and knowledge acquired through monitoring, and integrated or synthesized by theories, models, and constructs, must be very carefully thought through and well designed. Top management must be provided with a total organizational information capability—*selectively* and by *priority*. This means that executives will probably never need or want all the information on job positions, tasks, day-to-day errors, and so forth. But top management will want and need displays of trends, major changes, summaries, and selected specific information (immediately) should a critical question arise concerning, say, equal opportunity employment.

8

ADAPTIVE DESIGN AND MANAGEMENT

In a study of 800 of the nation's largest companies, it was found that long-range planning claimed most of the CEO's time and was expected to increase by 1985 (Trends, *Forbes,* November 24, 1980).

Most management consultants believe that over 90 percent of US companies have up to now proved incapable of developing and implementing meaningful corporate strategies. (*Fortune,* September 24, 1979, p. 118).

Increasingly, CEOs have been disappointed with the results of corporate, strategic, and long-range planning and concerned with the time, effort, and costs that have been devoted to these activities. Considering the nature of the world as it has been presented so far, such disappointment and concern is not at all unexpected. The picture shapes up as follows.

Strategic and long-range planning are indispensable to, and inextricably interwound with, adaptive organizational design. Planning and design are not synonymous—they are simply inseparable parts of a greater whole. Adaptive organizational design involves much more than planning, but without strategic and long-range planning there is no way to interrelate organizational performance and anticipated environmental changes.

Top management has found all too often that strategic or long-range plans, far from anticipating crises or other unpleasant surprises, have actually brought about problems the plans were supposed to prevent. Where there have been no counterintuitive or negative effects, it may be nevertheless quite difficult to demonstrate how the organization is better off as a result of costly planning efforts. Again and again, top management is caught by surprise—new competitors spring up seemingly from nowhere; old friends such as previous collaborators, suppliers, and customers suddenly turn into competitors; one's own lower management conspires to defeat the plan or else follows it slavishly and rigidly in spite of the most obvious demands for deviation. Ironically, it is those companies that have had the most experience with high-level planning and which have even experienced past successes, that now appear to be the most disillusioned.

Although there are some more specific reasons for these failures and disappointments, the overriding reason for planning failures and for corporate failures in general is rigid thinking rooted in past perceptions of the world.

Many organizations actually stifle creative and innovative thinking, which is perhaps the single most important resource of an organization. Some organizations are only now trying to understand, absorb, and utilize the concepts that arose in the 1960s and earlier 1970s. These concepts may have been applicable and helpful in those earlier and qualitatively very different times, but they are far too simple and limited for application in the environments of today and tomorrow. Some of these concepts may be familiar, for example, strategic portfolio analysis, strategic business until, the experience curve or learning by doing, and various kinds of growth-to-share matrices (growth of a product or strategic business unit plotted against market share). Both the experience and growth–share curves are negative, decreasing exponential-type curves, pointing out the severe constraints of monotonic views of the world. A monotonic function either goes up or down but not both.

Strategies for the 1980s will most certainly have to be more holistic, more anticipatory, and more creative. Yet, according to an article in *Fortune*, "most managers are still experimenting with the strategic tools developed in the Sixties, with mixed results."[1]

An adaptive organization must be flexible and resilient, open to ideas and perceptions from without, keep an eye on present and likely future environmental changes, learn from experience, and be quick in response. Yet much organizational planning rejects the very features necessary for viability and survival. Companies almost ritualistically remain fixed on outmoded assumptions and rely on standardized strategies that virtually telegraph the company's next moves to the opposition.

Management consultant J. Quincy Hunsicker comments both on a tunnel vision and a paralysis by analysis fostered by reliance on standardized strategies.[2] Users of the learning curve may fail to realize that competitors do not necessarily follow the same curve, and that differences in technology and orientation may render the learning curve irrelevant. Companies that depend too much on such standardized methodologies have been repeatedly hurt by competitors that act in innovative, unconventional, and unexpected ways.

Unadaptive organizational designs and management underlie most of these failures. Often the wrong people are responsible for planning. Analysis of data, statistics, and trends may contribute to planning but is never sufficient. Much more important is a holistic orientation and the hard-to-come-by skills of systems synthesis. Hunsicker writes:

> . . . the process of proposing a new idea, justifying it, and defending it against "challenges" by corporate staff and senior management is so intimidating that all but the most confident entrepreneurs are inclined to stick to less imaginative approaches that are easier to quantify and defend. Indeed, the more quantitatively oriented and sophisticated a planning process becomes, the harder it is for most managers to come up with fresh approaches. By its very nature, the system tends to suppress new ideas—ideas that may only be questions, vague feelings, or hunches at the start.

Although organizations—both business and government—were seldom if ever so large and powerful as they are today, their top managements appear to be more and more uncertain and more and more threatened by environmental pressures. A psychological defense mechanism is the quest for even greater exactness and predictability expressed in the forms of masses of data and quantified information, rationalized decisionmaking, and rigid control. This is no substitute for keeping an open mind and asking the right questions.

Finally, the failures of and disappointments with planning can be summarized as being due to:

Misunderstanding and misuse of mathematics, statistics, and of quantification in general.

Misuse of computers.

Resistance to change in ideas and concepts, resulting in acceptance of those ideas and concepts long after the time of usefulness has passed.

Persistence in using approaches and methodologies long after they have become outmoded.

Persistence in sticking rigidly to plans once developed as if these plans were lasting truths.

Confusion of long-range planning with things like the setting of five-year budgets.

Misunderstanding of human nature and the misuse of human resources, particularly the creative minds of people variously considered to be entrepreneurs, mavericks, troublemakers, boat-rockers, or too low in the organizational hierarchy to know anything of value.

BASIC DESIGN OF THE ADAPTIVE ORGANIZATION

The design of the adaptive organization begins with some simple models:

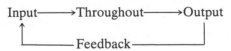

or alternatively,

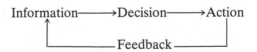

These basic cybernetic models were introduced and discussed in some detail earlier. Cybernetics is necessary but insufficient for the design of adaptive systems. And decision, of course, far transcends simple decisionmaking.

An expansion of this model, which reflects the structure of this book, is given in Figure 8.1. The figure should be considered to be three-dimensional in a

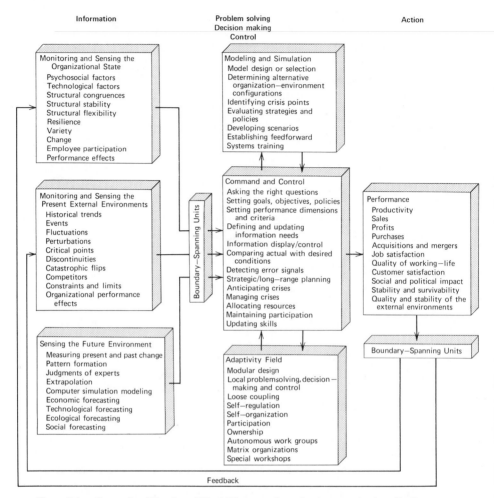

Figure 8.1. Generalized Top-Level Block Diagram of an adaptive organization. Similar structure recurs at various lower levels of the organization.

manner beyond what is shown here to indicate, in addition to the *top-management level* shown, the successive versions of the model at lower levels of the organization. These other versions are absolutely necessary in a design, an important feature of which is autonomous or semiautonomous subsystems. The diagram must *not* be construed as indicating that: (1) vertical communication is in only one direction, namely, up to down; (2) there are no other vertical channels of communication, for example, among various levels of *Modeling and Simulation* or the *Adaptivity Field;* or there are no lateral channels of communication at lower levels. Such an interpretation would destroy the very foundation of the adaptive organization.

Further, the diagram must *not* be interpreted as indicating centralization or militarization of problemsolving, decisionmaking, and control. Just as the basic design applies to the different levels of the organization, so it also applies to divisions or subsidiaries of a large organization. It is a generalized and flexible design that can be modified to fit local needs. In addition, many of the military debacles up to now have been due to "militarization" in the sense that this term has come to mean rigidity, lack of local initiative, inflexible rules and procedures, refusal to admit change, and unmodifiable preplanning.

An adaptive organization is at once a field of forces, a Gestalt, and a network. Figures using rectangles and other geometric symbols, lines, arrows, pluses and minuses, and so on can scarcely capture the holistic and dynamic nature of the organization. A blob, ameboid shape, abstract painting, or Rorschach ink blot might better convey the true nature of the organization, but these depictions could not communicate the specifies needed for discussion and design.

Referring briefly to each of the boxes in Figure 8.1, *Monitoring and Sensing the Organizational State* was discussed at length in Chapters 3 and 7. The boxes in the figure cannot of course encapsulate the scope provided there, but representative areas are given. Some of these areas are relatively straightforward, but others require more thought. Some of the areas have rather precise measurement concepts and tools; others will be more dependent on a general holistic grasp of the situation, perhaps involving intuition and hunch, and heuristic or rule-of-thumb methods. This is not necessarily a drawback. The first steps in any kind of problemsolving are the recognition that there *is* a problem and the identification of that problem. Reductionism, arbitrary isolation of problems from context, premature quantification, and premature imposition of decision rules *can* present a serious drawback.

Psychosocial factors and *technological factors* are examples of areas that are relatively straightforward and which possess well-thought-out measurement concepts, fairly precise measurement tools, and even bodies of fairly reliable data. The results of classical sociotechnical systems studies and longitudinal trends in job satisfaction can provide immediately usable information for organizational problemsolving.

It is important not to specify too much detail beforehand about the whats and hows of measurement, for this would introduce a rigidity that would defeat the very concept of an adaptive organization. For example, the flow of people, work, materials, and information will differ from organization to organization. So can the nature of job satisfaction or dissatisfaction which can be reflected in the design of a questionnaire. Although a *strategy for design* is presented here especially in this chapter, and although the strategy provides a framework for tactics, the tactics themselves and especially the local operations should be a matter of problemsolving within the individual organization or organizational level. As necessary, organizational problemsolving can be aided or supported by outside consultants or catalysts in the form of action research. But attempts should not be made to impose solutions either beforehand or from the ouside.

Several other areas of *Monitoring and Sensing the Organizational State* require newly developed or still undeveloped approaches and tools. *Structural–functional congruencies* refer to the degree of fit among the different subsystems and parts of the organization. For example, a level of management or the R&D group may have become technologically obsolescent and no longer fit the goals of a purportedly high-technology organization. Structure and function are of course closely interrelated, but to simplify the discussion the term structural will be used to mean structural–functional. There is no easy, practical way to determine congruency. People must develop a feel for it through experience and repeatedly asking the right questions. For example: why are people communicating less now that all that money has been invested in the new information technology?

Structural stability is an extremely important concept with regard to organizational viability and survival. The search for discontinuities, development of catastrophe theory models and measurements based thereon, and examination of systems dynamics oscillations are the key means of monitoring for structural stability.

Structural flexibility is an indicator of the variety and rapidity of necessary organizational responses. Once again, there is no one simple measure to apply here, but rather a repertory of possible measures is available to organizational problemsolvers. One key question might be: haven't we gone too far in attempting to codify everything? Or, why did we lose out several times in a row to those outfits that came out of nowhere?

Resilence is an indicator of the organization's ability to absorb or bounce back from external shocks or perturbations. The work of John Argenti on corporate failure and collapse provides a number of clues as to where to start in assessing organizational resilience. Catastrophe manifolds offer other insights. The equilibrium level at which the organization operates can provide one measure of resilience.

Variety is a key concept in cybernetics. Adaptation and survival of a system are closely related to the way the system incorporates and handles variety. Putting all one's eggs in one basket has long been known to be risky. Executives have of course long recognized this fact, and this is why corporations diversify into different industries, companies, divisions, and products. However, corporations often go to great lengths to reduce variety within the organization, for example, through standardization and hiring practices. There should be a congruence or fit between the variety within the organization and the variety of environmental challenges, opportunities, and threats. An organization with low variety is likely to be a poor problemsolver.

Change may appear to be so obvious that it is trite to put it in the box. Everybody knows today that organizations are changing and must change. But the acknowledgment of change is not the same as the measurement and control of change. For example, there may be no reference points for making comparisons. Also much change is latent, incipient, or subtle. Change is pervasive and applies to the other boxes in Figure 8.1. Having noted its importance, it will not be indicated in the other boxes.

Employee participation in problemsolving and decisionmaking is inherent in the concept of an adaptive organization, not just because this is the humanistic way to do things or because present fads say that this is proper management. No organization has the capability and resources to solve its myriad problems from the top. The more top management concerns itself with routine and local matters, the less capability it will have for things like strategic and long-range planning. Furthermore, the less the input of all organizational levels to higher-level planning, policymaking, and decisionmaking, the more likely will be the continuation of the present debilitating accompaniments of poor worksystem design. Without active monitoring and top management encouragement, employee participation may just erode away in the ordinary course of organizational change.

Organizational-performance effects represent one of the most critical areas of sensing and monitoring in a cybernetic design. It should be noted that the two preliminary figures in the text and Figure 8.1 show *closed-loop* systems. Organizational performance outputs are fed back to modify selected features of the organizational state. Or, to put it another way, actual performance is compared with desired performance. Or, outputs are compared with inputs. Comparison entails complex sets of processes at the level of the total organization. These processes will be discussed more fully later in this chapter.

Turning now to *Monitoring and Sensing the Present External Environments,* it should be noted that the properties of environments as a whole and the forces, trends, and configurations of the several dimensions of the environment and systems may suddenly reconfigure to produce unexpected new patterns. (Once again it should be noted that the items within each box as shown in the Figure in input-output terms *may* apply to other blocks or boxes. Items that may apply to two or more blocks are indicated either in the order of arrangement in and discussion of Figure 8.1 or in the block that best highlights their meaning.)

Historical trends provide indicators of change, for example, growth or decline from the past to the present. Trends may be continuous or continual (discrete). Trends, given the multifaceted data problem discussed in Chapter 4, give good first impressions of changes in technological, social, human resource, and other environmental factors.

Events are presumably one-of-a-kind or rare occurrences. Sometimes this is actually the case, but more importantly events may be the tips of the icebergs, surface indicators of an unknown or poorly understood subsurface field of forces. The interactions of forces within a field can lead to sudden and unexpected reconfigurations or changes in the total pattern of the field. This is the major theoretic explanation of the turbulence of environmental fields.

Changes in the nature of the forces, variables, and parameters that characterize the systems in the external environment are typically those not looked for up to now. These important indicators of emergent qualitatively different configurations are *fluctuations* in the field or in the behavior of specific systems, *perturbations* imposed on systems by external forces in the field, *critical points* on either side of which system behaviors are qualitatively and perhaps irreversibly different, *discontinuities* in trends, and *catastrophic flips* from one equilibrium level or surface to another. Executives, organization designers, planners, and environmental analysts should make a great effort to understand these concepts. Otherwise, they will fail to comprehend the real meaning of environmental turbulence and organizational evolution and adaptability.

Competitors consist mainly of other organizations. Competition between organizations and the search for the proper ecological niches was discussed earlier in Chapter 6. In a time of limits to growth, growth of one organization is very likely to come out of the hides of other organizations. Corporate strategy and tactics must increasingly be based on anticipatory knowledge of what the opposition is likely to do. And again, emergence and reconfiguration are of paramount importance as new coalitions form; new, small companies offer superior products to those of older, large, and established companies; and buyers or customers and suppliers suddenly turn into competitors. With environmental limits and increasingly formidable competitors—as the weaker or less competent (unless protected, say, by government) are squeezed out by the survival of the fittest—organizations will be cutting their own throats if they eliminate innovation through the misuse of power and control.

Constraints and limits are increasingly important at this late point in the present stage of societal evolution. This is quite a complex area, which must be viewed primarily in terms of evolution and which cannot be approached in terms of easy interventions to produce quick and desirable solutions. Part of this complexity is explained in Chapter 3 in a discussion of growth forms, especially of coalition formation and hyperbolic sociotechnical growth expressed through a series of S-curves encompassed by envelope curves. Such growth, especially after it has broken through local limits or ceilings is essentially irreversible. The links between social and technological forces and between, say, business and government organizations cannot easily be broken. Symbiotic new forms have emerged. Thus, business cannot universally decry government regulations because many regulations operate to the advantage of business. The many government practices that individually benefit selected interest groups—labor, retirees, veterans, farmers, persons on welfare—have evolved and become more firmly entrenched over the years. To maintain these links may break the country financially; to try to sever these links is to risk major societal upheaval, perhaps even insurrection or revolution. Constraints on the organization imposed by the political environment were treated in Chapter 6.

Finally, the organization must monitor the *effects* on the external environment *of its own performance*. This is an increasingly critical area. Indicators include such rather straightforward though perhaps debatable measures as market penetration, market share, total sales of goods or services, pollution and its effects, and use or destruction of resources, and more subtle measures such as changing attitudes and opinions toward business and government. Organizations must be especially attuned to long-range, cumulative, and irreversible impacts.

The adaptive organization will need a much better understanding of the external environment, an understanding that derives from more sophisticated information.

In looking at the block, *Sensing the Future Environment,* one sees that the many possible futures do not of course exist, so the future environment cannot be monitored. However, forces, trends, and configurations in the present can be sensed and forecast into the future. In Chapter 4 a number of forecasting methods were described and evaluated. The essential ingredients of this block are sensing and measuring the present and past, the recognition and formation of patterns, the judgments of experts, and forecasts of understood presents into the future, activities which are considered to be both extremely difficult and quite indispensable.

Measuring present and past change provides a basis for looking at the future as long as it is remembered that the past, present, and future will never be exactly alike, and as long as the measures include the fluctuations, perturbations, critical points, discontinuities, and catastrophic jumps or falls. Single indicators are rarely of value; hence, the importance of *pattern formation.* In viewing and interpreting past and present patterns of trends and events, one should be particularly alert for *precursory phenomena.* Once again it is possible to think in terms of isomorphies (structural or functional similarities between different kinds of systems) and general laws of nature. For example, changes in ground water, ground elevation, geomagnetism, and the concentration of radon gas seem to precede earthquakes. This gives a hint that one should look for precursory phenomena or early-warning signals in societal systems. One example could be human values, which appear to be more basic and permanent than attitudes or opinions. Measured changes in values could signal a change in attitudes or opinions to follow a certain amount of time later.[3] Familiar to most executives, as a rather rough approach, is the use of leading and lagging indicators in economic models.

The future will of course occur with or without human beings. However, the numbers, success, and impacts of humanity ensure that the future will be molded by humankind for at least some decades to come. Although nearly everybody foresees a human future of one kind or another, every form of scientific futures forecasting relies on the *judgments of experts.* The trouble is, there are often problems in deciding who is an expert. Experts have been very wrong in the past, and judgmental abilities differ among people as a function of cognitive and personality processes.

Past and present trends and patterns are *extrapolated* into the future, and events, judged to take place at given times, are superimposed to modify or be modified by the trends and patterns. Trends and patterns change within a field of forces, being amplified or attenuated or broken up and reconfigured, so that straightforward extrapolations are bound to be wrong. Events can have more than local or one-of-a-kind effects or impacts. Futures forecasting is still greatly limited by the failure to incorporate behavioral and social factors and the failure to reflect the reconfigurational nature of societal evolution into forecasts.

Computer simulation modeling is the only practical way to handle large numbers of dynamically interacting variables. We favor the systems dynamics approach. In Chapter 4 we stressed this preference.

In addition to these general methods, there are forecasts which can be applied to any of the specific external environments discussed earlier. Four examples are given in the box. *Economic forecasting* is by far the most commonly practiced despite its limitations. *Technological forecasting* is probably the most sophisticated method. *Ecological forecasts* are becoming increasingly common, but *social forecasts,* other than the naive and trivial, are unfortunately rare. The number and availability of forecasts, however, is no guarantee of their meaningfulness or usefulness. Plotting of hard technological data led to the concepts of families of S-curves encompassed by envelope curves and of stages or platforms of relatively little change separating stages of exponential or hyperbolic growth, which were highlighted in Chapter 3.

Ecological forecasts are often based on hard data on soil changes and erosion, deforestation, desertification, water composition, species numbers, and so forth. Social forecasting, more than any other type, requires an understanding of field-theoretic and emergent processes.[4] But hard data are rarely available.

Turning to the *Modeling and Simulation* block, it can be noted that this block is off-line to the major flow of information through the organization and also that there is no necessary reference to computers. An adaptive system need not embody a given technology or a given mechanization of processes. Modeling and simulation in this design have no direct interface with the external and internal environments. The block provides an indispensable support capability to the problemsolving activities highlighted in *Command and Control.* Note the two-way arrows. There is overlap in practice between *Sensing the Future Environment* and *Modeling and Simulation.* However, the overall functions are not identical. For example, measurements of changes in present systems could be made without referring the resulting data to a formal model.

Modeling and simulation are considered to amplify greatly human problemsolving capabilities in complex organizations. Although not necessary for all problemsolving or for all stages in a sequence of problemsolving, computers are essential to the overall design of adaptive large organizations in turbulent environments.

Model design or selection is a first step in utilizing this capability. Organizations differ in their resources for building and supporting models; hence, a spectrum ranging from no internal modeling capability to a very large capability can be visualized. At present no organization, not even a large national government, has a complete capability. Many large organizations today have mixtures of internally designed and externally supplied models. Such arrangements often introduce interface problems, and experience shows that executives resist using models that were "not invented here."

In Chapter 4 it was indicated that the construction of bottom–up models has not been very successful because of problems of interface and incompatibility and because of the sheer absence of submodels. Further, in the design of the adaptive organization, one can distinguish between *model services* whereby outside agencies provide information, for example, from econometric models, to key decisionmakers, and internal *interactive models* whereby organization members can design different organization–environment configurations and ask a variety of questions.

As discussed in Chapters 2, 4, and 6, the most difficult and important stages of model design are the initial conceptualization and formalization. Computerization must take a poor third place. Premature computerization is the reason for failure of many a model and many an information system. Furthermore, a good job of conceptualization and formalization itself may provide such valuable new insights that the organization can see its problems in an entirely new light. The organization may be able to do without a large computer capability. Small computers and small models, manually integrated by much more sophisticated persons, may well suffice in certain cases. And even in an organization that relies heavily on computer simulation modeling, there need be no necessary recourse to this methodology at all organizational levels.

These caveats aside, in large organizations in turbulent environments, computer simulation modeling is a necessity. Determining alternative organization–environment configurations provides one key approach to understanding and maintaining adaptability and maximizing chances for survival. It must be emphasized that the necessity for the use of this approach is not widely known. It goes far beyond the asking of *what if* questions and far beyond the policy manipulations of systems dynamics and other large models. *Determining alternative organization–environment configurations* is a way of incorporating contingency and variety into a computer simulation model. For example, various types of organizational structure could be simulated as a function of various environmental contingencies. Variations are made in both the organization and the environments. Decisionmaking is endogenous and affected by its results, not imposed exogenously by a policymaker, who, though the system or environment may change, remains unaffected by his own actions.

Properly designed and used models can be invaluable in the *identification of potential crisis points or situations.* Many models of course attempt or have attempted to do this; for example, *The Limits to Growth models* identified potential pollution and population-growth crises in the next century. The U.S. Government model, discussed in Chapter 6, forecast a number of serious environmental problems by the turn of the century. Gloomy as these and other prognostications may appear, they greatly underestimate the criticalness of happenings in the world-system field. As stated several times earlier, incorporation into dynamic computer simulation models of the constructs discussed in Chapters 3 and 5 would most likely move closer to the present and portray in intensified form a number of interacting world crises. Even without these systemic considerations, individual organizations will face a greater number of more intense crises, with one quickly following the other. These crises may appear in familiar areas—productivity, labor unrest, competition from other organizations, or economic instability, for example—but in surprisingly different forms. Imaginatively designed and utilized models can help organizations to anticipate and adapt to or ward off such crises.

Another important purpose for developing a sophisticated modeling and simulation capability is to *evaluate strategies and policies* before entering the real-world arena. For example, a market environment containing one or more products and one or more competitors could be simulated, and strategies tried out against the strategies and counterstrategies of various competitors. As a warning, this kind of evaluation of strategies and policies should not be allowed to deteriorate into another sterile exercise in game theory or other competition between rationalized decisionmakers. Emotional factors, seeming internal contradictions, and unpredictability are likely to be important elements.

The *development of scenarios,* discussed in Chapter 4, is a means not only of combining a number of inputs and interactions to produce alternative holistic pictures or patterns of a situation. It is also an important means of encouraging participation in problemsolving by all concerned parties. Thus, scenario development is a significant bridge between the social and technological capabilities of the problemsolving and learning organization.

When a measure of or information about the behavior or performance of a system is returned to the input, and added to or compared with that input, feedback is obtained. The term *feedforward* is often used to describe future planning situations. Feedforward involves the setting of goals based on the most realistic forecasts available, and then attempting to steer performance so as to meet these goals. In negative feedback, regulation and control attempt to narrow the disparity between present actual and desired behavior or performance. In actuality, lags and delays may prevent any simple relationship between the two measures, producing unstable or oscillating systems. In feedforward, regulation and control attempt to narrow the disparity between future goals and ongoing performance. Certain intermediary operations may be temporarily skipped, perhaps to be returned to as approach to them becomes more imminent. Or alternatively intermediate operations or projects may be dropped as better control information becomes available. With the passage of time, feedback becomes incorporated into the larger scheme of feedforward. In a sense feedforward is to feedback what strategy is to tactics. Both are indispensable to the adaptive organization. Like feedback, feedforward can be positive as well as negative.

Finally, an important function for modeling and simulation, not widely used outside military and space organizations, is *systems training*. This is an area in which improvements can be made. Organizations spend billions of dollars on training, but much of this is fragmented, misdirected, or questionable. Systems training can provide a valuable integrative framework for otherwise fragmented activities. Through systems training organization members can become better prepared beforehand to manage anticipated difficulties and crises. Group, person–computer problemsolving, not the acquisition of personal skills is meant here.

Look now at the two boxes labeled *Boundary-Spanning Units,* one between the three boxes providing environmental information and *Command and Control* and the other straddling the feedback loops between *Performance* output and information input. The concept of boundary-spanning units was introduced in Chapter 1 and amplified in Chapter 7. The expansion and formalization of these units is an important feature of the design, both in terms of the *people* involved and of the *processes* involved. Consider first the input side of Figure 8.1. The people are experts in the environments, measures, patterns, theories and models, forecasts, and so on. There necessarily must be a large number of these experts corresponding to the variety in the environments. Some of the experts will be exployees of the organization and others will be outside consultants or providers of information services. However, new specialists going their separate ways often producing mutually contradictory information or recommendations will perpetuate the situation decried in Chapter 2, albeit with *today's* concepts and approaches. Further, it is the job of these experts to provide the best information, support, and advice possible, not themselves to manage the organization.

This does not mean of course that experts and specialists should be excluded from participating in management. At some levels of the organization the information-acquirer, the decisionmaker, and the doer will be the same person. This is of course one of the essential points of the design of matrix organizations and of designs alternative to hierarchy. Here, however, is meant the top level of the total organization, which must confront all the environments in all their turbulence over the long range.

If some constraints are not put on the roles of disparate specialist experts, the intended adaptive organization may end up rather like the rigid, unmanageably complex organizations discussed earlier. And once again the importance of the role of Systems Integrator, a supergeneralist, who can tie together the strands provided by the specialists, is stressed.

The processes in boundary-spanning are those discussed under topics of the sequence of information flow and the data problem. Data and information can be misleadingly amplified, attenuated, biased, noisy, filtered, sporadic, and aggregated. It is too much to expect that perfect data and information will be available under all circumstances. Often data and information with *known* limitations are better than nothing at all. But information flowing into the problemsolving and decisionmaking functions should always be qualified, to the extent possible, in terms of deficiencies and limitations. Such qualification is not limited to considerations of statistical reliability.

Consider now the output side of Figure 8.1. Here the people and processes are those that facilitate the achievement of goals, the implementation of plans, and the improvement of performance. The people might be those who can resolve conflicts, bridge different constituencies, or communicate the organization's purposes to groups or organizations that are in a position to aid or impede the organization's actions. The people might be the varied members of a board of directors (or trustees, governors, or counselors) that is congruent with the variety of interests in the environments. The processes—political, economic, and social—are those that pave the way for the organization to reach its goals. A number of these are well known to most executives.

Command and Control is based on the concept of a computerized command, control, communications, and intelligence or information system (C³I system), which was discussed in Chapter 1. The concept of the C³I system is one valuable input to the overall design. These C³I systems have been remarkably successful in acquiring, processing, and displaying hard and soft information for command-and-control decisions. Rapidity and accuracy of response have been characteristic of these military and space systems.

Nor are military organizations, even in societies considered to be authoritarian, necessarily monolithic and inflexible. Len Deighton writes in *Blitzkrieg* that in 1940 the German panzer division was more complicated than any other division but far more versatile.[5] It had tanks, infantry, artillery, engineering, supply, transport, medical, maintenance, and administratve units or capabilities and thus had the variety to match the contingencies of the environment. The mixed nature of the division extended down into the subunits, which, being to some extent self-contained, could be reassembled and tailored to meet the demands of the particular battle. Furthermore, both German and British senior commanders agreed that German soldiers were more individualistic than were their opponents. In the fighting in North Africa the Germans were better able to improvise in emergencies than were their British opponents. The British gave up after losing all their officers, but German organization remained efficient down to the last few NCOs.

In their novel *The Third World War,* General Sir John Hackett and his top-ranking NATO colleagues predict the collapse and defeat of the Warsaw Pact forces, to a considerable extent because of a very high degree of centralization of command that leaves little autonomy and therefore initiative and resourcefulness to subordinate units of these forces.[6] Whether this is a realistic prediction or not of course remains to be seen.

To return to Figure 8.1 and the important representative functions of *Command and Control,* it must be reemphasized again in review that Figure 8.1, although shown in three dimensions, actually represents a four-dimensional system. The horizontal dimension is evident; this depicts inputs, throughputs, outputs, and feedback. In the front-to-back direction the blocks are boxes which possess their own variability and which themselves process inputs into outputs through appropriate transfer functions. The vertical dimension is implied; however, it indicates that the figure shows only one (the top) level of several to many levels. These levels are sometimes called *recursion* levels. Recursion is an important property of many mathematical and computer-programming techniques. Something is recursive if it is defined partially in terms of itself. Recursion as a concept fits well into a top-down, stepwise-refinement orientation to problemsolving. Taken too literally recursion could be the wrong approach to the design of adaptive systems, with its implication of one-way communication, hierarchical aggregation, and algorithmic anticipation of all finite consequences. The concepts of semiautonomous levels and lateral as well as vertical communications are more important elements in the design of adaptive systems.

The fourth dimension is time for dealing with dynamic systems. Thus, most of the functions and processes indicated in the boxes are iterative by design. However, the organizations are *evolving,* and slight variations, drifts, and fluctuations may progressively render exact iterations both difficult and meaningless. For convenience of discussion the items in the boxes are described in a certain sequence, but at any frame of time—except perhaps as an initial condition—there is no first step.

We start our closer examination of the *Command and Control* block with the function, *asking the right questions.* At the executive level these include questions about the mission or purpose, capabilities, history, continuity, change, environmental fit, and performance of the organization. For example: what is the *real* primary purpose this organization was founded to accomplish? What business *should* we be in? What were the *earliest* indicators that should have warned us that performance would subsequently decline so rapidly? Note the longitudinal and evolutionary perspective of these questions. Often today, with a rapid turnover of executives as well as other employees, organizational memory is lost. Thus, a new executive may amplify errors that could have been detected and damped had a longer-range historical perspective been utilized.

The mission or purpose defines the organization's *raison d'être.* However in many, especially older, organizations there is a disparity between the nominal and actual purposes. Often this disparity is not recognized by top management itself. Conflicting purposes, though, can lead to misperceptions about the world and a widening loss of environmental fit. This appears to be true of at least some of the U.S. auto makers, which could not distinguish among the acquisition and maintenance of power and money, the manufacture of quality cars to fit changing markets, and the necessity to rethink in the broader terms of the transportation business.

Setting goals, objectives, and policies enables organizations to move toward discharging their mission or purpose. Goals can be considered longer-range targets to be reached and objectives can be considered to be shorter-range targets (as in management by objectives). Policies can be considered to be rather specific (that is, they are parts of plans) means of accomplishing goals and objectives. Unfortunately, terminology is far from standardized, and definitions of goals, objectives, plans, policies, and so on vary greatly among users of the terms. Goals, objectives, plans, and policies must not be rigidly preprogrammed and unmodifiable—to design them so is almost a sure guarantee for failure and a defeat of the very concept of an adaptive organization.

Setting the dimensions and criteria of organizational performance adds rigor to the framework provided by *true* recognition or identification of purposes, goals, objectives, etc. A dimension is a qualitatively more or less distinguishable aspect of performance such as growth, productivity, profits, sales, return on investment (and other ratios), quality of work life, and stability and survivability. In terms of our design of an adaptive organization, performance is always multidimensional. Some of these dimensions are quite familiar to most executives; others stem from the concept of living systems and other concepts stressed here. Qualitatively distinguishable should not be interpreted as meaning that there is no interaction among these dimensions, and the possibilities of conflict among them is almost self-evident. A criterion defines the level, often a mean level, and range of tolerance of deviations of a dimension. Some dimensions may have multiple criteria. Setting dimensions and criteria further specifies the structural and operational requirements for achieving goals and objectives.

Defining and updating information needs adds further detail. Discharging this function improperly has led, as has been discussed, to the failure of management-information systems in general. Note that this is considered primarily a *Command and Control* function, not a *Boundary-Spanning* function, and certainly not a design requirement to be imposed from outside the organization by information-system specialists. As already discussed, information is the best possible coming from the environments, modeling and simulation, actual performance, and the *Adaptivity Field*. The word updating should be carefully noted. The environments are turbulent, so the most recent information is necessary; however, the need for updated information also stems from the practices internal to Command and Control and more importantly from organizational learning.

A greatly neglected and almost invariably poorly implemented functional requirement is *information display and control*. Here the problem can be one of equipment availability or human engineering or both. It is a pity that poor organization, presentation, and control over information is often the straw that breaks the camel's back in turning top management against information systems. Recent advances in computer-generated displays including graphics, television, and telecommunications provide the basis for a wide variety of display sizes, colors, formats, and placements. These advances make possible imaginative combinations, under real-time and interactive conditions, of pictorial, symbolic, and alphanumeric presentations from various video, computer, and manual sources at different geographic and organizational locations. Specific techniques include large-screen video and nonvideo displays; projection television; splitscreen television; cable television; fiber-optic ground communications; communications satellites; combinations of television, telephone, and keyboards; electronic blackboards that can sense and transmit the position and movement of a stylus; and computer graphics that provide for expansion, contraction, off-centering, greater detail, rotation, and three-dimensional appearance of the image.

Human engineering deficiencies can involve organization, presentation, and control and both the vendor and the client. An example of an organizational deficiency is the inability to provide to the user the particular pattern or combination of information that is needed for problemsolving and decision-making. An example of a presentation deficiency is poor visibility, legibility, or interpretability due to character design and placement with not enough contrast. An example of a control deficiency is the failure to provide the user with the capability to select information by priority or level of detail. If the equipment maker does not have a good human engineering capability, the buyer is usually stuck with whatever deficiencies the displays may have. Even well-designed equipment can be misused if higher-level human engineering is lacking. This is an important and promising field that needs more attention.

Comparing actual with desired conditions is at the heart of a cybernetic design. The success of this function of course depends on the successful discharge of antecedent functions, namely, that goals, objectives, policies, dimensions, and criteria have been realistically and properly established, and that the best possible information under the circumstances is available and properly displayed. Goals and objectives, within the constraints of criteria, express the desired long- or short-range conditions for the various dimensions of performance. Actual conditions are the *measured* performance outputs. The comparison process itself produces further information which is prerequisite to decision and action. The comparison process can be variously manual or computerized, depending on amenability to automation, cost considerations, and individual preferences. At the operational level of the organization, information, decision, and control action can be highly automated, as in automatic process-control in refineries and in the chemicals industry, in machine control of metals-processing and tooling, and increasingly in robotization of assembly lines. At the top-management level we are dealing with computer-*aided* problemsolving and decisionmaking. Comparison, decision, and control action can apply both to the present and simulated future.

Detecting error signals results from the comparison process. An error is the disparity between actual and desired conditions. Its magnitude depends on the criterion level set and the variation or level of tolerence of deviation from the criterion level. Within the tolerence levels, performance of many systems can be regulated automatically. This is especially true of the physical systems and person–machine systems used for industrial processing and of aircraft and other vehicles. Under these conditions only *exceptions* need be communicated to human monitors and controllers. The broad idea of exception–detection can also apply to management and to the design of the adaptive organization as a whole. Thus, in an organization comprised of semiautonomous, essentially self-regulating units, only critical exceptions (those beyond the capability of local control) need be communicated to successively higher levels of management. Unless this design is accepted, top management will be so swamped—as is the case with many present organizations—with decision and control details that it will be incapable of discharging the functions emergent at its own level.

Detecting and reporting exceptions from preset and fixed levels of tolerance may be necessary and adequate for certain processes or parts of the organization, but these measures are insufficient in the design of the adaptive organization as a whole. In turbulent environments exceptions show both great variety and great unpredictability.

The concept of error has some connotations deeper than those indicated above. There are three values involved, namely, desired condition, actual condition, and error or disparity. In some situations information is lacking on one or more of these values. For example, only error information may be available, and compensatory control may amplify an oscillation producing even greater system instability. These situations occur frequently when time lags lead to reversals of values in oscillating systems. Person and machine lags in the manual control of an aircraft, for instance, can lead to loss of control of the aircraft if pilot attempts to correct extremes of roll, pitch, and yaw coincide with swings of the plane *back* in the direction for which control is attempted. Even more complex situations can occur in organizations where control of several or many interrelated variables is required. In these cases systems dynamics theory should be applied. There are many challenges in organizations for these types of control actions.

Strategic and long-range planning, especially the *preparation* for these activities, are important subjects for concern. Almost anybody can make a plan, and almost everybody does plan to some extent. Whether a plan will work at all or work as intended, however, is a different story. Strategic and long-range are of course not synonymous, but the two terms encompass similar or overlapping scales, time frames, and organizational levels.

Well-designed plans should include these features:

Provision of a framework for good tactical and short-range planning and good policy design.

Flexibility and modifiability as future conditions may require.

Incorporation of enough *variety* to match or be congruent with the relevant environment.

Involvement of all the stakeholders who must implement or live with the plan.

Utilize as fully as possible early-warning and anticipatory information and knowledge.

To these five positives we must once again add a negative—avoidance of fascination with measurement of the evident and easily quantifiable factors and variables and avoidance of premature quantification and computerization.

To the above framework could be added a number of details in recipe ingredient fashion. For example, dates, lengths, divisions into subunits, points of accountability, and periodic and final reports could be specified. To do so would be a disservice. One organization's good plan could be another organization's disaster. Most important, organizational planning should be considered inseparable from organizational learning.

Anticipating crises, one of the important themes of this book, is briefly the use of information and knowledge about the dynamics of the world to avoid future harm to the organization. It has been stressed that the past, present, and future can never be identical, and that extrapolation of past and present trends and even patterns can yield an incorrect view of the future. Rather, basic laws and processes of nature that describe and explain causally phenomena like discontinuity, catastrophic jump, self-organization, and reconfiguration of fields have been emphasized. The use of effects, which the mass of organizational and societal data represent, unless these effects can at least tentatively be interrelated with causes, has been played down.

It is impossible of course ever to be able to anticipate and manage *all* possible crises. Some crises and catastrophes (in the literal sense of the term) *originate* exogenously to the world system. These large perturbations may then trigger reconfigurational changes predictable from field theory. However there may be nothing that can be done about the situation within the time frame of this book (roughly from now to 12:01 A.M., January 1, 2001!), if ever. Solar and other celestial phenomena that produce catastrophes on earth are possible, even if statistically rare. The most recent explanation of the intiation of and quite sudden ending to the worldwide extinction of dinosaurs, flying and marine reptiles, and large marine invertebrates at the end of the Mesozoic Era is based on a large asteroid's striking earth. The asteroid ploughed up such a vast amount of dust that the atmosphere soon was filled to the extent of cutting off the spectra of solar radiation necessary for photosynthesis. Severe disruption at the basic level of the ecological food web soon spread throughout that web.[7]

In Edwin Balmer's and Philip Wylie's *When Worlds Collide* and *After Worlds Collide,* written back in 1932 and 1934, respectively, two planets from outside the solar system were predicted to cross earth's orbit, one colliding with and destroying earth and the other swinging into earth's orbit. A group of U.S. entrepreneurs in a future civilization were able to save a few Americans by transporting them to the second planet—there to find themselves competing with the Japanese and Russians!

This brief digression into past and future catastrophes should not make one forget that there are plenty of imminent crises and catastrophes to deal with now. And concern with crisis should not cause one to forget that one is also concerned with the anticipation of opportunity.

Managing crisis is the logical extension of anticipating it. There are three basic factors or variables involved, which can be combined in different ways to produce several kinds of adaptive and maladaptive organizations.

1. Degree of anticipatory value in the input information and knowledge.
2. Degree of resiliency of organizational structure.
3. Degree of control attempted under the given circumstances.

A highly adaptive organization structures its information and knowledge inputs so that they have maximum anticipatory value, given limitations of the state of the art. An example of such varied and rich input would be the probabilistic systems dynamics trend-impact analysis used by General Electric (discussed in Chapter 4), greatly augmented by conceptual and mathematical models based on the field-theoretic and emergent forces presented in Chapter 5. The highly adaptive organization has built into its structure a great deal of resiliency. It can absorb major perturbations from the environment without fragmenting. Finally, the highly adaptive organization has a repertory of control strategies and tactics. It attempts to preclude the development of, ward off, and steer around major crises.

The maladaptive organization, at the other extreme, is constantly caught with its pants down. It tries to insulate itself from the environment, shut out all the bad news, and avoid any thought of early warning. Its rigidly hierarchical structure is brittle. It attempts to control threats in its environment through brute force.

Generalizing from the individual person to the organization, the adaptive system knows its capabilities and limitations, builds up a repertory of skills, remains flexible in the face of likely contingencies, and learns from experience. In the individual, anticipation of the poorly known, the uncertain, or the unknown may produce anxiety—or joy. In the face of anxiety, many individuals develop psychodynamic coping responses—substituting symbol for reality, misdirecting their energies, becoming overly hostile and aggressive, distorting information and communications, simplifying their environments, adopting ritualistic behaviors, and trying to control everything. Top managers are not immune to anxiety, and organizational anxiety can be part of the organizational climate. Thus, many organizations make strenuous attempts to reduce uncertainty, and correspondingly variety, through the adoption of ritualistic practices, rules, and procedures and through the standardization and homogenization of the worksystems. In these organizations the internal and external environments are greatly simplified, so that everything can be accounted for and controlled before any harm occurs.

Here, an adaptive system is one that has developed and maintains a capability for adaptation in the face of ongoing and future threats and opportunities. It can also be noted that a *one-time* adaptation—actually a maladaptation in the long run—in the face of threat that is perceived to be overwhelming, the system launches itself along a path of increasingly stereotyped behavior in the manner indicated above.

Because of both variety and turbulence in the environments, preprogrammed and rigid regulation and control, especially the brute-force and massive-commitment type, is bound to fail in the longer term. It will fail because it does not take into account the many environmental changes that are constantly eroding the pillars of support. It will fail because the concentration of resources comes at the expense of other vital activities.

Misuse of regulation and control—through preprogramming, introduction of inflexibility, and overcommitment—is widespread throughout the United States (and elsewhere) today. Few organizations are free of this misuse, even though some sore conflicts pit business and industry against government. Regulation and control has been misapplied to the economy, to specific businesses and industries, to the internal structure and employees of a given organization, and to various environmental factors. Regulation and control are important elements in struggles for position and power, but the players must recognize the inconsistencies and the likelihood of longer-term deleterious results.

No organization and no nation possesses unlimited resources. Misuse of regulation and control is just one way of losing resources. *Allocating resources* is another major function of Command and Control. Like most of the functions in the design, allocating resources is complex. It has attracted a great deal of attention over the years, but unfortunately most of the approaches have been mechanistic rather than organic. Thus, one doesn't hear too much today about cost-effectiveness analysis, benefit-cost analysis, and Program Planning and Budgeting System. These approaches simply haven't worked in organizational and societal settings because of both the great difficulty in the initial measurement of the relevant variables and the subsequent differential changes affecting these variables.

Some executives misinterpret the nature of resources, which most importantly are potentialities rather than specific and often fixed observables. Additionally, some management actions contribute to the destruction of the organization's own resources. A building or plant eventually becomes obsolete or may require prohibitive expenditures for operations and maintenance. Money once spent, may never be recouped. The most important resources of the adaptive organization are the human resources, which impart the creativity, innovation, flexibility, driving force, and proper use of supportive technology necessary for continuing resiliency, learning, and survivability. Yet squelching human potentiality has long been inherent in the design and operation of many organizations, leading inexorably to the destructive consequences of job dissatisfaction and alienation.

Allocating resources in an adaptive organization therefore boils down to the mutual working-out of a framework of possibilities and constraints at each organizational level. The framework should reflect organizational goals and objectives, requirements, and mutually agreed-upon tolerable ranges of financial, supply, performance, and other direct observables. Beginning with fixed budgets, strict accountability, and tight control is not the way to go about things in an adaptive organization. The allusion of course is here again to a design based partially on semiautonomous units.

The natural and social ecosystem is to the external environments what the psychosocial system is to the internal environment. In the ecosystem lies the potential for self-recovery and self-healing. The adaptive organization maintains a harmonious fit with the ecosystem. It does not allocate the use of resources in ways that are destructive of its future options.

Allocating resources is never without some risk. In the adaptive organization the risk in reduced through anticipation and shared through variety, resilience, flexibility, and autonomy. Formal risk-analysis programs may be appropriate for some actuarial situations, but even here, as noted in Chapter 7, economic and demographic change have wreaked havoc with Social Security as well as with many private pension plans. In the adaptive organization risk assessment will stem from experience, based on a fundamental learning capability of the organization as a whole and its constituent parts, reinforced by properly used qualitative and quantitative models. Risk assessment will not be based on relics of the 1960s.

To conclude the discussion of *Command and Control,* two further functions, *maintaining participation* and *updating skills* are noted. Although these functions are conceptually straightforward, they are not always acknowledged or acted on. All organizations possess a natural drift, part of their overall evolution. Participation is indispensable to adaptive organizations because it means mutual commitment. Skills rapidly become obsolescent in a world of social and technological change. Systems of people and machines, as well as of individuals, must both acquire new skills and receive training in the use of these skills. Unless top management actively pursues, encourages, and supports the two functions, they may wither away to the detriment of the organization as a whole.

Turning now to the box in Figure 8.1 entitled *Adaptivity Field,* note that this block, like *Modeling and Simulation,* is off-line to the general left-to-right flow through the organization. Also note the two-way arrows connecting the box with *Command and Control.* Like *Modeling and Simulation,* the *Adaptivity Field* provides support for the on-line functions of *Command and Control.* The *Adaptivity Field* could be a purely conceptual structure, but preferably it should be a place where members of workshops, representatives of semiautonomous groups, and top managers meet, supported by the necessary technology, to discuss new theories, concepts, constructs, and models and the feedback results of actual experience and to initiate new designs.

Ingredients of adaptive organizations were present even in prehuman primate societies, and humankind, almost by definition, would not have survived the millions of years of evolutionary stress without a high degree of adaptability. As long as evolving humankind maintained a good fit with a changing environment, its chances for survival were high. The loss of fit of many human organizations and societies through prehistory and history followed the loss of *relative* adaptability to changing environments, which in turn stemmed from entrenchment of ideas and practices combined with an inability or unwillingness to change. Inability to change was often dictated by the suddenness with which the known environment was enlarged or reconfigured, perhaps because of the invasion of competitors from afar. Since the first Industrial Revolution, inability and unwillingness to change have been related by many authors to hierarchical and bureaucratic structure and to Frederick W. Taylor's scientific management and its descendants. Other authors have stressed the decay internal to aging organizations which have grown to a point of diseconomies of scale.

In response to the deficiencies of large, aging, bureaucratic, "scientifically-managed," impersonal, and dehumanizing organizations, a number of compensatory designs have been introduced in recent years. These designs reinstate at least some local decisionmaking and control. Other designs stem from the overall processes of mechanization and automation, particularly from recent advances in control system engineering and from work in artificial intelligence including work on pattern perception and on robotization. There is now a large literature from the engineering, mathematical, and computer-science perspectives on self-regulating, intelligent, and adaptive systems. As discussed earlier, most of the actual implementations have been at the operational level of organizations. Unfortunately, the behavioral-social and engineering approaches to decision and control are not always reconcilable. This incongruence leads to ongoing sociotechnical systems problems, one of the concerns of problemsolvers in the *Adaptivity Field*.

The design of an adaptive organization presented here does not start from scratch. Constructs or building blocks from other sources have been incorporated if these building blocks were not in violation of the theoretic framework based on evolution, field theory, living systems theory, general applicability of natural laws, dynamic organization–environment interaction, and isomorphism between organism and organization leading to organismic organizational design. The theoretical orientation was presently mostly in Chapters 1, 3, 5, and 6 although throughout the book theory, analysis, evaluation, interpretation, and examples have been interwoven. In the next section of this chapter adaptive systems theory will be discussed more deeply.

In Chapter 2 some of the building blocks for the adaptive organization were discussed and some unpromising approaches were discarded. Even in utilizing the acceptable building blocks, it must be borne in mind that many of the properties of adaptive organizations are necessary but by themselves insufficient. This issue becomes particularly important when self-regulating and self-organizing systems are contrasted, when maintenance of the present state with evolution are contrasted, and when the limits of cybernetics are considered.

The highest-level property of the adaptive organization is the ability to change *purposely* the structure, function, and behavior of the organization in keeping with experience and with the actual and anticipated dynamic demands imposed by the environment. That is, the highest-level property is the ability to *learn*. Top-level learning is itself a function of structure including, recursively, the degree to which learning ability is distributed throughout the various levels and parts of the organization. As in other systems discussed, there are critical thresholds below which little learning and little adaptability are possible.

A further consideration is that a high level of learning ability in an organization leads to a high level of problemsolving ability. Of course the two terms are not synonymous. For example, an organization could theoretically possess a high level of learning ability and no memory and therefore a low level of adaptability because things had to be learned over and over again. The dangers attendant on the organizational memory loss which follows faulty archival recordkeeping and the rapid turnover of knowledgeable personnel also have been mentioned.

The adaptive organization therefore effectively learns and solves problems. It also does other things such as make decisions and implement controls, but maladaptive organizations do these things too. Decision and control in their more precise forms represent the wrong level of analysis with which to start the design of an organization. This level of approach was popular in the 1960s and most of the 1970s and still has a considerable following, but organizational problems are not amenable to such subsystem approaches.

Consider the people and person–machine ensembles responsible for anticipating and managing crises and opportunities and the people and ensembles responsible for maintaining ongoing adaptability and environmental fit as problemsolvers. As applied to the *Adaptability Field,* which represents a flow of ideas focusing on adaptability, consider the following constructs or building blocks.

Most basically, the design of the adaptive organization is *modular,* that is, at each level there are a sufficient number of functionally overlapping units so that malfunction or loss of any one unit does not produce crisis in the entire organization. Each unit is semiautonomous and imbued with its own creative and flexible thinking and learning and problemsolving abilities. Thus, congruence is maintained through *local problemsolving, decisionmaking, and control.* This does not, however, negate any necessary—where necessity itself is flexible and can change with circumstances—lateral, bottom–up, or top–down communication and control. Unit boundaries are permeable and not rigid, and *loose coupling* connects the various units. Thus, the way is paved for different lateral and vertical groupings of units or representatives of the units as problem contingencies might require. Modularity, local problemsolving, decision-making, and control, overlapping capabilities, nonrigid boundaries, loose coupling, and flexible configuration and reconfiguration together add resiliency to the organization. The resilient organization can absorb the shocks of perturbations, rather than have them spread like wildfire throughout the organization in the manner discussed in Chapter 5.

Self-regulation is a major feature of cybernetic designs. Examples can be found widely among the living prototypes of the biological world; in modern weapons, power and speed control in automobiles, autopilots in aircraft, and the thermostatic heat and air-conditioning systems in buildings; and in the basic operations of computers. However, self-regulation is a major feature but not the only important feature in adaptive organisms and organizations. By not understanding this limitation, many designers of adaptive systems are on the wrong track.

Let's look again at the higher organism. Cybernetic subsystems abound—reflex control of the curvature of the lens in the eye, reflex control of the diameter of the pupil in the eye, reflex control of respiration, temperature control, the myriad regulations in the internal environment by endocrine and neuroendocrine means. The 19th-century French physiologist, Claude Bernard, coined the term *milieu interne* to describe the internal environment. Around 1930 the American physiologist, Walter B. Cannon, coined the term *homeostasis* to describe the maintenance of constancy of the internal environment. Homeostasis, originally restricted in application to the intercellular spaces, was soon extended to cover most aspects of internal regulation and control, and some writers even described a social homeostasis. Norbert Wiener, the father of cybernetics, later incorporated the concept into his own framework.

Cybernetic systems including homeostatic systems are excellent at *doing what they have been told to do,* either by genetic preprogramming or by human design. They sense conditions that are out of tolerance, make comparisons, determine errors, and issue corrective control signals to restore equilibrium or steady-state. They do an excellent job, *within shorter time frames,* of regulating and controlling *preprogrammed functions.* In existing organisms and organizations, cybernetic systems have negligible effects on *structure* and structural changes such as differentiation. Robots that build other robots, are discharging preprogrammed functions far more than they are creating new structures.

This is of course the distinction between cross-sectional or short time frame and evolutionary or longitudinal perspectives. Neglecting immunological changes (greater resistance among some human individuals and races to certain diseases, development of drug-resistant microorganisms and poison-resistant rodents), structural–functional changes in evolution may take tens of thousands to millions of years. One of the accompaniments of evolution is the reconfiguration of older structures and functions and the emergence of new structures and functions.

In the adaptive organization, what took many thousands or millions of years to accomplish must be accomplished in months or a few years by imaginative human designers. This is the property of *self-organization,* whereby structures and functions are quickly reconfigured to meet anticipated environmental contingencies. Self-organization provides the ingredient for adaptivity that self-regulation by itself lacks. The two types of dynamic processes complement one another. Self-organization provides the framework for a given environmental fit, and self-regulation maintains function within desired ranges as indicated by the framework. However, self-regulation possesses little capability to determine new desired conditions in multidimensional environments in which qualitative changes in both organization and environment are of paramount importance.

The situation is of course more complex than this brief treatment might have indicated. Living systems consist of many levels of organization of matter and energy and many hierarchical levels of regulation and control. A system is *self*-regulating within the organism within a higher level of regulation and control, for example, neuroendocrine regulation and control. And self-organization in evolution is dependent on the feedback mechanisms of regulation and control.

One of the most important needs is the need to have at least some minimally acceptable degree of control over oneself, one's destiny, and one's environment. In Chapters 2 and 7, this need was discussed under the rubrics of self-actualization, power motivation, and learned helplessness. Human needs are of course functions of perceptions of what could be and what should be, which in turn are very often the results of comparisons between a person's actual state and other peoples' states. With vastly increased speeds, diversity, and distribution of communications and transportation, such social comparison processess have greatly increased in frequency, scope, and severity in recent years. These comparison processes underlie much of the world's malaise and active resentment including job dissatisfaction, lowered productivity, crime, the North–South international gap, and general world tensions. Without beating the point any further here, it should be evident that the present world *problématique* is a natural result of evolutionary changes in both the cybernetic and reconfigurational senses.

What should be stressed here is that there have been few if any successful and adaptive societies that totally deprived people of control. Even slaves, without some hope or motivation, could quickly learn to be just clumsy, stupid, and incompetent enough to thwart the system without being so obviously recalcitrant or useless as to risk severe punishment or death. In modern bureaucratic organizations and societies, depriving people of self-control by imposing layers of external controls has led to a loss of initiative, resourcefulness, and willingness to cooperate and resume self-control even when the organization changes or emergencies demand greater individual autonomy.

In the adaptive organization, control by the individual is expressed not only by autonomy but by *participation* and *ownership*. In the previous discussion of the blocks in Figure 8.1, it was emphasized that top management should actively ensure participation by at least the representatives of all the major stakeholders. These people can greatly help or greatly hinder, often in creative new ways, the achievement of organizational goals. Unfortunately, participative management has often degenerated into just another form of poorly disguised manipulation. Participants dutifully, if ritualistically, voice their concerns to management, which then may pay lip service to these concerns and perhaps make some token or cosmetic changes. Participants may feel some temporary cathartic relief, but nothing important changes. In the adaptive organization, participation means commitment by all concerned parties to active roles in design and operations.

Changes in the concept of ownership of organizations and of resources have been significant in recent years. One of the most significant changes in the history of modern organizations was a shift from owner-managers to hired managers. The question, who owns the modern organization? is even harder to answer than deep thinkers might believe because the answer to the question is tied in with the measures of performance in Figure 8.1.

Even within the strictly legal definition of ownership, however, the interesting and important problems are the actual or potential:

Ownership by thousands of isolated little stockholders.

Ownership by other large, but neutral, organizations like those that invest pension funds.

Ownership by other large, aggressive, organizations attempting a takeover.

In the adaptive organization ownership also includes all those people who devote much or most of their lives to the organization. Individual ownership is an important part of individual control. This should include hands-on ownership, shared with others, of the job and its products. This design resembles the democratization of work stressed from the beginning by classical sociotechnical systems scientists discussed in Chapter 2. However, the design transcends ideology, and, indeed, adaptive and also maladaptive subsystems have been found in authoritarian as well as in democratic societies. In this context, it should be noted especially that small, privately-owned plots of ground in Communist countries produce crop amounts that are far out of proportion to the amount of land. In any society it is difficult to develop and sustain motivation to work for an organization that is owned by others or in which ownership is remote and symbolic. Personal ownership demonstrates immediate control and immediate results.

In describing the *Adaptivity Field* thus far, it is concepts and constructs that have been dealt with. Another concern is the practical means of implementation of design concepts. Two of these are *autonomous work groups* and *matrix organizations,* discussed in Chapter 2. Another is *special workshops* to which further attention will be paid in the next section.

Now look at the final block in Figure 8.1, *Performance.* Performance is the proof of the pudding for organisms and organizations. If an animal cannot find and utilize sustenance, it starves, becomes much more susceptible to disease, or falls prey to other animals. Asset-poor, bankrupt, pathological, and merged or acquired organizations are also not uncommon. If an animal or plant species is in danger of extinction, human agencies often try to protect it. The same is true of many failing organizations. As discussed throughout this book, there are many similarities between the behavior of organisms and that of organizations. Limited space precludes further discussion, but consider the question: under what conditions of conflict and frustration does organizational performance become derailed, that is, misdirected from the primary goals and become pathological?

The definition and evaluation of performance is one of the most exciting as well as one of the most difficult areas in the study of organizations. Some reasons why are the following:

Within the organization, there are both explicit and implicit dimensions of performance

Dimensions of performance are not completely under the control of the organization itself, but are affected by the perceptions and wills of various stakeholders

Organizational performance is multidimensional, even though organizations often try to constrain it as one dimension

Dimensions of performance, like goals and objectives, typically conflict

Actual performance has both more or less expected and desired direct effects and unexpected and often undesirable side effects or *externalities*

Subsystem performance does not necessarily aggregate well into total system performance

Measures of performance include both the hard and the soft and the obvious and the subtle

Performance along any given dimension, as the final action of the organization in any one iteration or cycle, presupposes a web of antecedent activities including the proper setting of goals, objectives, and criteria and the building up and maintenance of motivation to perform. If one or more critical antecedent activities or the entire organizational web or field are deficient, as is the case in many organizations today, effective performance can hardly be expected.

The *Performance* block contains a number of dimensions. Some of these are quite familiar to executives who have had a great deal of experience with them. Others represent familar areas, but many people would not yet have thought of them as formal dimensions of performance. Still others have emerged from the theory and interpretations of this book—these may be the most important dimensions for long-term adaptability and survival.

Note again that *actual actions* are being discussed, not goals, objectives, or targets, levels, and criteria, which presumably have now been set, or effects or impacts that are yet to be fed back through the environmental sensors for eventual comparison between actual and desired conditions. For both developing better understanding of how the organization works and improving performance, it is necessary to look *holistically* at each action *stream,* and to remember, do no analysis without synthesis.

Some familiar dimensions and measures of performance are these:

Productivity in output per person–hour per product per plant. For different reasons, productivity may differ between blue- and white-collar workers, between low- and high-technology products, and between plants or companies of the same corporation. Here productivity is a microeconomic measure. In Chapter 7 productivity was discussed in macroeconomic terms.

Sales, or total net per product per plant.

Profits, or total per corporation (examples of both aggregated and disaggregated measures are provided; because of legal and taxation pressures, creative accounting, and so on, none of these measures is usually calculated in so straightforward a manner as this listing might suggest).

Purchases in specific amounts of raw materials, energy, or supplies per given price.

Acquisitions or mergers, or target companies per price per time frame.

Because these dimensions and measures are familiar does *not* mean that they can be always managed successfully or without unpleasant surprises. In fact many of the crises and failures mentioned or discussed in Chapters 1, 5, and 6 involved performance dimensions and measures with which most executives have had considerable experience. But in these cases the environment was misunderstood, because of imperfect knowledge of a relatively static environment or because of change, and poor judgments and policies were made.

The list above is not meant to be exhaustive. For example, many corporations base their assessments of performance on *ratios,* such as return on investment, return on equity, sales per total assets, working capital per total assets, or earnings before interest and taxes per total assets.

Familiar areas that are becoming recognized as *formal* dimensions of performance include:

Job satisfaction. This is an example of a dimension that has no single or simple means of measurement. Management efforts to improve performance could be measured, for example, by amounts of time spent on worksystem redesign. Mutual cause–effects are hard to disentangle, but the actual performance behaviors of workers can be measured by:

Questionnaires, surveys, and interviews for assessing attitudes, opinions, and feelings.

Overt behaviors like absenteeism, tardiness, job turnover, illnesses (almost all of which have some psychosomatic component), sick leave, pilferage, vandalism, sabotage, or quarrels or fights on the job.

Presumed interrelationships in models, say, between job satisfaction and productivity.

Quality of working-life. Here also there is a considerable subjective component and feedback loops of mutual causality may be hard to decipher. Quality of worklife is related to job satisfaction, but the two are not the same. For example, quality of worklife implies broader considerations of participation, ownership, control, and autonomy as well as of esthetics, safety, and health than does job satisfaction. Quality of worklife is a collective attribute of an organization, but job satisfaction may be an individual perception. In some cases people are satisfied with their jobs because they have not yet learned to be dissatisfied.

Customer satisfaction. This is not a recondite concept, but it has been slow to catch on as a performance dimension to be encouraged actively. It can be measured both by responses to questionnaires and by overt behaviors such as complaints, items returned, or goods or services for which customers "conscientiously" refuse to pay. There is still quite a bit of *caveat emptor* in the attitudes of some organizations. Low public opinion of large organizations in general, coupled with increasing competition, are likely to stimulate changes in these attitudes.

Social and political impact. This means performance action intentionally directed toward a target individual, group, organization, or population so as to control or influence the target. Such action has long been an important part of corporate behavior. Impact can be measured, for example, by key decisions made outside the organization, bills sponsored and passed in a legislature, and votes made in an election.

Some performance dimensions have been little recognized outside this book and a few other treatises. The dimensions are not specific outputs like many discussed above. Rather they pertain to the fundamental *immanent* needs of the organization for adaptation and survival. As stated before, problem recognition and identification are more difficult and important tasks than is problem solution in the sense that a well-recognized, well-defined problem or problem-set leaves room for the search for a variety of alternative solutions, whereas a solution to a poorly-recognized, poorly-defined problem is likely in our complex world to turn out to be a wrong solution at the wrong time and a creator of even worse problems. Formalizing the dimensions that follow is a step toward focusing management concern and attention onto them:

Stability and survivability are higher-order, longer-range, and emergent dimensions of performance. In any single iteration through Figure 8.1, *Command and Control* attempts to reduce the disparity between desired and actual performance thereby restoring one type of *immediate* stability. However, over time and many iterations, stability may be first gradually and then catastrophically lost and the chances of survival greatly lessened. A number of possible measures of stability and survivability have been discussed throughout this book. Here are examples:

Increasing frequency and amplitude of deviations from norms and much slower recovery times.

Decomposition of linkages among subsystems.

Rigidification of linkages among subsystems.

Irreversible results of practices, leading to a narrowing of options.

Catastrophic flips onto low levels of equilibrium that are more vulnerable to perturbations.

Quality and stability of the external environments have never before been defined as a *specific* organizational goal and performance dimension but are nonetheless in the longer term one of the most important, if not the most important, of the goals and dimensions. The arguments for such quality and stability are manifold. They include various value-based and therefore usually debatable issues such as public health, esthetics, the rights of our fellow living beings, and the type and degree of overall corporate responsibility. But the great power and high resistance to present human understanding and control of the forces of nature and society are, by and large, not debatable. For example, although one might argue the validity of catastrophe theory, one cannot deny the existence of catastrophes. As noted again and again, the results of many organizational actions, for instance, soil and water destruction, are practically irreversible, especially after critical thresholds have been exceeded. Ecosystem instability leads to political instability. Billions of Third World poor will scarcely provide markets for the kinds of goods that large U.S. companies produce—countries like South Korea, Taiwan, China, India, and Mexico will provide the bicycles, sewing machines, and transistor radios the poor will want (if even these items can be afforded). Capital plant and equipment can be competitively provided by Japan and West Germany. In Central America large areas of tropical forests have been cleared for cattle raising and, ironically, a large amount of the beef has gone to the growing American fast-food industry, while local beef consumption has decreased. Situations like this usually do not produce a legacy of goodwill. In the United States crime is proliferating as more and more people perceive the futility of ever narrowing the gap between Having and Not Having. The organization can never be independent of its environments. In fact, as discussed in Chapters 1, 6, and 7, much of the organizational structure and function is contingent on the environments. The anticipatory and adaptive organization will ensure as fully as possible that its very actions at present do not severely constrain its future choices and threaten its future survival.

In concluding the interpretation of Figure 8.1, it should be emphasized that output signals are just as susceptible to bias, noise, attenuation, and amplification as are input signals. For output signals also, time delays are usually troublesome. There can be many a slip 'twixt the *Command and Control* cup and the *Performance* lip and also between actual performance and fed-back knowledge of that performance. The severe effects of the time delays—asynchronism among variables or even complete loss of stability—can best be illustrated by a systems dynamics model or a model of a manual control system of an aircraft or other vehicle. At a next level of detail, Figure 8.1 could be refined to show the various distortions of the information–decision–action–feedback stream.

Finally, *our adaptive-organization design is a total system design, not a patch-up of presently deficient designs.* It is a *sociotechnical systems design,* but in a somewhat different sense of usage of that term. In a classical sociotechnical systems design, the production or technological subsystem is usually seen somewhat as the adversary around which the social subsystem is designed. In the design here the major technological subsystem is computer-communications technology, which symbiotically helps groups of problemsolvers. Flexible equipment is embedded in a flexible organic structure. Most classical sociotechnical systems designs have been focused at the operational level; this one is focused at the top management level.

It is seldom possible to build a large organization from scratch. Therefore, utilizing this design will require a period of interpretation of adaptive-organization design and present organizational designs. In turn this will require mutual cooperation among executives, planners, designers, and (at first) outside consultants in order that the evolving design meet the needs of the relevant stakeholders.

The remainder of this chapter will interpret further the *Adaptivity-Field* and *Performance* blocks and provide guidance on implementing the design.

FURTHER FOCUS ON ADAPTIVITY

The *Adaptivity Field* consists of ideas—theories, hypotheses, concepts, constructs, models—and the people who test and apply these ideas in order to maintain adaptive fit to the turbulent environment. In this section several of the key theories presented earlier will be further interrelated and qualified and then the characteristics of the problemsolving groups necessary for the maintenance of organizational adaptability will be described.

Compatibility, Contradiction, and Limitation in the Use of Theory for Design

Although it is impossible these days to design adaptive organizations and management without resource to theory and models, an executive or planner can become so dependent on one orientation that he is almost better off relying on intuition and hunch. Thus the very purpose of an adaptive system could be defeated if top management committed itself to a cybernetic design once and for all and subsequently refused to budge from that orientation. Top management must resist the allure of, and entrapment by, *the* seeming final panacea even though that panacea promises surcease from indefiniteness, ambiguity, uncertainty and, therefore, from anxiety.

Throughout, this book has stressed the inappropriateness of static and cross-sectional perspectives, theories, and models to today's and tomorrow's organizations and turbulent environments. However, even within the class of dynamic and longitudinal perspectives, theories, and models, there are still many inconsistencies, contradictions, and gaps in knowledge.

Briefly, the major systems theories stressed in this book can be outlined as follows:

I. Theories that deal with *changes* in form, structure, interrelationship, pattern, configuration, or function, especially the *sudden emergence* of

new forms, and so forth
  A. Second law of thermodynamics (Entropy Law)
  B. Field Theory
      1. Field theory in modern physics and the theory of critical phenomena
      2. Dissipative-structures theory—self-organization in nonlinear systems *far from thermodynamic equilibrium*
      3. Catastrophe theory
  C. Hyperbolic-growth or coalition-formation theory
II. Theories that deal with information processing and regulation and control in *existing* forms, structures, configurations, and so forth.
  A. Cybernetic theories
      1. Systems dynamics

These distinctions are of fundamental importance. Without understanding this fact, it is impossible to design meaningfully adaptive organizations and managements and institutional policies.

Distinction, however, does not mean mutual exclusiveness. In the long haul of evolution, organisms, ecosystems, and social systems adapt to environmental perturbations by changes in form, structure, interrelationship, pattern, configuration, or function. Changes in both systems and environments may be continuous or discontinuous and slow or sudden. In the shorter haul of day-to-day living, these systems have to get along as best they can in the evolutionary adaptations up to the present.

The natural world provides many interesting examples of structural and functional adaptations to special environments. For instance, mammals and birds have very narrow ranges of tolerance for concentrations and ratios of certain ions like sodium, potassium, calcium, and phosphate in the inter- and intracellular environments. Drinking seawater or eating salty prey thus poses a critical problem of physiology and survival. Many marine creatures excrete a very concentrated urine. Gulls have a special gland near the eyes that excretes almost crystalline salt. But human beings do not have these adaptive capabilities. The Ancient Mariner lamented in Samuel Taylor Coleridge's *Rhyme,* "Water, water, everywhere, Nor any drop to drink." If human beings were suddenly forced to live naturally on or in a marine environment, they would within a few days at most become extinct.

Some executives may still not see the significance of these seeming digressions. Such biological examples are provided because:

1. Some designers confuse total systems adaptability with homeostatic regulation and control, which is only the short-term component. Physiological measures and criteria and approaches to ranges of tolerance (which ignore fluctuations, one of the most important types of early-warning signals), used by themselves, are inappropriate bases for the design of adaptive systems and for long-range planning.

2. Some users of the term "organismic" confuse it with the anatomical and physiological. The term also incorporates the ecological. Structure and function are intertwined with evolution and anatomy, physiology, biochemistry, and psychology are intertwined with ecology.

3. Because of increasing turbulence in the world-system field, evolutionary time, and therefore options for trial and error and experimentation, is running out for most animals, plants, ecosystems, and societal systems. Vulnerable species, populations, organizations, nations, and systems—like the miners' canary—will be the first to go. But the pressures of the field of forces will successively knock out all but the most anticipatory and most adaptive systems.

There are several other features in the outline of theories given above that should be clarified. First, certain basic constructs or processes like information and feedback apply to most of or all the theories. For example, all cybernetic systems are based on (usually negative) feedback, but feedback can occur in systems that are not cybernetic. Positive feedback can lead to unrestrained growth or elaboration of new forms or configurations that do not possess the internal regulation and control of a cybernetic system. Rather, regulation and control may be imposed by the environment, by system breakdown, or by a newly reconfigured and higher-order system. This appears to be very much what is happening in the world right now.

Second, the two basic categories of theories are not separable on the basis of determinism or probability. Cybernetic systems are inherently deterministic although cybernetic models like systems dynamics can be modified by probabilistic inputs, as discussed in Chapter 4. In organisms a chance variation in homeostatic regulation, due perhaps, to birth injury, accident, or disease, is not passed on to the next generation. Likewise, a chance variation in the performance of a servomechanism, robot, or computer is not passed on to the next generation of devices. In each case a higher-order control is involved. In the case of the organism, in the simplest sense, a single gene controls and regulates a single enzyme or hormone which controls a single metabolic or homeostatic process. Feedback messages from the regulated process serve to turn the enzyme or hormone on or off and especially in early growth and development, morphogenesis, the gene itself. *Within the organism* the processes are deterministic and essentially cybernetic—the interrelationship between regulator and regulated process is more or less direct. However, the relationship between a controlled and regulated process (needed for survival) and the controlling gene, *outside the organism,* is very indirect and the uncertain pathways are strewn with randomness and chance. This contributes to the limitations of the strictly cybernetic paradigm.

Higher-order control based on human decisions is also greatly limited in purely cybernetic designs. Human designers can of course usually eliminate undesirable fluctuations in the performance of machines and try to ensure that such fluctuations do not appear in subsequent production batches, model changes, or generations. Quality control is one commonly practiced approach to the elimination of variances that are considered undesirable. But the imposition of the machine model onto organizations and societies, even if qualified in terms of requisite variety, lulls one into a sense of unwarranted confidence, a confidence based on dangerous oversimplifications. In the real world the pathways between controller and controllee are not well known, the controllee may respond in a quite unexpected and counterintuitive manner, and there are usually multiple loci of conflicting control.

Both cybernetics and catastrophe theory deal with systems near equilibrium. Once again, these are basically deterministic situations. That is, the one or more states of the system have been predetermined through evolution. But the antecedent evolutionary processes, themselves functions of stochastic events or processes, may be unknown. Even the alternate states of the system may be unknown. *This is an exceedingly important point.* Theorists, modelers, planners, policymakers, and decisionmakers may assume that the system has only one state and one equilibrium level, and that the system tries continuously to maintain that equilibrium or steady-state through quantitative adjustments to external perturbations. By tries is meant both inherent system responses and responses to human control attempts. Unfortunately, almost all social and economic planning and policymaking, assuming that it is dynamic and anticipatory at all, is in this vein. In reality the system may—and probably usually does—have two or more qualitatively different states and two or more equilibrium levels. Because of a combination of factors, the system may suddenly and unexpectedly jump to or fall from one state and level to another. The very concept of *stability,* an underpinning of both cybernetics and common sense and parlance, now comes into question.

Finally, none of the theories in the outline above is invariably wrong or necessarily always misapplied. To paraphrase and extend Kenneth Wilson's comments on multiple scales of organization in physics, discussed in Chapter 5: There are islets of cybernetic regulation and control in lakes of changing form on islands of cybernetic regulation and control (the second-order cybernetics of Heinz von Foerster[8] in seas of changing form on planets. . . .

It is the shores or boundaries, or thresholds for jumping from one type of system organization to another, that it is most important to recognize, first conceptually and then practically. It is perceiving one type of system organization when the system is actually in the other configuration that is by definition wrong, and the implementing of a design based on the incorrect perception that is inappropriate.

In pursuing this discussion of theory, we are assuming that a group of problemsolvers is concerned with establishing a theoretical basis for the design of an adaptive organization. We assume that they are holistically oriented and quite sophisticated in the sense of being far beyond the stage of incremental, ad hoc, or patchwork design thinking. We assume that they are aware of the mischievousness of most of the partial attempts at design for information–decision–and–control up to now.

Continuing, to examine cybernetics a little further it should be noted that the basic concepts of regulation and control go back at least to the ancient Greeks, and that MIT Professor Norbert Wiener first presented a formal, integrated theory of communications and control in 1948. The theory of cybernetics was greatly expanded by English scientist, Dr. W. Ross Ashby, and it is Ashby who is more often referred to.[9] Ashby was a remarkable man, trained as a physician, but his dedication to detached objectivity and the furtherance of scientific law led him to couch much of his language in terms of mathematical abbreviations. For the practical person, Ashby's examples are not particularly exemplary. Ashby's mathematics are not difficult, just his shorthand style of communicating. This may explain the limited dissemination of Ashby's theories to control systems engineering, where much of the practical design work is done. Nevertheless, Ashby has provided us with some good rules of thumb.

Ashby's theories have been extended and applied to organizational design and management by another English cybernetician, Stafford Beer.[10] Beer had the unique experience of directly participating in production planning at a national level, in this case for the government of Salvador Allende in Chile. This government was soon overthrown, and Allende's successor, General Augusto Pinochet, thereafter implemented a strict monetarist economic policy based on the ideas of Milton Friedman of the University of Chicago. Pinochet has succeeded in bringing under control much of the social and economic chaos that prevailed under Allende. However, despite the enormity of factors contrasting different countries and the same country at different times, one cannot but help speculate about an opportunity lost for trying out an alternative approach to societal system design.

The most important law in cybernetics is Ashby's *law of requisite variety,* which is often said to play the same role in cybernetics as the second law of thermodynamics plays in physics. The law most basically provides a *link* between information and control. Ashby defined the process of regulation to involve the interaction of five major variables: (1) a regulator, (2) a regulated system or process, (3) a source of external disturbances or perturbations, (4) a set of all possible outcomes of the disturbances, and (5) a subset of desired stable outcomes resulting from the regulator's reponses to the disturbances.

The law of requisite variety states that the capacity of a device—or structure or subsystem—as a regulator cannot exceed its capacity as a communications channel. Ashby himself put it, "only variety in the regulator can force down the variety due to the disturbances." The law thus imposes strict upper limits on the degree of controllability a regulator can achieve. Put another way, the control of a system requires at least as much variety in its actions as the system itself can exhibit. The law provides a valuable statement about the necessary or optimum fit between the organization and its environments.

By itself the law as just summarized is necessary but insufficient for the design of adaptive organizations. For example, a system's information-acquisition and -processing capability could be faulty so that it provides only a limited interpretation of the variety in the real world. The system's responses could therefore be accordingly limited. The variety of the regulator could equal or exceed the variety provided by the communications channel and the variety in the system's behavior. But the system would be poorly fitted to the real world. Thus the adaptive organizational design summarized in Figure 8.1 and implied throughout this book balances the variety in the environments with variety in sensing and monitoring and information-processing with variety in decision, control, and regulation, with variety in the dimensions of performance. In this usage, variety is a measure of alternative qualitative environmental conditions or configurations, organizational states or configurations, and organizational performance behaviors. As a problemsolver one should ensure that the variety of the environments is matched by the variety in design, and that the variety of solutions matches the inherent variety of the problems. This isn't usually the case these days.

Ashby of course was far too brilliant a thinker not to have envisioned control requirements beyond those of simple mechanical regulators. In his concept of *ultrastability* Ashby proposed some degree of anticipatory, as opposed to reaction, control. An ultrastable system has enough variety built in, in terms of possible internal modifications, to match much of the variety of environmental disturbances. Matrix organizations and autonomous work groups can provide the potential for such internal modification. Hence, some fairly sophisticated designs of adaptive organizations are now at this stage. However, as noted previously, this design capability is still not enough.

Ashby died in 1972. During the last years of his career he had brought classical cybernetics about as far as it could go, and he and his colleagues had turned their attention to the nature of *interactions* within the system and between the system and its environment. The work of Ashby and his colleagues on the organization of information and control began to converge with the work of "field theorists" on the organization of matter–energy. Among other things, Ashby and his colleagues and followers were able to prove mathematically that a system loosely coupled with its environment is more stable than is a system either unconnected with its environment or, at the other extreme, a system with each subsystem directly connected with the environment. In studying the limits to size and complexity, they were also able to show that, in randomly connected networks, the system is stable up to some *critical* size or complexity, but behond this *critical threshold* it suddenly becomes unstable.

In brief: from several directions of scientific endeavor, there is increasing theoretical justification for choosing one approach to adaptive-organizational design above others. Figure 8.1 shows a cybernetic design based on feedback regulation and control, expanded by the incorporation of an updated law of exquisite variety and by anticipatory feedforward control, and enriched by the breadth of field theory.

Before moving on to the last-mentioned element of the design, variety in regulation and control in terms of everyday decisions by top management should be looked at a little more fully. Two examples of the longer-term deleterious effects of highly centralized, top–down communications and control will be considered.

First, consider the acquisition of diverse companies by a large corporation. Typically, these companies had grown and developed in relationship to their local environments whether their managements formally recognized and acknowledged the importance of environment or not. A great deal of trial-and-error learning had taken place. Congruency among the internal subsystems and at least some fit with the environment had evolved. Successful companies had maintained some variety among managers, employees, and overall problemsolving capabilities. One or more crises may have developed in the end to precipitate the acquisition, but it is unlikely that the company would have become an attractive target for acquisition in the absence of a potential for further high performance, a potential based on variety. Across the many companies of a large corporation, there can be a great deal of variety.

Acquisition of diverse companies that possess a variety of problemsolving, learning, and adaptive capabilities—not just production capabilities—is a good corporate survival strategy. Nevertheless, many corporations helped kill the goose that laid the golden eggs. Local managers, many of whom still had the best knowledge of their business, were replaced with corporate people. Standardized rules and procedures were implemented, and the companies streamlined in a misguided attempt at greater efficiency. Local options were taken away. Overall, the company became just another deadened unit of a highly centralized bureaucracy. As a result company morale dropped, the remaining local managers and employees became recalcitrant, and productivity declined qualitatively or quantitatively or both. In the end it was necessary for the corporation to divest itself of the once promising company that had somehow turned out to be unexpectedly unprofitable.

The history of corporations is filled with examples of unplanned divestitures. Although the mismanagement just summarized was much more common practice during the great heyday of the conglomerates in the late 1960s and early 1970s, it continues today. The business literature provides current examples. The mere rumors of acquisition or merger continue to trigger feelings of anxiety and demoralization in targeted companies.

Although there were no police, lawyers, or government busybodies to record the fact, many corporations have violated the law of requisite variety! The capacity for regulation and control far exceeded the capacity for communications.

The second area of discussion deals with what has already been defined to be one of the most basic needs—the need for *perceived individual control*. This need for control may be two way. The feeling of being out of control over one's own self, one's destiny, and one's environment is frequently associated with attempts to influence, manipulate, and control others. Feelings of lack of control may lead to learned helplessness or to compensatory attempts to gain control by whatever means are available. Moreover, perceived lack of control is deleterious to overall health as well as to performance.

Misuse of control over individuals is common in organizations. There are many managers who, very insecure in their own lives, have obsessively–compulsively attempted to insure exactness and perfectly predictable behavior on the part of others. Management insecurity is often the primary motivation for implementing tight control systems, which, as discussed above, leads to a reduction in variety and therefore a reduction in long-term survivability.

Further, neither feelings of helplessness and greatly lowered motivation and performance nor active attempts to counter overcontrol are good for the health of an organization or of a society. It is highly likely that unhealthy organizational climates, lowered organizational and national productivity, and general social malaise are due to a considerable extent to misuses of control. Today nobody has a complete monopoly on control—increases in vandalism, crime (including a shift to apparently senseless crimes), and terrorism attest to this fact. Environmental or societal stress impacts on the most vulnerable individuals, groups, and organizations first, and the changes just noted should be seen as early-warning signals of possible conflagrations to come.

Psychologists Lawrence Perlmuter and Richard Monty provide experimental substantiation, in other animals as well as in people, of the great importance of perceived individual control.[11] The word perceived is critical here. Freedom of choice, in the absence of perception of that freedom, is insufficient to stimulate intrinsic motivation and learning. In addition, people compare their own amount of perceived control with that perceived in others. Low levels of perceived control can produce unpleasant, even dangerous, results.

Differences in the perception of control in the self and in others therefore underlie many of the day-to-day and persistent problems in organizations. Programs in participative management or consultative management often fail because employees do not perceive that they have any real control over their lives and environments. Executives may spend extra hours on the job at night and on weekends setting an example for employees. But the executive really can come and go as he wishes, and employees may perceive the executive's behavior as just one more form of manipulation. Everybody ends up with worse feelings toward others in such situations.

It is not possible to build adaptive organizations without designing in individual control within a framework for encouraging and maintaining individual dignity. This is as true in nominally authoritarian organizations and totalitarian societies as in nominally democratic ones. Earlier in this chapter the great flexibility and resourcefulness of German military units and personnel in the first year of World War II was described. The support for Solidarity, the consortium of new Polish trade unions is at least partly due to the neglect and perceived abuse of people by a faceless bureaucracy. Industrial workers and farmers report feeling unimportant and unneeded. The severe, perhaps imminently catastrophic, societal problems of Britain today stem to a considerable extent from mutual suspicion and disrespect between workers and management, which stem in turn from perceptions of past abuses of control.

In the developed Western and Communist countries, and increasingly in the rest of the world, more and more people, particularly younger people, no longer believe that the boss (father, teacher, priest, president, military commander, party, company president), simply by occupying a role or holding office, is the wisest or has the right to exercise control over others. These changes in attitudes and beliefs are part of the great pattern of irreversibility emphasized here. At the same time, people are often willing to impart to selected individuals a wisdom and a right to exercise power and control. These are ingredients of the cauldron in which radical societal transformation is being brewed.

Classical sociotechnical systems designers have from the beginning worked toward a democratization of organizations and alternatives to bureaucratic hierarchies. It can be argued that these aims are philosophically justified and that an improved quality of worklife leads both to greater job satisfaction and to improved productivity. However, as discussed earlier, the basic hierarchical, bureaucratic design has proved to be remarkably resistant to change. One important reason for this is that even if all stakeholders are locally committed to change, change is very difficult because bureaucracies are embedded in bureaucracies. An organization or society is the result of evolutionary processes, which up to now have led to increasing levels of control.

Organizational redesign for adaptability cannot smoothly be accomplished overnight. If the theoretical and practical interpretations made in this book are accepted by concerned executives, then *now* is the time for executives actively and explicitly to begin the planning for a new organization. Under any conditions we should expect in the next decade or two some crises of nearly irresistible forces meeting nearly immobile objects. Organizations that have successfully anticipated these crises and have designed in flexibility and resilience are most likely to adapt to societal transformations and to survive.

Before concluding this section, the problems of discontinuity, equilibrium, and catastrophe will be discussed further, and also one of the most innovative concepts in recent years—*resilience*. As mentioned in Chapter 6, the concept of resilience was introduced by Professor Crawford S. Holling and his colleagues.[12] The concept of resilience and the contrasting of resilience with stability can be thought of as a blend of catastrophe theory and empirical evidence from the study of ecosystems.

Almost every student of organizations acknowledges the importance of the environment and of organization–environment interaction. Many organization theorists hold that organizational structure is contingent on environmental factors. Few executives would deny the potential impacts of the natural resource, social, technological, and economic environments on their organizations. Cyberneticians state that the system must maintain stability in the face of the environmental pertubations, and that variety in these environmenal disturbances must be met with variety in regulation and control. The concept of the turbulent environment is widely accepted.

But very few people who study and work in organizations know very much about environments—especially about the dynamic forces that sweep across the environments. Even economists, sociologists, and political scientists have not been able to help much because their focus of investigation has usually been on institutions and structures rather than on forces. And the very orientation toward stability and its maintenance may be wrong or inappropriate in many situations today.

The people who do know the most about environmental forces are systems ecologists. Ecology is the science that deals with the interactions among organisms and environments. Ecology as a science should not be confused with the environmentalist movement. Like all sciences, ecology is or should be neutral, but can be put to good or bad uses by people.

Ecosystems are very complex and are now inextricably intertwined with societal systems. In fact, the distinctions between ecosystems and societal systems, as far as basic forces are concerned, are moot. However, a number of specific ecosystems have been studied long enough and intensively enough to provide models on how complex systems in general operate. Insights about the different equilibrium levels and catastrophic behavior in the spruce budworm–forest ecosystem in northeastern Canada and the Great Lakes fisheries provide guides to understanding national productivity, unemployment, crime, economic cycles, war, and other societal systems problems.

Most importantly, studies of ecosystems provide further evidence of the counterintuitive behavior of complex systems subjected to certain management strategies, tactics, or polices.

Consider the spruce budworm–forest ecosystem, the main components of which are (1) the spruce budworm, an insect larva which devours foliage; (2) parasites and predators of the budworm; (3) the balsam fir; (4) the spruce; and (5) the birch. An exogenous force impacting on the system is the weather. As is the case with all complex systems, it is important here to think in terms of patterns or configurations, not in terms of isolated variables or cause–effect mechanisms. Only when there is a concatenation of forces, does catastrophic reconfiguration take place.

The budworm, somewhat misnamed because it favors the balsam fir over the spruce, behaves at two different equilibrium levels, that of being rare and that of catastrophic outbreak in numbers or density. At the lower level budworm numbers are kept in check by parasites and predators. However, if by chance several dry years occur in succession, the budworm escapes local control, multiplies its numbers, and defoliates and kills large numbers of mature balsam fir. Immature balsam fir, most spruce, and all birch are not destroyed. With enough mortality among the mature balsam fir, a critical level is reached beyond which the high population density of budworms can no longer be supported and the population collapses.

Nasty bugs are destroying valuable natural resources! What would be a good strategy to deal with this situation? One that comes immediately to mind is to spray the larvae. But this would be a counterintuitive strategy, first, because of the well known capability of insects quickly to develop resistance to insecticides; second, because the pesticides might unfavorably impact on the predators that normally keep the budworm population in check, triggering even more frequent outbreaks; and third, the budworm is *necessary* for the maintenance of the forest ecosystem. It is necessary because, in its absence, the mature balsam fir would crowd out the spruce, birch, and immature balsam fir.

The budworm–forest ecosystem is highly unstable, but it has great resilience. *Stability* describes the ability of the system to return to a state of equilibrium after a temporary disturbance. The more rapid the return and the less the fluctuation, the greater the system stability. *Resilience* is a measure of the persistence of interrelationships within systems and their capability to absorb internal changes and external perturbations yet still maintain a structural–functional integrity. It is a measure of the persistence of interrelationships among populations as well as among state variables.

These distinctions are vitally important to the design of the adaptive organizations and of adaptive managements. They imply some major shifts in management thinking and practice from those up to now. Thus, the top-level, long-range goal and strategy of an organization should *not* be the maximization either of efficiency or of a particular goal or reward. It should be maintaining flexibility which encourages persistence or survival. Managers should not try to establish homogeneity in their organizations or to damp all fluctuations. Organizations with low variety and low fluctuations also have low resilience. The resilience orientation, moreover, does not require a capability to predict the future precisely. In Holling's words it requires "only a qualitative capacity to devise systems that can absorb and accommodate future events in whatever unexpected form they may take."

Holling contrasts two alternative strategies for societal (and organizational design):

1. A *fail-safe* strategy, emphasizing the quantitative and the optimal. This strategy leads to a design of highly optimal systems, which maximize specific yields while ignoring human and ecological constraints and in which variety and fluctuations are minimized, and attempts are made to minimize the probability of failure. This kind of strategy and design can gradually shrink the stability domain within which given conditions, say, the sociotechnical and economic practices of the world since World War II, can persist. The shrinking is not evident until an unexpected perturbation, once absorbable, no longer can be so. And in ecosystems and societal systems there is little knowledge as to where stability boundaries might be, the causes of these boundaries, and the duration of the boundaries. Holling writes that it is "almost inevitable that an attempt to reduce fluctuations would, at the same time, cause a shrinkage of the stability region through the action of cultural or natural selection."

2. A *safe-fail* strategy, emphasizing the qualitative and persistence and resilience. This strategy optimizes a cost of failure and designs in periodic minifailures to prevent evolution to inflexibility. In discussing the

Modeling and Simulation block of Figure 8.1, the importance of systems training for anticipated difficulties and crises was emphasized.

In most organizations some mixture of these strategies will be necessary.

Problemsolving Groups—Composition, Participation, Functions, Durations, Impediments

The design and management of the adaptive organization require both the acquisition and development of knowledge and the practical application of this knowledge. The latter, to which we devote this section, is easier said than done.

No person is omniscient. The learning and problemsolving capabilities of the organization permeate the organization and cannot be limited to top management and its staff advisers. In many organizations in recent years the numbers of management and especially of staff have grown disproportionately. Because of differences in education and experience—sales, marketing, finance, accounting, science, engineering—communications difficulties often arise between top management and specialist or functional areas.

No executive and no staff, even if his and their backgrounds are in the same areas as those of the workers, can constantly monitor and keep up with all the changes and problems in the daily operations of their complex organization. To try to do so represents an incorrect expenditure of human and other resources and a faulty organizational design. To oversimplify things through strict precontrol, strict accountability, and the generous use of rules and procedures is to produce an even more rigid and maladaptive design.

An organization that is continually putting out brushfires is not well designed. Even an organization that generally runs smoothly, but on occasions quickly has to set up ad hoc teams, has not been designed to its full potential.

The adaptive organization in the turbulent environment must have an *ongoing* capability for anticipation of organizational and evironmental reconfigurations, an *ongoing* capability for problemsolving, and an *ongoing* capability for managing difficulties and crises. However, the scope of anticipation, problemsolving, and management will differ throughout the organization. All members of subunits cannot spend their workdays worrying about every feature of a systems-level problem or about every possible long-range force that might someday impact on their work. To so spend their time would mean that no work at the operational level would be done.

The large and complex, but highly adaptive, organization must be designed to reflect a flexible compromise between the extremes of centralized control and regulation and vertical top–down communications on the one hand and local autonomy of control and regulation and lateral communications on the other. "Flexible compromise" means that the boundary between one type of structure and the other should be capable of being shifted as stresses and opportunities require.

Professor Karl Butzer has studied civilizations as adaptive systems, with over 5000 years of Egyptian history as one example.[13] Major external and internal crises over this period were successively overcome by reorganization of the political and economic superstructure. However, civilizations become unstable when a top-heavy bureaucracy makes excessive demands on the productive sector.

Sociotechnical systems scientist, Philip G. Herbst, is probably the leading advocate of "alternatives to hierarchies"[14] and writes: "The development of functioning horizontal linkages is an essential step in the transformation of hierarchical structures." This design orientation is certainly on the right track and, for small organizations and communities and for units within large organizations, it need not be questioned in principle. However, carried to extreme, decentralized control and lateral communications could spell the breakup of a large organization. Design should utilize semiautonomous units as fully as the experience and learning of the individual organization indicate as feasible.

Semiautonomous units should themselves develop through experience and learning as much capability for self-organization and self-regulation as possible. This is simply parsimony in design. Individuals, organizations, and nations have had to pay a high price for the luxury of overcontrol. Overcontrol leads to and continues to reinforce looking inward rather than looking outward. This is one reason for the failure of many organizations to keep up with changes in the external environment and the failure of long-range planning.

Arguments for the design of semiautonomous work units have been made by sociotechnical systems scientists over the past three decades. Sociotechnical systems scientists have long worked toward the improvement of the quality of worklife and the democratization of work as frequently noted. But the justification for semiautonomous units transcends these laudable goals. Every organization has limited resources. Top management resources spent on checking up on employees and making sure that they do things "right" are resources that are misspent in at least three ways—in terms of loss of variety, loss of time, and loss of orientation toward flexibility, resiliency, and survival in the face of environmental stress.

Therefore, semiautonomous work units and matrix organizations should be incorporated into design of the adaptive organization. As discussed in some detail earlier, to function effectively, people need some degree of control over their lives and their environments, and are demanding more recognition of their needs and work and more participation in decisions affecting their lives. Therefore, into the *Adaptivity Field* indicated in Figure 8.1, *ongoing* representation from the semiautonomous units will be designed and this participation will be part of the *Monitoring and Sensing the Organizational State*.

Briefly referring again to the nervous-system model, it should be noted that in moving from lower to higher levels of the nervous system, there is an *emergence of new properties*. The higher centers are not just a bigger and more inclusive version of the lower centers. There is *mutual* control between higher and lower centers. Mutual control should also be recognized in the design of the organization. There are emergent properties at the level of top management, which reformers should not attempt to destroy. On the other hand, top management becomes meaningless (except parasitically to perpetuate itself) in organizations beset with an underlying pathology.

The *composition* of problemsolving groups includes both organizational members and consultants or advisers from outside the organization. Few organizations will ever have the internal expertise to cover all possible anticipated organizational and environmental problems. The importance of the emergent role of Systems Integrator, discussed earlier, once more is clear.

Problemsolving groups at the level of top management—remember that other groups operate throughout the other organizational levels and divisions—are generally composed as follows:

1. Catalysts or action researchers (see Chapter 2) are those who *help* structure meetings, insure participation, provide preliminary agenda, guide discussions, suggest hypotheses for testing, formulate interim conclusions, prepare audiovisual and other display materials, and insure continual movement toward the agreed-upon objectives of the group. It should be emphasized again that these catalyst persons must take great pains not to appear to dominate or control the group and to impose solutions "not invented here," that are almost certain to be rejected. They should also go out of their way to avoid appearing arrogant or to appear to know it all.
2. The chief executive and members of the board to the extent possible.
3. The Director of Corporate, Strategic, and Long-Range Planning. If this role has not yet been formalized, an equivalent person can substitute.
4. The Systems Integrator. This role may be newly defined in the given organization, be combined with that of Number 3, or be provided by the outside catalysts.
5. Experts on the given organization:
   a. Management staff. Again a combination of roles is possible.
   b. Representatives of the semiautonomous units.
6. Experts on specific areas of the external and internal environments.
7. Experts on modeling, futures research, systems theory, and computer simulation. Again, a combination of roles involving Numbers 1, 3, 4, and 7 can be arranged.
8. Representative of outside stakeholders, as relevant.

Participation is critical to paving the way to continued smooth performance. That is why participation has been indicated as a required function of the *Monitoring and Sensing the Organizational State* and *Command and Control* blocks of Figure 8.1. Participation is particularly important in the cases of top management, employees, and outside stakeholders. Many an ostensibly problemsolving or policymaking group has fallen by the wayside because top management either expressed downright hostility or paid only lip service and abdicated responsibility, delegating it to a staff person. In the absence of employee participation, all the usual people problems discussed in this book and elsewhere will probably erupt. If representatives of outside stakeholders, or those who see themselves as stakeholders, are not included, some will undoubtedly feel that their ox has been gored and will eventually retaliate in one way or another.

A redistribution of power in American society and in the world has already taken place, and further redistributions can be expected. No one individual or institution has a monopoly on power, and a great many individuals, groups, and institutions have unexpectedly new power. This is part of the pattern of intersecting problems and crises, the *problématique,* of our times. Hubris expressed by any party can only generate friction and conflict, and although games are often fun, the price paid in terms of greatly increased stress on the adaptive capabilities of the parties may turn out to be too high.

It should be stressed, however, that with the right to participate comes *responsibility*. Participation is not license to wreck the organization, either through malice or through incompetence. In some cases participation will have to be restricted until the individuals or groups have demonstrated their good intentions and their qualifications.

The *functions* of problemsolving groups are those of marshalling knowledge, information, intuition, hunch, spontaneous creative innovation, and abilities and skills toward realization of an agreed-upon objective. Problemsolving groups help generate goals, strategies, and long-range plans, which provide the framework for the determination of objectives, tactics, policies, and short-range plans in more delimited and specific situations. Problemsolving must be open, fluid, and dynamic, yet must operate within the time and resource constraints that all organizations present. There are no fixed rules for problemsolving in dynamic organizations in turbulent environments. To offer such rules would defeat the very purpose of adaptive-organizational design. However, general guidance can help stimulate the development of a continuing organizational learning and problemsolving capability.

The functions summarized above may seem easy at first glance, but they are not necessarily so. Countless millions of dollars have been wasted in problemsolving gone awry. There are a number of possible *impediments* to effective problemsolving of which we can mention the following:

1. Failure to design the problemsolving group correctly. For example, the group could contain persons unwillingly assigned to it, hostile persons, overly dominating people, or technically unqualified persons. Management could employ the wrong catalyst group—the group must include people who know a great deal about systems, organizations, and behavioral and social science. They must *not* be psychologists or other

disciplinary specialists in organizational development, management development, sensitivity training, and other approaches who may be either obsolescent or too limited. It is of the utmost importance that enough *variety* be designed into the problemsolving group.

2. Starting with problemsolving as opposed to problem recognition and identification. Problemsolving begins with:

    a. Recognizing that there is a specific problem or set of problems *practically* dissectable out of a complex context and determining the scope and level of the problem.

    b. Defining the problem so that it can be dealt with given the resources of the group and of the organization that must implement the resulting policy or plan.

    c. Monitoring to make sure that the group has really selected and defined the problem correctly. The wrong problem correctly solved, filed away, and forgotten, a common result in organizations, is really quite a waste of time.

3. Misuse of models, computers, and quantification. A major function of the catalyst group is the creative generation of conceptual models and scenarios, the selection of appropriate formal modeling approaches, the computerization of the model as required, and the provision of an interaction or gaming capability in the model so that alternate designs, plans, policies, strategies, and tactics can be tested and evaluated. Models perceived as unrealistic, unusable, imposed by somebody else, threatening to an executive's self-respect or status and power, or overly abstracted and quantified are liable to be filed away and forgotten.

4. Allowing a rigid atmosphere, lacking in spontaneity, to develop. Much problemsolving is subconscious or preconscious, and the atmosphere should be open and fluid so that intuitions, hunches, and spontaneous ideas can be brought out and used. Once again, we reject that ogre of the 1960s, the rational decisionmaker who uses only quantitative facts. Even in the 1960s sophisticated systems analysts recognized that management has a strong subjective and intuitive component, but many other people never learned this lesson. In addition, creative problemsolving can be effectively inhibited by an atmosphere that provokes feelings of anxiety. Rigid agenda, keeping up the pressure for quick solutions, and constantly reminding participants of deadlines can effctly destroy creative problem-solving.

Finally, the *duration* of problemsolving groups in the adaptive organization will vary. The importance of ongoing learning and problemsolving has been emphasized. If the organization is designed according to the recommendations made throughout this book, a great many problems will be handled routinely and will not turn into brushfires. The real crises will be anticipated at least to some extent, and adaptive strategies will have been designed. Variety and levels of supplies, inventory, and spare parts; maintenance of equipment and facilities; availability and usability of job aids and tools; and worksystems that provide an acceptably safe, healthful, and motivational quality of life should be routinely regulated and controlled by the semiautonomous units. Should major *exceptions* arise suddenly and unexpectedly, for example, large-scale equipment breakdown or release of dangerous levels of pollution, emergency problemsolving teams will have to be established. The duration of these teams may be only a few days. It might, for example, turn out that the organization lacks the financial resources to replace worn-out plants and equipment, and that a plant has to be shut down. Problemsolving teams of longer duration may be necessary in situations that become crises.

We should note here that an anticipatory capability does not connote unlimited resources to do something about the anticipated situation. Here, the organization may have anticipated that the plant or equipment would eventually wear out but not know when and not have the resources to continually upgrade, replace, or modernize.

Long-anticipated crises or opportunities and long-range planning will require specific problemsolving groups, such as those the compositions and functions of which are summarized above, superimposed on the continual learning and problemsolving capability provided by the *Adaptivity Field* shown in Figure 8.1.

In a well-designed adaptive organization, the eventual need for specific new problemsolving groups will have been anticipated within reasonable time boundaries, and the lead time for setting them up greatly reduced as a result of ongoing experience and system training.

ORGANIZATIONAL PERFORMANCE: ASSESSMENT AND PREDICTION

The *Performance* block in Figure 8.1 shows a number of dimensions of organizational performance. These were discussed earlier, as well as the relationship between goals and objectives on the one hand and performance on the other, and the selection of criteria or standards of performance and of ranges of tolerance or variability away from a criterion level. It is assumed that the overriding purpose of the organization is to survive *so that* the agreed-upon goals and objectives can be met through effective performance. Sometimes organizations continue to try to survive long after they have lost all useful purpose. Sometimes organizations try so hard to be efficient, in the usual sense of this term in business and government, that they become no longer effective. These organizations are drastically in need of help.

There are few areas in the sciences that study humankind that have received more detailed attention than has performance. For many decades, individuals, groups, organizations, programs, policies, institutions, systems, subsystems, governments, and nations have been peered at, poked, probed, stimulated, dissected, and analyzed. Psychologists have studied individuals and groups for nearly 100 years. In the 1960s especially, a number of supposedly objective and scientific measures arose to assess programs, policies, and institutions. These included Program Planning and Budgeting System (PPBS), cost/benefit analysis, and benefit/cost analysis. We might also mention Management by Objectives. Many observers consider these approaches to have been failures. Overall, there are about as many unanswered questions about performance as there were decades ago. This is because much of the research over the years led to dead ends, was based on superficial observations or theory, required unavailable data, required measurements that could not be made, or simply involved far too great an abstraction of the real world. Even a simple ratio concept like benefit/cost analysis falls by the wayside because it is impossible realistically to equate benefits, say, of social programs to financial terms, and it may even be impossible to measure financial costs.

There is, therefore, no simple or invariant formula for measuring realistically, in today's world, total organizational performance and the contributions of the different dimensions of performance to total performance. A listing or ranking of performance dimensions and criteria and results is only of preliminary value. The dimensions are not just items on a list. They are subsystems, which may overlap, which interact, which may conflict, and the behaviors of which do not aggregate to unity. Further, performance dimensions and criteria, and of course actual performance, must never be regarded as fixed. Making tradeoffs among dimensions and adjusting actual performance and performance criteria to meet changing needs and demands are part of the ongoing learning of the organization. The continual monitoring and adjustment of performance are critical in the design of the adaptive organization.

One point should be stressed here—in many companies executive compensation plans reinforce defective behavior oriented to the short-term rather than long-term goals. High annual salaries and a guaranteed annual bonus (and dividends), often quite apart from *real* company performance, are part of a positive–feedback system that helps cripple long-term survivability. Minor changes in products, reducing R&D and capital spending, delay in paying bills, postponing maintenance—generous creative accounting—can make executive performance appear to be much better than it actually is. CEOs, in assessing the performance of their own and other companies, should be wary of apparently impressive changes in quarterly or even annual earnings. Newer incentive plans attempt to link executive performance and rewards more closely to strategic goals. But implementing these new plans is not easy because incentive planning is just one part of overall long-range planning. Companies need a great deal of help here.

The actual design for monitoring, updating, and upgrading performance must reflect the needs of the organization within a given time frame. In the large, complex organizations in turbulent environments to which this book is largely directed, the variety and complexity of this design should fit the variety and complexity of the environments and explanatory theories and models discussed earlier.

Can organizational performance, especially failure and collapse, be predicted? There is some evidence that it can or at least could be up to now. Financial and investment analysts, and banks and other lending institutions, have been generally successful until recently in sizing up an organization's continued potential for performance. These experts examine such things as the firm's available cash, type and amount of debt, market position, amount of R&D, and management experience. The standard methods of assessment, employed for over two decades of strong economic growth and relative environmental stability, must now be supplemented, modified, or even replaced.

Dr. R. van Frederikslust in Holland made a study of the predictability of corporate failure.[15] Basically, he used a variety of regression equations, and in one model he used two ratios as independent or predictor variables—a *liquidity* variable, defined as (cash balance in the preceding time step plus the "earned resources" from the preceding to the present time step)/short-term debt during the preceding time step, and a *profitability* variable, defined as the rate of return on equity. The dependent or predicted variable was then used as a discriminant to classify corporations into two categories, failed and not failed. The two categories reflected separate but overlapping probability distributions. Failure was considered to be the inability of the firm to pay its obligations when they fell due, or, cash insolvency. The crisis of failure was considered to occur mostly as a consequence of a sharp decline in sales. Corporations could anticipate such crises by monitoring the early-warning signals of probable failure, for example, loss of an important customer, shortage of raw materials, or management deficiencies.

Van Frederikslust compared predicted and observed values of the cash balance for matched samples of failed and nonfailed firms quoted on the Amsterdam Stock Exchange between 1954 and 1974. He concluded that, using purely financial ratios, corporate failure could be predicted up to five years in advance.

The time interval covered by this study should be noted carefully. It is doubtful that such predictive accuracy could be obtained today or tomorrow using van Frederikslust's methods. In addition, John Argenti concluded that change in financial ratios was an insufficient basis for prediction. Argenti's model is more holistic; van Frederikslust's model is more analytic. Argenti's model seems to imply the existence of multiple levels of equilibrium and of catastrophic flips. It is fitting that this book should conclude with this final example of alternative approaches that have been so heavily contrasted in the preceding pages.

SUMMARY AND FINAL THOUGHTS

This chapter has presented in fair detail a design for adaptive organization and management. The design represents an *interweaving* of a great many ideas, approaches, facts, personal experiences, examples, studies, and methods, which have been covered in the first seven chapters. In helping top managements to prepare their organizations for the years ahead, generous use of the following ingredients has been made:

1. A long-range, longitudinal, dynamic, and evolutionary perspective and a consequent emphasis on early-warning signals.
2. Theoretical underpinnings that explain both the maintenance of the older and the emergence of the newer.
3. An unshakable interrelationship between humankind and nature.
4. An isomorphism of organism and organization.
5. A holistic rather than a reductionistic, a synthetic rather than a purely analytic, orientation.
6. An emphasis on organization–environment interaction.
7. A full consideration of the many dimensions and dynamics of the external environment, not just a treatment of the external environment as a generalized abstraction.
8. A full consideration of the several subsystems within the organization.
9. A construction or selection of models that are consistent with the variety in the problem and that lead to divergent (many solutions, many alternatives) rather than convergent (a single optimal solution) thinking. A model package like that used at General Electric Company (see Chapter 4), modified by field theory, is a good choice.
10. A view of the organization as a continually learning system, with a consequent emphasis on dynamic problemsolving groups and semiautonomous units so organized that managers, workers, and machines do that and only that which thay can do best.

Collectively, these ingredients, interwoven into the design of the adaptive organization and management provides the basis for:

1. As great an *anticipatory* capability as it now possible, given the present state of the art.
2. A varied repertoire of potential strategies for *managing anticipated crisis* by preventing little difficulties from building up and reinforcing one another to become a crisis, by steering around a crisis, and by confronting an unavoidable crisis forewarned and forearmed.

Finally, the last 20 years of this century are very likely to be among the most critical in human history. I believe that we are in the midst of a major world transformation or reconfiguration, perhaps comparable to those that accompanied the end of Classical Mediterranean Civilization (climaxed by the fall of the Roman Empire), and the Renaissance and Reformation, and at least comparable to that which followed the first Industrial Revolution. I have presented this argument and justifications for it throughout this book, but particularly in Chapter 3 (hyperbolic growth), Chapter 4 (Kondratieff cycle), Chapter 5 (field-theoretic reconfigurations, of which catastrophic flips seem at present to be the most tractable for practical applications), and Chapters 6 and 8 (multiple equilibria, instability, and resilience).

For those organizations that already partly fit the design given in this chapter, the time to build in far more adaptability is *now*. For those organizations characterized by the design deficiencies pointed out in this book and in the references, the time was *yesterday,* but better late than never.

Unfortunately, policy throughout the world appears to be based on an almost incredible naiveté and oblivion to the *forces* that are reshaping our world. Policymakers appear to believe that all one has to do to change an undesirable situation, perhaps back to the way it was before, is to push here and pull there. It would appear that political organizations, at least, are *not* learning organizations. The direct effect of the failure to understand the behavior of a field of societal–ecological forces will be, with a high degree of likelihood, World War III before the turn of the century. Only the design of mutually adaptive organizations and environments worldwide has any possibility of deleting this final exclamation mark at the end of our present stage of transformation!

APPENDIX DIAGNOSTIC QUESTIONS

This book is devoted to executive problemsolving. It has frequently been emphasized, however, that one doesn't just jump in and solve the first problem that becomes apparent. Effective problemsolving requires the even more important antecedent:

1. Recognition of the existence of a potentially significant problem.
2. Contrasting the problem with the field or background in which it occurs while not losing sight of the interrelationships crossing the boundary between problem and field.
3. Defining the problem in terms such that its solution can be managed.
4. Placement of the problem in a context by criticality, urgency, or priority. The context might be, for example, a list, a matrix, or a diagram.

Only trivial, statically defined organizational problems have simple, easily obtained, easily quantified, once-and-for-all solutions. Real-world problems and solutions are intertwined by complex, continuing, dynamic feedback interrelationships. The main purpose of this appendix is to kick off the formation or stimulate the further development of sophisticated thinking and problemsolving activities involving top general management, line and staff corporate, strategic, and long-range planners, and other members of special teams.

The questions in the appendix are directed toward helping executives and their associates diagnose problems in their own organizations, within the external environments, and between their organizations and the external environments. The questions should be of value to other managers as well. When the book is used as a text, the questions can serve as points of departure for further elaboration by professors and as focal areas for student research and for course projects.

The questions are arranged by chapters. The whole chapter should be read before answering the questions. In addition, some questions in later chapters, in the light of further knowledge, refer back to questions asked earlier. Because problemsolving is iterative and dynamic, executives may want periodically to review the earlier questions and answers in the light of more information on and experience with attempted solutions. Questions are organized in blocks, in the same way problems occur in the real world. In almost all cases, the answers to the questions require careful thought and not just flipping through the pages where pertinent topics are discussed.

The Table of Contents as well as the questions can serve to structure seminars, short courses, and workshops.

The questions are mainly for *you,* the chief executive, functioning in the context of your organization and environments. Thus, the answers, solutions, criticalities, and emphases may differ among organizations. The questions contain much variety. Given questions may not apply to all organizations. There are few if any pat answers. The questions serve to help you to recognize the existence of and to define problems. The text as well as your experience and answers will help to structure your approaches to problem solutions. In some cases you may want to delve into the References for further information. The questions and answers, or problems and solutions, are merely first steps toward assessing the continuing health, viability, subsystem congruence, environmental fit, adaptability, and survivability of your organization. The purpose of the questions is that of a *guide* and a *catalyst.* Managers must not be handed solutions on a platter. They and their organizations must work out their own solutions. Otherwise, the solutions will be undervalued and impermanent.

CHAPTER 1. CONCEPTS OF ORGANIZATION AND MANAGEMENT

1.1 Is my organization anticipatory? What does this term mean to me? Is anticipation an important capability for an organization to have? In what concrete ways is my organization anticipatory or not? Did we purposely build in a capability for anticipation? In which way? What can we do now to increase our capability?

1.2 Since I have been in management, how have I seen organizations change, if at all? Is my present organization different from previous places where I have worked? In which ways? What specific qualitative and quantitative changes can I note down? Is the nature of change itself different qualitatively or quantitatively from what it used to be? How?

1.3 How have I seen the external environments change, if at all? What specific qualitative and quantitative changes can I note down? Is change itself in the environment qualitatively or quantitatively different from what it used to be? How?

1.4 What *is Nature?* How do the processes of nature carry over to the design of better organizations? How can I apply some of the results from studying nature to my organization, if at all?

1.5 What is field theory? How is an organization, an environment, or both together a field of forces? What specific examples can I cite from my organization and from current events that the world can indeed be well represented as a field of forces? What are the advantages to me of thinking in terms of field theory as opposed to alternative approaches?

1.6   What is the second law of thermodynamics or Entropy Law? Why has this law been applied so widely? Why hasn't it remained in physics, limited to the study of heat? How does my answer further embellish my answer to Question 1.4? Why has there been such an emphasis in recent years that organizations are open, not closed, systems?

1.7   How does the Entropy Law enter into long-range planning? Why has the concept of irreversibility become so important? What processes and outcomes in my organization and its environments are clearly reversible? Irreversible? If Professor Georgescu-Roegen's interpretation of the Entropy Law is correct, how will this affect our still being in business in 10 years? In 20 years? Let's prepare a chart listing the pros and cons of alternative economic theories, such as Entropy Law, Keynesian, and monetarist theories, and how application of these theories might affect the future of our firm. What impacts and what tradeoffs, for example, involving availability and price of resources, foreign trade, and side effects on the natural environment and on peoples' thinking do we want to consider?

1.8   How does evolution apply to organizations? What stages in the history and evolution of my organization can I identify? What are the characteristics of each stage? What specific kinds of breaks separate stages?

1.9   What kinds of symptoms could indicate that our organization is suffering from aging processes, is losing fit with its environments, or is even beginning to suffer from pathology? Do we have records or data on these symptoms? If so, let's plot frequencies over the years. Can we detect any trends? Any sudden changes or discontinuities?

1.10 What is regulation and control in the theoretical sense? What are the different types of feedback, and why are they important? How do I see feedback operating in the shorter and longer range in my company? What is a cybernetic organization? Is my company cybernetic? In which specific ways is it cybernetic, and in which not? How do we practice regulation and control in our company? Could we make our company more efficient by designing it to accord more with cybernetic principles?

1.11 What is the difference between open and open-loop? Closed and closed-loop? How specifically would I characterize the structure of my organization?

1.12 How does information flow through my company? Could I trace the flow of any given piece of information? Does information change as it crosses boundaries? Where? How? How reliable is the information I get for decisionmaking? What are the differences among data, information, and knowledge?

1.13 How can hierarchy be studied theoretically? In which way is my corporation hierarchical? What are the specific advantages and disadvantages of our present structure? Are there practicable alternatives to hierarchy that we are now using or that we should now consider?

1.14   What symbiotic interrelationship do we have with other companies? With government? With foreign companies and governments? How did these come about and grow? What could happen to break these interrelationships? What will happen if long-standing interrelationships are suddenly broken?

1.15   What are the 10 most important characteristics we can identify for each of the four main subsystems in our corporation? Are these subsystems congruent? Can we trace any major problems to misfits or lack of congruence among the subsystems?

1.16   Before reading this book, how would I have identified, in order of importance starting with the most important, my five most important functions? Would I still identify and rank these functions the same way? What changes have I made, if any?

1.17   Is my organization well fitted to its external environments? How so or not so? What improvements can we make?

1.18   How can I explicitly state my ideas about the ways in which an organization is adaptive and the ways in which it is not? How adaptive is my organization? What specific impediments to adaptiveness do we face, if any?

1.19   Is the structure of my organization contingent on identifiable external and internal factors? In which way?

1.20   What are the advantages and disadvantages or dangers in viewing our corporation as a C^3I system? How well do we perform the 11 indicated functions? How can we relate the overall performance of our organization to each of these areas?

1.21   Am I, to be completely honest, the right manager for my company at this time? What unique strengths and capabilities have I contributed to my company? Is the rest of management congruent with this organization in these environments at this time? Are we changing with the times? How do we actively induce change? How specifically can we improve our management capability?

1.22   Has my organization suffered any crises? What form did they take? When and how did they first become evident? In retrospect, were there any early-warning signals? Did we heed these signals? How did we handle these crises? Were we successful? Would we do things differently today? Do we now have a system that includes the eight capabilities identified in Chapter 1 as necessary for adaptive and anticipatory organizations?

1.23   What sorts of management behavior can actually induce or precipitate crises? Is such behavior practiced in our organization?

1.24   From my own experience and from what I know about the many organizational difficulties and crises given at the end of Chapter 1, should I have handled things differently? How?

1.25 From my present perspective, how do I see my organization and its environments on January 1, 2001? How can I justify my perceptions? What specific factors and forces will produce this configuration? Are we passively at the mercy of systems forces? What are we doing to shape our own future?

CHAPTER 2. MAJOR PITFALLS: PART APPROACHES TO ORGANIZATIONAL ANALYSIS AND DESIGN

2.1 What experience have I had with internal and external specialist consultants and expert advisers? Have the relationships been mutually rewarding? Has the advice I have received been consistent or contradictory? Has it been useful? Has it been widely applicable? Let's construct a matrix giving the pros and cons of various specialist approaches, the costs of each approach, the possible tradeoffs we made or could have made, and what we did with the advice provided. Have we ever been conned by specialist consultants or advisers? If so, what steps could we take to prevent a recurrence?

2.2 Has our company used behavioral scientists? If so, what kinds of orientations did they bring? Did I, and other top management, understand what they were trying to do? Were their promises fulfilled? Did the problems they solved stay solved? Were there unforeseen impacts elsewhere in the company?

2.3 Does my corporation have lots of "people problems"? What sorts? Why? How have we handled these problems? Were we successful? If not, where do we turn now?

2.4 Does our organization have problems of low motivation, morale, job satisfaction, and productivity? How can behavioral scientists help us in these areas, if at all? Let's contrast the approaches of job enrichment, behavior modification, and job enlargement. What do we find?

2.5 How do we select future managers? What specific criteria do we use? Are highly structured, formal methods any better than informal ones?

2.6 Do we have an organizational development program? What exactly do the OD specialists do? What results have they produced? How do we measure their impact? Are we going to expand or cut back or abolish any OD capability we do have?

2.7 The theory and practice of sociotechnical systems have been greatly stressed in the book. In which specific ways, at which levels, is or is not my organization a sociotechnical system? Considering the pervasive effects of technology today, let's list at least 10 ways in which technology is impacting on our organization. Let's indicate both direct and indirect impacts. Are all these impacts desirable? What control do we have over these impacts and over technology in general?

2.8 Are we currently using any of the six features of sociotechnical systems design discussed in Chapter 2? Have they helped us? Why? Could any improvements be made?

2.9 What is the quality of worklife, as other top management and I see it, in our corporation? How do we define and measure quality of worklife? Do our perceptions differ from those of the workers themselves? How do we find out? How do we get frank and honest answers from the workers? Do they trust us? Do we trust them? Do we really care who trusts whom or not?

2.10 What is industrial democracy? Is it worth considering for my company? What are the pros and cons? Considering widespread value change, what are the long-range alternatives? Is a concentration of power and status at the top levels of organizations a necessary prerequisite for corporate success and survival? If so, why?

2.11 What *is* human factors? How can it contribute to improved organizational design and performance? Do we use human factors principles and findings? Which? How? If we don't use these principles and findings, why not?

2.12 Do we have an operations research capability? Have we used operations research methods and findings? Which? How? To what degree of success? Has the usefulness of OR changed over the years? What is meant by the terms *optimization, maximization,* and *minimization?* What are the strengths and weaknesses of these terms?

2.13 What is an information system? What information systems do we have in our corporation? To what extent is each manual or computerized? Do we actually use these systems? In what specific ways? Are the systems easy to understand and use? Do they interface well with the people and with each other? Do we have corporate-level systems? What improvements can we make?

2.14 Why and how do we use computers in our company? Why and when did we acquire our particular hardware and software capability? Did introduction of our computers provoke a crisis? How did we handle it? Do our computers interface well with people? If not, why, and what can be done about the situation? What is the likely future of the use of computers in our company?

2.15 The book says a great deal about models. What is a model? What are some different types of models? Can modeling improve the performance of our organization? Specifically, how? Is modeling a panacea? If computer simulation modeling has any limitations, what are they? What is industrial or systems dynamics as one form of computer simulation modeling, and why does this particular approach receive emphasis in the book? What is an econometric model?

2.16 Can I readily answer questions like those posed so far, or must I do a lot of digging for the answers? In short: can I always say, honestly, that I know what's happening in my own organization?

CHAPTER 3. ORGANIZATIONAL DYNAMICS

3.1 What are the main forms of growth curves? What are the strengths and weaknesses of basing plans and policies on each form? What kinds of relevant data are available to us for demonstrating each form? Are there limits to growth? How? If there are no limits to growth, what specific arguments can we advance to substantiate this position?

3.2 Compare the longitudinal with the cross-sectional approach to the study of organizations. What are the strengths and weaknesses of each? What data do we have that apply to each?

3.3 How can oscillatory behavior be generated in an organization? Have oscillations occurred in the evolutionary history of our organization? Which and how? How can we prevent oscillatory behavior? How can we handle it once it has begun? Is oscillatory behavior always bad? Why not?

3.4 In what stage of evolution is my organization? Is its scale compatible with its purpose? How do our structure, behavior, and performance compare with those of the same stage in Greiner's model? Let's indicate 10 positive attributes and 10 problems characteristic of the present stage of our organization. How should we start to attack the problems?

3.5 Let's repeat Question 3.4 using instead the SRI International model.

3.6 Is there any indication that my organization has reached, or is about to reach, a limit of scale or complexity beyond which our present management methods are decreasingly applicable and productive? Have our methods worn out and become actually counterproductive? Is our organization in any way out of control? How are we handling the situation?

3.7 What is meant by the triggering effect of an event or a fluctuation in behavior in a field of forces? Let's trace some examples from our own experience of the explosive spreading of influence of a changed value, scientific discovery or innovation, introduction of a new product, government decision, military action, or availability of resources.

3.8 What are some examples, from our own experience, of antecedent or precursory events that in retrospect triggered reconfiguration of the world-field? Why were these early-warning signs ignored at the time? Were we caught off guard by sudden, unexpected changes? How did we respond? What did we learn? Can the same thing happen again?

3.9 Is my company part of an old industry or of an industry otherwise threatened by sudden and rapid change? What is the nature and source of that change? Let's consider such things as inflation, government deregulation, foreign competition, costs of labor and natural resources, interest rates, availability of capital, and market saturation. These are rather obvious types of changes. Did we anticipate them? Were we made oblivious to impending change by an overblown sense of our own power? Did we consciously refuse to heed the handwriting on the wall?

3.10 What are the strategies and their advantages and disadvantages with regard to further buildup in size, variety, and regulation and control? Why has the frequency of conglomeration decreased since the late 1960s? Considering the magnitude of intersecting crises discussed in this book, what are the likelihoods for future successes for strategies of acquisition and merger, conglomeration, and multinational operation?

3.11 The book proposes that the world has entered a stage of major transition, transformation, or reconfiguration and presents many theoretical and practical arguments to substantiate this proposition. What further arguments can I, the executive, offer for or against this proposition? What plans and policies does my company have to deal with the oncoming transformation and/or alternatively the maintenance of roughly the same conditions that characterize the present? What are the risks involved in ignoring or discounting the argument for transformation? What are the costs of anticipating and preparing for crises that might never occur?

CHAPTER 4. PRELIMINARY GUIDANCE TOWARD STEERING INTO THE FUTURE

4.1 Do we use the results of futures research in our company? Do we have an in-house capability? What forms do we use? What types of futures studies have I found most promising? Do I really understand what futures researchers are trying to do?

4.2 What is trend projection or trend extrapolation? What trends do we commonly use in our own planning, policymaking, and decisionmaking? Have the trends proved to be reliable indicators? How do we judge a useful trend? A misleading trend? How are the trends we use related to one another? Do we use leading and lagging economic indicators? Have the nature, reliability, and usefulness of trends appeared to change recently? Any discontinuities?

4.3 Why is the data problem emphasized so much in the book? How do raw data become useful information? Can I put my finger on any data and information when I want them? Are they presented in a form I can readily understand and use? Are they complete? Consistent or contradictory? What can we do to improve our acquisition, processing, and presentation of data and information? Is any problem mainly a computer problem or a human factors problem?

4.4 Let's compare economic, technological, objective social, and subjective social indicators. What are the strengths and limitations of each? Which specific examples can we provide of our own use of these indicators? How do we use these indicators in day-to-day decisionmaking? In short- and long-range planning?

4.5   What is the objectivity–subjectivity problem? How is the problem related to perception and to perceptual bias? How can this problem have such a great impact on my organization? Do I base my decisions only on the facts while other people let their emotions sway their decisions?

4.6   Continuing Question 2.15, how do models get started? What is a conceptual or mental model? What are some examples of mental models I use every day? Are Douglas McGregor's *Theory X* and *Theory Y* mental models? How does one go from mental models to more formal models? Why do many elaborate computer models have rather shaky underpinnings? Do the models used in our organization suffer from such deficiencies?

4.7   What are some ways to interrelate variables in a model? Which methods do we use in our company? Diagrams? Matrices? Correlation? Regression analysis? What is a causal model, and how does it differ from a correlational or regressional model? Let's list 10 specific examples of mutual causality evident from observing our organization and its environments.

4.8   How do human judgments enter into model-building? How do judgments limit the fidelity, validity, and usefulness of models? What methods can be employed for honing our judgments? What methods do we use in our company?

4.9   What is a "surprise-free" forecast? How does this differ from a straight extrapolation of the past? From our perspective in this corporation, is it more or less likely that our future will be surprise-free than was the case 10 years ago? In 1971 did we fairly well predict what 1981 would be like? What turned out to be our major unanticipated problems, if any?

4.10 What is the Delphi technique? It has been available for almost 20 years. Do we use it? How? For how long have we used it? With what results?

4.11 What is cross-impact analysis? What are some of its different forms? What has been our experience with this methodology in our company? If we haven't used cross-impact analysis, how and where might we apply it? Where could we obtain more information on the various forms and their costs? With regard to all methodologies, how can we avoid being sold something we don't need and can't use?

4.12 The term *value* has several different meanings or interpretations. How do we use the term in our organization? Are we communicating effectively with others? How do we set priorities of values? How do we deal with conflicts among values?

4.13 What is a scenario in futures research? What examples of scenarios can I provide? How is a scenario constructed? What are the relationships among imputs, throughputs, and outputs? Why are scenarios particularly useful for corporate, strategic, and long-range planning? Do we use scenarios in our corporation for these purposes? How? What has been our experience?

4.14   Continuing Questions 2.15 and 4.6, what is a computer simulation model? Why has the methodology received such an emphasis in a book on anticipatory and adaptive organizations? How is the theory of systems science related to the modeling of complex systems? Do we use computer simulation modeling in our corporation? What has been our experience?

4.15   What is an econometric model? Why have econometric models received such wide use in business and government? How have they been used in our company? What has been the recent experience at our company and elsewhere with econometric models?

4.16   Continuing Questions 2.15 and 4.6, what is systems dynamics? What are its key theoretical underpinnings? What kinds of natural processes is it best equipped to handle? What are its limitations? What are the main characteristics of the National Model? Have we had any experience with systems dynamics in our firm? Specifically, what?

4.17   What are the main economic cycles? How has my company experienced these cycles? Have we been caught off guard? Do the cycles seem to be changing qualitatively or quantitatively? In which specific ways? Do we have data to plot any changes? Continuing Question 3.11, how do these cycles fit into the proposition that the world has entered a stage of major transition or transformation?

4.18   What is a deterministic model? A probabilistic model? A stochastic model? How do deterministic and probabilistic/stochastic models appear to be interrelated? What examples can we provide of each type of model? Why is a blend of these models necessary in futures studies? How do we think, giving specific examples, deterministically or probabilistically in our company?

4.19   Our company has decided that it can use a larger computer simulation model of the external environment, particularly the economic environment. I am requesting that our planning staff provide critical comparisons of the Systems Dynamics National Model, the World Integrated Model, the SPECULATER model, and a large, traditional econometric model.

4.20   Does use of computer simulation models solve complex problems once and for all? Why do different models produce different, sometimes diametrically opposite, results? How do models contribute to policy-making and to political behavior in general? How do the objectivity–subjectivity (Question 4.5) and rational-decisionmaker problems enter in here? How do the answers to these questions impact on planning, policymaking, and decisionmaking in my organization? How will the Bariloche model and its spinoffs affect our doing business abroad?

4.21   FUTURSCAN has brought futures research applied to corporate and long-range planning about as far as it is possible to go up to now. Has our corporation had experience with this complex methodology? With a comparable methodology? What have been the specific benefits, costs, surprises, and side effects of using these methodologies?

4.22 The book has introduced a new corporate-level role or type of outside corporate consultant—that of the Systems Integrator. What are the pros and cons in our company for employing the services of a Systems Integrator? What should be the qualifications of this person? Is it likely that our top general managers of the future will be much like the Systems Integrator? Why, or why not?

CHAPTER 5. EMERGENCE

5.1 Can I define emergence in two different ways, giving five examples of each from my observation of happenings in my organization and its external environments? What is the fundamental difference between these definitions?

5.2 Continuing Question 1.5, with what kinds of phenomena and processes does field theory deal? What specific examples of each can I provide from my experience with my company's interacting with its environments? Why should our anticipatory management be especially alert for the occurrence of such phenomena and processes?

5.3 How can I define *crisis?* How do physical, biological, and social systems behave around critical points, thresholds, and ranges? What is meant by a reconfiguration of the field? How do my answers affect the way we anticipate and manage crisis? How do my answers relate to those I gave for Questions 3.7 and 3.8?

5.4 What is meant by equilibrium? By stability? What are some limitations to these concepts, and how have they become outmoded for many applications? How can our company plan for a nonequilibrium, unstable future? What conflicts can we expect with other organizations, most of whose planners think in equilibrium, simple cause-effect terms? What are the limitations of such theories as supply-side and demand-side economics?

5.5 What is a fluctuation? What are examples of fluctuations in biological and social systems? Why must management in an anticipatory organization try to detect and monitor fluctuations? What examples are there from our company and its environments? How can new order arise out of fluctuations?

5.6 The book stresses the importance of qualitative mathematics over quantitative mathematics. How can mathematics be qualitative? Let's provide several examples from the behavior in our organization and its environments.

5.7 The book stresses that complex organizations and environments often show discontinuities and sudden, spontaneous, and unexpected changes in trend, form, pattern, or configuration. Let's contrast a model of the future of our organization and its environments with models based on the scenarios discussed in Chapter 4. I'm asking our corporate planning staff to develop tentative alternative long-range plans based on the two approaches.

5.8 The book makes a number of fundamental distinctions. Continuing Questions 1.8, 1.10, 3.4, 3.5, 3.6, 4.18, and 5.6, can I distinguish between (a) quantitative and qualitative change, (b) deterministic and stochastic processes, (c) regulatory/cybernetic and evolutionary/morphogenetic processes, and (d) growth and development/emergence? What examples of each can I provide from my past, present, and potential future organizations and environments?

5.9 What is catastrophe theory? What are the underlying assumptions? What are the main properties or attributes? With what kinds of phenomena and processes does catastrophe theory deal? Let's provide some further examples, from our organization and its environments, of the fold, cusp, and butterfly catastrophes. How can we use these models for forecasting and prediction? Long–range planning? Management control?

5.10 What are collective phenomena? What is collective behavior? Continuing Questions 3.7, 3.8, and 5.1, how do these phenomena or behaviors emerge? How do natural and social scientists differ, if at all, in their explanations of the emergence of collectivities? What types of events can trigger the emergence of new collectivities in organizations and their environments? Let's provide some further examples based on our own observations and experiences. What is the likelihood of new, unexpected, *surprise-full,* perhaps dangerous collectivities impacting on our organization within the next 10 years?

5.11 What are some recognized conditions for corporate failure? For corporate collapse? What are Argenti's 12 main causes and symptoms? How many, if any, of these early-warning indicators apply to my organization? Can we identify any critical points indicative of potential failure or collapse? How do the concepts of fluctuations, perturbations, multiple equilibria, and catastrophes enrich Argenti's model? Is there any evidence our organization has fallen to a lower equilibrium level with regard to motivation, morale, job satisfaction, innovativeness, or productivity?

5.12 Does the model considered in Question 5.11 appear to apply to Chrysler Corporation? To Ford Motor Company? To some airlines and financial institutions caught by combinations of deregulation, inflation, and high interest rates?

CHAPTER 6. THE SIX MAJOR EXTERNAL ENVIRONMENTS

6.1 How do I assess my organization's external environment as a whole?

Simple and easy to understand? Complex? Static? Rich in variety? Rapidly changing? Turbulent? How is the environment likely to be in 10 years? In 20 years?

6.2 What is the total capability of my company for assessing and analyzing the external environment? Do I myself have a good grasp of the problems that may arise in the external environment and what is required for assessment and analysis?

6.3 What is ecology? What does the concept of ecology seem to rankle many businessmen? In which ways are business and ecology harmonious? Disharmonious? Is a division of camps between businessmen and ecologists logical, necessary, or inevitable? Does my firm have a policy regarding ecology? What is it in both the short and long terms? Do we work together with ecologists on common problems? How?

6.4 What *should* be our corporation's *active long-range* policy with regard to ecological *forces* like desertification, salinization, acidification, alkalinization, lateritization, soil erosion, water-resources loss, pollution, habitat destruction, species extinction, and recreational land loss? How do these forces produce reversible results? Irreversible results? What economic costs are involved in preservation as opposed to correction? How will these natural environmental changes affect our business in 10 years? In 20 years? How will our short- and long-range policies affect peoples' attitudes toward our corporation?

6.5 What is the counterintuitive behavior of complex systems? How does this idea affect our plans and policies? Let's provide 10 examples from our company and its environments of counterintuitive behavior.

6.6 What is resiliency? How does resiliency differ from stability? Is our organization resilient? In which ways?

6.7 In which ways is our company specialized and efficient? Generalized and possessed of excess capacity? How much variety does our company possess? In which way? Does our company possess any symptoms of structural inertia? Which? How do these factors affect the adaptability of our company? Is our company designed so as almost to guarantee counterintuitive behavior and performance?

6.8 Let's provide 10 arguments why the world-environment field is becoming more turbulent and 10 arguments why it isn't. How do these arguments affect our long-range planning?

6.9 Who are the environmentalists? What characterizes the environmentalist movement? What are the main arguments of environmentalists? How well thought out and documented are these arguments? Are environmentalist arguments logical and rational? Why, or why not? Why has the environmentalist movement grown so much in the last 10 years? Is it likely that it will continue to grow? Why? Continuing Question 4.12, how do values enter into the picture?

6.10   Let's comment on the *Global 2000* model. Does it represent a realistic forecast? Is the world in the year 2000 likely to be better or worse than that forecast? Specifically, why? How do the areas covered in the *Global 2000* study impact on our present long-range planning?

6.11   For our company what new technological opportunities and challenges are on the horizon? What alternative developments or uses can we visualize? What impediments or constraints may apply? What lead times are involved? What costs? What are the social and ecological side effects of our developing or using these new technologies? How do we assess the side effects or impacts?

6.12   What are the main factors contributing to technological development? Is the future likely to be different from the present or past? How? How will any changes affect our company?

6.13   What is the Japanese challenge? The Japanese model? What can we learn from the Japanese? Can we make mistakes trying to emulate them? How? Are the Japanese unique, or merely among the first and most prominent among many emerging new industrial competitors? Which nations might be among the possible new competitors? In what areas? Why?

6.14   Does our company have a risk-management or risk-assessment program? If so, what is its scope? How has it positively contributed? What are its drawbacks, if any? Does it apply to technological risk? Do I fully understand what the experts in the area are doing?

6.15   What is automation? Robotization? Technological change? How do these trends, events, and forces affect our company in terms of productivity, motivation and morale, job satisfaction, and quality of working life? Any unexpected results or side effects? Which? How do these forces affect our industry? Our society?

6.16   What variety of educational and skill levels does our corporation possess? How many people in each category? How do we assess these levels? Is the assessment meaningful? Have these levels changed over the years? In which way? Do we have any idea what our levels and mixtures of education and skills will be in 10 years? In 20 years? How do we determine our future requirements and sources? Are our methods realistic?

6.17   It is often said that people are becoming more antibusiness and antigovernment—in short, antibigness. To what extent have I found this to be true? How do we assess public attitudes toward our corporation, if at all? Do we really care what the public believes? Are we honest with the public? Am I really aware of how our employees interact with the public? What are the pros and cons of following these alternative scenarios: (a) public be damned, (b) pay lip service to meeting public needs and demands and hit 'em hard with advertising, or (c) business leadership in social reform?

6.18 What is a stakeholder? Which are the main stakeholders in my company? What policies and programs do we have for interacting with each?

6.19 Let's provide 10 arguments why the socioeconomic environment is changing rapidly both qualitatively and quantitatively and 10 arguments why it is not. How well does our company understand this environment? What long- and short-term indicators do we use? How successful have we been recently in basing our strategies and policies on these indicators?

6.20 What is the energy future of my corporation? Have we developed specific contingency plans and policies? Which? What tradeoffs did we make in developing these plans and policies?

6.21 How will social and sociotechnical change generally affect my company? In which specific ways? Are we going to fight change? Have we developed policies for adapting to change? Which ones?

6.22 How creative is our approach to our market environment? Do we anticipate changes in consumer education, values, attitudes, tastes, and preferences? How do we evaluate return on advertising? On market research? Do we really know why customers abandon or switch products or brands? How flexible are we in anticipating the need for future products or services, and switching quickly to their development? Let's identify 10 ways in which a company can lose market share. How do we stand in each area?

6.23 What is the boundary of my organization? What boundary-spanning capabilities do we have for each of the six main external environments? How can we make improvements?

6.24 What adaptive strategies have we developed for interacting with each of the six external environments? As a learning exercise, let's identify five maladaptive strategies for each environment.

CHAPTER 7. THE INTERNAL ENVIRONMENT

7.1 How well do I know the values, attitudes, and motivations of my own workforce? Are these factors changing, and if so how have they changed over the past 10 years? Is it important to me and to the company that I know these things? What means do we use to assess human behavior and behavioral change in our company? Could our assessment methods counterintuitively be provoking the very kinds of behavior we are trying to avoid? What policies and plans do we have for working with a changing workforce?

7.2 What is corporate social and environmental responsibility? Is it necessary for my corporation to be so responsible? Considering both the short and long range, why, or why not? What plans and programs, if any, do we have for developing greater responsibility? Who will be the beneficiaries? How?

7.3   Why, specifically and allowing for tradeoffs, do people work for my company? Similarly, why do I work here? Are the needs, goals, and demands of blue-collar workers, white-collar workers, professionals, and managers interchangeable? Why, or why not? Is a job, including my job, more or less rewarding than it used to be? More or less fun? Why?

7.4   How do I sense the organizational climate in my company? Are my sensations and perceptions most likely consistent with those of others? Are there lots of rumors going around? Is there lots of friction, hostility, footdragging, backstabbing, and open conflict? Why? Or is my company a "friendly" place? Why? What continuing, nonfad policies can we develop to improve our climate?

7.5   In which ways could our management plans and policies, implemented with the best of intentions for improving the company and helping its employees, backfire, that is, produce counterintuitive results? Have such things happened? Why? How does the concept of intrinsic versus extrinsic motivation enter the picture?

7.6   What is rational human behavior? When is behavior rational? Irrational? Are some people more rational than others? How? When? What are the strengths and weaknesses of the rationality model applied to our organization?

7.7   As an executive, what are my main psychological needs? How do I satisfy these needs in this organization? Does satisfying my own needs mean that other people have to give up meeting their needs? How do I justify, if this is the case, meeting my own needs at the expense of others?

7.8   Continuing Question 7.5, how do modern motivation theories contribute to our understanding of the decline in productivity? In my company to what extent can the workforce be characterized in terms of learned helplessness? Overemphasis on extrinsic rewards and punishments? Killed intrinsic motivation? Lack of enjoyment? Do these characteristics seem related to lowered productivity? What plans and policies do we have to rectify such situations?

7.9   How can automation improve our productivity? What are the costs and benefits of automation? What has been the experience with automation in our organization? Are we planning or implementing an office of the future? What sociotechnical systems problems are involved? How will we handle these problems?

7.10 How is our company handling the opportunity for tradeoff of computer-communications systems against transportation systems? What benefits and difficulties have arisen, if any? How are we handling any problems? Where could we look for further help?

7.11 Let's identify and discuss the factors that are held to contribute to the productivity slump. What arguments can we present for and against the proposition that the United States and other countries and particular industries may have reached a structural saturation level beyond which much increase in productivity is impossible without catastrophic reconfiguration.

7.12 What sensing and monitoring capabilities does my company have for each of the external environments and subsystems in the internal environment? What techniques and specialists do we use? Do we obtain environmental information firsthand or through secondary sources? How do we monitor our monitoring capabilities? In short: do we really know what's happening around us and why?

CHAPTER 8. ADAPTATIVE DESIGN AND MANAGEMENT

8.1 What has been the experience in my company with strategic, corporate, and long-range planning? Are our planning methods nonexistent, old-fashioned, or up-to-date? In which ways?

8.2 What *are* the characteristics of a good long-range plan? What steps have we taken to design such plans? With what results?

8.3 Continuing Question 1.10, what is the basic cybernetic paradigm? In which ways must an adaptive organization be cybernetic? What are the limitations of the cybernetic approach to design? In which ways is our organization now cybernetic? In which ways not? Could cybernetic principles further improve our design and performance? How?

8.4 Let's start a series of workshops to study in detail the possibilities of implementing the adaptive organizational design (Figure 8.1) at our corporation. Who will be the workshop participants? Who will concentrate on which blocks? What will be our time frames?

8.5 Why are structural flexibility, resilience, and variety particularly important characteristics of an adaptive organization? To what degree does our company possess these attributes? How can we make improvements? Where can we turn for any needed help?

8.6 How do communications, regulation and control, employee participation, and autonomy differ in adaptive and nonadaptive organizations? How do these features apply in our organization? How can we make improvements? Where can we turn for any needed help?

8.7 Let's continue our response to Question 7.12 in the light of further information on monitoring provided in Chapter 8.

8.8 How can crises be managed? What methods do we practice in our organization? To what effect?

8.9 What is the difference between self-regulation and self-organization? How do both attributes fit into our corporation?

8.10   How can control be used most effectively in our company? Misused? What are the major consequences of misuse of control? Why is participation stressed in the book? Let's contrast lip-service participation with real participation. How do these features apply to our company?

8.11   Who owns our corporation? How has the concept of ownership changed recently? Is reevaluation of this concept in order for our corporation? Why, or why not?

8.12   What are the dimensions of performance at our company? What contributes to each dimension? How do we measure performance? How do we make tradeoffs among different dimensions? Do we use feedback and feedforward to improve performance? How? With what success?

8.13   Let's summarize and contrast the main systems-theoretical bases for the design of adaptive organizations and the understanding of turbulent environments. Let's specifically indicate how these theories do or do not relate to our organization interacting with its environments. Are the theories complete? If not, what additions or modifications should be made?

8.14   What is the law of requisite variety? How does the law relate to adaptive organizational design and to organization–environment interaction? How does the design of our organization accord with this law?

8.15   Continuing Question 6.6, let's constrast stability and resiliency further. Let's consider applications of these concepts to productivity, unemployment, job satisfaction, economic inflation and depression, crime, agriculture, forestry, fisheries, organizational failure and collapse, and war and peace.

8.16   Let's contrast fail-safe with safe-fail strategies. How can these strategies be implemented? Which strategy better fits the adaptive organization? What is the practice in our organization? What improvements can we make? Where or to whom can we turn for further help?

8.17   What is organizational problemsolving? Learning? How do they relate to planning, policymaking, and decisionmaking? Is our organization a problemsolving and learning organization? How specifically do we achieve these ends? Especially, what groups or teams do we use and what computer-communications system support? How do we set up these efforts? To whom can we turn for further help?

8.18   Let's summarize the main themes of the book and how these themes do or do not fit our organization. Are there likely to be changes in fit within the next one to 10 years? The next 20 years? Specifically, how?

NOTES

CHAPTER 1

1. A *continuous* function can be drawn as a graph without lifting the pencil from the paper; it has no jumps, breaks, or wild fluctuations. In the calculus, continuity of a function at a given point is defined in terms of the *existence* of limits by which the point is approached from the left and from the right and the *equality* of the two limits at that point. A *discontinuous* function shows a *jump* at a given point, or, in another sense, it has no finite limit as a value approaches that point. A step function is a discontinuous function. A *discrete* sequence or distribution consists of distinct events or activities.

2. Tires can of course be retread or recycled, but this requires the expenditure of additional matter/energy. The continued efficiency, feasibility, and viability of a process or organization must always be viewed in terms of the ratio of effort going in to what is gotten out. In a simple way, cost/effectiveness and benefit/cost ratios illustrate this type thinking. Arthur D. Little, founder of the company of the same name, literally made two silk purses out of sows' ears. One purse is at company headquarters, the other in the Smithsonian Institution.

3. Best references on the Entropy Law are references 10 and 16.

4. Tolstoy quote is from reference 17.

5. Miller reference is 15.

6. For more on the theory, analysis, and properties of systems, see, for example, references 6 and 7 and the references included therein; the journals *Behavioral Science* and *IEEE Transactions on Systems, Man, and Cybernetics;* and the *Proceedings* of the annual meetings of the Society for General Systems Research (Systems Science Research Institute, University of Louisville, Kentucky) and proceedings of the meetings (every other year) of the Austrian Society for Cybernetic Studies (Vienna) released as volumes of *Progress in Cybernetics and Systems Research.*

7. Some of this material was presented earlier as reference 8. The whole book edited by Burack and Negandhi provides a wealth of material on organizational design.

8. Chandler reference is 4.

9. Child reference is 5.

10. Woodward reference is 18.

11. Burns and Stalker reference is 3.

12. A good further reference on contingency theory is 13.

13. For more on matrix organizations and alternatives to pure hierarchial designs see references 11 and 12.

16. For more on C^3I systems see references 6; for more on societal information-systems see reference 7.

17. The single best source on transactional analysis is, reference 2. Notice the subtitle!

18. Beer reference is 1.

19. I prefer to give examples of recognizable organizations when propriety permits. These

cases, for the most part, represent combinations of abstractions from sources available to the general public such as the electronic media, *Forbes, Fortune, Time,* and the Los Angeles *Times.*

CHAPTER 2

1. Consider, for example, the interdisciplinary and systems-theoretic articles published in *Behavioral Science.*
2. The best descriptions of Herzberg's work still are some of the earlier articles in the *Harvard Business Review.* See references 24, 28, and 30.
4. Reference 25 is an excellent summary of the points that divide behaviorism and phenomenology (a congeries of descriptive holistic theories including psychoanalysis and Gestalt psychology).
5. Reference 31 is a good, popularly written overview of assessment centers.
6. For more on sociotechnical systems see references 10, 12, 15, 16, 22, and 23. These references collectively provide a comprehensive discussion of the theory, methodology, earliest definitive studies, and subsequent expansions into new areas.
7. Guest reference is 20.
8. For more on the theory and applications of industrial democracy see references 7, 15, and 23.
9. Examples are from reference 7.
10. For more on human factors/ergonomics see references 9, 11, 12, and 13.
11. For recent criticisms of OR/MS see references 3, 4, 5, 6, 8, and 14.
12. Ackoff reference is 1.
13. Lucas reference is 26.
14. Reference 32 is an excellent summary of many things of great importance and interest about computer-communications systems including hardware, software, history, trends and projections, new technologies, and impacts on man and society.
15. Davis reference is in 32, pages 1096–1102.
16. References to Corporate Simulation Models are 21 and 29.
17. The "Bible" of industrial or systems dynamics is reference 17. Reference 18 is a workbook that shows how the basic building blocks are used. Reference 19 presents an industrial dynamics model that depicts growth and stagnation of a new product. These dynamics take place because of differential control and lack of synchronization involving three main loops—salesmen hiring, market, and capacity expansion.

CHAPTER 3

1. Some readers may prefer to substitute "change" for "growth."
2. References 1, 2, 9, 12, and 14 discuss in more detail the growth curves, the differential equations describing these curves, and the solutions (integrations) to the equations. Although its examples are taken almost exclusively from the biological and physical sciences, reference 2 is an outstanding introduction to or overview or review of the mathematics underlying many of the phenomena and processes discussed in this book.
3. Long known to scientists and engineers, these ideas were popularized by *The Limits to Growth* models.
4. In hyperbolic growth the curve is a hyperbola. Such growth is also called hyperexponential or superexponential.
5. Strassmann reference is 13.

6. Freeman and Hannan reference is 5. This system could also be studied using an allometric model. The reference provides a good example of the use and interpretations of regression analysis, especially for terms indicating autocorrelation, autoregression, and change. The multiple regression model allows the separation of the effects of initial size and change during a given period. It is of the form

$$Y_t = \alpha_0 + \alpha_1 Y_{t-k} + \alpha_2 X_{t-k} + \alpha_3 \Delta X_t + \mu_t$$

where Y_t = the size of the teacher or administrator component at time t; it is the dependent variable.

Y_{t-k} = the size of the same component measured k periods earlier than t; it is an independent variable.

X_{t-k} = either the size of school enrollments or the size of the teacher component k periods earlier than t; it also is an independent variable.

$\Delta X_t + X_t = X_{t-k}$ is the change either in the size of enrollments or in the teacher component; it also is an independent variable.

μ_t = a stochastic or random error term at the time.

t = The α (alphas) are coefficients to be estimated by least-squares methods.

7. Reference to elementary features of systems dynamics structure and function is 8. Related models are discussed in Chapter 4.

8. These ideas were presented by Professor Forrester during a course in systems dynamics at the Massachusetts Institute of Technology which I attended in the summer of 1976.

9. Roberts reference is 10 and the quotation is from page 58 of this reference.

10. References 1 and 7 deal extensively with stochastic and Markov processes.

11. Greiner reference is 6.

12. Stanford Research International reference is 4.

13. Reference to multinationals is 11.

14. Reference to information loss in Conglomerates is 3.

CHAPTER 4

1. Other recent general references to futures research are Armstrong [1, Ascher [2, and the handbook edited by Jib Fowles (see [30]). Ascher presents an excellent critique of *errors* in forecasting. Fowles is an especially good compendium of the view of some 45 experts.

2. Some of these problems have been given special names by econometricians. For example, the absence of enough data is called the *degrees-of-freedom problem*, the bunching together of data the *multicollinearity problem*, the similarity of data from nearby time periods the *serial correlation problem*, the effects of discontinuous change in the world the *structural change problem*, and the inaccuracies in measuring the *errors-of-measurement problem*. Exponential smoothing, spectral-density detemination, and distributed-lag estimates may remedy some of these problems. Techniques like Box-Jenkins do not assume a particular pattern of past time-series data. Box-Jenkins often deals with moving averages and autoregression or autocorrelation. Autocorrelation deals with interdependence rather than independence of past observations. This overcomes one deficiency of regression analysis.

3. Columbus and a number of nobles were seated around the dinner table. One noble scoffed, "*Anybody* could have discovered America. What's so hot about that?" Columbus thought for a minute, then passed around an egg. "Can anybody make this egg stand on end?" Each noble tried but without success. Columbus then tapped the egg at one end, slightly breaking its shell. The egg stood upright. "Its easy," said Columbus, "now that I've showed you *how* to do it."

4. Emphases added. A collection of issues of the "Monthly Summary" covering 5 to 10 years gives a good impression not only of changing business conditions, but also of strengths and weaknesses in the methodologies used.

5. The polygraph controversy, however, illustrates the ongoing real difficulty of relating the objective and subjective. The correlation between specific feelings and specific physiological variables is not great.

6. Professor Rokeach [27, p. 5] defines a *value* as "an enduring belief that a specific mode of conduct or end-state of existence is personally or socially preferable to an opposite or converse mode of conduct or end-state of existence." Further, modes of conduct define *instrumental values* and desirable end-states define *terminal values*.

7. The best source on Delphi is 15.

8. Helmer reference is 9.

9. Futuzer group references are 10 and 28.

10. Structural Model reference is 18.

11. The term value is used in different ways. It may have a very precise meaning, e.g., as defined by Rokeach in [27]. Further, value is often viewed as an objective measure, with utility its subjectively perceived equivalent.

12. An overview of multi attribute utility measurement is [5].

13. This formula is from reference [5]: $U_i + \sum_j w_j \cdot u_{ij}$

   where U_i = the aggregate utility of the ith entity
   $\sum_j w_j = 100$,
   w_j = the normalized importance weight of the jth dimension of value
   u_{ij} = the rescaled position of the ith entity on the jth dimension.
   Thus, w_j is the output of Step 7 and u_{ij} that of Step 8.

14. Martino quotation is from 21.

15. Lenz reference is 19.

16. Wilson reference is 30. Ian Wilson has pioneered the use of futures research for strategic and long-range planning in companies. This section on scenarios reflects a number of his ideas.

17. From: *Models in the Policy Process: Public Decision Making in the Computer Era* by Martin Greenberger, Matthew A. Crenson, and Brian L. Crissey, p. 104. © by Russell Sage Foundation. Reprinted by permission of the publisher.

18. I make a strong distinction between *fidelity* and *validity*. Fidelity reflects the way realworld phenomena are correctly perceived and interpreted and then related qualitatively and quantitatively in model structure and behavior. Fidelity is an expression of how well we really understand the system. Validity asks if the model describes or predicts what it purports to do. Poor fidelity may be one cause of model invalidity. However, other things such as computer programming errors may contribute to model invalidity. A model may be valid, according to one concept of validity, in that the behavior of its parameterized variables correlates with the behavior of historical data. However, this model may lack fidelity in that *both* the model variables and historical data reflect only superficial observations of more important underlying phenomena, differential reporting, overly aggregated data, and so on.

19. One way of computing the size of an econometric model involves considering the number of stochastic equations as well as the number of endogenous and exogenous variables. A large model would have between 150 and 200 equations plus variables, a very large model would have over 300. Examples of large commerical models are those of Wharton Econometrics Forecasting Associates, an affiliate of the University of Pennsylvania; Chase Econometric Associates; and Data Resources, Incorporated. These companies offer services to corporations at $125,000 or more per year.

20. For more on national expectations theory see reference 12.

21. Reference to National Model is 14.
22. Gordon reference is 6.
23. Reference to the Mesarovic Pestel Model are references 15, 16, and 23.
24. Reference to this study is reference 16.
25. Further information on SPECULATER can be found in 17.
26. For more on the Bariloche Model see 14.
27. References to the Work at Science policy Research Unit are 3, and 4.
28. Donnella H. Meadows reference is 22.
29. The term surficial, not to be confused with superficial, comes from geology. I use it to describe those phenomena and data which, even though relatively evident and easy to measure, tell us little about the underlying structure and structural changes of organizations and societies.
30. Limits Modelers quotations are from *Models of Doom: A Critique of the Limits to Growth*, ed. by H.S.D. Cole, Christopher Freeman, Marie Jahoda, K.L.R. Pavitt, Universe Books, New York, 1973. (N.B. published in Great Britain by Chatto & Windus Ltd. under the title "Thinking About the Future.")
31. Peter C. Roberts reference is 26.
32. As examples of such surveys see references 8, 11, and 24.
33. "FUTURSCAN: *Toward a Manageable Future*." Copyright © General Electric Company. Courtesy of General Electric Company.
34. Ideally these new careerists should be developed within the organization. However, at first the role may have to be filled by outside consultants. And of course outside consultants will always be needed to provide fresh insights or outside-in perspectives.

CHAPTER 5

1. Recent, perhaps revolutionary, advances in field theory in physics, and in the study of critical phenomena specifically, have resulted from using *lattice* and *renormalization-group* techniques. These approaches are among the most esoteric and mathematically sophisticated in all science. However, the following example illustrates some points of concern in our dealing with the organization and its environments. Physical field theory references are 1 and 29. The first is esoteric and very mathematical; the second is understandable to the lay leader. For some of my own interpretations published elsewhere see references 11–14.

    Many studies are made with models of real systems, for example, real ferromagnets. Models can be classified by the number of dimensions they have, for example, length, width, and depth. A lattice of the two-dimensional Ising model (named after a German worker of the 1920s) of a ferromagnet has long been utilized. If, in this model, a single electron spin is *perturbed*, say, thermally, *the disturbance of order can propagate neighbor-to-neighbor over a large area of the lattice.* Distant spins, now oriented the same way, are said to be *correlated. Correlation length* represents the maximum distance over which a correlation can be detected.

    At a very high temperature the correlation length is near zero, and the spins are nearly randomly distributed. The system is not magnetized. As the temperature decreases, however, the coupling strength between adjacent electron spins increases, and correlations covering greater distances can be observed. These correlations represent spin fluctuations—patches in which the several spins point is generally the same direction. These are *small pockets of order in a field of randomness.* The system as a whole is still unmagnetized, yet lattice structure is much different from its structure near infinite temperature.

    As the temperature approaches the critical (Curie) point, the correlational length grows rapidly. The basic reactions remain the same and connect only adjacent lattice sites, *but long-range order has emerged from short-range forces.* At the Curie temperature itself, the correlation length becomes infinite. The system still remains unmagnetized, *but it is hypersensitive to small perturbations, the effects of which can nearly instantaneously engulf the whole field.*

In this type of modeling a means is sought for *predicting the macroscopic emergent properties of the system from the known microscopic properties.* Important qualitative insights at the higher level can be obtained without recourse to the precise form of fundamental interactions. Ferromagnetism, and the other qualitatively new phenomena like superfluidity and superconductivity, emerge out of the basically simple force laws of mechanics, quantum mechanics, and thermodynamics. The macroscopic collective behaviors occur at a statistical level, and only probabilistic predictions are made as to the behavior of any given individual element of the system.

In the renormalization-group transformation, all fluctuations, say, in electron spin direction whose scale is smaller than a given size are eliminated from the lattice through a repeated averaging process. With repeated transformations the behavior of the system at successively larger scales is elucidated. The larger-scale or longer-range behavior of each newer, thinned-out lattice can be viewed as equivalent to the behavior of the original lattice at a "higher temperature."

The fact that superficially very different physical systems behave identically in the vicinity of their critical points is called the *universality hypothesis.* The critical behavior of these systems is determined by only two quantities: (1) the dimensionality of space (usually of two or three dimensions), and (2) the dimensionality of the *order parameter.* Systems that share these dimensions have identical *critical exponents.*

The order parameter represents a macroscopic property emergent from interactions at a microscopic level. Examples are (spontaneous) magnetization, magnetic susceptibility, correlation length, density differences between the liquid and gaseous phases of a fluid, and concentration differences. In the order parameter field occur the strong fluctuations that characterize these phase transitions.

The macroscopic properties of these thermodynamic systems are functions of the amount by which the system departs from the critical temperature. Critical phenomena are proportional to a value called the reduced temperature raised by the values of the critical exponents.

2. The assembly of a newly synthesized molecule into a composite structure is largely under thermodynamic control. That is, each molecule is considered to search for its state of lowest chemical potential. (We have seen that minimization of a potential is an important feature of many systems.) Because of certain unique properties of complex hydrocarbon molecules in water solution, the molecules aggregate to form a micelle, which contains about 100 molecules. Formation of the micelle is a highly cooperative process. There is a critically narrow range of molecular concentration below which no micelles exist and above which almost every added molecule of the appropriate type enters the micelle. The critical concentration depends mainly on the size of the water-repelling portion of the molecule. The need to maintain balance between water-repelling and other molecular forces leads, through processes we can ignore here, to the formation of semipermeable cellular membranes and to the ability of cells to undergo deformation and penetration [24].

The organization of cells into more complex structures also exhibits field-theoretic behavior. Differences in adhesion and mobility among cells appear to account for a number of morphogenetic processes. Some of these processes are the sorting out of mixed-cell aggregates, the engulfment of one tissue by another, and the hierarchical ordering of various equilibrium configurations. Tensions at phase interfaces between different kinds of cells transmit forces over long distances. The final cellular configuration corresponds to minimum free energy at the surface. In order to achieve this thermodynamic equilibrium, there must be maximum adhesion of cell surfaces within the aggregate 22.

3. This discussion is partially based on reference 27.

4. Walls reference is 26. Walls uses the term "agitators" rather than "proselytizers."

5. The work of Professor Ilya Prigogine and his colleagues is given in references 17, 19, and 20. The first and third are hard reading; the second can be understood by the mature reader with some exposure to differential equations.

6. These reactions involve catalytic steps, and in particular *auto-catalysis* (self-catalysis) is associated with the self-organizing features of dissipative structures.

   An example of autocatalysis is the conversion of trypsinogen into the intestinal digestive enzyme trypsin. Under certain conditions, this reaction is possible only if trypsin itself is initially present. The reaction follows a logistic growth curve, and indeed many of the growth forms discussed in Chapter 3 find further expression in the chemical kinetics of autocatalysis.

   Chemistry provides many examples of emergent new forms. These include wave forms, differential concentrations, and oscillations. All these dissipative structures display collective behavior on a supermolecular level, and their lengths and periodicities are large when compared with times and sizes at the molecular level.

7. The diagram on this page is from reference 17, page 442.

8. Professor Prigogine cites studies of slime molds, of termites, and of army ants. (Citations to the original research on slime molds, termites, and army ants are given in reference 17). Slime molds are protozoans related to ameobas. They can exist either as isolated individuals or as collectivities possessed of some cellular differentiation. Formation of the collectivity is triggered when the chemical attraction of cyclic adenosine monophophate overcomes the random movements of the individual organisms. Above this critical point the individuals move closer together, centering on the area where the first fluctuation in density took place. Self-organization has emerged from the instability of the spatial distribution of the individuals at the critical point.

   Nonlinearities in the interaction mechanisms of termites when building nests can also yield the spontaneous formation of coherent structures. A chemical *communicator* is also involved in termite nest-building. This chemical is mixed with the building material when it is deposited randomly. When the density of the mixture reaches a critical value, the random and uniform distribution of the material no longer offers a stable solution to the equations controlling density (in the mathematical model of the system). Above a critically large size of deposit, the termites select this chance fluctuation for preferential further deposition. Continuing construction requires some proximity of deposits. If the initially largest deposit is so far removed from the others as to prevent connection, construction will stop and the termites will select another site.

   In the case of spacing of army ants, the chemical communicator is a hormone-like attractor called a pheromone. (Readers may be familiar with the use in agriculture and forestry of pheromones to lure to sterile individuals or to traps certain moths and other insects considered to be pests.) Above a critical density of army ants, the uniform distribution in space becomes unstable and the colony will branch into various types of paths.

   If these types of *reconfigurations* applied only to physiocochemical systems and to organisms other than humankind, they would warrant little attention in this type book. However, as I first emphasized in Chapter 1, there are laws, isomorphies (explanations of the same type structural/functional phenomena arising independently in different sciences), and—at the very least—highly suggestive analogies that apply to essentially all types and levels of systems.

9. The original research on the Kachin tribesmen is cited in reference 17.

10. Carneiro quotation is from reference 6, page 1021. Copyright New York Academy of Sciences. Courtesy of Dr. Robert L. Carneiro.

12. Thom reference is 25.

13. Further reading on catastrophe theory is given in references 8, 9, 15, and 30. I consider reference 15 to be the most valuable in that it says the most in the shortest space, with the least mathematical digression, and has the most relevant examples. Reference 30 is recommended as a starter.

14. I presented this cusp catastrophe example earlier in reference 11.

15. In my discussion of the Iranian revolution and all other issues in this book, I remain a strictly neutral, impartial, and objectve observer and interpreter. My sources of information on the Iranian revolution were open and available to everybody who wished to use them.

16. Social science references and perspectives on collective behavior are references 16, 18, 21, and 28. The sequence of activities leading to a new collectivity is partially based on the Neil Smelser theory of collective behavior as presented, updated, and interpreted in reference 16.

17. Battelle-Columbus Laboratories reference is 3.

18. Stanford Reseach International reference is 23.

19. Argenti reference is 2.

CHAPTER 6

1. These concepts were published earlier, but the most recent references are 7 and 8.

2. Jurkovich reference is 12.

3. Tosi, Aldag, and Storey reference is 18.

4. Terreberry reference is 17.

5. Emery quote is from reference 7, page 19.

6. Holling reference is 11.

7. More on ecosystems principles can be found in, for example, reference 19.

8. These alternative stability paths, showing the responses to perturbation, are now sometimes illustrated by *phase portraits*. The abscissa and ordinate may represent two different populations like predator and prey, two competitors, or herbivore and food. The trajectories show the moment-by-moment changes of the two variables, given one starting point. Phase portraits can be generated by fairly simple coupled differential equations. Like all such models, they should be interpreted qualitatively, not quantitatively. They are not intuitively easy to understand, and I prefer to use catastrophe manifolds.

9. The examples of the Great Lakes fisheries and Peruvian cotton come from reference 11, which also provides citations to the original research as appropriate. A number of other examples come from my *Sociotechnical Systems,* reference 7 in Chapter 1.

10. Hannan and Freeman reference is 10.

11. Emery reference is 7.

12. *The Global 2000 Report to the President* reference is 3. Quotes are from pp. iii-iv, 1.

13. For an example of a sophisticated mathematical and statistical study of invention and innovation, see reference 15.

14. Freeman reference is 9.

15. White and Graham references are 20.

16. Lawless reference is 13.

17. For a sophisticated look at technology assessment, see reference 1.

18. Starr and Whipple references are 16.

19. For a thoughtful philosophical analysis and interpretation of autonomous technology, see reference 21.

20. For a further look at the interrelationship between technological change and manpower resources, see reference 4.

21. Professor R. Joseph Monsen [14] has written a very good synthesis of different views on American capitalism and has produced several scenarios as to its future.

22. DeGreene reference is from 5.

23. DeGreene references are 2 and 5.

CHAPTER 7

1. The Opinion Research Corporation reference is 3; The Opinion Research Corporation is an Arthur D. Little Company.

2. Smith, Frank, Roberts, and Thelin references are 15.

4. Bowman and Haire material (including quotation) is from reference 2 © (1975) by the Regents of the University of California. Reprinted from *California Management Review,* Volume XVIII, no. 2, pp. 41 to 47 by permission of the Regents.

5. Part of this discussion is based on reference 14.

6. Another division of motivation theories is into *content* theories, concerned more with the origin of needs, and *process* theories, concerned more with what happens once the organism is aroused. Examples of the former include the theories of Herzberg and of McClelland. An example of the latter is the theory of Vroom.

7. This argument is excellently pursued in reference 5.

8. McClelland reference is 7.

9. Maccoby reference is 6.

10. Atkinson reference is 1.

11. Seligman reference is 12.

12. Csikszentmihalyi reference is 4.

13. Stokols reference is 16.

14. Human thinking and problemsolving vis-à-vis the computer, and artificial intelligence, are discussed excellently, but from different points of view, in references 8, 9, and 17.

15. Samuelson, Kjell, Miller references are 11.

16. Several points in this section were suggested in reference 10.

CHAPTER 8

1. Kiechel, reference is 17.

2. Hunsicker reference is 16. Quotation is from this reference, pages 13 and 14. New York, AMACOM, a division of American Management Associations, 1980.

3. I have discussed precursory phenomena earlier in references 8 and 9.

4. Two examples of the rare sophisticated approaches to social forecasting are references 11 and 18.

5. Deighton reference is 10.

6. Hackett reference is 12.

7. Alvarez, Walter, Frank and Helen references are 1.

8. Von Foerster, Heinz references are 21.

9. Ashby references are 2 and 3.

10. Beer references are 4 and 5.

11. Perlmuter and Monty references are 19.

12. Holling references are 14 and 15.

13. Butzer reference is 6.

14. Herbst reference is 13.

15. Frederikslust reference is 20.

REFERENCES

CHAPTER 1

1. Beer, Stafford, 1973. "The Surrogate World We Manage." *Behavioral Science,* **18** (3), 198–209.
2. Berne, Eric, 1973. *What Do You Say After You Say Hello?: The Psychology of Human Destiny.* New York: Bantam.
3. Burns, Tom and G.M. Stalker, 1966. *The Management of Innovation* (2nd ed.). London: Tavistock.
4. Chandler, Arthur D., Jr., 1962. *Strategy and Structure: Chapters in the History of Industrial Enterprises.* Cambridge, MA: MIT Press.
5. Child, John, 1972. "Organizational Structure, Environment, and Performance: The Role of Strategic Choice." *Sociology,* **6**, 1–22.
6. De Greene, Kenyon B. (Ed.), 1970. *Systems Psychology.* New York: McGraw-Hill.
7. De Greene, Kenyon B., 1973. *Sociotechnical Systems: Factors in Analysis, Design, and Management.* Englewood Cliffs, NJ: Prentice-Hall.
8. De Greene, Kenyon B., 1977. "Organizational Best Fit: Survival, Change, and Adaptation." In Elmer H. Burack and Anant R. Negandhi (Eds.), *Organization Design: Theoretical Perspectives and Empirical Findings.* Kent, OH: Kent State University Press.
9. Galbraith, Jay, 1973. *Designing Complex Organizations.* Reading, MA: Addison-Wesley.
10. Georgescu-Roegen, Nicholas, 1971. *The Entropy Law and the Economic Process.* Cambridge, MA: Harvard University Press.
11. Herbst, Philip G., 1974. *Socio-technical Design: Strategies in Multidisciplinary Research.* London: Tavistock.
12. Herbst, Philip G., 1976. *Alternatives to Hierarchies.* Leiden, The Netherlands: Martinus Nijhoff.
13. Kast Fremont E. and James E. Rosenzweig, 1973. *Contingency Views of Organization and Management.* Chicago: Science Research Associates.
14. Lawrence, Paul, R. and Jay W. Lorsch, 1967. *Organization and Environment: Managing Differentiation and Integration.* Cambridge, MA: Harvard University Graduate School of Business Administration.
15. Miller, James G., 1978. *Living Systems.* New York: McGraw-Hill.
16. Rifkin, Jeremy with Ted Howard, 1980. *Entropy: A New World View.* New York: Viking.
17. Tolstoy, Leo, 1869. *War and Peace,* Book XI, Chapter 1.
18. Woodward, Joan, 1965. *Industrial Organization: Theory and Practice.* London: Oxford University Press.

CHAPTER 2

1. Ackoff, Russell L., 1967. "Management Misinformation Systems." *Management Science,* **14** (4), B-147–B-156, December.

2. Ackoff, Russell L., 1970. *A Concept of Corporate Planning*. New York: Wiley.

3. Ackoff, Russell L., 1973. "Science in the Systems Age: Beyond IE, OR, and MS." *Operations Research,* 661–671, May–June.

4. Ackoff, Russell L., 1977. "Optimization + Objectivity = Opt Out." *European Journal of Operational Research*—1–7.

5. Ackoff, Russell L., 1979. "The Future of Operational Research is Past." *The Journal of the Operational Research Society,* **30** (2), 93–104.

6. Ackoff, Russell L., 1979. "Resurrecting the Future of Operational Research." *The Journal of the Operational Research Society,* **30** (3), 189–199.

7. Bernstein, Harry and Joanne Bernstein, 1979. *Industrial Democracy in 12 Nations*. U.S. Department of Labor, Bureau of International Labor Affairs, Monograph No. 2. Washington, D.C.: U.S. Government Printing Office.

8. Bevan, R. G. and R. A. Bryer, 1978. "On Measuring the Contribution of OR." *The Journal of the Operational Research Society,* **29** (5), 409–418.

9. De Greene, Kenyon B., 1970. *Systems Psychology*. New York: McGraw-Hill.

10. De Greene, Kenyon B., 1973. *Sociotechnical Systems: Factors in Analysis, Design, and Management*. Englewood Cliffs, NJ: Prentice-Hall.

11. De Greene, Kenyon B., 1977. "Has Human Factors Come of Age?" In Alan S. Neal and Robert Palasek (Eds.) *Proceedings of the Human Factors Society 21st Annual Meeting,* Pages 457–461. Santa Monica, CA: Human Factors Society.

12. De Greene, Kenyon B., 1979. "Societechnical Systems, Ergonomics, and Industrial Plant Design in an Explosively Changing World." Paper given at the VIIth Congress of the International Ergonomics Association, August 27–31, Warsaw, Poland.

13. De Greene, Kenyon B., 1980. "Major Conceptual Problems in the Systems Management of Human Factors/Ergonomics Research." *Ergonomics,* **23** (1), 3–11.

14. Eilon, Samuel, 1980. "The Role of Management Science." *The Journal of the Operational Research Society,* **31** (1), 17–28.

15. Emery, Fred E., 1977. *The Emergence of a New Paradigm of Work*. Canberra: Centre for Continuing Education, Australian National University.

16. Emery, Fred E. and Eric L. Trist, 1973. *Towards a Social Ecology: Contextual Appreciation of the Future in the Present*. New York: Plenum.

17. Forrester, Jay W., 1961. *Industrial Dynamics*. Cambridge, MA: MIT Press.

18. Forrester, Jay W., 1968. *Principles of Systems*. Cambridge, MA: Wright-Allen Press.

19. Forrester, Jay W., 1968. "Market Growth as Influenced by Capital Investment." *Industrial Management Review,* **9** (2), 83–105.

20. Guest, Robert H., 1979. "Quality of Work Life—Learning from Tarrytown." *Harvard Business Review,* 76–87, July-August.

21. Gupta, Shiv and Laurence D. Richards, 1979. "A Language for Policy-Level Modeling." *The Journal of the Operational Research Society,* **30** (4), 297–308.

22. Herbst, Philip G., 1974. *Socio-Technical Design: Strategies in Multidisciplinary Research*. London: Tavistock.

23. Herbst, Philip G., 1976. *Alternatives to Hierarchies*. Leiden, The Netherlands: Martinus Nijhoff.

24. Herzberg, Frederick, 1968. "One More Time: How Do You Motivate Employees?" *Harvard Business Review,* 53–62, January–February.

25. Hitt, William D., 1969. "Two Models of Man." *American Psychologist,* **24** (7), 651–658.

26. Lucas, Henry C., 1975. *Why Information Systems Fail*. New York: Columbia University Press.

27. Luthans, Fred and R. Kreitner, 1975. *Organizational Behavior Modification*. Glenview, IL: Scott-Foresman.

28. Myers, M. Scott, 1964. "Who Are Your Motivated Workers?" *Harvard Business Review*, 73–88, January.

29. Naylor, Thomas H. and Daniel R. Gattis, 1976. "Corporate Planning Models." *California Management Review*, **18** (4), 69–78.

30. Paul, William J., Jr., Keith B. Robertson, and Frederick Herzberg, 1969. "Job Enrichment Pays Off." *Harvard Business Review*, 61–78, March–April.

31. Rice, Berkeley, 1978. "Measuring Executive Muscle." *Psychology Today*, 95 ff., December.

32. *Science*, **195** (4283), the entire issue of March 18, 1977 devoted to "Electronics."

CHAPTER 3

1. Bartholomew, D. J., 1973. *Stochastic Models for Social Processes* (2nd edition). New York: Wiley.

2. Batschelet, Edward, 1976. *Introduction to Mathematics for Life Scientists* (2nd edition). New York: Springer-Verlag.

3. Boyle, Stanley E. and Philip W. Jaynes, 1972. *Conglomerate Merger Performance: an Empirical Analysis of Nine Corporations*. Washington, D.C.: U.S. Government Printing Office. November.

4. Elgin, Duane S., 1977. "Limits to the Management of Large, Complex Systems." Part IV, Volume II of *Assessment of Future National and International Problem Areas*. Menlo Park, CA: Stanford Research International, Center for the Study of Social Policy. February.

5. Freeman, John and Michael T. Hannan, 1975. "Growth and Decline Processes in Organizations." *American Sociological Review*, **40**, 215–228, April.

6. Greiner, Larry E., 1972. "Evolution and Revolution as Organizations Grow." *Harvard Business Review*, 37–46, July–August.

7. Leik, Robert K. and Barbara F. Meeker, 1975. *Mathematical Sociology*. Englewood Cliffs, NJ: Prentice-Hall.

8. Mass, Nathaniel J. and Peter M. Senge, 1974. "Understanding Oscillations in Simple Systems." System Dynamics Group Paper D-2045-1. Cambridge, MA: Massachusetts Institute of Technology, Alfred P. Sloan School of Management.

9. Meyer, François and Jacque Vallee, 1975. "The Dynamics of Long-Term Growth." *Technological Forecasting and Social Change*, **7** (3), 285–300.

10. Roberts, Edward B., 1967. "The Problem of Aging Organizations: A Study of R&D Units." *Business Horizons*, 51–58, Winter.

11. Rose, Sanford, 1977. "Why the Multinational Tide Is Ebbing." *Fortune*, 111–120, August.

12. Sørensen, Aage B., 1978. "Mathematical Models in Sociology." *Annual Review of Sociology*, **4**, 345–371.

13. Strassmann, Paul A., 1976. "Stages of Growth." *Datamation*, **22** (10), 46–50.

14. Taagepera, Rein, 1979. "People, Skills, and Rsources." *Technological Forecasting and Social Change*, **13** (1), 13–30.

CHAPTER 4

1. Armstrong, J. Scott, 1978. *Long-Range Forecasting: From Crystal Ball to Computer*. New York: Wiley.

2. Ascher, William, 1978. *Forecasting: An Appraisal for Policy-Makers and Planners.* Baltimore: The Johns Hopkins Press.

3. Clark, John and Sam Cole, 1975. *Global Simulation Models: A Comparative Study.* New York: Wiley.

4. Cole, Sam, Christopher Freeman, Marie Jahoda, and K. L. R. Pavitt, 1973. *Models of Doom: A Critique of the Limits to Growth.* New York: Universe.

5. Edwards, Ward, 1976. *How to Use Multi-Attribute Utility Measurement for Social Decision Making.* Social Science Research Institute Technical Report 001597-1-T. Los Angeles: University of Southern California, August.

6. Environmental Analysis Staff, Corporate Strategic Planning and Studies, General Electric Company, 1976. *FUTURSCAN: Toward a Manageable Future.* Fairfield, CT: General Electric Company.

7. Forrester, Jay W., Nathaniel J. Mass, and Charles P. Ryan, 1976. "The System Dynamics National Model: Understanding Socio-Economic Behavior and Policy Alternatives." *Technological Forecasting and Social Change,* **9** (1&2), 51–68.

8. Fromm, Gary, William L. Hamilton, and Diane E. Hamilton, 1975. *Federally Supported Mathematical Models: Survey and Analysis.* Washington, D.C.: U.S. Government Printing Office.

9. Gordon, Theodore J. and Olaf Helmer, 1964. *Report on a Long-Range Forecasting Study.* Paper P-2982. Santa Monica, CA: The RAND Corporation, September.

10. Gordon, Theodore J. and John Stover, 1976. "Using Perceptions and Data about the Future to Improve the Simulation of Complex Systems." *Technological Forecasting and Social Change,* **9** (1&2), 191–211.

11. Greenberger, Martin, Matthew A. Crenson, and Brian L. Crissey, 1976. *Models in the Policy Process: Public Decision Making in the Computer Era.* New York: Russell Sage.

12. Guzzardi, Walter, Jr., 1978. "The New Down-to-Earth Economics." *Fortune,* 72–79, December 31.

13. Helmer, Olaf, 1977. "Problems in Futures Research: Delphi and Causal Cross-Impact Analysis." *Futures,* **9** (1), 2–31.

14. Herrera, Amílcar O. and Nine Others, 1976. *Catastrophe or New Society: A Latin American World Model.* Report IDRC-064e. Ottawa: International Development Research Center.

15. Hughes, Barry, 1977. *General Structural Description of the World Integrated Model (WIM).* Unpublished paper. Cleveland, OH: Systems Research Center, Case Western Reserve University, October.

16. Hughes, Barry B. and Mihajlo D. Mesarovic, 1978. "Population, Wealth, and Resources Up to the Year 2000." *Futures,* **10** (4), 267–282, August.

17. Interdisciplinary Systems Group, 1975. *Land Use, Energy Flow, and Policy Making in Society,* NSF GI-27 Final Report. Davis, CA: University of California.

18. Lendaris, George G., 1980. "Structural Modeling—A Tutorial Guide." *IEEE Transactions on Systems, Man, and Cybernetics,* **SMC-10** (12), 807–840.

19. Lenz, Ralph C., Jr., 1977. "Technological Forecasting: State-of-the-Art, Problems, and Prospects." In Wayne I. Boucher (Ed.), *The Study of the Future: An Agenda for Research,* pp. 68–75. Washington, D.C.: U.S. Government Printing Office, July.

20. Linstone, Harold and Murray Turoff (Eds.), 1975. *The Delphi Method.* Reading, MA: Addison-Wesley.

21. Martino, Joseph P., 1975. *Technological Forecasting for Decisionmaking.* New York: Elsevier.

22. Meadows, Donnella H., 1977. "The Unavoidable A Priori: A Discussion of Major Modeling Paradigms." In Jørgen Randers and Leif K. Ervik (Eds.), *The System Dynamics*

Method—The Proceedings of the 1976 International Conference on System Dynamics, Geilo, Norway, August 8–15, 1976, pp. 161–240. Oslo, Norway: Resource Policy Group.

23. Mesarovic, Mihajlo and Eduard Pestel, 1974. *Mankind at the Turning Point.* New York: Dutton/Reader's Digest.

24. Naylor, Thomas H. and Horst Schauland, 1976. "A Survey of Users of Corporate Planning Models." *Management Science,* **22** (9) 927–937.

25. Office of Federal Statistical Policy and Standards, Bureau of the Census, U.S. Department of Commerce, 1977. *Social Indicators 1976.* Washington, D.C.: U.S. Government Printing Office.

26. Roberts, Peter C., 1978. *Modelling Large Systems: Limits to Growth Revisited.* New York: Halsted.

27. Rokeach, Milton, 1973. *The Nature of Human Values.* New York: Free Press.

28. Stover, John G. and Theodore J. Gordon, 1978. "Cross-Impact Analysis." In Jib Fowles (Ed.), *Handbook of Futures Research,* pp. 301–328. Westport, CT: Greenwood Press.

29. White House Conference on the Industrial World Ahead, 1972. *A Look at Business in 1990.* Washington, D.C.: U.S. Government Printing Office.

30. Wilson, Ian H., 1978, "Scenarios." In Jib Fowles (Ed.), *Handbook of Futures Research,* pp. 225–247. Westport, CT: Greenwood Press.

CHAPTER 5

1. Amit, Daniel J., 1978. *Field Theory, the Renormalization Group, and Critical Phenomena.* New York: McGraw-Hill.

2. Argenti, John, 1976. *Corporate Collapse: The Causes and Symptoms.* Maidenhead, Berkshire, England: McGraw-Hill (UK).

3. Battelle-Columbus Laboratories, 1973. *Science, Technology, and Innovation.* Columbus, OH: Battelle-Columbus Laboratories, February.

4. Boffey, Philip M., 1978. "Investigators Agree N.Y. Blackout of 1977 Could Have Been Avoided." *Science,* **201** (4360), 994–998.

5. Carneiro, Robert L., 1968. "Ascertaining, Testing, and Interpreting Sequences of Cultural Development." *Southwestern Journal of Anthropology,* **24** (4), 354–374.

6. Carneiro, Robert L., 1969. "The Measurement of Cultural Development in the Ancient Near East and in Anglo-Saxon England." *Transactions of the New York Academy of Sciences,* Series II, **31** (8), 1013–1023.

7. Carneiro, Robert L., 1981. "Successive Reequilibrations as a Mechanism of Cultural Evolution." In William S. Schieve and Peter M. Allen (Eds.), *Self-Organization in Dissipative Structures: Applications in the Physical and Social Sciences.* Austin: University of Texas Press.

8. Casti, John L., 1979. *Connectivity, Complexity, and Catastrophe in Large-Scale Systems.* New York: Wiley.

9. Cobb, Loren, Rammohan K. Ragade, and B. G. Ash (Eds.), 1978. "Applications of Catastrophe Theory in the Behavioral and Life Sciences." *Behavioral Science,* **23** (5), entire special issue.

10. Curvin, Robert and Bruce Porter, 1979. *Blackout Looting: New York City, July 13, 1977.* New York: Gardner.

11. De Greene, Kenyon B., 1978. "Force Fields and Emergent Phenomena in Sociotechnical Macrosystems: Theories and Models." *Behavioral Science,* **23** (1), 1–14.

12. De Greene, Kenyon B., 1978. "Field Theory as a Framework for the Computer Simulation Modeling of Complex Societal Systems." In *Proceeding of the International Conference on Cybernetics and Society, Tokyo-Kyoto, Japan, 3–7 November 1978*, Vol. I, pp. 338–345. New York: Institute of Electrical and Electronics Engineers.

13. De Greene, Kenyon B., 1979. "Reconfigurational Processes in the Evolution of Social Systems." In Richard F. Ericson (Ed.), *Improving the Human Condition: Quality and Stability in Social Systems*, pp. 50–61. Louisville, KY: University of Louisville, Society for General Systems Research.

14. De Greene, Kenyon B., 1981. "Limits to Societal Systems Adaptability." *Behavioral Science*, **26** (2), 103–113.

15. Isnard, C. A. and E. Christopher Zeeman, 1976. "Some Models from Catastrophe Theory in the Social Sciences." In Lyndhurst Collins (Ed.), *The Use of Models in the Social Sciences*, pages 44–100. Boulder, CO: Westview.

16. Marx, Gary T. and James L. Wood, 1975. "Strands of Theory and Research in Collective Behavior." *Annual Review of Sociology*, **1**, 363–428.

17. Nicolis, Gregoire and Ilya Prigogine, 1977. *Self-Organization in Nonequilibrium Systems: From Dissipative Structures to Order through Fluctuations.* New York: Wiley.

18. Oberschall, Anthony, 1978. "Theories of Social Conflict." *Annual Review of Sociology*, **4**, 291–315.

19. Prigogine, Ilya, Peter M. Allen, and Robert Herman, 1977. "The Evolution of Complexity and the Laws of Nature." In Ervin Laszlo and Judah Bierman (Eds.), *Goals in a Global Community: The Original Background Papers for Goals of Mankind, A Report to the Club of Rome.* Vol. 1, *Studies on the Conceptual Foundations*, pp. 5–63. New York: Pergamon.

20. Prigogine, Ilya, 1980. *From Being to Becoming: Time and Complexity in the Physical Sciences.* San Francisco: Freeman.

21. Quarantelli, E. L. and Russell R. Dynes, 1977. "Response to Social Crisis and Disaster." *Annual Review of Sociology*, **3**, 23–49.

22. Rogers, Gary, 1977. "Modeling Cellular Movements for Computer Simulation." In M. H. Hamza (Ed.), *Proceedings of the International Symposium SIMULATION '77*, pp. 475–478. Calgary, Alberta, Canada: Acta Press.

23. Stanford Research International, 1977. *Assessment of Future National and International Problems Areas*, Research Report CSSP 4676-14, Volume 1. Menlo Park, CA: Stanford Research International, Center for the Study of Social Policy, February.

24. Tanford, Charles, 1978. "The Hydrophobic Effect and the Organization of Living Matter." *Science*, **200** (4345), 1012–1018.

25. Thom, René, 1975. *Structural Stability and Morphogenesis; An Outline of a General Theory of Models.* Reading, MA: Benjamin.

26. Walls, D. F., 1976. "Non-Equilibrium Phase Transitions in Sociology." *Collective Phenomena*, **2**, 125–130.

27. Weidlich, W., 1972. "The Use of Statistical Models in Sociology." *Collective Phenomena*, **1** (1), 51–59.

28. Weller, Jack M. and E. L. Quarantelli, 1973. "Neglected Characteristics of Collective Behavior." *American Journal of Sociology*, **79** (3), 665–685.

29. Wilson, Kenneth G., 1979. "Problems in Physics with Many Scales of Length." *Scientific American*, **241** (2), 158–179.

30. Zeeman, E. Christopher, 1976. "Catastrophe Theory." *Scientific American*, **234** (4), 65–83.

CHAPTER 6

1. Armstrong, Joe E. and Willis W. Harman, 1977. *Strategies for Conducting Technology Assessment.* Stanford, CA: Stanford University, Department of Engineering-Economic Systems, December.

2. Chestnut, Harold and Kenyon B. De Greene (Special Editors); 1982. "Special Issue on Supplemental Ways for Improving International Stability—Editorial Overview." *IEEE Transactions on Systems, Man, and Cybernetics,* **SMC-12** (2).

3. Council on Environmental Quality and Department of State, 1980. *The Global 2000 Report to the President* (in 3 volumes). Washington, D.C.: U.S. Government Printing Office.

4. De Greene, Kenyon B., 1975. "Technological Change and Manpower Resources: A Systems Perspective." *Human Factors,* **17** (1), 52–70.

5. De Greene, Kenyon B., 1980. "Anticipating Critical Reconfigurations in World Societal Fields." Paper given at the Workshop on Supplemental Ways for Improving International Stability, University of Virginia, Charlottesville, October 26–28. Also in press in 1982, *IEEE Transactions on Systems, Man, and Cybernetics,* **SMC-12** (2).

6. De Greene, Kenyon B., 1981. "Limits to Societal Systems Adaptability." *Behavioral Science,* **26** (4), 103–113.

7. Emery, Fred, 1977. *Futures We Are In.* Leiden, The Netherlands: Martinus Nijhoff.

8. Emery, Fred and Eric L. Trist, 1973. *Towards a Social Ecology: Contextual Appreciations of the Future in the Present.* New York: Plenum.

9. Freeman, Christopher, 1979. "The Determinants of Innovation." *Futures,* **11** (3), 206–215, June.

10. Hannan, Michael T. and John Freeman, 1977. "The Population Ecology of Organizations." *American Journal of Sociology,* **82** (5), 929–964, March.

11. Holling, Crawford S. (Ed.), 1978. *Adaptive Environmental Assessment and Management.* New York: Wiley.

12. Jurkovich, Ray, 1974. "A Core Typology of Organizational Environments." *Administrative Science Quarterly,* **19**, 380–394.

13. Lawless, Edward W., 1977. *Technology and Social Shock.* New Brunswick, NJ: Rutgers University Press.

14. Monsen, R. Joseph, 1979. "The Future of American Capitalism." *California Management Review,* **XXI** (3), 5–16, Spring.

15. Sahal, Devendra, 1978. "The Distribution of Technological Innovations." *Proceedings of the International Conference on Cybernetics and Society, Tokyo-Kyoto, Japan, November 3–7, 1978,* Vol. I, pp. 573–579. New York: Institute of Electrical and Electronics Engineers.

16. Starr, Chauncey and Chris Whipple, 1980. "Risks and Risk Decisions." *Science,* **208** (4448), 1114–1119, June 6.

17. Terreberry, Shirley, 1968. "The Evolution of Organizational Environments." *Administrative Science Quarterly,* **13**, 590–613.

18. Tosi, Henry, Ramon Aldag, and Ronald Storey, 1973. "On the Measurement of the Environment: An Assessment of the Lawrence and Lorsch Environmental Uncertainty Subscale." *Administrative Science Quarterly,* **18**, 27–36, January.

19. Watt, Kenneth E. F., 1973. *Principles of Environmental Science.* New York: McGraw-Hill.

20. White, George R. and Margaret B. W. Graham, 1978. "How to Spot a Technological Winner." *Harvard Business Review,* **56** (2), 146–152, March-April.

21. Winner, Langdon, 1977. *Autonomous Technology: Technics-Out-of-Control as a Theme in Political Thought.* Cambridge, MA; MIT Press.

CHAPTER 7

1. Atkinson, John W. and Joel O. Raynor, 1978. *Personality, Motivation, and Achievement.* New York: Halsted.

2. Bowman, Edward H. and Maison Haire, 1975. "A Strategic Posture Toward Corporate Responsibility." *California Management Review,* **XVIII** (2), 49–58, Winter.

3. Cooper, Michael R., Brian S. Morgan, Patricia M. Foley, and Leon B. Kaplan, 1979. "Changing Employee Values: Deepening Discontent." *Harvard Business Review,* 117–125, January–February.

4. Csikszentmihalyi, Mihaly, 1977. *Beyond Boredom and Anxiety.* San Francisco: Jossey-Bass.

5. DeCharms, Richard and Marion S. Muir, 1978. "Motivation: Social Approaches." *Annual Review of Psychology,* **29,** 91–113.

6. Maccoby, Michael, 1976. *The Gamesman: The New Corporate Leaders.* New York: Simon and Schuster.

7. McClelland, David C., 1975. *Power: The Inner Experience.* New York: Irvington.

8. Mowshowitz, Abbe, 1976. *The Conquest of Will: Information Processing in Human Affairs.* Reading, MA: Addison-Wesley.

9. Newell, Allen and Herbert A. Simon, 1972. *Human Problem Solving.* Englewood Cliffs, NJ: Prentice-Hall.

10. Renshaw, Edward F., 1976. "Productivity." In Vol. 1, *Productivity,* pp. 21–56, of *U.S. Economic Growth from 1976 to 1986: Prospects, Problems, and Patterns.* Washington, D.C.: U.S. Government Printing Office.

11. Samuelson, Kjell, James G. Miller, Edward J. Kazlauskas, and Kenyon B. De Greene, 1980. *Informatic Communication and Multi-Way Video* (four separate papers). In Alan R. Benenfeld and Edward J. Kazlauskas (Eds.), *Communicating Information, Proceedings of the 43rd Annual Meeting,* Vol. 17, pp. 129–142. White Plains, NY: Knowledge Industry Publications.

12. Seligman, Martin E. P., 1975. *Helplessness: On Depression, Development, and Death.* San Francisco: Freeman.

13. Sethi, S. Prakash, 1975. "Dimensions of Corporate Social Performance: an Analytical Framework." *California Management Review,* **XVII** (3), 58–64, Spring.

14. Simon, Herbert A., 1980. "The Behavioral and Social Sciences." *Science,* **209** (4452), 72–78, July 4.

15. Smith, Frank, Karlene H. Roberts, and Charles L. Hulin, 1976. "Ten Year Job Satisfaction Trends in a Stable Institution." *Academy of Management Journal,* **19** (3), 462–469, September.

16. Stokols, Daniel, 1978. "Environmental Psychology." *Annual Review of Psychology,* **29,** 253–295.

17. Weizenbaum, Joseph, 1976. *Computer Power and Human Reason: From Judgment to Calculation.* San Francisco: Freeman.

CHAPTER 8

1. Alvarez, Luis W., Walter Alvarez, Frank Asaro, and Helen V. Michel, 1980. "Extraterrestrial Cause for the Cretaceous-Tertiary Extinction." *Science,* **208** (4448), 1095–1108, June 6.

2. Ashby, W. Ross, 1956. *An Introduction to Cybernetics.* London: Chapman and Hall.

3. Ashby, W. Ross, 1960. *Design for a Brain: The Origin of* Adaptive Behavior (2nd editon). New York: Wiley.

4. Beer, Stafford, 1972. *Brain of the Firm: A Development in Management Cybernetics.* New York: McGraw-Hill.

5. Beer, Stafford, 1979. *The Heart of the Enterprise.* New York: Wiley.

6. Butzer, Karl W., 1980. "Civilizations: Organisms or Systems?" *American Scientist,* **68** (5), 517–522, September–October.

7. De Greene, Kenyon B., 1977. "Organizational Best Fit: Survival, Change, and Adaptation." *Organization and Administrative Sciences,* **8** (1), 117–133, Spring.

8. De Greene, Kenyon B., 1979. "Reconfigurational Processes in the Evolution of Social Systems." In Richard F. Ericson (Ed.), *Improving the Human Condition: Quality and Stability in Social Systems—Proceedings of the Silver Anniversary Meeting,* London, England, August 20–24, 1979, pp. 50–61. Louisville, KY: University of Louisville, Society for General Systems Research.

9. De Greene, Kenyon B., 1981. "Limits to Societal Systems Adaptability." *Behavioral Science,* **26** (4), 103–113.

10. Deighton, Len, 1980. *Blitzkrieg: From the Rise of Hitler to the Fall of Dunkirk,* New York: Knopf.

11. Emery, Fred E., 1977. *Futures We Are In.* Leiden, The Netherlands: Martinus Nijhoff.

12. Hackett, General Sir John and Other Top-Ranking NATO Generals and Advisors, 1978. *The Third World War: August 1985.* New York: Macmillan.

13. Herbst, Philip G., 1979. "Community Conference Design: Skjervøy Yesterday, Today, and Tomorrow." Paper presented at the *Conference on Hierarchical/Non-Hierarchical Systems and Conditions for Democratic Participation,* Dubrovnik, Yugoslavia, January 1979. Oslo, Norway: Work Research Institute.

14. Holling, Crawford S., 1976. "Resilience and Stability in Ecosystems." In Erich Jantsch and Conrad H. Waddington (Eds.), *Evolution and Consciousness: Human Systems in Transition,* pp. 73–92. Reading, MA: Addison-Wesley.

15. Holling, Crawford S. (Ed.), 1978. *Adaptive Environmental Assessment and Management.* New York: Wiley.

16. Hunsicker, J. Quincy, 1980. "The Malaise of Strategic Planning." *Management Review,* **69** (3), 9–14.

17. Kiechel, Walter III, 1979. "Playing by the Rules of the Corporate Strategy Game." *Fortune,* **100** (6), 110–118, September 24.

18. Miles, Ian, 1974. "Social Forecasting: From Impressions to Investigation." *Futures,* 240–242, June.

19. Perlmuter, Lawrence C. and Richard A. Monty, 1977. "The Importance of Perceived Control: Fact or Fantasy?" *American Scientist,* **65** (6), 759–765, November-December.

20. Van Frederikslust, R. A. I., 1978. *Predictability of Corporate Failure.* Leiden, The Netherlands: Martinus Nijhoff.

21. Von Foerster, Heinz, 1974. *Cybernetics of Cybernetics.* Urbana-Champaign: University of Illinois, Biological Computer Laboratory.

INDEX